W9-AFO-195

PAUL

Apostle of Liberty

PAUL

Apostle of Liberty

by Richard N. Longenecker

HARPER & ROW, *Publishers*
NEW YORK, EVANSTON
AND LONDON

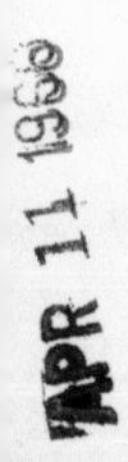

To Fran
My Beloved
for
We Are Fellow Workers
in God's Service
« I Cor. 3:9 »

FIRST EDITION

LIBRARY OF CONGRESS CATALOG CARD NUMBER: 64-19500

L-O

Contents

Abbreviations

BOOKS AND JOURNALS

Ap. and Ps.	*The Apocrypha and Pseudepigrapha of the Old Testament*, ed. R. H. Charles
B. A.	*Biblical Archaeologist*
B.A.S.O.R—S.S.	*Bulletin of the American Schools of Oriental Research—Supplementary Studies*
E.G.T.	*The Expositors' Greek Testament*
E.Q.	*The Evangelical Quarterly*
E.T.	*The Expository Times*
H.D.A.C.	*Hastings' Dictionary of Apostolic Church*
H.D.B.	*Hastings' Dictionary of the Bible*
H.D.C.G.	*Hastings' Dictionary of Christ and the Gospels*
H.J.	*The Hibbert Journal*
H.N.T.	*Handbuch zum Neuen Testament*
H.T.R.	*Harvard Theological Review*
I.C.C.	*International Critical Commentary*
J.B.L.	*Journal of Biblical Literature*
J.E.	*The Jewish Encyclopedia*
J.J.S.	*The Journal of Jewish Studies*
J.Q.R.	*Jewish Quarterly Review*
J.T.S.	*Journal of Theological Studies*
M.N.T.C.	*Moffatt New Testament Commentary*
N.T.S.	*New Testament Studies*
R.B.	*Revue Biblique*
S.J.T.	*Scottish Journal of Theology*
Str.-Bil.	*Kommentar zum Neuen Testament aus Talmud und Midrash*, Hermann L. Strack and Paul Billerbeck
Z.N.W.	*Zeitschrift für die neutestamentlich Wissenschaft*
Z.T.K.	*Zeitschrift für Theologie und Kirche*

TALMUD

General

j.	Jerusalem or Palestinian Talmud	Mish.	Mishnah
b.	Babylonian Talmud	Tos.	Tosephta
R.	Rabbi or Rabbah		

Tractates

Aboth	Pirke Aboth	Keth.	Kethuboth	Shebu.	Shebuot
Ab. Zar.	Abodah Zarah	Kid.	Kiddushin	Sheka.	Shekalim
Bab. Bath.	Baba Bathra	Meg.	Megillah	Sot.	Sotah
Bab. Mez.	Baba Mezia	Men.	Menahoth	Suk.	Sukkah
Ber.	Berakoth	Mak.	Makkoth	Teb. Yom	Tebul Yom
Dem.	Demai	Nid.	Niddah	Yeb.	Yebamoth
Eduy.	Eduyoth	Pes.	Pesahim	Yom.	Yoma
Hag.	Hagigah	Sanh.	Sanhedrin		
Kel.	Kelim	Shab.	Shabbath		

PHILO

De Abr.	De Abrahamo
De Cherub.	De Cherubim
De Congr.	De Congressu Eruditionis Gratia
De Decal.	De Decalogo
De Ebriet.	De Ebrietate
De Exsecrat.	De Exsecrationibus
De Fuga	De Fuga et Inventione
De Gigant.	De Gigantibus
De Jos.	De Josepho
Leg. ad Gai.	Legatio ad Gaium
Leg. All.	Legum Allegoria
De Migrat. Abr.	De Migratione Abrahami
De Mutat. Nom.	De Mutatione Nominum
De Post. Cain.	De Posteritate Caini
Quis Rer. Div. Heres	Quis Rerum Divinarum Heres sit
Quod Det. Pot. Insid.	Quod Deterius Potiori Insidiari Soleat
Quod Deus Immut.	Quod Deus sit Immutabilis
De Sacrif. Ab. et Cain.	De Sacrificiis Abelis et Caini
De Somn.	De Somniis
De Spec. Leg.	De Specialibus Legibus
De Virt.	De Virtutibus
De Vita Mos.	De Vita Mosis

DEAD SEA SCROLLS

1QS	Manual of Discipline (serek hay-yoḥad)
1QH	Psalms of Thanksgiving (hodayot)
1QM	War Scroll (milḥamah)
CDC	Cairo Damascus Document (6QD and 4QD[b] of Qumran)
IQHab.	Habakkuk Commentary
IQSa	A Formula of Blessing

References are given according to column and line. CDC references are also given according to chapter and verse in parenthesis, as in *Ap. and Ps.*

JOSEPHUS

Life	Vita Josephus	War	The Jewish War
Antiq.	Antiquities of the Jews	Contra Apion	Contra Apion

NOTICE: Texts used in this study are Kittel and Nestle, unless otherwise indicated. Undesignated translations of nonbiblical material are those of H. Danby, *The Mishnah*; the Soncino edition of *The Babylonian Talmud,* ed. I Epstein; F. H. Colson and G. H. Whitaker, *Philo* (The Loeb Classical Library); Wm. Whiston, *The Works of Flavius Josephus; The Apocrypha and Pseudepigrapha of the Old Testament,* ed. R. H. Charles; and T. H. Gaster, *The Scriptures of the Dead Sea Sect.*

Introduction

THE APOSTLE Paul has never ceased to excite the interest of both scholar and layman. From a purely biographical perspective, he is a favorite in that "there were probably exceedingly few people of the Imperial age of Rome whom we can study so exactly as we can Paul through his letters."[1] For the historian interested in the origin of the Christian religion, the teaching and work of the Apostle is secondary only to that of his Lord. In a very real sense the maxim is true: "Explain the origin of the religion of Paul, and you have solved the problem of the origin of Christianity."[2] In the field of comparative religions, he stands at the crossroads of Hebraicism and Hellenism—yet lifts his eyes above and beyond. Theologically, his influence upon Christendom is unparalleled. Heretics and saints—Marcion, Augustine, Luther, Baur, and Barth, to name only a prominent and assorted few —have claimed theological impetus from him. There is, as many still discover today, a divinely inspired timelessness about his message which grips men and leads them on to their Lord.

As a result of this interest, a great body of literature has arisen about the name of Paul. So diligently and thoroughly has he been investigated that most consider the literary and personal profile of the Apostle to be unmistakably set in bold relief. And yet there have always been claims that scholarship has grossly misinterpreted even the main outlines of his teaching and life.[3]

The present study stems from a conviction that, while previous scholarly efforts have resulted in a generally faithful reproduction of

---

[1] A. Deissmann, *Paul,* trans. W. E. Wilson (London: Hodder & Stoughton, 1926), p. 25; also published as a Harper Torchbook, p. 19.

[2] J. Gresham Machen, *The Origin of Paul's Religion* (London: Hodder & Stoughton, 1921), pp. 4-5. Cf. F. C. Baur, *Paul, His Life and Works,* trans. E. Zeller (London: Williams & Norgate, 1875), Vol. I, pp. 3-4.

[3] The recent work of H. J. Schoeps begins on this premise: "The apostle Paul is a truly great figure. His greatness is shown in the very fact that he has found no congenial interpreter and probably never will. From Marcion to Karl Barth, from Augustine to Luther, Schweitzer or Bultmann, he has ever been misunderstood or partially understood, one aspect of his work being thrown into relief while others have been misunderstood and neglected" (*Paul,* trans. H. Knight [Philadelphia: Westminster, 1961], p. 13).

the Pauline profile, there still remain areas of ambiguity which need clarification. It is therefore the purpose of this work to investigate a matter which can truly be said to be distinctively Pauline: the legality-liberty dialectic of the Apostle. And in three areas of this subject it has appeared needful to sharpen our understanding of Paul: (1) in his pre-Christian days under the legal system of Judaism; (2) in his Christian teaching regarding legality and liberty; and (3) in his personal practice of liberty as an apostle of Christ.

Perhaps the most obvious difficulty relating to the historical profile of the Apostle is that concerning his actions as represented in the Book of Acts. Did the apostle of liberty really continue in such Jewish practices as those ascribed to him, e.g., taking upon himself Jewish vows, keeping up the Jewish customs, worshiping in the Temple, claiming Pharisaic privileges, and accepting guidance from the elder apostles in Jerusalem? And if so, how can this be explained? Were these practices performed hypocritically or with tongue in cheek; are they evidences of inconsistency and vacillation; or is there an inner consistency of faith and life in the Apostle which we have failed to notice and which, when understood, can aid us in the ordering of our Christian lives?

But enroute to a consideration of the problem practices of Acts, many questions must be clarified. What did his "all things to all men" maxim mean for his Gentile mission and pastoral ministry? What attitudes did he have toward the Jerusalem apostles, the Jerusalem Church, and the Jewish nation, and how cordial were his relations with each? What did he teach regarding legality, nomism, and liberty? As a young rabbi, where did he stand in respect to the Judaism of his day? What was the spirituality of that Judaism like? How satisfying was his preconversion religious experience? What tensions did he feel in his early life? These are matters which must be clarified if we are to view the profile of Paul without distortion.

I

The Problem of Sources

IN THE STUDY of Paul's background, teaching, and practice, it is necessary first of all to delineate the sources of primary significance. Two areas must be identified: (1) the writings that truly represent the Pharisaism of Paul's day, and (2) the extent of the genuinely Pauline literature.

TALMUDIC LITERATURE

Talmudic literature has been variously evaluated.[1] Older Gentile scholars, such as W. Bousset and A. Schweitzer, have insisted that it was not representative of predestruction Pharisaism at all.[2] Many modern writers have agreed, arguing that the Judaism of R. Johanan b. Zakkai, or of R. Akiba, or later yet of Judah the Patriarch, was sufficiently different from that of before the first destruction to be called a new religion.[3] An element within liberal Judaism, too, has

[1] "Talmudic literature" is here used in its broader meaning: the Mishnah, the two Gemaras, the earlier Midrashim, and the Tosephta. It is used to include those codifications and writings from about A.D. 200-600. Thus the term excludes the (probably) earlier Targums and the later cabalistic and ethical writings. In its narrow sense, "Talmud" refers to the Gemaras: Palestinian or Jerusalem, c. A.D. 400, and Babylonian, c. A.D. 500-600.

[2] W. Bousset, *Die Religion des Judentums im neutestamentlichen Zeitalter* 2d. ed., (Berlin: Reuther & Reichard, 1906), p. 541; A. Schweitzer, *Paul and His Interpreters,* trans. W. Montgomery (London: Black, 1912), pp. 48-49. Schweitzer graphically says: "The picture which they draw for us shows only sun-scorched plain, but this yellow, wilted grass was green and fresh once. What did the meadows look like then?"

[3] Cf. B. S. Easton, *Christ in the Gospels* (New York, Scribner's Sons, 1930), pp. 89-108; F. C. Burkitt, "What Christians Think of Jews," *H. J.,* Vol. XXVIII, No. 2 (Jan., 1930), pp. 267-69.

its doubts that the rabbinic Judaism of the first century can be adequately described from the Talmudic sources.[4] On the other hand, most Jewish and some Gentile scholars maintain that we can form a picture of predestruction Judaism from the rabbinical writings in our possession.[5] Thus the monumental work of George F. Moore is based on the premise that "the task of Johanan ben Zakkai and his fellows was one of conservation, not of reformation."[6] Moore insists that since the writings give no hint of a new departure or a new religion, we must accept them as possessing a basic continuity with that earlier time—though undoubtedly there has been a shifting emphasis within this fundamental solidarity through four or five centuries of thought and persecution. But though there has been a development within the Talmud, there is, he maintains, "no indication that the development was on new lines or on different principles from that which preceded it."[7]

Objections against this latter position fall into four categories: (1) the late date of the Talmudic materials, (2) the influence of Christianity upon the records, (3) the impact of the first and second destructions on Judaism, and (4) the possibility that later medieval Judaism again altered the original literature with an eye to religious and political opposition in that day.[8]

The argument from lateness of date is, in itself, not convincing; especially when we consider that such a treatise as Pirke Aboth probably had its origin in the days of the first-century rabbi, Johanan b. Zakkai. It is true that, as the codifications and formulations become more and more removed from the predestruction period, the argument would seem to become more telling. And yet we are dealing

[4] E.g., C. G. Montefiore, *Judaism and St. Paul* (London: Goschen, 1914), pp. 14-15.

[5] E.g., L. Finkelstein, "The Book of Jubilees and the Rabbinic Halaka," *H. T. R.*, Vol. XVI, No. 1 (Jan., 1923), p. 39; G. F. Moore, *Judaism in the First Centuries of the Christian Era* (Cambridge, Mass.: Harvard University Press, 1927-30), Vol. I, pp. 71, 87, 172-73; Vol. III, p. 17.

[6] *Ibid.*, Vol. I, p. 131.

[7] *Ibid.*, Vol. III, p .22.

[8] The first three arguments are best voiced by W. D. Davies in his *Paul and Rabbinic Judaism* (London: S. P. C. K., 1955), pp. 3-4. H. L. Strack insisted that the fourth must be seriously considered as well (*Introduction to the Talmud and Midrash* [Philadelphia: Jewish Publication Society of America, 1931] pp. 78, 85-86).

with a religious attitude which took great pride in the preservation of tradition. While changes through forgetfulness and differing circumstances would occur, this desire to preserve the traditional—barring other considerations—minimizes the temporal element.

The factors of religious opposition and political disaster, however, cannot be accounted as equally negligible. Though Moore has maintained that "neither the Nazarenes in Palestine, . . . nor Gentile Christianity made any mark on Judaism,"[9] it is hard to believe that this was the case. The very rise of a postcanonical body of opposing religious expression, i.e., the Christian New Testament, was probably a major factor in the original desire of the Tannaitic rabbis to bring together their traditions so as also to have authoritative postcanonical documents from their point of view.[10] Furthermore, the success of this new religious position, claiming as it did to be truly representing the Old Testament and the religion of Israel, undoubtedly forced Judaism to look within itself and solidify what it believed to be its positions of strength.[11] Certainly the unity of God and the importance of the Torah were emphasized as they never were before. At this time the Shema was invested with the importance of a confession of faith, the *eḥad* given special prominence.[12] And from this time arise the many explanations of the plural names, pronouns, and adjectives used in connection with the Divine Being in the Old Testament.[13] Likewise, the extreme glorification of the written Law[14] and the attribution of

[9] *Judaism,* Vol. I, p. 92.

[10] Cf. R. A. Stewart, *The Earlier Rabbinic Tradition* (London: Inter-Varsity Fellowship, 1949), pp. 20-21.

[11] Cf. S. Schechter: "New laws were enacted and old ones revived, with the object of resisting Christian influences over the Jews. To expand the Oral Law, and give it a firm basis in the Scriptures, were considered the best means of preserving Judaism intact" (*Studies in Judaism* [London: Black, 1896], p. 232).

[12] Cf. E. G. Hirsch: "To controvert their [the Jewish Christians'] departures from the fundamental positions of Judaism, the Palestinian synagogue, as did all later Judaism with the exception of the cabalists, laid all the greater stress on the unity of God" ("God," *J. E.,* Vol. VI, p. 5).

[13] See R. T. Herford, *Christianity in Talmud and Midrash* (London: Williams & Norgate, 1903), pp. 250-320, for the reproduction of Talmudic texts on this point.

[14] Cf. S. Schechter, *Some Aspects of Rabbinic Theology* (New York: Macmillan, 1909), p. 123, n. 5, where the Jewish doctrine of the Law's continued full existence in the Messianic Age is suggested to be such a reaction. Cf. *infra,* pp.130, 185.

divine inspiration to the oral[15] seem to be reactions to the national losses and Christian opposition. As Akiba's rejection of the LXX and his encouragement of Aquila to produce a new Greek translation were clearly in opposition to what he felt to be the misuse of the LXX by the Christians,[16] so other attitudes and doctrines in the Talmud appear to bear this same stamp. The explicit Tannaitic rejection of the miraculous as evidence,[17] the Talmudic suspicion of mysticism,[18] the suppression of eschatological study, and the purging of apocalyptic speculation,[19] to mention only a few, seem to fall within this category. In our growing knowledge of diversity within early Judaism, we are led more and more to the conviction that Palestinian Pharisaism had within it more tendencies and variations than are readily seen in its later literature.

As to the fourth objection, it certainly is possible that medieval Judaism again altered some words and phrases in its literature. But a sweeping revision of the material at that time seems unlikely.

What then can be used from the Talmudic literature in an attempt to understand the Pharisaism of Paul's day? It would seem from the sweeping indictments above that we have little reason to trust any of it. Yet there are portions of that literature which can be used by the historian and are beyond the realm of reasonable doubt—portions and passages from which, it is true, a detailed picture is impossible, but from which a general impression can be obtained. These are the passages which seem to come from an early time and appear to be

[15] Cf. L. Finkelstein, "The Pharisees: Their Origin and Their Philosophy," *H. T. R.*, Vol. XXII, No. 3 (July, 1929), p. 245.

[16] Cf. H. B. Swete, *An Introduction to the Old Testament in Greek* (Cambridge, Eng.: The University Press, 1900), pp. 30-42.

[17] B. Bab. Mez. 59b. Cf. Schechter: "When the Rabbis saw their dangerous consequences, they insisted that miracles should have no influence on the interpretation and development of the Law" (*Studies in Judaism*, p. 231; see also *Aspects of Rabbinic Theology*, pp. 6-7).

[18] Cf. W. L. Knox: "Mysticism was associated with an interest in cosmogony which might easily lead to theosophy or even to Christianity" (*St. Paul and the Church of the Gentiles* [Cambridge, Eng.: The University Press, 1939], p. 102). See also Moore, *Judaism*, Vol. I, p. 413.

[19] Cf. D. Daube, *The New Testament and Rabbinic Judaism* (London: Athlone Press, 1956), pp. 135-36. Daube says, in comment upon b. Yeb. 47b, that very possibly it was considered that "speculation about eschatology was dangerous because it might lead to inquiry into or even acceptance of the Christian tenets."

above reasonable suspicion of having been written in reaction to Judaism's political and religious misfortunes. The following four categories of such portions are here proposed,[20] and upon them this study will to a large extent base its conclusions regarding the theology of predestruction Palestinian Pharisaism:

1. Practices and rules deemed by Johanan b. Zakkai and his followers to be very ancient, or, as Moore says, to be "customs the origin of which was lost in antiquity."[21] Quite often these are introduced by such a phrase as "Our rabbis taught," or "It has been taught," though in each case the context must be noted as well.

2. Actions and teachings of certain named persons who lived before the first destruction, or who personally had their roots in that earlier period.[22] The chief authority of this class is the tractate Pirke Aboth, with its Haggadic teachings attributed to specific teachers. Of principle importance in the Aboth are chapter 1, dealing with the teachers up to A.D. 70, and chapter 2, treating mainly Johanan b. Zakkai, whose roots were firmly planted in the predestruction period, and his disciples. And while "for a knowledge of the ideals of rabbinical ethics and piety, no other easily accessible source is equal to the Abot,"[23] there are other passages of this type scattered throughout the Gemaras, Midrashim, and Tosephta.

3. Passages and portions which have no reason to be a reaction to either religious opponents or political trials, and which do not seem to have been influenced by a particular local situation or passing fancy, but have parallels elsewhere in the literature. Here it is that the subjective element of interpretation enters most. Yet here are passages which must not be overlooked.

4. Ancient liturgies, confessions, and prayers: the Shema, the Shemoneh Esreh (the "Eighteen Benedictions" or "Prayers"), and the broad outlines of the 613 Commandments. It is true that the Benedictions were revised by Gamaliel II, but probably only revised.

[20] The debt to A. Lukyn Williams' *Talmudic Judaism and Christianity* (London: S.P.C.K., 1933), pp. 38-43, is clearly evident in points 1, 2, and 4.

[21] Moore, *Judaism,* Vol. I, p. 29; cf. Vol. III, pp. 6 ff.

[22] While it can never be proved, there seems no reason to doubt that "the authorities in whose names statements are quoted are a help, if not an infallible index, to fixing their date" (Finkelstein, "Book of Jubilees and Rabbinic Halaka," *op. cit.,* p. 39).

[23] Moore, *Judaism,* Vol. I, p. 157.

Except for the confessional insertion, there is no reason to doubt their predestruction quality. The antiquity and importance of the Shema as a recognized confession is attested by its inclusion on the Nash Papyrus and on a phylactery from the Wadi Murabbaat finds.[24] And in regard to the 613 Commandments, we can at least accept the broad outlines therein presented.

NONCANONICAL LITERATURE

The question concerning the importance of the apocryphal and so-called pseudepigraphical writings in the study of Pharisaism in particular, and first-century Judaism in general, has not ceased to interest and confound investigators of every type and ability. And with the information from Qumran continuing to pour forth, such interest has been greatly revived. Definite conclusions are impossible, especially in view of the importance of the finds from the Qumran libraries for this area of study and the great amount of material from the caves that has yet to be evaluated.[25] Tentative opinions, however, must be expressed.

Certain extreme views need not detain us here: as, for example, that all noncanonical writings except Sirach were wholly unknown to real Pharisaism,[26] or, on the other hand, that they were probably more

[24] The Nash Papyrus, a small piece of papyrus containing the Decalogue and the Shema, has been variously dated from the second century A.D. back to the second century B.C. Of late, scholarship has tended to favor the latter half of the first century B.C. for its date (cf. H. H. Rowley, *The Zadokite Fragments and the Dead Sea Scrolls* [Oxford: Blackwell, 1952], p. 13, for an excellent summary on the various dates assigned). The finding in the Wadi Murabbaat caves of a phylactery containing the three passages, Exod. 13:1-16, Deut. 11:13-21, *and* Deut. 6:4-9, and this in close conjunction with an apparent marriage contract dated in the seventh year of the reign of Hadrian (c. A.D. 124), offers further evidence for the antiquity of this celebrated prayer (cf. Y. Yadin, *The Message of the Scrolls* [London: Weidenfeld & Nicholson, 1957], p. 70).

[25] The relevancy of the Qumran finds for pre-Christian Judaism has been disputed by S. Zeitlin, G. R. Driver, J. L. Teicher, and P. Kahle. But their dating, ranging from the third century A.D. to the Middle Ages, has failed to convince in the face of the evidence from archaeology and paleography. See W. F. Albright, "Postscript," *B.A.S.O.R.—S.S.*, Nos. 10-12 (1951), pp. 57-60, for a brief, early, and altogether reliable summary of the evidence both pro and con.

[26] E.g., Schechter, *Aspects of Rabbinic Theology*, p. 5.

representative of early Pharisaism than is the Talmud.[27] Nor should we view all of these writings as representative of one type of thought or piety. The solution is not to be found in so simple a statement as that they are Pharisaic, or not Pharisaic.

With the exception of Sirach, G. F. Moore classes all of the apocryphal books as outside "the schools" and "not intrinsically of immense importance" in the study of first-century Pharisaism.[28] Yet it does not follow that the apocryphal works neither reflect nor have influenced early Pharisaism, even though it be true that they originated outside the "schools" of official Judaism. Akiba, at the beginning of the second century A.D., "protested strongly against the canonicity of certain of the Apocrypha, Ecclesiasticus, for instance"; yet he had "no objection to the private reading of the Apocrypha, as is evident from the fact that he himself makes frequent use of Ecclesiasticus."[29] That an early second-century rabbi felt compelled to express himself against official acceptance of the Apocrypha indicates that at least until his time the apocryphal writings had some influence within Palestine. So too, in view of his own practice of reading in private the Apocrypha, his assertion that the reading of "external books"—i.e., those outside the canon—invalidates one for a share in the world to come[30] must be viewed as denouncing only the reading of such books as if they possessed the authority of Scripture and/or the reading of them aloud in public study and liturgical recitation.[31] In all likelihood, the Pharisaic attitude was similar to that of Qumran: i.e., a giving of great care and attention to the Scriptures and the traditional interpretations within the group while taking a lesser interest, though still definitely an interest, in those works classed as outside the canon.[32]

[27] E.g., Schweitzer, *Paul and His Interpreters,* p. 50.

[28] Moore, *Judaism,* Vol. I, pp. 126-27.

[29] L. Ginzberg, "Akiba ben Joseph," *J. E.,* Vol. I, p. 305; cf. also G. F. Moore, "Apocrypha," *J. E.,* Vol. II, p. 6. See Mish. Sanh. 10.1 and b. Sanh. 100b.

[30] Mish. Sanh. 10.1.

[31] Cf. W. D. Davies, "The Jewish Background of the Teaching of Jesus: Apocalyptic and Pharisaism," *E. T.,* Vol. LIX, No. 9 (June, 1948), p. 237.

[32] F. M. Cross, Jr., points out that while the biblical portions of the Qumran texts usually "have a standard format and are written in an elegant book hand; scribal treatment of non-canonical works is rarely as careful or fine" (*The Ancient Library of Qumran* [London: Duckworth, 1958], p. 29). This purely

It seems wisest, therefore, to acknowledge the Apocrypha's inferiority to both canonical Scripture[33] and oral tradition, but also to insist that as popular devotional literature it had some influence upon Pharisaism generally and perhaps partially reflects the thought of some individual Pharisees. On the whole, there is the same stress upon and delight in the Law in the Apocryphal books as in the Talmudic literature.[34] It has every appearance of being commendable to a Pharisee's interest and in some cases expressive of a Pharisaic mind. Thus, our study will use much of the Apocrypha as a secondary source in understanding Pharisaism: the pseudohistorical treatise I Esdras, the wisdom of Sirach, the popular tales of Tobit and Judith, and the histories of I and II Maccabees as influencing first-century Palestinian thought;[35] I Baruch and IV Ezra as reflecting aspects of early Pharisaic theology. The precise placing of the Wisdom of Solomon as preceding or contemporary with the Judaism of Paul's day is very uncertain.[36] Probably it is best to view it as "newly published when Paul was a student."[37] The other additions included in the LXX's listing are all, with the possible exception of Susanna, insignificant.

Of the remaining apocryphal, ethical, polemic, and popular works which are extant from this period and which lie outside the realms of the canon and so-called Apocrypha, none except the Letter of

---

mechanical feature probably reflects the attitude of the sect toward the literatures in its possession (cf. J. van der Ploeg, *The Excavations at Qumran* [London: Longmans, Green, 1958], p. 154).

[33] The Prologue to Sirach, Contra Apion I. 8. 38-42, and possibly II Macc. 2:13-14, evidence the Apocrypha's inferiority to Scripture.

[34] See R. Marcus, *Law in the Apocrypha* (New York: Columbia University Press, 1927), esp. pp. 52-59.

[35] The fact that Qumran has not as yet yielded copies of I and II Maccabees, coupled with the realization that "the Qumran library has not produced works composed in Jewish circles hostile to the sectarians" (Cross, *Ancient Library of Qumran,* p. 148, n. 5), is a possible argument from silence for the nonsectarian character of these works.

[36] See *Ap. and Ps.,* ed. R. H. Charles (Oxford: Clarendon Press, 1913), Vol. I, and Swete, *Intro. to the O.T. in Greek,* pp. 265-88, for discussions regarding the dating of the apocryphal works. The conclusions arrived at in these works have been generally followed here.

[37] C. H. Dodd, *Romans,* M. N. T. C. (London: Hodder & Stoughton, 1933), p. 81.

Aristeas and the Story of Ahikar has sufficient evidence behind it to claim direct influence upon or representation of Pharisaism. Jewish and some Christian scholars have long insisted that "each of these books comes from circles which represented special interests, and were apparently of limited influence. None of them is written with the responsibility attaching to authors who had any official position in Judaism."[38] The Qumran finds have now indicated the sectarian nature of such works as Enoch, Jubilees, the Ascension of Isaiah, the Martyrdom of Isaiah, [39] and the Damascus Document,[40] besides, of course, the distinctive Qumran literature itself. Probably the Psalms of Solomon must also be assigned to this class.[41] And yet we must not suppose that these works are entirely foreign to the spirit of Pharisaism. Apocalypticism, for instance, is speculatively carried further in these extraneous books than it would be in Pharisaism, but basic eschatology is common to both.[42] There is a difference of emphasis between Apocalypticism and Pharisaism, but "it is grievously erroneous to enlarge this difference into a cleavage."[43] The heavily

[38] L. Finkelstein, "The Oldest Midrash: Pre-Rabbinic Ideals and Teachings in the Passover Haggadah," *H. T. R.*, Vol. XXXI, No. 4 (Oct., 1938), p. 293; see also "Book of Jubilees and Rabbinic Halaka," *op. cit.*, pp. 39-40.

[39] Not that these works are definitely Essene, but they are of a common background and mentality. See M. Burrows, *Dead Sea Scrolls* (New York: Viking Press, 1956), pp. 220-21; K. G. Kuhn, "The Two Messiahs of Aaron and Israel," *The Scrolls and the New Testament,* ed. K. Stendahl (London: S.C.M. Press, 1958), p. 257.

[40] One of the first to point out the relationship between CDC and IQS was K. G. Kuhn, "Die in Palästina gefundenen hebräischen Texte und das Neue Testament," *Z. T. K.*, Vol. XLVII, Heft 2 (1950), pp. 196 ff.

[41] See Burrows, *Dead Sea Scrolls,* pp. 221-22, for a moderate and reserved evaluation and conclusion that "in their attitudes and their points of view the Psalms of Solomon and the Dead Sea Scrolls have much in common." This similarity of outlook is suggested in Ps. of Sol. 17:17-19: "There was not among them [the rulers?] one that wrought in the midst of Jerusalem mercy and truth. They that loved the synagogues of the pious fled from them, as sparrows that fly from their nest. They wandered in deserts that their lives might be saved from harm."

[42] See J. Bloch, *On the Apocalyptic in Judaism* (Philadelphia: Dropsie College, 1952), where the extraneous character of these sources for Pharisaism is advocated and yet the overlapping of the two movements on the question of eschatology is pointed out.

[43] W. D. Davies, "The Jewish Background of the Teaching of Jesus: Apocalyptic and Pharisaism," *op. cit.*, p. 237.

apocalyptic Daniel and Ezekiel were accepted as canonical in Pharisaism,[44] and from the response of the Pharisaic IV Ezra, the non-Pharisaic apocalypses seem to have made some impression. As in the case of the rabbinically read Sirach which also was read at Qumran,[45] so there seems to have been an interpenetration on matters eschatological as well as ethical. We cannot assume a Pharisaic acceptance of much of the extreme apocalyptic thought then current. But neither can we deny its awareness of this thought, nor its basic eschatological agreement with and limited absorption of the popular apocalypticism of the day. Such opposition to this view as the Talmud affords must be explained as the result of disastrous false hopes, political ruin, and opposition from a rival religious movement claiming to be the fulfillment of Israel's destiny. And yet, at best the so-called pseudepigraphical evidence is only indirect and secondary.

From the nature of the Letter of Aristeas and its use by Josephus,[46] it seems probable that this work was current and accepted in Palestine. The Letter is not only a glorification of the Jewish nation and its literature, but also an apology to the Palestinians for the LXX. It appears to have been written with an eye to the Hebraic attitude toward translating the sacred into the vulgar. Possibly its author was a former Palestinian Pharisee living in Egypt who well realized the reaction back home to the translation of the LXX, and who knew how to soften the blow. And it appears that it accomplished its purpose. Likewise, the Story of Ahikar was probably accepted as edifying reading. It seems to have been assumed by Jesus as common knowledge.[47] And the attitude of just revenge on the part of some of the Pharisees would give it a receptive audience, if it had not already had a part

[44] Ezekiel was at one time, in light of the popularity of the apocalyptic extremists, considered too troublesome for public use. Even its canonicity was questioned. But its withdrawal was at no time based upon a question of its sacredness, its inspiration, or its prophetic authorship. Rather, it was considered "expedient to withdraw the book from public use lest the unlearned or the half-learned be stumbled by the apparent discrepancies between it and the Law" (Moore, *Judaism,* Vol. I, p. 247). The fact that it remained in the canon must be considered significant.

[45] Cf. Burrows, *Dead Sea Scrolls,* p. 219.

[46] Antiq., Preface 3 and XII. 2. 1-15.

[47] Jesus' parables of the Wicked Servant and the Prodigal Son, and His teaching on overcoming evil with good, seem to have the Story of Ahikar in mind, as pointed out by J. R. Harris, A. S. Lewis, and F. C. Conybeare, "Story of Ahikar." *Ap. and Ps.,* Vol. II, p. 719.

in the forming of such an attitude. If it had not earlier been introduced into Palestine, the introduction given it by the Book of Tobit would have made its entrance inevitable.[48]

Regarding the Testaments of the Twelve Patriarchs, the very relevancy of the material makes it both important and difficult to assess its relation to early Judaism. The older view was that it is a Christian work. During the last century it has been generally accepted as Jewish with extensive Christian interpolations.[49] Since Qumran it has often been viewed as an Essene writing, either with Christian additions[50] or strictly Essene.[51] And lately, M. de Jonge has argued that in its present form the work is a Christian composition.[52] Upon the basis of a literary analysis, and without reference to the Qumran evidence which came to light after the writing of his dissertation, De Jonge at first concluded that "the author knew a Jewish Testament of Levi and a Jewish Testament of Naphtali and used these as examples and as sources of material for the composition of his 'Testaments of the Twelve Patriarchs.' "[53] And in seeming confirmation of his thesis came the announcement from the Rockefeller Museum Scrollery in Jerusalem of the identification of Aramaic fragments of a Testament of Levi and Hebrew fragments of a Testament of Naphtali among the scrolls, with no evidence to date of any other "Testaments."[54] Recently De Jonge has retracted his original position, and now views the work as a Jewish composition which has undergone a thoroughgoing Christian redaction;[55] i.e. not a Christian writer using Jewish sources

[48] Tobit 1:21, 2:10, 11:17-18, and 14:10 refer explicitly to the characters and plot of the Story of Ahikar.

[49] Charles, *Ap. and Ps.*, Vol. II, in agreeing with the earlier work of Schnapp and Bousset, has been most influential in establishing this position in the English-speaking world.

[50] Cf., e.g., Kuhn, "Two Messiahs of Aaron and Israel," *op. cit.*, p. 58.

[51] Cf., e.g., A. Dupont-Sommer, *The Jewish Sect of Qumran and the Essenes,* trans. R. D. Barnett (London: Vallentine, Mitchell, 1954), pp. 38-57, 165-66, and *The Dead Sea Scrolls,* trans. E. M. Rowley (London: Blackwell, 1952), pp. 94-96.

[52] *The Testaments of the Twelve Patriarchs* (Assen: Van Gorcum, 1953).

[53] *Ibid.*, p. 117.

[54] J. T. Milik, "Le Testament de Levi en Arameen," *R. B.*, Vol., LXII (1955), pp. 398-406. F. M. Cross, Jr., in 1958 wrote, "The Testament of Naphtali is unpublished and only recently identified" (*Ancient Library of Qumran,* p. 34, n. 62; see also p. 150, n. 7).

[55] Cf. H. H. Rowley, *The Relevance of Apocalyptic,* rev. ed. (London: Lutterworth Press, 1963), pp. 68-69.

or Christian interpolations on a Jewish theme, but an extensive reworking of an earlier Jewish composition so that the entire product reflects Christian theology. Definiteness at this time is impossible. The Testaments of the Twelve Patriarchs may be a Jewish writing; in its present state it may be Christian.[56] Whatever the final answer—and here we must await the joint efforts of Bedouin and scholar for further word from the Dead Sea scrolls—it seems precarious to use the Greek version of the Testaments to illustrate *any* section of pre-Christian Judaism.

We may conclude, therefore, that I Esdras, Sirach, Tobit, Judith, I and II Maccabees, the Story of Ahikar, and the Letter of Aristeas had a direct influence upon first-century Palestinian Pharisaism; while I Baruch and IV Ezra reflect aspects of such thought. The other writings of the day must be viewed as without sufficient evidence to be any more than at best indirect and remote witnesses to Pharisaic Judaism's theology. Therefore I shall use the major portion of the Apocrypha, the Letter of Aristeas, and the Story of Ahikar as sources in the attempt to understand first-century Palestinian Pharisaism, though with the recognition that they are of value secondary to the evidence from the Talmud, and with the realization that the sectarian literature I have excluded may still furnish indirect aid in the quest.

THE HISTORICAL ACCOUNTS

For a knowledge of the religious situation of first-century Palestine, Josephus is somewhat disappointing. While his works promise much and are valuable historically, they reflect the fact that their author had little interest in religion for its own sake. Josephus' value as a source for understanding first-century Hebrew theology is minimized by his evident aloofness from the main stream of Judaism. And thus, when it comes to theological thought, he must always be used in a purely

[56] This is the view of J. T. Milik, *Ten Years of Discovery in the Wilderness of Judaea,* trans. J. Strugnell (London: S. C. M. Press, 1959), pp. 34-35, which has been accepted by M. Burrows, *More Light on the Dead Sea Scrolls* (London: Secker & Warburg, 1958), pp. 179-80, and J. van der Ploeg, *Excavations at Qumran,* pp. 205-206. J. B. Lightfoot had argued earlier that the work was definitely that of a Christian author, possibly from the Nazarene sect (cf. *Epistle to the Galatians* [London: Macmillan, 1890], pp. 319-21).

secondary measure and suspected of telling us no more than what was popularly held by the Jewish people and what would be acceptable to the better of the pagan thinkers.

In the canonical Gospels we have an historical record that is in many respects just the reverse of that of Josephus. Here the purpose is primarily religious, with the chronological recounting of historical events treated in a subsidiary fashion. They were in a very real sense "written out of faith and for faith." It is therefore necessary to view all the references in the Gospels to the contemporary religious scene in Palestine as secondary to and conditioned by the Christian perspective. But the recognition that the Gospels are not without bias and are not primarily interested in Judaism *per se* is not to discredit their trustworthiness in the area of our present concern. In fact, I agree with G. F. Moore that "the Gospels themselves are the best witness to the religious and moral teaching of the synagogue in the middle forty years of the first century."[57]

The trustworthiness of the Acts account as an indirect witness to authentic Jewish tradition and an accurate representation of the life and preaching of the Apostle Paul has been often denied. Many have pointed to the evident "conciliatory purpose" of the work as being a detriment to an objective treatment of history and thus fatal to a true representation of events and statements. And indeed, it seems that one of the aims of the writer was to counter a pre-Marcionism by laying stress on the parallels and unity between Peter and Paul. But the recognition of this purpose does not necessarily reflect upon the credibility of the account. J. B. Lightfoot has correctly observed that "such a purpose is at least as likely to have been entertained by a writer, if the two apostles were essentially united, as if they were not. The truth or falsehood of the account must be determined on other grounds."[58] The primary argument against the historicity of Acts is that it completely breaks down the moral character of the Apostle Paul, presenting him as quite a different person than he appears in his own letters. Events and speeches which have only a loose correspondence to actuality were invented according to the purpose of the author and the pattern of the day. But is this really so? Adolf

[57] Moore, *Judaism,* Vol. I, p. 132.
[58] Lightfoot, *Galatians,* p. 359.

Harnack's work on Acts is the notable exception to this view.[59] The last chapter of the present work will consider the relation of Paul's practice and speeches in defense, as represented in Acts, to his teaching as given in the Epistles. Much that could be said here is better left for that later discussion. Suffice it here to anticipate the conclusions of that exploration by saying that such features of Acts as the Tübingen scholars have insisted were entirely non-Pauline are not quite so incredible as has been claimed. Here is one of those areas in the profile of Paul which needs clarification, and which I hope to penetrate and explicate in the present study. And thus, since I believe that "the most weighty reason"[60] against the trustworthiness of the Acts presentation is in reality faulty, this study will make use of that record in conformity to the rule of J. Weiss:

> It should be considered an axiom that a document must be read in the sense and in the form in which it stands until proof is brought forward that this is impossible. One should first see whether, assuming its genuineness, there is a convincing historical picture; whether the writings suit the setting in which they are placed; and only when this is shown to be impossible should it be declared spurious.[61]

Yet, because of its nature as being at least one step removed from the innermost mind of the Apostle, the historian must always consider the Acts as secondary to the Epistles for a knowledge of Paul's thought. And further, while it claims to be an accurate account of history, it must be remembered that it does not claim to be, nor can it be viewed as, presenting a verbatim and complete record of

[59] See *Luke the Physician,* trans. J. R. Wilkinson (London: Williams & Norgate, 1907); *The Acts of the Apostles,* trans. J. R. Wilkinson (London: Williams & Norgate, 1909); *The Date of the Acts and of the Synoptic Gospels,* trans. J. R. Wilkinson (London: Williams & Norgate, 1911). Regarding the historicity of the geographical and cultural details in Acts, see Wm. Ramsay, *St. Paul the Traveller and the Roman Citizen* (London: Hodder & Stoughton, 1908).

[60] Baur, *Paul,* Vol. I, p. 11.

[61] J. Weiss, *The History of Primitive Christianity,* trans. by "four friends," ed. F. C. Grant (London: Macmillan, 1937), Vol. I, p. 153; though of course Weiss used this argument only in connection with the radical criticism that denied the authenticity of all the Pauline epistles. He really believed that the non-Pauline elements in Acts were conclusive evidence against the position that the work was written by Luke and is to be considered trustworthy (cf. *ibid.,* pp. 4-11).

speeches and events. From an historical perspective it should be accepted as an honest and sincere attempt to relate the affairs of the early Church and of Paul, and on that basis be constantly tested as to its correspondence to the Pauline letters and as to what we know of the historical and cultural situation of the times.

THE PAULINE CORPUS

Although the Tübingen school accepted only the *Hauptbriefe* (Galatians, I and II Corinthians, Romans) as authentic, there is now general agreement regarding the Pauline authorship of I Thessalonians, Colossians, Philemon, and Philippians as well. Second Thessalonians has been held in question primarily because of the apocalyptic section of 2:1-12, which is such an integral part of the letter and its purpose that it cannot be regarded as a later interpolation. But with the realization that, though the Apostle's eschatology was reorientated, it was not abandoned, the main argument against this epistle becomes quite weak. The general nature and style of the so-called Epistle to the Ephesians, coupled with its striking similarity to Colossians, have led many to view it as a summary of and an introduction to the letters of Paul by a later Paulinist.[62] For the purpose at hand, we need not enter into this dispute; though I do believe that the hypothesis of a circular letter written at the same time as the Colossian letter is at least as good an explanation for these peculiarities as any other. Suffice it here to point out that even those who most staunchly oppose its Pauline authorship insist upon its faithfulness to the Pauline teaching.[63] And this is all we really need to be concerned about in the present study.

Of letters claiming Pauline authorship, the most problematic are

[62] In addition to James Moffatt and the list of Continental scholars which he cites (*An Introduction to the Literature of the New Testament,* 3d ed. rev. [Edinburgh: T. & T. Clark, 1918], p. 375), note: J. Weiss, *Primitive Christianity,* Vol. I, p. 150; E. J. Goodspeed, *The Key to Ephesians* (Chicago: University of Chicago Press, 1956); W. L. Knox, *St. Paul* (Edinburgh: Davies, 1932) pp. 147-48, and *St. Paul and the Church of the Gentiles,* pp. 182-84; M. Dibelius, *Paul,* trans. F. Clarke (New York: Longmans, Green, 1953), p. 8; C. L. Mitton, *The Epistle to the Ephesians: Its Authorship, Origin and Purpose* (Oxford: Clarendon Press, 1951).

[63] Goodspeed says that while it was written between A.D. 90 and 100, "every sentence of it owed its vital quality to him" (*Key to Ephesians,* p. xiv);

the pastorals. In 1807 Schleiermacher questioned their genuineness; while in 1922, after a century of debate, the statistical analysis of P. N. Harrison was published.[64] To most scholars, Harrison's presentation convincingly demonstrated that the three works are the effort of another writer who incorporated genuine fragments of earlier Pauline correspondence. Harrison's methodology, however, has come under cogent criticism; especially by W. Michaelis in 1929 and Bruce M. Metzger in 1958.[65] And lately, scholarship has witnessed the beginning of a return to Pauline authorship on the part of some investigators.[66] The question as to whether the Pastorals are the product of a later author or editor using Pauline fragments, the expression of the Apostle himself in a situation of which we know nothing, or the result of an aged or infirm Apostle giving greater liberty to an unknown amanuensis, is of great significance in a study of first-century ecclesiology and the mission of Paul. But it is not vitally important for the present work. It is in the accepted epistles, principally the *Hauptbriefe,* that the essential features of the Apostle's thought regarding our subject are found. Thus, while I personally believe all thirteen epistles to be authentic writings of the Apostle Paul, we may, for the purposes of this study, leave the problem of the pastorals somewhat open. That they are Pauline is all we need assert at the present, since they are only subsidiary documents for the subject at hand.

The case of Hebrews is both dissimilar and somewhat similar to that of the pastorals. It is dissimilar from the above thirteen at least in that the epistle does not claim Pauline authorship explicitly. It is

---

and W. L. Knox insists that the non-Pauline authorship "must not be taken as depreciating the value of the letter. The writer combines a real measure of originality with a deep understanding of Paulinism and a thorough loyalty to it" (*St. Paul and the Church of the Gentiles,* p. 184).

[64] P. N. Harrison, *The Problem of the Pastorals* (London: Oxford University Press, 1922).

[65] W. Michaelis, "Pastoralbriefe und Wortstatistik," *Z. N. W.*, Vol. XXVIII, Heft 1 (1929), pp. 69-76; B. M. Metzger, "A Reconsideration of Certain Arguments Against the Pauline Authorship of the Pastoral Epistles," *E. T.*, Vol. LXX, No. 3 (Dec., 1958), pp. 91-94.

[66] E.g., J. Jeremias, *Die Briefe an Timotheus und Titus* (Göttingen: Vandenhoeck & Ruprecht, 1949), pp. 4-5; and J. Behm, in his revision of P. Feine's *Einleitung in das Neue Testament* (Leipzig: Hinrichs, 1950), pp. 206-18.

similar to Ephesians and the pastorals in that its content adds little to the considerations of this study. Questions regarding the authorship and provenience of the Book of Hebrews are of real and vital concern to an understanding of the book itself and of other issues in theology, but they need not detain us in our study of Paul's legality-liberty dialectic.

Background

II

A Hebrew of the Hebrews

To UNDERSTAND Paul rightly, reference must be made to his Jewish background and the influence of that background upon him. But since the Judaism of the predestruction period was a complex within a unity, a general summary of Jewish thought offers little real understanding without some indication of Paul's early relationship to it. Saul, "who is also called Paul,"[1] must be located in the thought of his day; the nature of his Judaism must be designated before it can be analyzed.

A great deal of investigation and debate has entered into this question. As each aspect of ancient thought has become known (e.g., apocalyptic, Mystery Religion, rabbinic, and lately Essene), the process of trial and error—thesis, antithesis, and synthesis—has been repeated. There have been many false starts, and many diverse interpretations are current. But a general concurrence of thought seems to be forming. It is not my purpose here to outline the history of that investigation, nor to point out every influence upon or similarity to Paul from these fields. I shall restrict the discussion to the Hebraic biographical claims made in the New Testament regarding Paul and to the criticisms made against them; allowing such positive evidence as is available for the Hebraic character of Paul's preconversion Judaism to appear later in this study where it is pertinent. In this chapter, therefore, the Pauline assertions will set the theme with the objections to them calling the tune.

THE BIOGRAPHICAL CLAIMS

It is not necessary to refer to all the explicit biographical claims in the Pauline literature, for many of them could be ascribed to either

[1] Acts 13:9.

a Hellenistic or a Hebraic Pharisee.[2] But three are pertinent: three which associate, or at least imply a thorough acquaintance of, Paul's pre-conversion Judaism with that religious orientation acclaimed the most Hebraic of the day.

A Hebrew of Hebrews. Phil. 3:5 and II Cor. 11:22 both state that Paul was a Hebraicist as opposed to a Hellenistic Jew. The phrase "a Hebrew of Hebrews" (*Hebraios ex Hebraiōn*) in Philippians certainly means more than simply of Israelite stock, since the Apostle has just previously traced his lineage by saying "an Israelite by race, of the tribe of Benjamin." It need not, however, be taken in the other extreme to mean a Jew born in Palestine of parents also born in Palestine. On the one hand, we must insist that the phrase claims more than just Jewish descent. On the other, we cannot assert that it means more than a Hebraic religious background. It is best rendered "a Hebrew born of Hebrews" (RSV), or more freely "a Hebrew son of Hebrew parents" (Moffatt). In the II Corinthians passage, Paul matches qualification to qualification against the best that can be produced by Jew or Jewish Christian. In such a context, "Are they Hebrews? So am I!" (*Hebraioi eisin? kagō*) can only mean a Hebraicist as against a Hellenist.

At the feet of Gamaliel. Acts 22:3 represents Paul as saying that he was educated "at (*para*) the feet of Gamaliel." This is the famous Gamaliel I, who, like Hillel his grandfather,[3] was highly esteemed by his people: "Since Rabban Gamaliel the elder died there has been no more reverence for the law; and purity and abstinence died out

[2] Such as being circumcised on the eighth day, of the people of Israel, of the tribe of Benjamin, as to the Law a Pharisee, as to zeal a persecutor of the Church. Even such statements as "as to righteousness under the law blameless" (Phil. 3:6), "educated according to the strict manner of the law of our fathers" (Acts 22:3), and "I advanced in Judaism beyond many of my own age among my people, so extremely zealous was I for the traditions of my fathers" (Gal. 1:14), could be honestly said by a Pharisee whose only frame of reference was a Hellenized Diaspora Judaism. As C. G. Montefiore has said, a Hellenistic Jew "could fancy himself perfectly orthodox" (*Judaism and St. Paul,* p. 94).

[3] Or, possibly, his father. For the position that Hillel was the father of Gamaliel, see: E. Schürer, *The Jewish People in the Time of Jesus Christ,* 2d ed., trans. J. MacPherson (Edinburgh: T. & T. Clark, 1890), Div. II, Vol. I, p. 363 and n. 164; H. L. Strack, *Intro. to the Talmud and Midrash,* p. 109. Probably, however, Hillel as Gamaliel's grandfather is the better view; cf. R. T. Herford, "Pirke Aboth," *Ap. and Ps.,* Vol. II, p. 694, and W. Bacher, "Gamaliel I," *J. E.,* Vol. V, pp. 558-59.

at the same time."[4] Such a qualification, if we may accept the Acts account as a faithful report in this instance and Paul's words as true, would go far toward establishing that the Apostle was well acquainted with the best in Palestinian Pharisaism.

Brought up in this city. Acts 22:3 also indicates Paul's early residence in Jerusalem. There is some difference of opinion regarding the proper reading of this verse. Nestle's text places the comma after the phrase "in this city" and thus has Paul saying: "Brought up in this city, at the feet of Gamaliel educated according to the strict manner of the law of our fathers."[5] Punctuating the verse thus, one could view the passage as claiming that Paul's infancy was spent in Jerusalem and that he was therefore a resident of the city even before his training under Gamaliel. Alexander Souter inserts the comma after the phrase "at the feet of Gamaliel" and thus represents Paul as saying: "Brought up in this city at the feet of Gamaliel, educated according to the strict manner of the law of our fathers."[6] This latter reading connects the Apostle's residence in Jerusalem with his education under Gamaliel. But however we punctuate the verse, the claim is still made that Paul came to Jerusalem in his youth; whether as a child before his instruction under Gamaliel or primarily for the purpose of rabbinic training.

Needless to say, these statements have not gained universal acceptance. In light of their understanding of first-century Judaism, Jewish scholars have rejected these claims of one who they believe rejected them and the ancestral faith.[7] And many of those working in

[4] Mish. Sot. 9.15.

[5] So Moffatt's translation.

[6] So the AV and RSV.

[7] The liberal Jewish scholar C. G. Montefiore has been most vociferous in this regard. Though he cannot claim to represent Orthodox Judaism on many points, on this question he has shouted what all Judaism has muttered down through the centuries—especially the Orthodox. His insistence is that Paul's Judaism "was not Rabbinic Judaism, but Diaspora Judaism," and that as such it was of a "poorer and inferior type" to that which existed in Jerusalem (*Judaism and St. Paul,* p. 93; cf. also Samuel Sandmel, *A Jewish Understanding of the New Testament* [New York: University Publishers, 1956] pp. 37-51 and *passim*). Paul's view of the Messiah, his concern for the Gentile, his "pessimism," his theory of the Law, his ignorance of the rabbinic doctrine of repentance, his mysticism, his soteriology, his religious psychology—all these are opposite to true rabbinic thought (*Judaism and St. Paul,* pp. 58-60). "For these phenomena Paul's individual genius and the conversion at Damascus do not

the field of comparative religion have looked askance at the Hebraic claims, preferring to argue from the analogies between Paul's Christian theology and the Mysteries to his early dependence on Hellenistic thought.[8]

The question is pertinent. The position that is taken regarding Paul's preconversion position in the complex of Pharisaism will affect one's whole understanding of his teaching and practice—both as a Jew and as a Christian. If his later Christian theology is dependent upon

---

suffice. Paul must have been less than a Rabbinic Jew, and more. To explain him are needed: (1) a Judaism which was other than Rabbinic; (2) religious influences, conceptions and practices which were not Jewish at all" (*ibid.*, p. 66). The argument is not that Paul consciously adopted the concepts of Hellenism and the Mystery Religions, for these he viewed with horror; but that he unconsciously assimilated their views and outlook, so that his religion differed from rabbinic Judaism in Jerusalem "in those very points which constitute the essence and bloom of a religion, different less in dogma than in attitude, less in creed than in outlook and emotion" (*ibid.*, pp. 94-95). Thus Montefiore is "disposed to look with much suspicion upon the statement in the Acts . . . that Paul 'was brought up in Jerusalem, at the feet of Gamaliel, instructed according to the strict manner of the law of our fathers' " (*ibid.*, p. 90). And he regards Phil. 3:4-6 as having "no genuine Jewish ring" (*ibid.*, p. 94). To Judaism, it is the fact of Paul's background in Diaspora Judaism, a religion which was "poorer, colder, less satisfying and more pessimistic than Rabbinic Judaism" (*ibid.*, p. 126) which underlies the reason why "his profoundly religious nature had not been given the nurture it required" (*ibid.*, p. 127), and why he later "sets up imaginary ninepins in order to knock them down" (C. G. Montefiore, "Jewish Concepts of Christianity," *H. J.*, Vol. XXVIII [Jan., 1930], p. 251). This approach has been taken over by a few Gentile scholars as well, e.g., James Parkes (cf. esp. *Jesus, Paul and the Jews* [London: S.C.M. Press, 1936], p. 124 and *passim*).

[8] With R. Reitzenstein and W. Bousset leading the field, scores began to turn their attention to the analogies between Greek and Christian thought. In the excitement of discovery, superficialities were so stressed and analogies so used as proof of necessary dependence that some began to ask "whether Comparative Religion has hunted down its game according to fair forest-law, or whether its 'bag' is poached" (A. Schweitzer, *Paul and His Interpreters*, p. 194). But not all were "poachers," and in the endeavor to adjust the excitement of discovery to a saner perspective much thought was expended. So much so that in 1928 A. D. Nock said in lighthearted irony: " 'Saviour-gods' and mysteries probably did not bulk so large in the life of the first century A.D. as in modern study" ("Early Gentile Christianity and Its Hellenistic Background," in *Essays on the Trinity and the Incarnation*, ed. A. E. J. Rawlinson [London: Hodder & Stoughton, 1928], p. 81). But all the effort has not been in vain, for today can be seen what appears to be a gathering of ideas flowing in one general direction; though of course Bultmann and his followers still argue for popular Greek philosophy and Diaspora theology as the real intellectual and spiritual rootage of Paul.

Hellenistic thought at few or many places—and not rooted in Palestinian Judaism, his conversion experience, and/or his Christian understanding of the Old Testament—then the extent to which it is dependent upon such Hellenism is the extent to which the biographical claims to Hebraic Judaism must be viewed with suspicion. The answer to this question determines the sources and analogies to be stressed and the interpretive principles to be employed in understanding the religious life of Rabbi Saul and in appreciating much of the Pauline theology.

It is useless at this point to bring in general arguments for either the authenticity or the nonhistorical character of the speeches in Acts and the letters of Paul. We can only test the Pauline assertions by comparing what is known of his training, actions, attitudes, concepts, expressions, and hermeneutics with what is known of Hebraic and Hellenistic thought.

A DIASPORA HOME

The most obvious objection to Paul's Hebraic background is the fact of his Diaspora home.[9] Acts 21:39 represents him as calling himself "a Jew of Tarsus of Cilicia"; Acts 22:3 has it "a Jew born in Tarsus of Cilicia"; in Acts 9:11 the words of the Lord in the vision to Ananias refer to Paul as "a man of Tarsus"; and in Acts 9:30 and 11:25 he first flees to and then is called from Tarsus. Yet his Diaspora home is not as obvious a sign of his Hellenism as would first appear.

The scene of Paul's upbringing. The problem is complicated by the uncertainty of the proper reading of Acts 22:3. Is the participle *anatethrammenos* to be separated by a comma from the instruction at the feet of Gamaliel, and thus possibly to refer to a pre-educational rearing in Jerusalem? Or is the participle to be connected to both its succeeding phrases, "in this city" and "at the feet of Gamaliel," and

[9] Many consider this conclusive, believing it evident that "by the circumstances of his birth and upbringing Paul belonged to the liberal Hellenistic side of Judaism" (S. H. Hooke, "Christianity and Mystery Religions," *Judaism and Christianity,* Vol. I, ed. W. O. E. Oesterley [London: Sheldon Press, 1937], p. 241). Cf. also T. R. Glover, *Paul of Tarsus* (London: S. C. M. Press, 1925), pp. 5-23; M. Dibelius, *Paul,* pp. 15-26; K. Kohler, "Saul of Tarsus,"*J. E.,* Vol. XI, pp. 79-80.

thus temporally equivalent to the participle *pepaideumenos*? The first reading allows the possibility that Paul's infancy or every early childhood was spent in Jerusalem in the household of his elder sister.[10] The second connects his coming to Jerusalem with his education, and the question then depends upon when he came to be so educated.

Both readings are possible. The second, however, seems more probable, for then all the verbal nouns in the line of qualifications presented in verses 3 and 4 would each uniformly precede its clause. To separate *anatethrammenos* from "at the feet of Gamaliel" would require *pepaideumenos* to function verbally for that phrase and the next, and would land the participle right in the middle of its clause—disrupting the uniform pattern. Now such disruption is certainly possible. But, all else being equal, certainly symmetry and order should tell.[11]

The question thus turns on the age of Paul when he, or his family for him,[12] sought an education at the Pharisaic school in Jerusalem. And here the evidence is definitely inadequate. That the Mishnaic time schedule of "five years old for the Scripture" and "ten years for the Mishnah"[13] reflects Pharisaism's practice in Paul's day, or that Josephus' educational schedule was normative,[14] are both debatable.

[10] So W. C. van Unnik, *Tarsus or Jerusalem,* trans. G. Ogg (London: Epworth Press, 1962). Cf. Acts 23:16.

[11] This exegesis is not necessarily opposed by the *apo archēs* of Acts 26:4. The "from the beginning" need not refer to more than "among my nation," with "and in Jerusalem" indicating a chronological extension of thought.

[12] If Paul's father and (possibly) grandfather had been Pharisees (cf. Acts 23:6), then such a family decision would have been natural—if not inevitable.

[13] Mish. Aboth 5.21. The fact that the Qumran "Two-Column Fragment," which probably preceded and was attached to 1QS, enumerates the same age divisions as Mish. Aboth 5.21 makes it more plausible that this is a true reflection of an earlier age. In the "Fragment," one is to study the "Book of Study" for ten years, and then at twenty to undergo an examination preparatory to his admission into the community. CDC 14.3-12 (17.1-8) also corresponds to Pirke Aboth in its age requirements for those in governing and officiating positions.

[14] Josephus, Life, 2: "When I was a child, and about fourteen years of age, I was commended by all for the love I had to learning; of which account, the high priests, and principal men of the city came then frequently to me together, in order to know my opinion about the accurate understanding of points of the law. And when I was about sixteen years old, I had a mind to make trial of the several sects that were among us." He then goes on to tell of his accelerated course in Pharisaism, Sadducean thought, Essene life and under a desert dweller named Banus, and that he returned to live as a

We do know that education in the Scriptures and the Law was stressed in every city for the Israelite boy,[15] and this at a quite early age.[16] And we know that there were also special Pharisaic schools where, it seems, prospective rabbis were trained more intensively.[17] Thus it would not be at all improbable that the Mishnah and Josephus both indicate the approximate situation; i.e., an early education in the Scriptures and the traditions in each city through the co-operation of the synagogue school, the synagogue, and the home,[18] with the possibility of further intensive schooling commencing in one's teens at one of the rabbinic schools. In view of the lack of conclusive evidence for a pre-educational residence in Jerusalem and the known educational schedules for a Jewish boy, it seems best to view Paul as having been reared with his family at Tarsus until sometime in his teens,[19] and then taking up studies under Gamaliel at Jerusalem. In thus accepting an early Tarsian training for the Apostle, the extent of Hellenistic influence upon him because of his Diaspora home must be investigated. The answer involves an understanding of both the Judaism of Tarsus and that of Paul's own immediate family.

Tarsian Judaism. Recent studies have emphasized the fact that we must be careful not to divide Judaism into an absolute geographical dichotomy; i.e., to distinquish too sharply between Palestinian and Diaspora Judaism.[20] And this emphasis is needful in light of earlier

---

Pharisee. We need not agree with him as to the extent of his knowledge or his comparison of the Pharisees to the Stoics, but the ages he relates are interesting.

[15] Cf. Josephus, Antiq. IV. 8. 12, Contra Apion I. 12; Mish. Kid. 4.13; Mish. Keth. 2.10; Mish. Shab. 1.3; b. Bab. Bath. 21a.

[16] Josephus, Contra Apion II. 18: "From our first consciousness" *(apo tēs prōtēs euthus aisthēseōs);* Philo, Leg. ad Cai. 210 (Cohn and Wendland, Vol. VI, p. 194): "From earliest youth" *(ek prōtēs hēlikias).*

[17] The schools at Jamnia and Beth Shea'rim, of a slightly later time, reflect this practice (cf. b. Sot. 49b).

[18] Cf. Schürer, *Jewish People,* Div. II, Vol. II, pp. 44 ff.

[19] R. Eliezer ben Hyrkanos was told he was too old to learn Torah at twenty-two (Aboth de R. Nathan, I. 6 and II. 13) or twenty-eight (Pirke de R. Eliezer, ch. 1), though R. Akiba began rabbinic studies at forty (Aboth de R. Nathan, I, 6 and II. 12, 14b, 15a).

[20] W. L. Knox, *Some Hellenistic Elements in Primitive Christianity* (London: Oxford University Press, 1944), *St. Paul and the Church of Jerusalem* (Cambridge, Eng.: The University Press, 1925); C. A. A. Scott, *Christianity According to St. Paul* (Cambridge, Eng.: The University Press, 1927); W. D. Davies, *Paul and Rabbinic Judaism;* W. D. Stacey, *The Pauline View of Man* (London:

presentations of a self-contained Hebraic Judaism within Palestine and a syncretistic Hellenistic Judaism beginning near the borders of Palestine and extending outward. The geographical factor in the understanding of Judaism is important, but must be recognized as not all-important.

But while denying the absoluteness of the equations "Palestinian Judaism equals Hebraic Judaism" and "Diaspora Judaism equals Hellenistic Judaism," we must be careful not to overlook the truth implicit in them: that there were differing mental climates within the basic unity of Judaism. Two factors are involved here, (1) geography and (2) attitude and outlook. While it is true that Judaism cannot be neatly bisected, the position that seeks only to lessen the force of the geographic factor without reference to differing mental climates confuses while it explains. It is probably truer to view Judaism as "drawn and quartered" within a unity. The horizontal cleavage of geography must be noted. But more important is the vertical break between Hebraic and Hellenistic inclinations in both Palestine and the Diaspora. The geographical distinction of Palestinian and Diaspora, and the demarcation of mental climate between the Hebraic and the Hellenistic, are at the same time both distinct and interrelated matters. We must not equate the two sets of terms and believe that in dealing with the one we have also treated the other. A good rule to follow is: Do not erase the distinction between the Hebraic and the Hellenistic in lessening that between Palestine and the Diaspora; nor emphasize the cleavage between Palestine and the Diaspora in insisting that Hebraic and Hellenistic outlooks are different.

It is certainly true that on the basis of geography and increased external pressures, Diaspora Judaism could be more readily characterized as Hellenistic than that of Palestine. Certainly the Diaspora had its Philo and Palestine produced the Mishnah. But Jerusalem also had its Hellenistic synagogues,[21] while Corinth had its Hebraic Jews[22]

Macmillan, 1956). Though this is a more modern emphasis, it is not a discovery new to either Christian or Jewish scholarship; cf. H. A. A. Kennedy, *The Theology of the Epistles* (London: Duckworth, 1919), p. 22, and I. Abrahams, *Studies in Pharisaism and the Gospels* (Cambridge, Eng.: The University Press, 1917), p. 82.

[21] Acts 6:9. See E. Schürer, "Alexandrians in Jerusalem," *J. E.*, Vol. I, pp. 371-72.

[22] II Cor. 11:22. Cf. W. Schmithals, *Die Gnosis in Korinth* (Göttingen: Vandenhoeck & Ruprecht, 1956), p. 36: "Nennen sie sich betont *Hebraioi,* so

and Babylon yielded to none as a center of Hebraic thought. Both Jewish heretics and Jewish patriarchs bore Greek names,[23] and both could have come from a Diaspora city and carried their city's name with them throughout their life.[24]

To characterize all of the Diaspora as either lax[25] or hyperstrict[26] in its outward observance of the Law is precarious indeed. We might expect a more humane application of the laws in the Diaspora. But the emphatic rejection by the chief Hellenist himself, Philo, that the Law's demands are to be taken lightly or allegorized away puts us on our guard against assuming a general laxity in the Diaspora.[27] "Absence makes the heart grow fonder" is as true as "out of sight, out of mind." And the former seems to some extent indicated by the Diaspora Jew in his enthusiasm to pay the temple tax while the Palestinian collections were made with difficulty.[28] The author of the

---

bezeichnen sie sich damit (im weitesten Sinne) als Palästinajuden. Sie mögen bereits in der Diaspora wohnhaft gesehen sein, wie das bei Pls ja auch der Fall war, ohne doch die innere und äussere Bindung an die palästinische Heimat verloren zu haben." Whatever one thinks of Schmithals' main thesis cannot blunt his point here.

[23] E.g., the Jewish heretics Stephen and Philip, the patriarch Antigonus of Socho (Mish. Aboth 1.3). Though Antigonus was probably a proto-Sadducee, and certainly not a patriarch in the sense of a descendant of Hillel, he is listed in the Aboth as a pillar of Pharisaism.

[24] E.g., Saul of Tarsus and Hillel "the Babylonian." It is recorded that Hillel's Babylonian origin was once mocked by two men who attempted to make him angry in order to test his patience (b. Shab. 31a).

[25] As, e.g., W. L. Knox, *St. Paul,* p. 24.

[26] As, e.g., Montefiore, *Judaism and St. Paul, passim.*

[27] Though Philo emphasized the rightness of the soul's disposition before God as the necessary condition in performing the ritual of the Law acceptably before God (De Spec. Leg. i, 271 f.), and though his presentation to his Gentile readers was an allegorized rendering of the meaning of the Law, "he roundly condemned those Jews who ignored the literal meanings of the Law as being worthless in favour of a symbolic meaning" (Davies, *Paul and Rabbinic Judiasm,* p. 96). He believed that circumcision should be allegorically interpreted, yet must be practiced literally (De Migrat. Abr. 89-94). He insisted upon the eternality of the Law (De Vita Mos. 44) and rebuked those who did not practice it (De Exsecrat. 138 f.).

[28] De Spec. Leg. i. 3 speaks of the Diaspora's enthusiasm; Mish. Dem. *passim,* De Spec. Leg. i.5, and Judith 11:12 ff. relate the situation in Palestine. This difference cannot all be attributed to the wealth of the Diaspora as against the poverty of Palestine. A truer reason could be the Palestinian disgust with some of the sham and hypocrisy surrounding the Temple and the idealism of those far removed. Cf. W. L. Knox, *St. Paul and the Church of the Gentiles,* pp. 32-33.

fictional Tobit looks toward Jerusalem as "the goal of all his hopes,"[29] and sets the keeping of the Law as the ideal for Israel.

All of these, it is true, are external matters. But they do suggest that we cannot conclude that we understand Diaspora Judaism by reference only to the map.[30] The strength of Jewish orthodoxy varied not according to geography so much as according to mental climate.

The Judaism of Paul's home. We actually know very little about either the social situation or the mental climate of Paul's family. Deissmann's insistence that Paul's training in tent-making and his continual occupation with that trade show him to have come "from the unliterary lower classes and remained one of them"[31] has failed to convince.[32] Both the attitude of Judaism toward manual labor[33] and the tone of Paul's references to his labor and his acceptance of

[29] D. C. Simpson, "Tobit," *Ap. and Ps.,* Vol. I, p. 185: "Distance lends enchantment to Jerusalem, the goal of all his hope."

[30] To the synagogue, with its system of traveling teachers from Jerusalem, must go the credit in large measure for preserving the coherency of a Judaism that was both centered and scattered. Regarding the synagogue as the external unifying factor in Judaism, see F. J. Foakes-Jackson and K. Lake, *Beginnings* (London: Macmillan, 1920-33), Vol. I, pp. 159 ff.; O. Michel, *Paulus und seine Bibel* (Gütersloh: Bertelsmann, 1929), p. 111; Davies, *Paul and Rabbinic Judaism,* p. 7. Regarding the basic unity between Temple and synagogue, see Abrahams, *Studies in Pharisaism and the Gospels,* pp. 2 ff.

[31] A. Deissmann, *Paul,* p. 48.

[32] See J. G. Machen, *Origin of Paul's Religion,* p. 45; C. H. Dodd, *The Mind of Paul: A Psychological Approach* (Manchester: John Rylands Library, 1934), pp. 7-8. Deissmann's romantic figure of the horny-handed, sweating stitcher looking up from his work to greet friends and dictating letters in the midst of hard toil falls a little flat in view of the Talmudic statement: "A man should always teach his son a clean and not laborious trade. What, for example? R. Hisda said: Needle-stitching" (b. Ber. 63a).

[33] R. Gamaliel II is credited with saying: "Excellent is Torah study together with worldly business, . . . all Torah without work [i.e. manual labor] must fail at length, and occasion iniquity" (Mish. Aboth 2.2). A disciple of R. Akiba is even called "R. Johanan, the sandal-maker" (Mish. Aboth 4.14). Also b. Kid. 99a: "Whosoever doth not teach his son work, teacheth him to rob." The earliest explicit statement of this nature seems to be Sirach 7.15: "Hate not laborious work, nor husbandry, for it was ordained of God." G. H. Box and W. O. E. Oesterley "Sirach," *Ap. and Ps.,* Vol. I. p. 339, n. 15, point out the parallel between Sirach 7:15 and Job 7:1 in the phrase "hate not a warfare of work." The reference to "the carpenter's son" of Matt. 13:55, Mark 6:3 is not opposed to this; for there the objection is not raised because of Jesus' or Joseph's manual labor, but because of His supposedly known lineage.

money[34] argue against an early proletarian status. Rather, it appears highly probable that he came from a well-to-do bourgeois home; for if he were born a Roman citizen,[35] then we must credit his family with some wealth and social standing.[36] Wealth and standing in society imply contact with the Gentile world. And indeed we must assume a fair share of this on the part of Paul's family. But more important than the external contacts are the inward attitudes. Anderson Scott has stated this concisely and well:

> The position of a Jewish family in such a city was not really analogous to that of a family of any other race. Probably the strongest thing in the consciousness of such a family would be the sense of difference, of separateness, of occupying a higher plane religiously and ethically than the Gentiles round about. All the outward expressions of family life, the common meals, the festivals, the study of the Law, the worship of the Synagogue, would tend to preserve and foster this separateness. Even under modern circumstances it is characteristic of many Jewish homes that they retain the Jewish atmosphere with little modification from without. And there is good reason to believe that Paul's home was one of this type.[37]

There is the tradition recorded by Jerome[38] which suggests that Paul's parents originally came from a town in Galilee called Gishala,[39] and that they fled to Tarsus during the Roman devastation of Palestine. If this be true, it would appear that the family went to

[34] Dodd's words are apposite. Of I Cor. 4:9–13, he says: "A man born to manual labour does not speak self-consciously of 'labouring with my own hands.' . . . Surely we miss the point of this unless we read it as the utterance of one whose natural place in society is the exact reverse of all this" (*Mind of Paul: A Psychological Approach,* p. 7). Of Phil. 4:14–19: "Here Paul is trying to say a graceful word of thanks for a gift of money. How much he hated taking it, we may infer from I Cor. 9:15–18. He can scarcely bring himself to acknowledge that the money was welcome to him, . . . This was a man who had chosen poverty as his lot for ideal ends, but could never feel himself one of the 'poor,' to whom alms might be offered without suspicion of offence" (*ibid.*, pp. 7–8).

[35] Acts 22:25–29.

[36] Cf. Dodd, *Mind of Paul: A Psychological Approach,* p. 7.

[37] C. A. A. Scott, *Christianity According to St. Paul,* pp. 3–4.

[38] Comm. on Philemon 23.

[39] The criticism that Galilee was, after all, closer to apocalyptic thought than Pharisaic is partially countered by W. D. Davies, "The Jewish Background of the Teaching of Jesus: Apocalyptic and Pharisaism," *E. T.,* Vol. LIX, No. 9 (June, 1948), p. 233.

Tarsus not because of the opportunities presented or out of Hellenistic leanings but of "stern necessity."[40] This would further portray them as first-generation colonists, whose motto could easily have been: "In the world, but not of the world."[41]

Thus, while it is true that a Hellenistic Judaism could be expected to be more common in the Diaspora than in Palestine and a more tolerant attitude toward the inconsequential practices of the Gentile seems obligatory for the existence of a Diaspora Jew, we must yet insist that "no hasty conclusions must be drawn from the fact that Paul was born in Tarsus."[42] It was possible for a thoroughly Hebraic Jew to be born and reared in the Diaspora.

DISPUTED ATTITUDES AND ACTIONS

Montefiore has asserted that Paul's preconversion Judaism differed from Hebraic Judaism "less in dogma than in attitude, less in creed than in outlook and in emotion."[43] It is necessary, therefore, to consider the four main arguments in this area against the Apostle's claimed Hebraic background.

[40] W. Barclay, *The Mind of St. Paul* (London: Collins, 1958), p. 28: "We cannot think that at some time Paul's father had emigrated to Cilicia in search of fame and fortune; a Pharisee would never willingly have lived away from the sacred soil of the Holy Land; it must have been some stern necessity which brought him there."

[41] Possibly such an attitude lies behind the recorded Pauline references to Tarsus. When addressing Jews, as recorded in Acts 22:3, he just names the city. But when speaking to a Gentile officer, as in Acts 21:39, his reference is more profuse. Rendel Harris has pointed out that Euripides' reference to Athens as "a not ignoble Greek City" (cf. Ion, line 8: *ouk asēmos Hellēnōn polis*; and Dionys. Hal. ant. Rom. 2.35: *poleis ouk asēmoi, genos echousai to Hellēnikon*) was well known in the Greek-speaking world, and has argued in explanation of Paul's usage in Acts 21:39 that other prominent cities used the same words in order to compare themselves favorably with Athens (R. Harris, "Did St. Paul Quote Euripides?" *E. T.*, Vol. XXXI, No. 1 [Oct., 1919], pp. 36–37). But if this be so, it is interesting that in Acts 21:39 Paul is quoted as speaking of Tarsus as "a not ignoble city" (*ouk asēmou poleōs*)—but not "a not ignoble *Greek* city." If Paul were following a common form of speech, it is significant perhaps that he could not bring himself to say, with Euripides and the common designation, "of the Greeks"—even to a Gentile soldier. It is possible that here he expresses a homebred attitude: a recognition of certain excellencies within the Gentile world, but a refusal to credit the pagan world for them or to associate oneself too closely with them.

[42] Kennedy, *Theology of the Epistles,* p. 14.

[43] Montefiore, *Judaism and St. Paul,* pp. 94–95. Cf. Schoeps, *Paul,* pp. 24–50.

The persecution of the Church. The Tübingen school and others have denied that Paul was trained under Gamaliel on the ground that his harsh attitude and action in Acts 8:1, 3 and 9:1, 2 are not worthy of a pupil of so tolerant-minded a teacher. It is certainly true that Gamaliel's words in Acts 5:34-39 are an example of moderation in the midst of frenzy. And they are in the tradition of true Hebraic Pharisaism.[44]

Klausner's explanation of the relationship of Paul to Gamaliel was that Paul was "that pupil" mentioned in late Talmudic sources as arguing with Gamaliel regarding the material element in the Messianic blessing. Thus he acknowledged the association of the two while

[44] In opposition to J. Weiss' insistence that the words of Gamaliel in Acts are "an historical mistake" and not true to the Pharisaic character (*Primitive Christianity,* Vol. I, p. 185), it must be noted that Antiq. XIII. 10. 6 speaks of the gentleness, mildness, and justice of the Pharisees. The statement of the second-century R. Johanan that "any assembling together that is for the sake of Heaven shall in the end be established, but any that is not for the sake of Heaven shall not in the end be established" (Mish. Aboth 4.11), stresses the policy of wait and see the end result, even as do Gamaliel's words in Acts 5. And there is every reason to believe that this sentiment ran right through the best in Pharisaism.

Such a policy sprang not only from the natural tolerance of the Hasidim, but also from the lessons of history. The Hasmonean Simon's Messiahship (I Macc. 14:4 ff.), the pretensions of the Hezekiah whom the youthful Herod put down in Galilee (Antiq. XIV. 9. 2), the nationalism of Judas the Galilean from Gamala (Antiq. XVIII. 1. 1 and 6; XX. 5. 2; War II. 8. 1 and 17.8), and the prophetical claims of Theudas (Antiq. XVII. 10. 5 or XX. 5. 1) had all had their day and in the end were proved invalid. Possibly significant as well is b. Sanh. 98b, 99a, where it is twice stated that "Hillel . . . maintained that there will be no Messiah for Israel, since they have already enjoyed him during the reign of Hezekiah." The statement in 99a has added: "May God forgive him [i.e. Hillel, for so saying]." J. Klausner (*The Messianic Idea in Israel,* trans. W. F. Stinespring [London: Allen & Unwin, 1956], p. 404) and G. F. Moore (*Judaism,* Vol. II, p. 347, n. 2) believe this to be a reference to another than Hillel the Elder. But S. Mowinckel (*He That Cometh,* trans. G. W. Anderson [Oxford: Blackwell, 1956], p. 284, n. 6, following H. Gressmann, *Der Messias* [Göttingen: Vandenhoeck & Ruprecht, 1929], pp. 449 ff.) and M. Buttenwieser, "Messiah," *J. E.,* Vol. VIII, p. 508, insist that this is the great rabbi. If this be truly the Hillel of Herod the Great's day, then there was in Gamaliel's own family a tragedy of mistaken identity which would strongly urge upon Gamaliel a policy of moderation. The further question of whether this Hezekiah was the king of Judah, as the Talmud insists, or the insurrectionist from Galilee is somewhat inconsequential; though, in view of Akiba's recognition of Simon ben Kosebah, the latter possibility cannot be discounted. If it had been the Galilean, Hillel's position in the eyes of his posterity would have been even more tragic.

accounting for the difference.[45] The identification of "that pupil" with Paul, however, is far from settled. At best it would be but a much later Jewish explanation for the roots of the Apostle's theology; i.e., his argumentative and pernicious character. Thackeray's explanation is more probable: "It is not paradoxical to suppose in the case of a man of St. Paul's temperament . . . that the same doubt which inclined Gamaliel to leniency only heightened the fervour of persecuting zeal in the Apostle."[46]

And yet there appears to be a more evident answer in the Acts account itself. Previous to Gamaliel's advice, it is recorded that the central issues of the witness of the Church had been concerning the Saviorship, Lordship, and Messiahship of Christ—His heaven-ordained death, His victorious resurrection, and His present status as exalted Redeemer. William Manson has well characterized the disciples' early functional theology in saying: "The stream of thought flowed in an intense but narrow channel; carrying in its flood much that for the time remained in solution in the sub-conscious rather than in the conscious region of the Christian mentality."[47] To the Sanhedrin, and especially to the Sadducean and priestly element who instigated the early suppressions, such teaching not only caused turmoil to orderly rule, but, more important, impinged upon their authority. To the more noble and tolerant of the Pharisees, however, the Jerusalem Christians were yet within the scope of Judaism and not to be treated as heretics. The divine claims for Jesus the Christ as yet lay in the subconsciousness of the Church, and the Jewish Christians gave no evidence of laxness in the observance of the Law because of their new beliefs. Other sects were tolerated within Judaism. Deluded Messianic followers could be countenanced as well. "The Pharisees might wish all men to be even as they were; but that result could be attained only be persuasion."[48]

But between Gamaliel's advice and Paul's action there appeared from the substrata of Christian conviction an ominous element of Jewish apostasy. In Acts 6, Stephen began to apply the doctrine of

[45] Klausner, *Messianic Idea in Israel,* p. 507, n. 24, and *From Jesus to Paul,* trans. W. F. Stinespring (New York: Macmillan, 1943), pp. 309–11.

[46] H. St. J. Thackeray, *The Relation of St. Paul to Contemporary Jewish Thought* (London: Macmillan, 1900), p. 10.

[47] W. Manson, *Jesus the Messiah* (London: Hodder & Stoughton, 1943), p. 52.

[48] A. D. Nock, *St. Paul* (New York: Harper, 1938), pp. 35-36.

Christ's Messiahship to the area of Jewish Law. He probably was baited on this topic by returning Diaspora Jews who had moved to the homeland with a desire to keep the Law more rigidly, and who now were concerned by the Christians' attitude toward it.[49] And undoubtedly he had a real interest in the subject himself. But here was a dangerous path to tread. It was one which even the apostles were not ready to take. Stephen's message was Jewish apostasy indeed! And it was especially to be opposed since voiced by a Hellenistic Jew who probably claimed to have returned to the Holy City out of religious ardor, but was now most vociferous against what he had formerly professed. Had Rabbi Gamaliel faced this aspect earlier, his attitude would surely have been different. With the whole basis of Judaism thus threatened, Paul's action could have been taken with Gamaliel's full approval.

Paul's action could also have been easily justified biblically. Numbers 25:12-13 recounts the turning away of God's wrath by one man who was zealous to put apostasy out of Israel—even to the killing of the offenders—and the praise of God that came to him for his action. To Paul, the situations then and now could easily have been analogous: Israel's near-entrance into the land with Israel's near-Messianic kingdom, and the similar apostasies which could but further delay God's blessings.[50] The exhortation of II Maccabees 6:13 may even have rung in his ears: "For indeed it is a mark of great kindness when the impious are not let alone for a long time, but punished at once."

[49] B. Reicke speaks of Stephen's opponents as "zionistischen Diasporajuden" ("Der geschichtliche Hintergrund des Apostelkonzils und der Antioch-Episode," *Studia Paulina,* ed. W. C. van Unnik and G. Sevenster [Haarlem: Bohn, 1953], p. 178).

[50] "Sins cannot completely frustrate the redemption; but they can delay it. This is the prevalent view in the Talmud" (Klausner, *Messianic Idea in Israel,* p. 430; cf. pp. 428-32). See *Str.-Bil.* (Munchen: Beck, 1922-28), on Acts 1:7, for the various positions taken within Judaism.

The idea that Israel must not be allowed to drift apart into apostasy in the face of near Messianic blessing seems well embedded in the thought of Judaism. "R. Simeon b. Yohai said: Like as when a man who brings together two ships, and binds them together with ropes and cords, and builds a palace upon them; while the ships are lashed together, the palace stands; when they drift apart it cannot stand. So only when Israel does God's will is His heavenly palace secure" (Sifre Deut., Berakah, 346, trans. *A Rabbinic Anthology,* ed. C. G. Montefiore and H. Loewe [London: Macmillan, 1938], p. 35). The fact that Qumran reveals parallel thought, e.g., 1QS 9.20-21, makes it probable that this sentiment characterized the Judaism of Paul's day as well.

This situation had every aspect of a holy war in which the best of Pharisaism could, and possibly should, participate.[51]

An interest in Gentiles. The correlation between the nation's election and a Gentile mission had always been a problem for the Jew; this in spite of the blessing to the nations included in the Abrahamic covenant,[52] the promise of light to the Gentiles in Isa. 49:6, and the words regarding the turning of the Gentiles to the worship of God in Isa. 55:6-7, Zeph. 3:9-10, and Zech. 8:22.[53] For the homeland, the problem was not as acute, since contacts with Gentiles were fewer,[54] but for the Diaspora the Gentile question was constantly pressing. Hence the well-known and often mentioned missionary interest among Diaspora Jews.[55] The success of such activity is indicated in Josephus' noting of the many proselytes in Antioch[56] and the women sympathizers in Damascus,[57] and in Paul's constant encounter with *hoi sebomenoi* in the Diaspora synagogues.[58] We must not suppose, however, that there was no missionary interest in Palestine itself.

The fact that the Pharisees accepted the Book of Ruth, in which David and his dynasty—and hence the Messiah also—are traced back to a converted Moabitess, is witness to the fact that "the Pharisees and their successors, the Tannaim, could not have been at all opposed to proselytes in general."[59] And the Gospels speak of Palestinian Pharisees traversing "sea and land to make a single proselyte,"[60] and

[51] Such a combination of withdrawal to godliness and zeal for holy war is paralleled in the Qumran community and has for its precedent many cases in Israelite history; cf. ch. IV, "Zealously Persecuting," pp. 102-3.

[52] Gen. 22:18, 26:4, 28:14.

[53] Isa. 60 is not in the same class as these passages, for there the emphasis is upon Israel's blessing through subjugation of the nations.

[54] Yet Gentile contacts were not unknown to Palestinian Pharisaism. The Talmud gives many instances of laws regarding Jewish and Gentile partnerships in agricultural pursuits (e.g., b. Shab. 150a) and Jews bathing with Gentiles (e.g., b. Shab. 151a). Regarding the agricultural associations, H. Loewe has remarked: "Even if all these Jews were not Pharisees, the recognition of their association with Gentiles was Pharisaic" ("Pharisaism," *Judaism and Christianity,* Oesterley, ed., Vol. I, p. 112).

[55] Cf. Schürer, *Jewish People,* Div. II, Vol. II, pp. 304 ff.; Foakes-Jackson and Lake, *Beginnings,* Vol. I, pp. 164 f. and Vol. V, pp. 74 f.

[56] War, VII. 3.3.

[57] War, II. 20. 2.

[58] Acts 13:14, 43, 50, 17:4, 17.

[59] Klausner, *Messianic Idea in Israel,* p. 478.

[60] Matt. 23:15.

of at least one worshiper in Jerusalem, the aged Simeon, believing that God's blessing contains universal implications.[61] The clearest expression of such concern in the Talmud is probably that of Hillel: "Be of the disciples of Aaron, loving peace and pursuing peace, loving mankind and bringing them nigh to the Law."[62] But if Hillel's ethical maxims[63] were originally "missionary maxims . . . turned into general rules of seemly conduct in strict harmony with the legalistic attitude," as David Daube has argued,[64] we have further evidence of a Hebraic missionary interest.[65] The statement of R. Eleazar manifests contact with Gentiles and an interest in making a proper answer to them: "Be alert to study the Law and know how to make answer to an unbeliever [lit. "Epicurean"]."[66] And at a time when the combination of Gentile persecution and the traitor tactics of proselytes turned the heart and eyes of Judaism away from the outside world, resulting in the inauguration of legislation to hinder any proselytizing attempts,[67] agony and concern over the fate of the majority of mankind were expressed by the writer of IV Ezra.[68]

It is therefore not true to say that Paul's interest in the Gentile could only have arisen had he been a Hellenistic Jew. While it might have had sufficient roots in the experience and call associated with his conversion, coupled with the historical commands of his new Lord, it is also fully possible that it was originally planted and cultivated in the soil of Hebraicism.

A mystic temperament. Paul's Christian mysticism has also been set

[61] Luke 2:32.

[62] Mish. Aboth 1:12. Cf. N. N. Glatzer, "Hillel the Elder in the Light of the Dead Sea Scrolls," *Scrolls and the N. T.*, ed. K. Stendahl, p. 241, for an excellent summary of Hillel's interest in proselytes.

[63] Tos. Ber. 2.24; Derekh Eretz Rabbah 8.4; Derekh Eretz Zuta 5.5.

[64] D. Daube, *N. T. and Rabbinic Judaism*, p. 340.

[65] For further implicit Talmudic evidence of such a Hebraic interest, see the articles in *J. E.*: "Proselyte," Vol. X, p. 222, by E. G. Hirsch; "Conversion," Vol. IV, p. 250, by K. Kohler; and "Judaism," Vol. VII, p. 366, by K. Kohler. The thesis of these articles is that "in pre-Christian times very determined efforts were made toward proselytizing the heathens; but as soon as the Church took up the task, following the methods of Paul, . . . the zeal of the Jews diminished, the 'conversion of the Gentiles,' . . . became obnoxious to the Synagogue" (Vol. IV, p. 250).

[66] Mish. Aboth 2.14.

[67] Cf. Hirsch, "Proselyte," *op. cit.*, p. 224.

[68] Esp. chap. 7.

against his Hebraic claims. Montefiore has insisted that the rabbinic Judaism of the Apostle's day did not foster a mystic temperament, though mysticism was not altogether foreign to it.[69] Others have gone further in claiming that "the Jewish mind and character, in spite of its deeply religious bent, was alien to Mysticism."[70] The problem is twofold: (1) Could a mystic temperament have sprung from the Hebraic Pharisaism of Paul's day? (2) Was Paul's Christian mysticism really different from a possible Hebraic type?

The picture painted by the nineteenth-century Jewish historians of predestruction Hebraic Pharisaism is devoid of any mystical element. And this portrayal has often served as the basis for twentieth-century comparisons of Paul and Judaism. However, a voice of one crying in the wilderness has been raised from the Hebrew University in Jerusalem. It is G. G. Scholem's thesis that the rationalistic and mystical tendencies within Judaism have throughout history been "interrelated and interdependent. Neither were they from the start manifestly opposed to each other, a fact that is often overlooked."[71] He insists that both the compiler of the Halakic traditions, the pronounced rationalist Judah the Patriarch,[72] and the nineteenth-century historians, as Graetz and Zunz, saw mysticism as an ally to Judaism's foes and a detriment to the type of religion each desired to make dominant in his day. For the historians as well as for R. Judah, mysticism

> epitomised everything that was opposed to their own ideas and to the outlook which they hoped to make predominant in modern Judaism. Darkly it stood in their path, the ally of forces and tendencies in whose rejection pride was taken by a Jewry which, in Steinschneider's words, regarded it as its chief task to make a decent exit from the world.[73]

And Scholem's thesis seems even more convincing today in view of the information from Qumran. Since 1948 it can no longer be said that "mysticism does not thrive where no other service of the

[69] *Judaism and St. Paul,* pp. 50-51.

[70] W. R. Inge, *Christian Mysticism* (London: Methuen, 1921), p. 39. Cf. Dibelius, *Paul,* p. 35.

[71] G. G. Scholem, *Major Trends in Jewish Mysticism* (New York: Schocken, 1941), p. 23.

[72] *Ibid.,* p. 42.

[73] *Ibid.,* pp. 1-2.

eternal God is known than the fulfilling of his commandments."[74] The Talmud still possesses its faintly glowing embers of the mystical spirit in Hillel's esoteric statement,[75] the account of the four rabbis who entered Paradise,[76] and the vision of R. Joseph.[77] But it does seem that somewhere along the line of rabbinic succession the crude but flaming piety has been extinguished by a more enlightened mind. "The sea of the Talmud," it is true, still possesses "its gulf stream of mysticism."[78] But that stream has been relegated to subterranean passages. The finger of accusation points to R. Judah.[79] But as long as the "O taste and see that the Lord is good" of Psalm 34:9 is embedded in Hebrew literature, we cannot say that there was no foundation for a Hebraic mysticism.

Yet Paul's Christian mysticism is not just to be equated with the piety of the Old Testament sages or the best that we can imagine in Pharisaism. Its roots are in the Hebrew concepts of identification and the corporate community of God and His people. But it goes beyond that. And the fact that it goes beyond would be no surprise to the convert Paul. His whole insistence is that the new covenant in its entirety, though having its roots in the old, goes far beyond it.[80] Personal communion of the type where one can speak of himself as "in Christ" or "being changed into his likeness" stems not from the old but from that established in and through Christ.[81]

It must then be insisted that a sense of immediacy between God and man was possible in the Hebraic Pharisaism of Paul's day, but that Paul's Christian mysticism is most probably explained by his experience of Christ.

[74] Dibelius, *Paul,* p. 35. Such a belief died in the same year as its author, when Qumran broke its silence. Cf. ch. III, "The Religion of a Nomist."

[75] B. Suk. 53a: "If I am there [God speaking?], all are there, and if I am not there, who is there?" Cf. Lev. R. 35.1. W. Bacher uses this one statement to illustrate "the almost mystic depth of his [i.e. Hillel's] consciousness of God" ("Hillel," *J. E.,* Vol. VI, p. 399).

[76] Tos. Hag. 14b.

[77] B. Pes. 50a.

[78] S. Schechter, *Studies in Judaism,* Preface, p. xxix.

[79] Davies, *Paul and Rabbinic Judaism,* pp. 14-15, agrees with Scholem that the absence of mystical elements in the Mishnah is the result of the rationalism of R. Judah.

[80] II Cor. 3:7-11.

[81] II Cor. 3:18.

The demands of the Law. Probably the most repeated objection to Paul's Hebraic background is that of his "pessimistic" view of the demands of the Law; i.e., that man is under a curse in not keeping the Law *in its entirety*. Galatians 3:10 and 5:3 have been variously described as "Paul's misrepresentation of Pharisaism"[82] or "his overstrained definition of the requirements of the Law."[83] And many have insisted that here he shows himself familiar with only a variation of Judaism and not the real Hebraicism which he claims.[84] The Jewish objection is summarized by Moore:

> How a Jew of Paul's antecedents could ignore, and by implication deny, the great prophetic doctrine of repentance, which, individualized and interiorized, was a cardinal doctrine of Judaism, namely, that God, out of love, freely forgives the sincerely penitent sinner and restores him to his favor—that seems from the Jewish point of view inexplicable.[85]

Thus, to insist that one must do all the Law is to ignore Hebraic Pharisaism's central doctrine of the infinite and unceasing willingness of God to forgive the repentant sinner, and therefore to show an unawareness, or at best a faulty comprehension, of that doctrine and the Pharisaism to which it was basic. If Paul had really known the Judaism he claims, he could never have misrepresented it so rankly.

Now it is possible to argue that this attitude is the result of his Christian reinterpretation of the Old Testament; i.e., that as a Christian he sees the whole Law in a new and different perspective. Whereas before he could visualize himself as being more capable of keeping the Law and view God as more tolerant, now, knowing righteousness in Christ and seeing Himself in His intense light, he sees the awful claims of the Law as he never saw them before and God's grace more abundant because of man's inability. His statements in Galatians, therefore, are not supposed to represent the accepted theology of the best of Judaism, but his Christian understanding. The truth of this position lies in stressing Paul's heightened understanding

[82] Nock, *St. Paul,* p. 29.

[83] G. F. Moore, *Judaism,* Vol. III, p. 150, n. 209. Cf. K. Lake, *Paul: His Heritage and Legacy* (London: Christophers, 1934), pp. 70 ff.; W. H. P. Hatch, "The Pauline Idea of Forgiveness," *Studies in Early Christianity,* ed. S. J. Case (New York: Century, 1928), p. 347.

[84] E.g., Montefiore, *Judaism and St. Paul,* pp. 72-73.

[85] Moore, *Judaism,* Vol. III, p. 151.

of both grace and law as a Christian. But we need not insist that this understanding was entirely different from that of Pharisaism.

It should be noted that this doctrine of the necessity of doing all the Law is not absent in Palestinian Judaism. The Mishnah speaks of being "heedful of a light commandment as of a weighty one,"[86] running "to fulfil the lightest duty even as the weightiest,"[87] and recounts how the reader at the scourging of an apostate or immoral man is to read the ominous words of Deut. 28:58 f.: "If thou wilt not observe to do all the words of this law," etc.[88] The Gemaras and Midrashim tell of R. Huna's teaching that adultery is the transgression of all the commandments,[89] Gamaliel II's turmoil over Ezek. 18:1-9, "he that does *all* these things shall live,"[90] and R. Jose's teaching that liability is incurred for any infraction.[91] The Tosephta, arguing on the principle that the Law and all of life are a single whole stemming from God, insists that the breaking of a commandment reveals a previous denial of the Almighty.[92] On this same principle, IV Maccabees has the aged Eleazar say to his torturer Antiochus, "The transgression

[86] Mish. Aboth 2.1.

[87] Mish. Aboth 4.2.

[88] Mish. Mak. 3.14. Even if Gal. 5:3 had not been part of Paul's Pharisaic theology, the five occasions when these words were forcibly hurled at him as a Christian (note II Cor. 11:24) could have convinced him of their Pharisaic nature; cf. Deissmann, *Paul,* pp. 61-62.

[89] E.g., Num. R. 9.12, on Num. 5:14.

[90] B. Sanh. 81a. R. Akiba, however, quoted to him Lev. 18:24, and insisted that since one does not have to do all the abominations enumerated to be defiled so one does not have to do all the commands to live (an argument directly countered by Haggai 2:11-13); a conscientious and on the whole successful keeping of the Law was what was meant. The interesting aspect is that here a grandson of Paul's claimed teacher is cited as accepting, or at least as being troubled by, the very doctrine which the Christian Paul proclaims, while Akiba, who was so influential in the molding of Jewish thought in his day and that of the later codified Mishnah, opposes him. In the parallel passage, b. Mak. 24a, Gamaliel's perplexity arises from Ps. 15.

[91] B. Shab. 70b. R. Jose, commenting on the phrase in Lev. 4.2, "if a soul shall sin through ignorance against any one of the commandments of the Lord," says: " 'Of one of them' teaches that liability is incurred for one complete act; for one which is but part of one; for performing labours forbidden in themselves, and for labours whose prohibition is derived from others.

[92] Tos. Shebu. 3.6: "No man denies the derivative (i.e., the separate commandments) until he has previously denied the Root (i.e., God), and no man sins unless he has denied Him who commanded him not to commit that sin." (Translation and parentheses from Montefiore and Loewe, *Rabbinic Anthology,* p. 122).

of the Law, be it in small things or in great, is equally heinous; for in either case equally the Law is despised."[93] So also in the Qumran texts the emphasis is upon doing all the commandments.[94] In the New Testament, James, whose roots were in Pharisaism, parallels Paul's statement by saying that guilt in all results from failure at one point.[95] It therefore seems that Daube has not overstated the case in saying that "the inter-dependence of all precepts, their fundamental equality, the importance of even the minor ones, or apparently minor ones, because of their association with the weightiest—these were common themes among the Tannaites."[96]

Further, the forgiveness of God is not necessarily minimized by a belief in the condemnation of the whole Law resting upon one who breaks it at one point. For the writer of IV Ezra, the realization of man's utter inability, because all men have broken God's law at one point or more and thus are under God's judgment, only sets the stage for God's mercy: "For in this, O Lord, shall thy righteousness and goodness be declared, if thou will compassionate them that have no wealth of good works."[97] Judaism could accept both the condemnation of the whole Law for offense at one point and the forgiveness of God which shows itself abundant in the face of human inability.

As with IV Ezra, so with Paul. It is not a pessimism that is presented, but a pessimistic optimism; i.e., man's case is hopeless of itself, but in God there is abundant hope. In Galatians 3:10 and 5:3 the pessimism of human effort is expressed and emphasized to those who would make human endeavor an avenue to righteousness. But Paul's total message is not limited to this point, nor is this aspect of his proclamation non-Pharisaic.

One must insist here, as for the previous three objections of this

[93] IV Macc. 5:20-21. The passage in Sirach 7.8, if the secondary Syriac reading of "former sins" be rejected, would add further noncanonical evidence: "In respect of one sin thou are not without guilt."

[94] E.g., 1QS 1.14. W. D. Davies, "Paul and the Dead Sea Scrolls: Flesh and Spirit," *Scrolls and the N. T.*, ed. K. Stendahl, p. 281, n. 80, says that he counted 73 instances in 1QS alone where the expression "all" is used in connection with doing the law.

[95] Jas. 2:10.

[96] Daube, *N. T. and Rabbinic Judaism*, p. 251. Daube's comments on pp. 119 ff. and J. B. Mayor's summary, *The Epistle of St. James* (London: Macmillan, 1892), p. 86, are excellent treatments of this whole problem.

[97] IV Ezra 8.36.

type, that the case against the Pauline Hebraic claims from his attitudes and actions is at best inconclusive. The inquiry now turns to his ideas and expressions, and their Hellenistic affinities.

DISPUTED CONCEPTS AND EXPRESSIONS

A major matter of interest and controversy in New Testament studies since the latter half of the nineteenth century has been the relation of the concepts of Christianity to those of the religious movements within the Hellenistic world.[98] Much that has been revealed in the investigations in this area is pertinent here. It is, however, not my purpose to cover so vast an area in a few pages, nor even to attempt a summary of Paul's relation to the Mystery Religions. Our interest here is exclusively in whether Paul's Christian expression betrays an earlier influence of Hellenistic Judaism.

It cannot be doubted that much had transpired in Paul's life between his student days and his later Christian writings. And it is always precarious to argue from a later attitude to an earlier one, especially when the two situations are separated by a great personal revolution of aim and action. Yet there is a point of view from which it is legitimate to consider the objections to Paul's Hebraic claims from the standpoint of his Christian expression. It must be considered axiomatic that the extent to which his writings reveal rabbinic or Hellenistic affinities is the extent to which his Hebraic claims can be accepted or must be looked upon with suspicion. It is to be expected that his conversion would have made him less rabbinic, but it is hardly a possibility that it made him more so. Thus, whatever rabbinic affinities there are in his theology must be assumed to have been carried over from his past. Whatever Hellenistic elements there are could have been picked up later, but their presence still must cast a valid suspicion upon his claims to a Hebraic past. Our concern is therefore to investigate Paul's writings along the lines set by the objections raised.

The nature of religion. In the epistles of Paul, the word "mystery" (*mustērion*) is used twenty times, with the majority of this usage having reference to the nature of the gospel which the Apostle pro-

[98] Note Schweitzer's extended survey of this issue in German scholarship through the turn of the century, *Paul and His Interpreters.*

claimed.[99] The Mystery Religions likewise used the term with reference to the nature of their message. In Hellenistic thought the term strictly denoted the rite or rites of the service, which could not be divulged to the uninitiated; but popularly it connoted "the spiritual meaning . . . to justify the crude and primitive practices of barbarous religion."[100] Some have explained Paul's use of the term as being analogous to and showing dependence upon the Mysteries.

It should be noted in passing that Philo's agreement with Hellenism is clear at this point. Of his thirteen uses of the word *mustērion* and one of *mustis,*[101] all explicitly convey, or are not contrary to, the concept of a secret and sacred knowledge of divinity open only to the initiated and sanctified, and not to be revealed by them. In eight of the fourteen, the revelation of God through Moses, or an aspect of it, is described as a holy mystery in this sense.[102] He can speak of Sarah learning that "being admitted into the inmost mysteries" she is "not to blab or babble them thoughtlessly but to store them up and guard them in secrecy and silence,"[103] and can exhort the initiated to receive the truth through Moses "into your souls as holy mysteries indeed and babble not of them to any of the profane."[104] The Essenes likewise spoke of true religion as "mystery," the nature of which they were to keep hidden[105] even in the face of torture and death.[106] So also Wisdom 6.22 shows its acquaintance with such a definition, and possibly this is entailed in the description in Wisdom 2.2 of those who did not know the mysteries of God.

With Paul, however, the term takes the Palestinian sense of Amos 3:7, Psalms 25:14, Proverbs 3:32, and Sirach 3:20; i.e., of a hitherto unknown aspect of God or His dealing which has now become known,

[99] Rom. 16:25-26; I Cor. 2:6-13, 4:1, 15:51; Eph. 3:3-10, 6:19; Col. 1:26-27, 2:2, and 4:3.

[100] W. L. Knox, *St. Paul and the Church of the Gentiles,* p. 183, n. 1.

[101] As cited by I. Leisegang, "Indices," Vol. VII of L. Cohn and P. Wendland, *Philonis Alexandrini Opera* (Berlin: Reimer, 1896-1930).

[102] De Cherub. 48-49; Quod Deus Immut. 61; Leg. All. iii. 3, 27, 100; De Sacrif. Ab. et Cain. 60, 62.

[103] De Sacrif. Ab. et. Cain. 60.

[104] De Cherub. 48.

[105] See esp. 1QS 9.16-19. Also 1QS 8.18, the uncorrected text of 1QS 10.24 (where the original scribe wrote "conceal," but a later scribe changed it to "relate"), and CDC 15.10 (19.10).

[106] War, II. 8. 7.

either to all or to those who will accept such revelation.[107] Paul's emphasis, as also that of the Talmud,[108] was not on the hidden or secret nature of the revelation, but on its present manifestation. He spoke of "the mystery hidden for ages and generations" only to emphasize "but now made manifest to his saints."[109] He used the term in the sense of an unrevealed and unrevealable divine secret in I Corinthians 14:2, but from the context it is clear that just such a concept is what he was censuring and subjugating to the principle of open and intelligent edification. Only in I Corinthians 2:6-16 and II Corinthians 4:3-4 does he approach the idea of a secret and hidden gospel. But that secrecy is never attributed to the intent of the Gospel itself but to the fall of man from the norm God has established. The spiritual Gospel is hidden from man because of the unspiritual character of man, not because it is essentially secret or meant to be kept hidden. It is to be proclaimed to all, even the spiritually dead, as Paul's missions and defenses illustrate. In all,[110] Paul's usage of "mystery" conforms more closely to Hebraic thought than to Hellenistic.

A further and closely related objection raised against the Apostle at this point is in regard to what is considered his sacramental definition of religion. His teaching regarding baptism and the Lord's Supper have appeared to some to have the savor of the Mysteries; i.e., that the essence of religion in its manward aspect is that of intrinsically efficacious rites.[111] It must be questioned, however, whether the Hellenistic concept of efficacious rites made any real impression on *any* form of Judaism; even though a priestly ritualism often threatened to

[107] Cf. H. A. A. Kennedy, *St. Paul and the Mystery Religions* (London: Hodder & Stoughton, 1913), pp. 124 ff.; W. L. Knox, *St. Paul and the Church of the Gentiles,* pp 183 f.; C. A. A. Scott, *Christianity According to St. Paul,* pp. 127 f.; and J. S. Stewart, *A Man in Christ* (London: Hodder & Stoughton, 1935), p. 74.

[108] Cf. b. Shab. 88b: "That secret treasure [i.e. the Torah], which has been hidden by Thee for nine hundred and seventy-four generations before the world was created, Thou desirest to give to flesh and blood!"

[109] Col. 1:26.

[110] The sense in Eph. 5:32 is not that of a secret spiritual meaning, but is probably to be taken more in our modern sense of that which is intrinsically difficult to understand: ". . . the two shall become one. This is a great mystery, and I take it to mean Christ and the church, however, . . ."

[111] E.g., E. Hatch, *The Influence of Greek Ideas and Usages upon the Christian Church* (London: Williams & Norgate, 1914), pp. 281-96; Kohler, "Saul of Tarsus," *op. cit.*, p. 83.

dominate in the religion of Israel and in Judaism. Not only did the most Hellenized forms of Judaism we know reject the rites of the Mysteries,[112] but such as Philo and the Qumran bards also denounced the idea that access to true religion could be gained purely by ritual.[113] For them, the rites had value only when preceded by a correct inner disposition and faith.[114] And those rites, while performed in modesty and propriety, were not secret.[115]

On this question Paul is at one with the leading proponents of Judaism, whether Hebraic, Hellenistic, or sectarian. Surely the uncertain reference to baptism for the dead in I Corinthians 15:29 is countered by his many insistences on *fides sola*. For Paul, life in Christ was to be lived as a sacrament;[116] but it was not gained by sacramentalism. Nor need we press too hard his use of Mystery terminology. Terms were in the air, and meanings differed.[117] Anderson Scott's words regarding Paul's use of "mystery" are pertinent:

> In fact, a careful examination of the Apostle's use of the word rather raises the question whether he would have used it so freely in a non-technical sense if he had had any consciousness of a relation between Christian rites and what were specifically described as "mysteries," or indeed if the technical sense of the word were in such universal use as is commonly supposed.[118]

[112] Wisdom of Solomon 14.15, 23 connects the Mysteries with the solemn rites of the rankest idolatry, and 14.16 speaks of the Mysteries as an "ungodly custom." In De Spec. Leg. i. 319, Philo equates their rites with "clap-trap and buffoonery" and exhorts Moses' disciples and friends to stay clear of these "ceremonies belonging to the darkness of night" (H. A. A. Kennedy's trans. in his *Philo's Contribution to Religion* [London: Hodder & Stoughton, 1919], p. 220).

[113] Note De Spec. Leg. i. 271 f.; also ch. III, "The Religion of a Nomist," pp. 80-81.

[114] Quis Rer. Div. Heres 18.

[115] Regarding the Jewish rites of circumcision, baptism, and sacrifice, see Abrahams, *Studies in Pharisaism and the Gospels,* pp. 36 ff., and Schürer, *Jewish People,* Div. II, Vol. II, pp. 319 ff.

[116] Cf. Rom. 12:1-2.

[117] E.g., to the Mysteries *gnōsis* brought salvation, cf. R. Reitzenstein, *Die hellenistische Mysterienreligionen* (3d. ed.; Leipzig: Teubner, 1927), p. 114; to Philo, "knowledge" is a chief human factor in gaining salvation but is ineffectual unless aided by God, cf. De Migrat. Abr. 170 f. and Kennedy, *Philo's Contribution,* p. 199; to Paul, "knowledge" is not a path to but a consequence of salvation.

[118] C. A. A. Scott, *Christianity According to St. Paul,* pp. 127-28.

Dualism. There are many contrasts made in the Pauline literature that could be given a dualistic label. But the question here is, are there any which reflect distinctive Greek dualism?

The Apostle's reference to "the first man Adam" (*ho prōtos anthrōpos Adam*) who is "of the earth, earthy" (*ek gēs choikos*) and "the last Adam" (*ho eschatos Adam*) who is "from heaven" (*ex ouranou*)[119] has often been compared with Philo's distinction between "the heavenly man" (*ho ouranios anthrōpos*) and "the earthly" (*ho gēnios*).[120] Many have seen in it certain evidence for a common background.[121] However, besides the fact that his terminology differs slightly, the order of Paul's presentation and his emphasis in the comparison are exactly reversed from that of Philo's. Paul's "first man" is a "living soul" even though "from the earth," and his emphasis is entirely upon the greater "last man." Philo looked to the past prototype, whereas Paul's eyes were upon the echatological man who had been revealed in the present. The Apostle's reversal of the Greek order—"but it is not the spiritual which is first but the physical, and then the spiritual"—speaks volumes against a similar mental background of the two. The Jew of Alexandria could never have fitted his Platonism into Paul's order.[122]

Another Pauline contrast is that of those who are "spiritual" (*pneumatikos*) and those who are "fleshly" (*sarkikos*).[123] Philo has a similar distinction, though he would speak of "the man controlled by reason" (*logistikos*) and "the bestial man" (*haimatikos,* to coin an adjective).[124] Some have seen in these distinctions of both Paul and Philo undertones of the Hellenistic divinity-versus-mortality motif.[125] Yet for neither Paul nor Philo does man ever become divine. Philo verges the closest to that position in saying that the good man "becomes

[119] I Cor. 15:45-49; cf. Rom. 5:15-21.

[120] Leg. All. i. 12, 31 ff., 53 ff., 88 f.

[121] E.g., Reitzenstein, *Hellenistischen Mysterienreligionen,* pp. 346 ff.; Dibelius, *Paul,* p. 32; Kohler, "Saul of Tarsus," *op. cit.,* p. 79.

[122] Cf. Manson, *Jesus the Messiah,* Appendix D, pp. 174-90, and Michel, *Paulus und seine Bibel,* p. 23.

[123] I Cor. 2:14—3:3.

[124] Quis Rer. Div. Heres 57; Quod Deus Immut. 56, 143; De Gigant. 28-31; De Abr. 155; and others.

[125] E.g., E. Hatch, "Pauline Idea of Forgiveness," *op. cit.,* 346-47, and *The Pauline Idea of Faith* (Cambridge, Mass.: Harvard University Press, 1917), p. 40.

no man." But he likewise insists: "But clearly neither is he God"; he is "on the borderline."[126] Paul spoke of participating in the "blood" and "body" of Christ,[127] but he never divorced the spiritual man from humanity. The orientation of the spiritual man is heavenward and he awaits glorification, yet never shall that glorification become absorption or quantitative identity. This usage of similar thought forms by Paul and Philo is an example of common employment of infiltrating terms and expressions of the Greek world without any necessary acceptance of all that those expressions might convey in the world outside.[128] There is no direct correlation between these two Jewish thinkers and Hellenism on this point, nor need there have been any between the two men themselves.

A third disputed comparison between Paul, Diaspora Judaism, Hellenism, and Hebraic Pharisaism in this area is in the distinction between the material and the nonmaterial in man. Both Paul and Philo speak of man as twofold in his constitution. Paul contrasts the "inner man" (*esō anthrōpos*)[129] and the "external man" (*exō anthrōpos*).[130] In respect to the former, "spirit" (*pneuma*) and "mind" (*nous*) often[131] and "soul" (*psuchē*) sometimes[132] are used synonymously; whereas in the latter case "flesh" (*sarx*) is generally used as its equivalent,[133] with "body" (*sōma*) at times serving that function.[134] Philo's usual distinction is between "soul" (*psuchē*) and

[126] De Somn. ii. 230-31.

[127] I Cor. 10:16-17; cf. Heb. 3:14, 6:4; II Pet. 1:4.

[128] W. L. Knox, *Some Hellenistic Elements,* p. 37: "Both St. Paul and Philo have an essentially superficial acquaintance with Greek thought; they are completely indifferent to philosophy as such, and only employ it as a handmaid in the service of a revealed religion which they have accepted for reasons which have nothing to do with philosophy. Philo's knowledge is of course infinitely wider in range than St. Paul's so far as we can judge; it is also far less Jewish; but it is equally superficial." See also *St. Paul and the Church of the Gentiles,* Preface, p. x, and p. 90.

[129] Rom. 7:22; II Cor. 4:16; and Eph. 3:16.

[130] II Cor. 4:16.

[131] Rom. 7:23, 8:10, 16; I Cor. 2:11, 7:34, 14:14; II Cor. 7:1; I Thess. 5:23.

[132] Usually "soul" is used by Paul to refer to this present life in its totality (e.g., Rom. 11:3, 16:4; I Cor. 15:45; II Cor. 1:23; Phil. 2:30). But at least once (I Thess. 5:23), and possibly again (I Thess. 2:8), it is used in this more technical sense.

[133] Rom. 8:10-11; I Cor. 6:13-20, 7:4, 34, 9:27, 13:3; etc.

[134] Usually "body" refers to life in its totality in its outward form of appearance, its *aussere Erscheinungsform.* But in Rom. 8:10, 13 and II Cor. 5:6, 8 it takes on this narrower meaning.

"body" (*sōma*);[135] though he also contrasts *pneuma* and *haima,*[136] *nous kai logos* and *sōma,*[137] *psuchē* and *sarx,*[138] and similar combinations. But, Hellenistically influenced as this may appear, the division of man into two component parts is not necessarily dependent upon Greek thought. Hebrew psychology, it is true, insisted upon the fundamental unity of the human personality. Yet division within that unity was not an incompatible concept. The Old Testament speaks of man becoming a "living soul" by the combination of the "breath of lives" and the earthy substance.[139] In the thought of the Old Testament, life and personality cease where soul and body are separated,[140] and life recommences where these are again joined.[141] Hillel spoke of his soul as a "guest in the house" of his body.[142] And the Beth Hillel and Beth Shammai distinguished between the "two formations" of upper and lower elements in man, and discussed the nature of man's body and soul in the next world.[143] To an Israelite, life indeed meant both. But the aspects could be distinguished. The fact that such a distinction is made by both Paul and Philo is not of itself indicative of Hellenism for either. Both have their roots in a similarly distinguishing Judaism. It is their views regarding the body, not their recognition of an external aspect in the constitution of man, that prove significant.

The body. That matter as such is evil is an important concept in Greek dualistic philosophy.[144] And because it is so basic, we should expect to find evidence of such a view in both Diaspora Judaism and Paul if they be truly influenced by Greek thought. To many in the past century, and to some in the twentieth, that is just what is found in Paul's use of "flesh."[145] Important distinctions, however, must be made between Hellenism, Hellenistic Judaism, and Paul.

[135] De Ebriet. 69; Leg. All. iii. 161.

[136] Quod Det. Pot. Insid. 82.

[137] *Ibid.,* 83.

[138] De Gigant. 42.

[139] Gen. 2:7.

[140] Gen. 35:18, where Rachel's *nephesh* departs her body.

[141] I Kings 17:22, where life accompanies the return of the child's *nephesh* to its body.

[142] Lev. R. 34.3.

[143] B. Sanh. 91a, 91b and Gen. R. 14.3 and 5 on Gen. 2:7.

[144] Epictetus' illustration of man as a snail in a shell (Dissertations I. 20. 17) is probably more apt than the modern characterization of the Greek concept as of "an angel in a slot machine."

[145] Cf. Schoeps, *Paul,* pp. 15-23, 26, where Hellenistic tendencies are stressed.

It is a mistake to characterize Philo as regarding matter as evil *per se*.[146] He is too good a Jew for that. Matter is a direct creation of God, and its intrinsic depravity would have serious implications for its Creator. No matter how opposite the flesh is to the soul, Philo can never regard it as the opposition of inherent evil to created good.[147] And yet he can verge exceedingly close to such a position in describing the flesh as being both corrupted and corrupting, both defiled and defiling.[148] Evil, for Philo, is not just resident in the flesh and using the fleshly nature, but it is rooted and finds its origin in the material body as well.[149] While we might desire to see in his usage only a reference to the fleshly appetites and urgings as being contaminated by sin, he leans more to the position of the earthy substance itself as being both captive *and* culprit. He comes very close to equating "body" and "flesh" with sin. So, too, the Qumran texts use "flesh" in such a manner that "it becomes almost synonymous with evil."[150]

For Paul, while the flesh is corrupted it is not of itself corrupting.[151] In the process of exonerating the Law as the corrupting element, Romans 7 also clears the material substance of man. Although verse 18 does speak of nothing good in the flesh, the following verses go on to insist that the flesh is not the culprit but that the enemy is sin which has found lodging and an avenue of expression in the flesh.[152] "It is

[146] Kennedy has rightly insisted that there is in Philo neither a "perfectly clear conception of Matter" nor evidence to show that he regarded matter as evil *per se* (*Philo's Contribution,* p. 74).

[147] Cf. De Gigant. 42, where *psuchē* and *sōma* are spoken of as being as opposite as night from day, light from darkness, odd from even, etc., and yet "because they have been the subject of creation, we do find fellowship and kinship of each with its opposite." Here Philo is being pulled between his Greek philosophy and his Hebrew theology.

[148] Quo Deus Immut. 142.

[149] Quis Rer. Div. Heres 268.

[150] K. G. Kuhn, "New Light on Temptation, Sin and Flesh in the New Testament," *Scrolls and the N. T.,* ed. K. Stendahl, p. 101. See 1QS 11.7-12 and IQM 4:3. Cf. Davies, "Paul and the Dead Sea Scrolls: Flesh and Spirit," *ibid.,* pp. 161-62.

[151] The opposition between flesh and spirit in passages such as Rom. 8:1-9, Gal. 5:17-24, etc., is not that of material substance versus immaterial, but of fleshly nature versus spiritual.

[152] Cf. H. W. Robinson: in Paul "the ultimate enemy of the Spirit of God is not the flesh but the Sin of which the flesh has become the weak and corrupted instrument" (*The Christian Doctrine of Man* [Edinburg: T. & T. Clark, 1911], p. 117).

clear that Paul took over the Old Testament conception of *basar* as being weak and prone to sin. His use of *sarx* does not imply that the physical element in man is of necessity evil as is implied in Hellenistic dualism."[153] In fact, the teaching that the body is to be redeemed[154] strongly suggests that it is not itself the culprit but under the influence of the culprit.

Because of his view of the corrupting nature of the material body, Philo viewed communion with God to be a matter for the soul alone. The body might be indirectly purified by the initiated and pure mind,[155] but it never enters directly into fellowship with God. Therefore in the soul's spiritual exercise, one must make himself "a stranger . . . in judgment and purpose" to "the earthy matter that encompasses."[156] And regarding physical exercise, it is "as a menace to the soul" while the

> pale, wasted and withered, so to speak, are the children of discipline. They have made over the bodily muscles to serve the powers of the soul and in fact are resolved into a single form, that of soul, and become unbodied minds. Naturally then the earthly element is destroyed and dissolved when the mind in all its powers has a fixed purpose to be well pleasing to God.[157]

True man—i.e., man in relation to God—is made up of only *nous kai logos;* "the living creature of two natures" cannot really be called man.[158]

In De Ebrietate 87, Philo gives us a very revealing glimpse of the relation of his views to those of his countrymen. He tells us that the priest in making sacrifice must recognize that the thousands of Jewish offerers believe the body to be secondary to the soul, *but still good*. Thus the priest must not despise the ideas of the people by attempting to make a purely spiritual offering and neglecting the physical sacrifices. But when the priest goes in to the inner altar, in the

[153] Davies, *Paul and Rabbinic Judaism,* p. 19. See also Wm. Sanday and A. C. Headlam, *Romans, I.C.C.* (Edinburgh: T. & T. Clark, 1900), p. 181; Machen, *Origin of Paul's Religion,* p. 276; Stacey, *Pauline View of Man,* p. 161.
[154] Rom. 8:23.
[155] De Somn. i. 177.
[156] De Migrat. Abr. 7—9.
[157] De Mutat. Nom. 33.
[158] Quod Det. Pot. Insid. 83.

presence of God alone and away from the eyes of the people, he acts only for the soul.[159] Thus the more the mind "soars aloft" and is "initiated in the mysteries of the Lord," the more it "judges the body to be wicked and hostile,"[160] and the more it sees that "it is impossible for one who is possessed by love for all that is incorporeal and incorruptible to dwell together with one who leans towards the objects of sense-perception doomed to die."[161] And thus Philo has no objection to the body of Moses being "stripped off him like a shell that has grown about the soul" and his soul as stripped naked set free to ascend to heaven.[162]

The attitude of the Qumran sectarians toward the resurrection of the body is as yet uncertain.[163] But they did lay more emphasis than did Philo upon the spiritual cleansing and purification of the flesh.[164] For them, the material aspect joined in the fellowship with God.[165] Theirs was not an escape from the earthly in order to purify it.

Paul's view of the physical body is hinted at in his references to bodily exercise as an illustration of some aspect of the Christian

[159] In this Philo offers some confirmation for Simpson's claim that "the major portion of the Jews in Egypt were probably never deeply influenced by Greek Philosophy, and many of them remained unaffected by the rising tide of Hellenism" (D. C. Simpson, "Tobit," *Ap. and Ps.*, Vol. I, p. 186). Cf. also Moore, *Judaism*, Vol. II, pp. 298-99, and Davies, *Paul and Rabbinic Judaism*, p. 12.

[160] Leg. All. iii. 71.

[161] De Migrat. Abr. 13—15.

[162] W. L. Knox, *St. Paul and the Church of the Gentiles*, p. 137, n. 3, citing De Virt. 4.

[163] For summaries regarding Qumran and the resurrection, see M. Burrows, *Dead Sea Scrolls*, pp. 270-72, and A. Dupont-Sommer, *Jewish Sect of Qumran and the Essences*, p. 8. Probably the truth lies somewhere between Josephus' assertion that they believed only in the immortality of the soul, as also argued by J. van der Ploeg (*Excavations at Qumran*, pp. 108-12), and Hippolytus' claim that they believed in a bodily resurrection, as insisted upon by Dupont-Sommer. Burrows, in agreeing with Vermes, is probably correct in saying that the Qumran community "expected the final judgment before the end of their own generation, and therefore were not concerned about the resurrection of the body. What they expected was neither the resurrection of the body nor the immortality of the soul alone, but the 'assumption' of the whole person in a purified body" (*Dead Sea Scrolls*, p. 270).

[164] 1QS 3.6 ff., 4.20. Cf. Kuhn, "New Light on Temptation, Sin, and Flesh in the New Testament," *op. cit.*, p. 101; and Davies, "Paul and the Dead Sea Scrolls: Flesh and Spirit," *ibid.*, p. 162.

[165] IQH 3.20-21: "So walk I on uplands unbounded and know that there is hope for that which Thou didst mould out of dust to have consort with things eternal."

life.[166] Like Hillel,[167] his interest in its care was quite different from that of Philo.[168] Nor could he agree with Philo regarding the place of the body in communion with God. For him the body enters into the working of God's salvation by becoming a temple of the Holy Spirit[169] and by being a medium through which one can glorify God.[170] The exhortation is even given not to disassociate body and soul in the worship of God, but to present the body as "a living sacrifice, holy and acceptable to God, which is your spiritual worship."[171] His prayer is that God will sanctify the Christian entirely—*pneuma, psuchē,* and *sōma.*[172] His expectation is that in the soul's goal of conformity to Christ, the body shall fully enter in; it shall be redeemed,[173] given life,[174] and be changed into the likeness of His glorious body.[175] Even his sighing with this body and longing to be out of such a body[176] was not that the soul might rise alone to God, but that it might the sooner gain its immortal body.[177] Hebraic Judaism had an intense dislike for being unclothed.[178] And Paul's thought lies along these lines rather than those of Hellenism or

[166] I Cor. 9:24-27; Gal. 2:2, 5:7; Phil. 3:14. As Hillel's reference to the monarch's statues (see note below) need not imply an approval of them, so Paul's references to the games need not indicate his approval of or previous attendance at them. Glover goes beyond the evidence in speaking of Paul as "this reprobate Jew, who had in his boyhood watched the Greek heathen at their sports, forgetful of old Jewish proprieties and Greek indecencies" (*Paul of Tarsus,* pp. 11-12).

[167] In Lev. R. 34. 1 ff., Hillel is recorded as comparing the human body to the statues of the king. If they must be kept clean and cared for, so must the body which was created in the image of the Almighty.

[168] Paul's reference to the beating and subduing of his body in I Cor. 9:27 must be interpreted in the light of his analogy of an athletic training which recognizes the value of the body. In fact, he severely denounces "self-abasement and severity to the body" as being "of no value in checking the indulgence of the flesh" (Col. 2:23). Even the statement in I Tim. 4:8 which most resembles Philo recognizes value in bodily exercise; and rather than censuring it, puts it in its proper relation to godliness.

[169] I Cor. 3:16, 6:15, 19.

[170] Phil. 1:20; I Cor. 6:20.

[171] Rom. 12:1.

[172] I Thess. 5:23.

[173] Rom. 8:23.

[174] Rom. 8:10.

[175] Phil. 3:21.

[176] II Cor. 5:4; Phil. 1:23.

[177] II Cor. 5:1-5.

[178] Mish. Ber. 3:5; b. Shab. 150a.

Hellenistic Judaism. "Paul was too good a Jew and too poor a Hellenist to describe the soul as being delivered from the clothing of the body so that it might ascend to heaven naked."[179]

Thus, Philo can view the material element in man as both defiled and defiling, and desire to escape from it that communion might be had with God. Qumran can agree with Philo regarding the nature of the body, but would not follow him regarding the need for soul-escape. Paul, however, can never brand the material flesh as the culprit. It is for him the neutral entity which has been taken captive by sin, but which can be used for God's glory and share in all of His blessings when it is presented unto Him. It does seem that Sanday and Headlam over seventy years ago spoke truly in saying:

> The controversy may now be regarded as practically closed. Its result is summed up by Lipsius in these decisive words: "The Pauline anthropology rests entirely on an Old Testament base; the elements in it which are supposed to be derived from Hellenistic dualism must simply be denied."[180]

Natural theology. The fact that Paul gives validity to a type of natural theology in the opening chapters of Romans seems to imply an influence from Hellenism. Greek metaphysical thought was early dominated by Aristotle's method of arguing through a succession of effects and causes back to "some first principle," a "First" or "Final Cause."[181] To the Greeks this Final Cause, or Unmoved Mover, was separated from the obvious effects by a series of causes and effects, with the effects being the unconscious but necessary repercussions of that First Cause. And in Romans 1:19-20 and in Philo's discussions of how Abraham came to recognize the true God,[182] it appears that this thought had either partially penetrated or been partially paralleled in Judaism.[183]

[179] W. L. Knox, *St. Paul and the Church of the Gentiles,* p. 137.

[180] Sanday and Headlam, *Romans,* p. 181.

[181] Aristotle, Metaphysics, Bk. II.

[182] De Abr. 13 ff.; De Migrat. Abr. 32 ff.; De Gigant. 13 ff.

[183] "Partially," since, however much a Jewish thinker might evidence agreement with Greek theistic thought, the Greek metaphysical ascriptions of non-personal motivation and indirect causation could never be accepted. For both Paul and Philo, God's action in the creation and preservation of the world was personal and direct; for both there was the possibility of theistic induction only because God had Himself consciously implanted a revelation of Himself in the world (Rom. 1:19: "For God hath showed it unto them"; Quod Det.

The Apostle's agreement with Philo, and their measure of agreement with Hellenism, however, do not necessarily indicate that Paul's roots were in a Hellenistic type of Judaism. Similar theistic speculation in such Hebraic passages as Gen. Rabbah 38.13 and 39.1 argues against this. The fact that theistic argumentation had a wide acceptance among various branches of Judaism is further indicated by the agreement of Josephus[184] and the sectarian Jubilees[185] with Philo and the midrash on Genesis. All four agree that Abraham was awakened to a consciousness regarding the true God by way of theistic inference. And perhaps the possibly Palestinian "Third Wisdom" (i.e., Wisdom of Solomon 11.2—19.22), in its acceptance of theistic argumentation,[186] is pertinent here as well. It seems that all we need conclude regarding Paul's agreement with Philo on the validity of theistic speculation is that both men were of Jewish stock and training.

But while there is agreement, there is also a definite and significant difference between Paul and Philo regarding the nature of theistic inference. Samuel Sandmel has pointed out that whereas all of the Palestinian references refer to the possibility of theistic inference from the created world of nature, Philo's insistence is that such inference can only be made from the order and rule seen within man himself.[187] For Philo, the revelation in creation is planted by God *in man alone,* and it is only because man is in the world that such revelation is also in nature.[188] It is therefore to the order and rule within himself that man must look if he is to see God's revelation in creation. All beholding of nature itself is of "Bezalel class."[189] On the

---

Pot. Insid. 86: "He breathed . . . from above of His own Deity. The invisible Deity stamped . . . the impress of Itself.").

[184] Antiq. I. 7. 1.

[185] Jubilees 12.16 ff.

[186] Wisdom, chap. 13. See S. Holmes, "Wisdom of Solomon," *Ap. and Ps.,* Vol. I, pp. 518, 524-25, for a survey on the question of Wisdom's authorship. The Testament of Naphtali 3.2 also reflects Palestinian thought, though the question is whether it is a Jewish or a Christian Palestinianism.

[187] S. Sandmel, "Abraham's Knowledge of the Existence of God," *H. T. R.,* Vol. XLIV, No. 3 (July, 1951), pp. 55-60. See De Abr. 72-74, De Gigant. 62-64.

[188] Quod. Det. Pot. Insid. 86: "The invisible Deity stamped on the invisible soul the impress of Itself, to the end that not even the terrestrial region should be without a share of the image of God."

[189] Leg. All. iii. 102; De Abr. 77. Cf. J. Drummond, *Philo Judaeus* (London: Williams & Norgate, 1888), Vol. II, pp. 5-6.

other hand, Paul manifests that his roots are not sunk in the same soil as those of Philo. That this distinction separates Hellenistic Judaism from Hebraic seems uncertain from the evidence. Nor can we declare that it necessarily divides Palestinian from Diaspora Judaism. It could very easily be Philo's own divergence from Jewish thought. But at least it does warn us to go slow in equating Paul with Philo, and thus with Hellenistic Judaism, at this point.

It is further noted that Paul agrees with Philo regarding the "conscience" (*suneidēsis*) as being the innate possession of every man and a real moral factor in the awakening of a man to God.[190] Yet in view of Judaism's acceptance of a limited and qualified natural theology, this agreement need carry no necessary implications either way regarding Hellenistic affinities between Paul and Philo. The background for both of them on this question is a Jewish heritage that has agreed to an extent with Hellenism.

Forms of expression. The parallels that have been cited between Paul and Hellenism are many. Not only such aforementioned terms as *mustērion, gnōsis, psuchē, pneumatikos,* and *nous,* but also such others as *doxa, teleios, sōtēria, psuchikos, phusis,* and *autarkēs* are proclaimed to reflect Greek thought in the Apostle's writings. And in confirmation of this judgment, it is pointed out that: (1) four times Paul explicitly quotes a Gentile saying or author;[191] (2) at times he makes use of the form of the Stoic diatribe;[192] and (3) his argumentation and expression can be paralleled in places by the Hellenized "Sapientia."[193] The atmosphere of Tarsus has been seen to manifest itself in the Pauline literature at these points.

But we need to be careful here lest we assume the old geographical dichotomy of a self-contained Palestinian Judaism and a syncretistic Diaspora. That Palestine and Jerusalem were not as invulnerable to

[190] Rom. 2:15. De Decal. 87; De Fuga 131, 203 f.; Quod Det. Pot. Insid. 22f.; Quod Deus Immut. 134ff.; De Jos. 47f. Cf. Kennedy, *Philo's Contribution,* pp. 111-15, and Stacey, *Pauline View of Man,* p. 36.

[191] Acts 17:28 (twice); I Cor. 15:33; and Titus 1:12.

[192] Rom. 9-11 and 2:1—3:20 are two of the longest where this form of familiar and lively interchange of question and answer, ironical apostrophe and personal appeal, is used.

[193] The comparisons between Rom. 1:18-32 and the Wisdom of Solomon are well laid out by Sanday and Headlam, *Romans,* pp. 51 f.

the penetration of Hellenism as some have proposed has been well pointed out by Emil Schürer and expanded by others.[194] This penetration need not be explained as the irresistible power of intellectual influences scaling the immovable wall of Hebraic isolation. The deepest reason for a limited acceptance of Greek thought within Hebraicism lay in the very nature of Pharisaic theology itself.[195] As an ethical religion, Judaism was in no position to counter completely a speculative philosophy and/or a highly philosophic theology. It was not able to fight fire with fire. Nor had it a desire to do so. Such alien thought must be definitely and staunchly resisted where it stood in opposition to the tenets and ethics of Judaism. But where it expressed truth, it could be accepted and worked into that religious fabric. For Israel, "the significance of the borrowed ideas [lay] not in their pre-history or antecedents but in Israel's understanding of them and in the use to which it [could] put them in the service of its religion."[196] The situation is exemplified clearly in Alexandria where the populace was willing to suffer death rather than accept the mystery cults or the objectionable Greek practices,[197] yet used Greek thought as an aid to Hebrew theology. And it was so also in Palestine. The Hebraic opposition to enforced Hellenization does not mean an absolute antagonism to every Greek term, idea, or form of expression. It is both interesting and instructive at this point to note that the Talmud speaks of a rabbinic training in the second century A.D. as

[194] Schürer, *Jewish People,* Div. II, Vol. I, pp. 29-50. Cf., e.g., Davies, *Paul and Rabbinic Judaism,* pp. 5-8; Stacey, *Pauline View of Man,* pp. 25-26. Some of the more pertinent evidence includes: (1) the statement of I Macc. 1:11-15 that certain of the people took on Grecian ways; (2) the Talmudic references to Greek clothing, ornaments, music, architecture, recreation (baths and games), municipal organization, legislation, courts, and coinage; (3) the fact that the name for the Jewish high court is a transliteration of the Greek word *sunedrion*; (4) the over 1,100 Greek words that have been counted in the Talmudic literature; (5) the Mishnah's statement that certain Temple vessels were marked with Greek letters (Sheka. 3.2); (6) The use of Greek in the LXX and the exhortations given in the synagogue; and (7) the permission to say the Shema in Greek.

[195] Cf. Schürer, *Jewish People,* Div. II, Vol. I, p. 350.

[196] Manson, *Jesus the Messiah,* p. 18; though with a change in tense, as indicated by the brackets.

[197] Cf. III Macc. 2:27 ff. True, this work is propaganda; but it surely contains some basis of fact.

including the study of the "wisdom of the Greeks."[198]

Undoubtedly W. L. Knox is right in insisting that Hebraic Judaism was sufficiently permeated by Hellenism to account for all of the Hellenistic forms found in the Pauline literature.[199] Paul's knowledge of Gentile literature, thought, terminology, and forms of presentation could have been quite easily gained through his rabbinic training in Jerusalem.[200] What he knew of real philosophic Hellenism was probably meager.[201] And all he accepted from Hellenism was accepted because it could convey *his* meaning, and not with reference to what it really meant outside. He used terms and forms which were current in the Gentile world, but he used them in accordance with what he had known and experienced in Judaism and Christianity. "The elements in his thinking to which parallels have been found in non-Jewish literature, in Greek religion or in pagan mysteries, are obviously secondary. They belong to the surface rather than to the core of this thought and teaching."[202]

DISPUTED HERMENEUTICS

The problem of the Pauline hermeneutics has not suffered from a lack of scholarly interest. Its study has followed in the wake of the former question regarding the conceptual and terminological affinities between Christianity and Hellenism, and the positions taken in that area have been followed also in this. In the renewed interest in Greek religious philosophy, Paul's exegetical methodology and interpretive principles were seen rooted in a Judaism similar to that of Philo. Siegfried, while refusing to be decisive, at least implied a

[198] B. Sot. 49b reports that R. Simeon b. Gamaliel II had five hundred youths learning the wisdom of the Jews and another five hundred learning the wisdom of the Greeks. The numbers may be distorted, but the establishment of such a dual curriculum need not be doubted.

[199] W. L. Knox, *Some Hellenistic Elements,* pp. 30-34; *St. Paul and the Church of Jerusalem,* pp. 126 ff.; *St. Paul and the Church of the Gentiles,* p. 91. Cf. Davies, *Paul and Rabbinic Judaism,* pp. 7-8.

[200] W. L. Knox suggests that such knowledge could have been obtained through a Greek anthology drawn up by the rabbis.

[201] His four quotations are but "conventional quotations" (W. L. Knox, *St. Paul and the Church of Jerusalem,* p. 115, n. 16); "the common property of popular philosophers" (M. Dibelius, *Paul,* p. 31).

[202] C. A. A. Scott, *Christianity According to St. Paul,* p. 10. Cf. J. S. Stewart, *Man in Christ,* pp. 56-64.

Pauline dependence upon such a Judaism.[203] And to many since, the hermeneutical comparisons between Paul and Philo have seemed conclusive.

As in the previous sections, it is not my purpose here to attempt an exhaustive treatment of the relation of Paul's hermeneutics to Hellenistic or Hebraic thought. Nor need we be detained by those Pauline affinities to Philo which have at least as many close parallels in Hebraic literature,[204] or the correlations to rabbinic methodology which have no parallel in Philo.[205] It is in those hermeneutical features of Paul which seem to correspond to what we find in Hellenistic writings, but not in Hebraic, that we are interested: allegorical exegesis and charismatic interpretation.

Allegorical exegesis. In Galatians 4:21-27, the allegory of Hagar and Sarah, and in I Corinthians 9:9-10, the application of the Deuteronomic law of not muzzling the ox to the sphere of apostolic rights, Paul comes the closest to Alexandrian exegesis. Michel insists that in Gal. 4 Paul has misspoken in saying, "These things are an allegory," for here "Paulus denkt mehr typologisch als allegorisch im eigentlichen Sinne."[206] But accepting the definition of typology as "linkages between events, persons, or things *within the historical*

[203] C. Siegfried, *Philo von Alexandria* [Jena: Dufft, 1875], pp. 304-10.

[204] E.g., I Cor. 10:4, the rock which followed in the wilderness, and Gal. 3:16, the distinction between "seed" (*sperma*) and "seeds" (*spermata*). Siegfried pointed out these instances as Philonic parallels (*ibid.*, p. 305). But the Apostle's insistence that "that Rock was Christ" in I Cor. 10:4 is also paralleled by b. Ber. 5b, "It has been taught: And 'rock' is nothing else than the Holy One, blessed be He," and the Targum on Num. 21. See E. Ellis, *Paul's Use of the Old Testament* (Edinburgh: Oliver & Boyd, 1957), pp. 66-70, for other Palestinian and Hebraic parallels. A slightly different designation, but with the same idea behind it, is found in CDC 6.3 (8.6): "The 'well' in question is the Law." The essential idea to all Jews was that the divine presence, as represented by the gushing rock, was with the people in the wilderness. To Judaism, it was the Holy One and/or His instruction; to Paul it was that too, but more particularly it was Christ. Paul's use of the singular noun in Gal. 3:16 is paralleled by Philo's treatment of *teknon* in De Mutat. Nom. 145 ff.; but also by b. Shab. 84b, in its distinction between "seed" and "seeds," and b. Sanh. 37a, where "blood" and "bloods" are differentiated.

[205] E.g., Paul's near-equal quotation from the Torah, Nebiim, and Kethubim, and his method of threefold quotation (Rom. 11:8-9, 15:10-12). Cf. Gamaliel's use of threefold quotation in b. Sanh. 90b, and see W. O. E. Oesterley, "The Exegesis of the Old Testament," *Record and Revelation*, ed. H. W. Robinson (Oxford: Clarendon Press, 1938), pp. 403-26, for further rabbinic parallels.

[206] Michel, *Paulus und seine Bibel*, p. 110.

framework of revelation," and of allegory as "the search for a secondary and hidden meaning underlying the primary and obvious meaning of a narrative,"[207] we must reject Michel's view that Hagar and Sarah are treated here merely typologically. Allegory has entered in. It is true that the Apostle's statement begins by being rooted in the historical situation, but verse 24 definitely goes beyond the historical to stress the hidden and underlying meaning. Similarly, in I Corinthians 9:9-10, Paul leaves the literal and primary sense of the words and insists that they were written for a reason not obvious in the passage itself. Here he quotes Deut. 25:4, which speaks of not muzzling the ox that treads out the grain, and then asks: "Is it for oxen that God is concerned? Does he not speak entirely for our sake? It was written for our sake."

Now it is true that there are many examples of allegory in the Talmudic literature,[208] but all those examples are to be distinguished from Philo's usage in that "bei allem Allegorisieren behält der Wortsinn stets seine volle Geltung."[209] For Philo, "der buchstäbliche Sinn ist lediglich der körper, der den allegorischen als die Seele umschliesst";[210] the literal and historical is only "a symbol of the religious and moral development of the human soul."[211] While in the Talmud, the rule is stated that "a verse cannot depart from its plain meaning."[212] The exegesis of Qumran, as many have pointed out, "has no real parallel either in Rabbinic Judaism, or in Philonic Judaism."[213] The commentaries to Micah 1 and Habbakkuk 1 and 2 seem to verge close to Philo, for there the prophetic history is all made applicable to the sect. Nevertheless, history is not abandoned, since for Qumran all that was written was meant for the community. It is strictly typological with Qumran and never breaks down into allegory. It appears, therefore, that Paul manifests greater affinity

[207] K. J. Woollcombe, "The Biblical Origins and Patristic Development of Typology," *Essays on Typology* (London: S.C.M. Press, 1957), p. 40.
[208] Cf. *Str.-Bil.,* Vol. III, pp. 388-97.
[209] *Ibid.,* Vol. III, p. 397.
[210] Michel, *Paulus und seine Bibel,* p. 106.
[211] C. Siegfried, "Philo Judaeus," *J. E.,* Vol. X, p. 7. Cf. *Philo von Alexandria,* pp. 165-68, regarding the Philonic canon.
[212] B. Shab. 63a. Even Josephus speaks of the "worthless shifts" which the Greek allegorists employ (Contra Apion, II, 36).
[213] F. M. Cross, Jr., *Ancient Library of Qumran,* p. 163.

with Philo in leaving the historical situation in Galatians 4 and in denying the literal meaning in I Corinthians 9.

Yet while he is not quite in line with what we know of Hebraic thought at this point, Paul is not quite Philonic either. In the first place, it is not altogether inappropriate to point out that there are only two such parallels to Philonic exegesis in Paul's letters;[214] whereas allegory permeates Philo's thought. Secondly, Paul's presentation does recognize the historicity of the event, though he later goes on to leave it. In his usage, the event and the use of that event are distinguished; and the historical nature of the event is not minimized by the following allegory. On the other hand, Philo ignores the historicity of the narrative. In all his treatments of Hagar and Sarah,[215] as well as in his treatments of each separately, what was historical to Paul is treated as myth whose symbols—"Hagar" and "Sarah"—convey truth for the present situation. Thirdly, while Paul in I Corinthians 9 does seem to leave the rabbinic method of arguing "If, then, so and so is true about A, how much more must it be true about B,"[216] his argumentation is not entirely non-Hebraic. The passage customarily cited in Philo as parallel to I Corinthians 9:9-10 is De Sacrific. Ab. et Cain. 260:

> You will discover that all this minuteness in reference to the animal shadows forth by means of symbols the improvement of your character. For the law does not exist for irrational creatures, but for those possessing mind and reason, so that its concern is not for sacrificial animals, to provide that they be without blemish, but for those who offer the sacrifices, that they be not disquieted by reason of any passion.

A comparison of the following two passages from the Midrash, however, indicates that Philo is not the only one with whom Paul is to be compared:

> The precepts were given only in order that man might be refined by them. For what does the Holy One, blessed be He, care whether a man kills an

[214] One must reject Woollcombe's view that there are three, including I Cor. 5:6-8 ("Biblical Origins and Patristic Development of Typology," *op. cit.*, p. 55), and Barclay's inclusion of I Cor. 10:4 (*Mind of St. Paul*, p. 16).

[215] Leg. All. iii. 244; De Cherub. 3—8; De Post. Cain. 130; De Congr. 1—23, 71—73, 121—122; and De Mutat. Nom. 255.

[216] Montefiore and Loewe, *Rabbinic Anthology*, Preface, p. ix. Cf. b. Bab. Mez. 88b.

animal by the throat or by the nape of its neck? Hence its purpose is to refine man.[217]
This [i.e., Prov. 30:5 with Deut. 14:4] means the precepts were given for the express purpose of purifying mankind.[218]

These statements are about 150 years later than Paul's day, it is true. Yet it does seem that "Entirely for our sake was it written!" could have been said by a Hebraic Jew as well as a Hellenistic one.[219]

The problem thus narrows down to the allegory of Gal. 4. But before Paul is relegated to Hellenism on the basis of this passage, more must be known regarding early hermeneutical interaction between Palestine and Alexandria. Siegfried and Kennedy have shown that "there can be little question that Philo stood in a long succession of allegorical interpreters of the Old Testament. The practice has been reduced to a kind of science."[220] The question is, how much did this succession of Alexandrian exegesis affect Palestinian methodology? We cannot assume complete isolation of Palestine from Alexandria. The fact that the Palestinian "sophists of literalness" rejected Philo's work,[221] and that possibly Philo was read by the community at Qumran,[222] shows at least some Palestinian awareness of the methodology of Alexandria. It could also have been that the Letter of Aristeas, with its one use of allegory comparable to that of I Corinthians 9,[223] was the means of bringing a mild allegorism into even the most closed recesses of Judaism.

Before drawing a final conclusion, we must recognize the signifi-

[217] Gen. R. 44.1.

[218] Lev. R. 13.3.

[219] Both these passages are attributed to R. Judah, but there is no reason to assume that such a treatment was original with him within Hebraic thought. Cf. Lev. R. 30.13, where R. Judah again, in regard to the command of Exod. 27:20, "take a light," says: "It is only in order to make you worthy and to atone for your souls."

[220] Kennedy, *Philo's Contribution,* p. 32. See also pp. 32-34, and Siegfried, *Philo von Alexandria,* pp. 16-37.

[221] De Somn. i. 16-17, 102. Cf. De Cherub. 12, 42; De Somn. ii. 301.

[222] R. de Vaux draws attention to the medieval Karaite writer Qirqisani and his reference to books of the "Alexandrian" being found in a cave of a Jewish sect which dwelt in caves ("A Propos des Manuscrits de la Mer Morte," *R. B.,* Vol. LVII [1950], pp. 421-25).

[223] Letter of Aristeas, 150: "For the division of the hoof and the separation of the claws are intended to teach us that we must discriminae between our individual actions with a view to the practise of virtue."

cance of Michel's words: "Die vorphilonische und vorpaulinische Tradition und Methodik müssen noch Fragen lösen, die bisher ungeklärt blieben."[224] There is the possibility that a limited use of allegory was not frowned upon within predestruction Hebraicism. Perhaps a moderate allegorism was part of an authentic Hebraic heritage, but just not incorporated to any extent in the Talmudic traditions. Or it may even be that there was a reaction to allegorism in rabbinic Judaism similar to that of the Antiochian versus Alexandrian schools of Christian interpretation, and thus a former moderate allegorism is not reflected fully in Judaism's literature. But at least, in view of Paul's very limited use of allegory and our meager knowledge of the interrelation between Palestine and Alexandria, it is precarious to refute Paul's Hebraic claims on this basis.

Charismatic interpretation. The real point of contact between Paul and Philo is in their mutual agreement that Scripture cannot be correctly interpreted by reference to the "letter" alone. For both, Scripture was intrinsically the revealed Word of God. But also for both, it is only the Word of God to the individual when its interpretive principle is the Spirit. Interpretation of Scripture must be a divine prophetic gift, not just a laborious and methodical investigation and presentation. The same Spirit who inspired must also illumine, or the "letter" is dead and destructive. And while the locus of revelation is the written Word, without the charismatic element *to gramma* becomes set against *hai graphai.* In this Qumran voices its agreement. Scripture as the Word of God is both letter *and* Spirit. In the midst of all interpretation, the Spirit must pervade. This meant, for Philo, the letter of the Old Testament as interpreted allegorically; for Qumran, the letter as interpreted by the Right Teacher; for Paul, the letter as interpreted by Christ through the Spirit.[225] But Christian charismatic interpretation is not Hellenism.

Other objections to Paul's Hebraic claims could be raised,[226] but

[224] Michel, *Paulus und seine Bibel,* p. 111.

[225] Cf. the emphases of Michel, *ibid.,* and Ellis, *Paul's Use of the O. T.*

[226] E.g., R. Bultmann's objection based upon Paul's statement in Gal. 1:22 that he was "unknown by sight to the churches of Judaea which are in Christ." Could he have really been unknown to them had he been trained in Jerusalem and taken the leadership in persecuting them? (cf. *Theology of the New Testament,* trans. K. Grobel [London: S.C.M. Press, 1952], Vol. I, p. 187). But Martin Dibelius is surely correct in saying it "is a naive assumption that

those listed in the foregoing pages are the main ones. Have they really discredited or nullified his claims? I think not. I believe there is little or no reason to doubt that Paul was a Hebrew of the Hebrews and trained at the feet of Gamaliel in the city of Jerusalem. It will therefore be legitimate to attempt to understand Hebraic Pharisaism in part from the Pauline references, and Paul's pre-conversion experience in part by Hebraicism's literature.

---

the victims of the persecution must have known personally the man who was carrying it on" (*Paul,* p. 47; cf. also Nock, *St. Paul,* p. 33, and E. D. Burton, *Galatians,* I.C.C. [Edinburgh: T. & T. Clark, 1921], p. 63). Further, if the persecution was directed primarily against the Hellenists and resulted in their expulsion, it is not too surprising that years later the persecutor should be "unknown by sight" to the remaining native Jewish Christians.

III

The Piety of Hebraic Judaism

PAUL'S BACKGROUND is not understood simply by designating the nature of his early Judaism. We must also analyze the theology and piety of that Judaism. But judging from the very diverse opinions expressed, an analysis of the spirituality of pre-destruction Hebraic Judaism seems well-nigh impossible. On the one hand, the majority of Christian scholars have followed the position popularized by Emil Schürer; i.e., that first-century Pharisaism's motivation lay in its "faith in Divine retribution,"[1] its ethic and theology being "swallowed up in jurisprudence"[2] resulting in a "fearful burden which a spurious legalism had laid upon the shoulders of the people."[3] Thus it is not difficult to find statements in Christian writings which easily equate Pharisaism with "legalistic Judaism" or "legalism."[4] There are likewise direct assertions that the Pharisee of the first century lacked "inwardness, a sense of relative values, unity and peace of his religious and moral life" while he lived in an atmosphere of "externalism, superficiality, casuistry, and unsatisfactory religious fellowship."[5] On the other hand, most Jews agree with Solomon

[1] E. Schürer, *Jewish People,* Div. II, Vol. II, p. 91.
[2] *Ibid.,* p. 120.
[3] *Ibid.,* p. 124.
[4] E.g., R. H. Charles, *Ap. and Ps.,* Vol. II, p. 786; J. S. Stewart, *A Man in Christ,* pp. 83-92; H. W. Robinson, "The Theology of the Old Testament: The Characteristic Doctrines," *Record and Revelation,* ed. H. W. Robinson, p. 348; E. Stauffer, *New Testament Theology,* trans. J. Marsh (London: S.C.M. Press, 1955), pp. 92-93.
[5] F. V. Filson, *St. Paul's Conception of Recompense* (Leipzig: Hinrichs, 1931), p. 7. The assertion of C. H. Dodd that "the Pharisaic God was for practical purposes an Absentee" (*The Meaning of Paul for Today* [London: Fontana, 1958], p. 37) is but another example of this approach.

Schechter and Israel Abrahams, insisting that "it is hardly an exaggeration to maintain that there is no noble manifestation of real religion, no expression of real piety, reverence and devotion, to which Jewish literature would not offer a fair parallel."[6] And concurrently, some Christian scholars argue that "the Judaism of the Pharisees, from which Christianity tore itself away, was no obsolete formalism, but a religion having the power to satisfy the spiritual wants of those who were faithful to it."[7] Christians have traditionally laid stress on the Halakic portions of the Talmud and the practice of Pharisaism as recorded in the New Testament and by Josephus. The Jews have stressed the Haggadah and the principles of Judaism. Neither group has failed to consider all the evidence, but their emphases have been different. To the first, it is the preponderance of dark elements in the literature and histories that is significant; to the other, the streaks of light in the shadows. And thus scholarship has been divided to this day.

The renewed attempt, which this chapter takes up, to understand the spiritual climate of the Pharisaism of early Roman times is not necessarily an endeavor to reconcile these two opposing views or to advocate either. As most previous investigators have done, so we desire to evaluate the piety of first-century Hebraic Judaism on the basis of what we believe to be its valid sources and with an eye to both the principles of the system and its practice—to both its possibilities and its actualities. And in view of the analogous evidence unearthed at Qumran, such a re-examination of Pharisaism's spirituality is pertinent at this time.

EXTERNALISM AND FORMALISTIC PIETY

Probably everyone is more ready to see the flowers in his own garden,[8] and the weeds in that of his neighbor. And yet it is poor

[6] S. Schechter, *Studies in Judaism,* p. 173.

[7] R. T. Herford. *Pharisaism* (London: Williams & Norgate, 1912), p. 2. G. F. Moore and F. C. Burkitt, for example, have expressed similar sentiments.

[8] I. Abrahams' sentiments could be just as fervently expressed by any religionist in favor of his own position: "Amidst the weeds of Pharisaism are flowers, amidst the Evangelic flowers are weeds. I cannot overcome my preference for the flowers. I am no gatherer of weeds" (*Studies in Pharisaism and the Gospels*, p. vii).

gardening to dwell on either to the exclusion of the other. While we might desire flowers, we must first of all deal with the weeds. And weeds there were in predestruction Pharisaism.

The testimony of the Talmud. The legalistic externalism of the great proportion of the statements in the Mishnah and the quibbling casuistry of the major portion of the Gemaras have caused many interpreters to view all Jewish piety as formalistic.[9] And it is not difficult to see why, when even the earliest and noblest tractate contains such views as: "The rules about Bird-offerings and the onset of menstruation—these are essentials of the Halakoth";[10] or "Which is the straight way that a man should choose? That which is an honour to him and gets him honour from men."[11] Both these statements, however, are credited to rabbis later than our time of interest; the first to R. Eleazar Hisma, from the beginning of the second century A.D., and the second to R. Judah at the end of the same century. It is therefore not my purpose to include them here as evidence. Nor shall I include the great amount of material of similar externalistic nature in the later Talmudic writings.[12]

When we dismiss all those writings which do not definitely have their roots in the predestruction period, we are left with a pitifully small amount of direct Talmudic evidence. And of this remaining material there are more statements manifesting an inward piety than a mere externalism. Yet there are expressions that reveal a purely commercial view of righteousness which can rightfully be assigned to that period before A.D. 70; e.g., the saying ascribed to antiquity that "a man should always regard himself as though he were half guilty and half meritorious: if he performs one precept, happy is he for

[9] E.g., P. P. Bläser cites as an example the fact that the short passages in the Pentateuch regarding the Sabbath rest (Exod. 16:23, 30; 31:12-17; 34:21; 35:1-3; Num. 15:32-36) are expanded to 39 articles and 1521 passages in the Mishnah (*Das Gesetz bei Paulus* [Münster: Aschendorff, 1941], p. 39).

[10] Mish. Aboth 3.19.

[11] Mish. Aboth 2.1a.

[12] Cf. C. G. Montefiore and H. Loewe, *Rabbinic Anthology*, pp. 202-32, for quotes and comments on what Montefiore elsewhere calls "the cheap doctrine of tit for tat and measure for measure" ("The Old Testament and Judaism," *Record and Revelation*, ed. H. W. Robinson, p. 447). All but one of the examples cited by Montefiore and Loewe are later than our time of interest. Also note the many expressions of justification by works and laboring for reward attributed to R. Akiba and his disciples in Mish. Aboth 2.16, 3.2, 3.16-17, 4.10-11.

weighting himself down in the scale of merit; if he commits one transgression, woe to him for weighting himself down in the scale of guilt."[13] The words ascribed to R. Eleazar, who personally and through his teacher R. Johanan b. Zakkai had his roots in the early period, also lean in this direction: "Know before whom thou toilest and who is thy taskmaster who shall pay thee reward of thy labour."[14]

The testimony of the Gospels and Josephus. The greater quantity of evidence revealing a formalistic piety in predestruction Pharisaism is contained in the Gospels and in the writings of Josephus. Many clashes between Jesus and the Pharisees over sabbath observance and ritual purity are recounted in the Gospels,[15] and at least one parable portrays the "elder brother" of Judaism as missing the significance of the occasion in his pride and self-pity.[16] Such accounts are primarily setting forth the Jewish failure to appreciate God's greater revelation and working in their midst in and through His Son; though, of course, in the light of this failure the Gospels cannot view the Pharisaic righteousness as anything but externalism. The damning evidence from the Gospels against Pharisaic spirituality, however, is contained in (1) John the Baptist's denunciation of them as a "brood of vipers" who take pride in the external matter of their descent from Abraham;[17] (2) Jesus' characterization of them as evil at heart while attempting to appear good;[18] (3) Jesus' contrasts in the Sermon on the Mount between the Pharisees' formalism and true righteousness;[19] (4) His application to the Pharisees of Isaiah 29:13, "This people honor me with their lips but their heart is far from me";[20] and (5) His long listing of woes pronounced upon the scribes and Pharisees—these who are proclaimed to be "hypocrites."[21] There is no need to

[13] B. Kid. 40b.
[14] Mish. Aboth 2.14.
[15] Cf. Mark 2:23-28 and par., Mark 3:1-5 and par., John 5, John 9.
[16] Cf. the latter part of the Prodigal Son.
[17] Matt. 3:7-9; though here it is also directed to the Sadducees, and in Luke 3:7 to the whole multitude.
[18] Matt. 12:33-37.
[19] Matt. 5:20—6:18.
[20] Mark 7:1-23; Matt. 15:1-20.
[21] Matt. 23:1-35; Luke 11:39-44. A. Lukyn Williams has sought to soften our Lord's criticism, arguing that "hypocrites" *(hypokritai)* should be translated by the more innocent "play actors" rather than transliterated by the harsher

say that these denunciations arose from a later *Lebensitz* of the Church, for the Talmud itself speaks of similar hypocrisy within Pharisaism and similarly condemns it.[22]

Josephus' account of the Jerusalem Pharisee Ananias, who hypocritically used the pretense of a religious fast to accomplish his political ambitions, indicates that at least one Pharisee's religion was but formal.[23] And the earlier indication in this Jewish war that the sacred seasons in Jerusalem were often used by the religious leaders

---

"hypocrites" *(Talmudic Judaism and Christianity,* pp. 63-78). His case rests upon the distinction between the "habitual action" of pretense on the part of the hypocrite and the "for the occasion only" action of the play-actor. But the distinction is rather thin when applied to the Gospels' portrayal.

If we were to consider only a part of the evidence, a case could be made for *hypokrisis* and *hypokritēs* as having a broader meaning in Matt. 23 than "hypocrite," or even Moffatt's "impious." Both forms of the word were used previous to and during the first century in Jewish literature to mean play-acting and actor; e.g., the case of the noble Eleazar in facing persecution, and the appeal of his friends to play the part of an apostate in light of his advanced age (II Macc. 6:21, 24, 25; IV Macc. 6:15, 17). And the context of many passages in the Gospels would not demand that *hypokritēs* be equated with anything more than "superficialists" (e.g., Luke 12:56, Mark 7:6); though that is a fairly severe charge of itself. The descriptions of Matt. 23:16 and following are all of superficiality, and the two in verses 13-15 of the same chapter are not necessarily adverse to such an interpretation. If we possessed only this evidence, we might agree that the term should better be translated "play-actors" or "superficialists"; though how this would materially ease the accusation against the Pharisees is difficult to see, since the context of Matt. 23 makes it plain that their action was neither innocent pretense nor unconscious naïveté. Yet there are other passages which warn us to go slow in rejecting the rendering "hypocrisy." The descriptions of the *hypokritēs* as "spies feigning themselves to be righteous" (Luke 20:20), giving alms "that they may have glory of men" (Matt. 6:2), praying "that they may be seen of men" (Matt. 6:5), fasting "that they may appear to men so to fast" (Matt. 6:16), double-hearted (Sir. 1:29), deceitful beguilers (Pss. of Sol. 4:22-25), and both a curse to others and cursed themselves (Job 34:30, 36:13) indicate that we have not misread the text. A. G. Hebert has well said: "The word *hypokrites* with the meaning of 'actor' belonged to the Greek drama, and so was alien to the Jewish tradition and the Aramaic language. The true meaning is deeper and more penetrating" ("Hypocrite," *A Theological Word Book of the Bible,* ed. A. Richardson [New York: Macmillan, 1950], p. 109).

[22] See b. Sot. 22b, j. Ber. 9.14b, and j. Sot. 5.20c. Also H. Loewe, "Pharisaism," *Judaism and Christianity,* Vol. I, ed. W. O. E. Oesterley, p. 186, where a summary of passages is given in support of the thesis that "the Pharisees were just as prone as Jesus to blame ostentation in religion."

[23] Life 56. Cf. Life 39.

for purposes of sedition and political advantage implies that Ananias' action may not have been an isolated incident.[24] Certainly externalism is evident in the historian's insistence, which he implies is the accepted view within the Jewish nation, that "the purposing to do a thing, but not actually doing it, is not worthy of punishment."[25] These words are spoken in connection with the attempt of Antiochus Epiphanes to plunder the temple of Diana in Persia. But Josephus clears him of all guilt, since—though he tried his hardest to get the treasure—he did not succeed. Now it is true that Josephus is a poor spokesman for the theology of Judaism. Yet it is probable that this view had a wider acceptance than just that of Josephus' own personal Pharisaism. This same principle is stated by fairly early Gemaras,[26] and some modern rabbis speak with approval of "the principle adopted for Israel that an evil thought is not to be viewed as an evil deed."[27] Probably of a similar nature is Josephus' representation of the Jewish view of retaliation: "Let him that is smitten be avenged immediately, by inflicting the same punishment on him that smote him."[28]

It does seem, therefore, that even though we disregard the later foliage of Judaism, much of which undoubtedly had its roots if not its flower in the early period, there were still weeds in the piety of predestruction Hebraic Judaism. But we must not linger over the weeds.

INWARDNESS AND PROPHETIC SPIRIT

The most difficult aspect of early Pharisaism for Christian scholars to see is that of inwardness. But in all fairness it must be noted that the Judaism of the predestruction period was not all externalism.

The testimony of the Talmud. The statement attributed to Antig-

[24] In recounting the Jewish opposition to Alexander Jannaeus, Josephus says: "The nation of the Jews made an insurrection against him at a festival, for at those feasts seditions are generally begun" (War, I. 4. 3).

[25] Antiq. XII. 9. 1.

[26] Note b. Kid. 40a: "Evil intention is not combined with deed"; which I. Epstein explains as: "There is no punishment for mere intention" (*The Babylonian Talmud* [Soncino], Seder Nashim VIII, p. 198, n. 14). Cf. j. Peah 1.1.

[27] E.g., Z. H. Chajes, *The Student's Guide Through the Talmud,* trans. J. Shachter (London: East & West Library, 1952), p. 169.

[28] Antiq. IV. 8. 33. Cf. the Story of Ahikar, and Matt. 5:38-39.

onus of Socho probably was first directed against the doctrine of a future life. Antigonus is usually classed as a proto-Sadducee of the third century B.C. But in that he is listed with the pillars of Pharisaism in the Aboth, it seems that in some way his person had been disinfected by the Pharisees and his words turned into an ethical maxim. Thus his teaching, "be not like slaves that minister to the master for the sake of receiving a bounty, but be like slaves that minister to the master not for the sake of receiving a bounty; and let the fear of Heaven be upon you,"[29] seems to have been understood by the rabbis as an appeal for inward motivation in the service of God. And the negative aspect of this thought was repeated by at least Hillel, Zadok, and Johanan b. Zakkai.[30] But better evidence for a Pharisaic inwardness of orientation can yet be cited.

In the discussions of proselyte baptism, there is the significant statement of R. Johanan b. Zakkai insisting that one did not really become clean by the water of separation nor unclean by a corpse; yet the provisions regarding cleanliness must be kept since this was the will of God.[31] Here the performance of external rites is rooted in the divine will and request, not the efficacy of the action itself. Further, Johanan b. Zakkai highly commends the expression of his pupil Eleazar that a good heart is the foundation of all good and an evil heart of all evil.[32]

More pertinent still is the evidence from several sources of a realization in predestruction Judaism that one must start from the mercy and love of God, returning that love and manifesting it to one's fellow man, if religion is to be meaningful. Probably the most important single factor in impressing mercy and love upon the con-

[29] Mish. Aboth 1.3.

[30] Hillel: "He that makes worldly use of the crown (i.e., the Torah) shall perish" (Mish. Aboth 1.13, 4.5); Zadok: "Make them (i.e., the words of the Law) not a crown wherewith to magnify thyself or a spade wherewith to dig" (Mish. Aboth 4.5); Johanan: "If thou hast wrought much in the Law claim not merit for thyself, for to this end wast thou created" (Mish. Aboth 2.8). Cf. Daube, *N. T. and Rabbinic Judaism*, p. 395, regarding the date for Zadok. Also b. Ab. Zar. 19a, where Antigonus' admonition is repeated in later literature, and Exod. R. 30.24, where merit is de-emphasized.

[31] Num. R. 19.8 on Num. 19:2. Cf. Daube, *N.T. and Rabbinic Judaism*, p. 107.

[32] Mish. Aboth 2.9. Cf. b. Shab. 63a and b. Ber. 6a, 13a, 20, where, in the literature of a later time, intent is stressed as the basis of all action and that which God judges.

sciousness of the Jew in this early period was the daily recitation of the Shema. After the recital of the unity of God, and before the commands regarding obedience, the significant words of Deut. 6:5 were repeated: "Thou shalt love the Lord thy God with all thine heart, with all thy soul, and with all thy might." These same elements of (1) confession of God, (2) love from God to man and/or man to God, and (3) obedience to God's instruction, appear in the same order in the Shemoneh Esreh[33] and in the enumeration of the 613 Commandments.[34] They were possibly included as well by many early Pharisees in the opening words of the "Ten Commandments."[35] There is also abundant evidence that at least Hillel made much of the *ḥesed* of God, both as revealed by God to man and as ought to be manifested by the man of God to his fellow men.[36] In this respect, he was a true follower of the Hasidic movement.[37] And although a nonritualistic emphasis was bound to arise with the enforced discon-

[33] The first words of the Shemoneh Esreh (the Eighteen "Benedictions," "Blessings," or "Prayers") regard the person and majesty of God; the first activity cited is that of His graciousness. It is not until the fifth Benediction that there is mention of service on the part of man.

[34] The listing of the 613 Commandments begins: (1) "To know that the Lord God exists"; (2) "To acknowledge His unity"; (3) "To love Him"; (4) "To fear Him." Though the list was only finally compiled by the medieval Maimonides, there is reason to believe that its roots are very ancient. See I. Broydé, "The 613 Commandments," *J. E.*, Vol. IV, pp. 181-86, for Tannaitic and Palestinian Amoraic testimony to its antiquity and for a listing of the commandments.

[35] In New Testament times "it is possible that many experts even then considered the verse 'I am the Lord, which have brought thee out of the house of bondage' to be one of the ten portions forming the whole" (Daube, *N. T. and Rabbinic Judaism*, p. 249). Cf. b. Mak. 24a. The listings in Antiq. III. 5. 5 and in the Targums could be interpreted either way. If the "Ten Words" were then ordered as they are in modern Judaism, the Decalogue began with: (1) a declaration of the Person of God; (2) an expression of God's gracious activity; and then, and only then, (3) commands to obedience. This same emphasis on beginning with God and His mercy is continued in the later writings; e.g., Mish. Ber. 2.2, where Deut. 6:4-9 is so interpreted, and b. Ber. 63a, where a similar stress is found in Prov. 3:6.

[36] For an excellent treatment of Hillel on this point, and a bringing together of the many Talmudic references, see N. N. Glatzer, "Hillel the Elder in the Light of the Dead Sea Scrolls," *Scrolls and the N.T.*, ed. K. Stendahl, pp. 233-34.

[37] Here is where Hillel and the Essenes came the closest to one another. The affinity is most easily explained by a common foundation in the Old Testament and in the Maccabean Hasidim.

tinuance of the sacrificial system, it is still significant that R. Johanan b. Zakkai took the words of Hosea 6:6 as his motto after A.D. 70: "I desire *hesed* and not sacrifice."[38] This appears to be but a re-emphasis of what was already accepted in at least some Hebraic circles before the fall of Jerusalem. Further, it should be pointed out that at least two Talmudic passages ascribed to antiquity—b. Sot. 31a and b. Shab. 88b—speak of the proper and best motivation in the religious life as being that of the love of God.[39]

Even those who most hotly dispute the element of inwardness as a real factor in predestruction Hebraic Judaism must at least agree with Bacher that the "love of man was considered by Hillel as the kernel of the entire Jewish teaching."[40] The statements ascribed to Hillel show him to have possessed a true inward spirituality, whatever characterization might be given to the rest of Judaism.[41] But the fact that one of R. Johanan b. Zakkai's students is credited with a similar expression of the Golden Rule as is attributed to Hillel,[42] and that the same sentiment is contained in the Letter of Aristeas,[43] makes it probable that the concept of love and consideration for one's fellow

[38] Aboth de R. Nathan I. 4.

[39] B. Sot. 31a: "It has been taught: R. Meir says: It is declared of Job 'one that feared God,' and it is declared of Abraham 'thou fearest God'; just as 'fearing God' with Abraham indicates love, so 'fearing God' with Job indicates from love. Whence, however, have we it in connection with Abraham himself [that he was motivated by love]? As it is written, 'The seed of Abraham who loved me.' " The passage then goes on to contrast the motivation of love and that of fear; and concludes that while both engender righteousness, the motivation of love is greater.

B. Shab. 88b: "Our Rabbis taught: Those who are insulted but do not insult, hear themselves reviled without answering, act through love and rejoice in suffering, of them the Writ saith, 'But they who love Him are as the sun when he goeth forth in his might.' "

[40] W. Bacher, "Hillel," *J. E.*, Vol. VI, p. 398.

[41] Hillel's famous statements are: (1) "What is hateful to thee, do not unto thy fellow man: this is the whole Law; the rest is mere commentary" (b. Shab. 31a); (2) "Be of the disciples of Aaron, loving peace and pursuing peace, loving mankind and bringing them nigh to the Law" (Mish. Aboth 1.12); and (3) "Trust not in thyself until the day of thy death, and judge not thy fellow until thou art come to his place" (Mish. Aboth 2.5).

[42] Mish. Aboth 2.10: "R. Eliezer said: Let the honour of thy fellow be dear to thee as thine own."

[43] Letter of Aristeas 207: "As you wish that no evil should befall you, . . . so you should act on the same principle towards your subjects and offenders."

men had a broader acceptance within early Pharisaism than we sometimes imagine.

The testimony of the Gospels and Josephus. Though much is said to the contrary in the Gospels and the writings of Josephus, there is still the recognition within both sources of what may be called a more noble element in Palestinian Pharisaism. Mark's Gospel recounts with approval the agreement of one scribe with Jesus that to love God and to love one's neighbor was of far greater importance than all external action.[44] And not all the Pharisees are presented in the Gospel narratives as in bitter opposition to Jesus.[45] Josephus likewise relates that Alexander Jannaeus still recognized a godly element in Pharisaism, even though he characterized the group as a whole as scoundrels.[46]

It seems, therefore, that we can recognize within predestruction Pharisaism not only the element of formalistic piety, but also at least a bit of true inwardness of spirit. It appears that there were Pharisees who could insist that "doing is a deadly thing—unless it is the result of heartfelt faith."[47]

THE CORRELATION OF THE TWO ELEMENTS

With the recognition of both a formalistic and an inward spirit within predestruction Hebraic Pharisaism, the question arises as to how these two elements are to be viewed in the over-all religious situation of the day. And it is at this point, in the interpretation of the data more than in the recognition of the elements, that divergence of opinion has arisen.

Past perspectives. Various positions regarding the relation of these factors in the over-all picture of Judaism have been advocated; in order to clarify the discussion, I list them as follows:

1. Some Jewish scholars have taken the line of whimsically shrugging off the baser elements in the Talmudic literature, insisting that

[44] Mark 12:28-34.

[45] Note the cases of certain Pharisees who warn Him to flee (Luke 13:31), Joseph of Arimathea (Mark 15:43), Nicodemus (John 3:1, 19:39), and, possibly, the chief Pharisee who had Jesus to dinner (Luke 14:1).

[46] Antiq. XIII. 15. 5.

[47] Williams' phraseology, *Talmudic Judaism and Christianity,* p. 32.

they are "only the expression of a momentary impulse, . . . or were meant simply as a piece of humorous by-play, calculated to enliven the interest of a languid audience."[48]

2. Other Jewish apologists refer all of what they believe to be base or exaggerated to the realm of the incidental, "made in the heat of polemics and through zeal for the preservation of a national unity," and thus never a part of true Judaism.[49]

3. Some Christian writers ignore the evidence from the Gospels and Josephus, either by excluding it as evidence or explaining away the denunciations found therein, and minimize the objectionable features in the Talmud.[50] The result is thus a general agreement with the first two Jewish positions; some going so far as to insist that "the Rabbinic Judaism of 4 B.C. to A.D. 70 was . . . as bright and happy a religion as the world has seen."[51]

4. A few have suggested that an individual Jew could, at one and the same time, believe that love was the only acceptable motive for service and yet that the motivation of desire to win God's favor was rewarded by God.[52]

5. The vast majority of Christian scholars have minimized the evidences of an inward piety and insisted that "Judaism believed in salvation through the observance of the Torah; the deliverance by an

[48] Schechter, *Studies in Judaism,* p. 240. Schechter continues: "The greatest fault to be found with those who wrote down such passages as appear objectionable to us is, perhaps, that they did not observe the wise rule of Johnson, who said to Boswell on a certain occasion, 'Let us get serious, for there comes a fool.' "

C. G. Montefiore mentally resurrects a jovial ancient rabbi and creates his apology as follows: "As you know, we Rabbis in those days loved to argue with one another. We liked to use the words of Holy Scripture to prove our various assertions, as they chanced to crop up in our minds. If one of us said A, the other loved to say B. It was such fun. We had not so many outlets for fun in those days. But you must not take our different and differing sayings so seriously. We never thought of them like that. They were just the outcome of the moment, and we did so enjoy the arguing" (Montefiore and Loewe, *Rabbinic Anthology,* p. xlvi).

On pain of being classed a humorless fool, this author cannot believe that the rabbis ever "thought of them like that." It is true that there are light touches in the Talmud, but the work is a basically serious one. And it was meant to be taken seriously.

[49] J. Z. Lauterbach, "Nomism," *J. E.,* Vol. IX, p. 328.

[50] E.g., G. F. Moore, R. T. Herford, A. L. Williams.

[51] Williams, *Talmudic Judaism and Christianity,* p. 53.

[52] E.g., J. Parkes, *Jesus, Paul and the Jews,* p. 70.

act of God was not the foundation of Judaism, but only a devotional accessory."[53]

The problem of religious orientation. In evaluating the spiritual climate of any religious group or system, it is not enough simply to balance baser elements against nobler ones and accept the verdict of the weightier quantity. Theology is more than mathematics. In dealing with spirituality we are dealing primarily with motives, not just expressions; though of course any investigation regarding motives has only the expressions as factual evidence on which to base its judgments. Yet the investigator must always realize that he is dealing with religious outlooks and orientations, and must accept the fact that there can be differing religious orientations within a given religious group or community.

We find such differing religious orientations at variance within our own souls even before we see them manifested within a particular religious form of expression; but we can also view them at work in all the spiritual and ethical activities of man—whether individual or formal and organized. These differing orientations can be grouped roughly into two classes or types. To borrow Deissmann's distinction in regard to mysticism, they are the "acting" religious orientation and the "reacting" religious orientation; that attitude which makes religion *a means in order to* and that which sees it as *an expression because of*. Deissmann's words regarding mysticism are also pertinent here:

> In both cases an action takes place. But in the first type the action is spontaneous performance of the individual or of the community, intended to produce in response to it a performance on the part of the deity, effective through its own execution, effective as *actio acta,* as *opus operatum.* In the second, the reacting type, on the other hand, the action of

[53] W. L. Knox, *St. Paul and the Church of the Gentiles,* p. 98. Wm. Barclay has said: "When Paul laid such stress on grace, he set out on a road of thought which was quite strange to the orthodox Jewish teaching of his day. It is true that in its highest and most devotional moments Jewish religion did rest in the mercy of God and in nothing else. . . . But that is not representative of the teaching of the orthodox Rabbis in the days of Paul" (*Mind of St. Paul,* pp. 155-56). For similar expressions, see also H. St. J. Thackeray, *Relation of St. Paul to Contemporary Jewish Thought,* p. 85; R. Bultmann, *Theology of the N. T.,* Vol. I, p. 314; Stauffer, *N.T. Theology,* pp. 35-36.

the man is an action in response, a reaction. Here it is God Himself who is really the *Leitourgos*, the *Theourgos* in the highest sense; the individual or the community only says the amen.[54]

In the constant demand for value judgments which comparative religion and theology as a whole make upon us, it is of the utmost importance to recognize the possibility of such differing orientations —indeed, even of opposing outlooks. Yet we must be aware that positive identification and precise analysis become extremely difficult, if not impossible. Precision of identification becomes impossible because such orientations cross all external lines and because the nature of our human knowledge is such that we can know nothing fully—least of all the human spirit, which defies the most skilled human scientific analysis. Yet we are forced to recognize as best we can, make value judgments, and view the details in their total perspective. This is what we must endeavor to do in understanding the piety of predestruction Pharisaism.

Acting and reacting tendencies in Hebraicism. All our sources recognize differing religious orientations within predestruction Hebraic Judaism, though they express the recognition differently. The Talmud distinguishes between the "reckoning Pharisee, who casts up his account of sins and virtues," and the "God-fearing Pharisee" and "God-loving Pharisee."[55] It speaks of both the *ish ḥesed* Hillel[56] and the goodhearted Johanan b. Zakkai,[57] but also warns regarding the bite and wounds of the mere formalists.[58] The Gospels speak of the Pharisees as hypocrites and lacking the love of God,[59] and yet commend a Pharisaic scribe for realizing that love of God and neighbor is basic to all spirituality. They can portray the Pharisees as agitating

[54] A. Deissmann, *Paul,* pp. 117-18; cf. *Religion of Jesus and the Faith of Paul,* trans. W. E. Wilson (London: Hodder & Stoughton, 1923), pp. 195 ff.

[55] B. Sot. 22b.

[56] Lev. R. 34.3: "A man of mercy [*ish ḥesed*] benefits himself (Prov. 11:17) —this refers to Hillel the Elder."

[57] Mish. Aboth 2.9.

[58] Mish. Aboth 2.10b: "Warm thyself before the fire of the Sages, but be heedful of their glowing coals lest thou be burned, for their bite is the bite of a jackal and their sting the sting of a scorpion and their hiss the hiss of a serpent, and all their words are like coals of fire." Mish. Sot. 3.4 speaks in the same breath of "a woman that is a hypocrite and the wounds of the Pharisees."

[59] John 5:42.

for Jesus' death,[60] and yet present cases of Pharisaic sympathy and tolerance.[61] Likewise, Josephus distinguishes between the genuine and the formalistic among the Pharisees.[62]

The distinction in these contrasts often falls between what I shall call an "acting legalism" and a "reacting nomism";[63] i.e., between an ordering of one's life in external and formal arrangement according to the Law in order to gain righteousness and/or appear righteous, and the molding of one's life in all its varying relations according to the Law in response to the love and grace of God. To both classes, the Law was of great importance; but it was important for different reasons.[64] To both "the joy of the commandment" was very real, but it sprang from different sources.

In interpreting the elements of formalistic and inward piety in predestruction Hebraic Judaism as stemming from acting and reacting religious orientations, there is the intriguing temptation to go

[60] The endeavor to disassociate the scribes from the Pharisees and to attribute the opposition to Jesus and the desire for His death only to Sadducean scribes (e.g., J. Bowman, "The Pharisees," *E. Q.*, Vol. XX, No. 1 [Apr., 1948], p. 133) is not convincing. L. Finkelstein's penetrating analysis of Pharisees and Sadducees, "The Pharisees: Their Origin and Their Philosophy," *H. T. R.*, Vol. XXII, No. 3 (July, 1929), pp. 185-261, well substantiates his opinion that "almost all of the scribes were of the Pharisaic persuasion" (p. 215). Cf. also G. F. Moore, *Judaism*, Vol. I, p. 66.

[61] Luke 13:31; Mark 15:43 and par.; John 3:1 ff. and 19:39; Luke 14:1.

[62] Antiq. XIII. 15. 5.

[63] The terms "legalism" and "nomism" are certainly synonymous in their primary and strict meanings; and are often so used interchangeably. Yet there is both a denotation and a connotation, an explication and a secondary meaning, to the terms. The primary meaning of both refers to the control of life in conformity to a rule or standard. But a secondary idea is also associated suggesting only a formal arrangement of the external aspects of life in order to gain righteousness and/or appear righteous. It is therefore necessary to distinguish between the primary and the secondary meaning. And this I shall endeavor to do throughout this work by allowing "nomism" to refer solely to the primary idea and "legalism" to carry the secondary connotation.

[64] Josephus spoke for the whole of the nation in saying: "We think it to be the most necessary business of our whole life to observe the laws that have been given us, and to keep those rules of piety that have been delivered down to us" (Contra Apion, I. 12). But within this unanimity, the concluding words of R. Safra's prayer are significant: "May it be Thy will, O Lord our God, to establish peace . . . among the disciples who occupy themselves with Thy Torah whether for its own sake or for other motives; and may it please Thee that all who do so for other motives may come to study it for its own sake!" (b. Ber. 17a).

further in an effort to pinpoint individuals who portrayed each tendency and to determine the extent of the influence of each element over the Pharisaism of the day. The first line of inquiry can lead nowhere, for, as I have noted above, our human powers of perception and analysis are at best inadequate in this area of motives and attitudes. Even if our sources were voluminous, unimpeachable, and transparent, the best that could be done would be to point out a few individuals who seem beyond doubt to have possessed a reacting faith. Regarding the second investigation, matters are just about as bad. But judging from the legalistic emphasis that followed the repulsion of the Seleucid attempt at Hellenization,[65] it was probably the case that each oppression and disaster from that time through at least the period before A.D. 70 only strengthened the forces of legalism. It was no accident that the Oral Law centered about those elements which had been previously attacked; i.e., sabbath observance and ritual purity.[66] It might be suggested that the distinction between Shammai and Hillel corresponds to these tendencies; and it is true that the one could be said to be "precise" and the other "kindly." Yet both precision and kindness could spring from either motivation. These tendencies cut across all external lines and temperaments. All that can be said with certainty is that there was within predestruction Hebraic Judaism both a formalistic piety and an inward spirituality; an acting legalism and a reacting nomism. It remains to analyze more closely and to portray these tendencies.

THE RELIGION OF A NOMIST

Much that has been written regarding predestruction Pharisaism has portrayed it as basically one in spirituality; i.e., a bleak and striving legalism. And though legalism can have a beneficial effect upon human society,[67] its net result may be so described. But in recogniz-

[65] Cf. Schürer, *Jewish People,* Div. II, Vol. I, pp. 51-56; though of course many Jews insist that such an emphasis began with Ezra (cf. A. Cohen, *Everyman's Talmud* [London: Dent & Sons, 1932], p. xvii).

[66] Cf. C. H. Dodd, *History and the Gospel* (London: Nisbet, 1938), p. 130.

[67] The Jewish insistence is that Christian investigators have closed their eyes to the fact that "the constant reminder of God's presence such as the precepts supply can not fail to have a beneficial influence upon man's morality" (M. Friedländer, *The Jewish Religion* [London: Shapiro, Vallentine, 1922], p. 234).

ing a distinction of motive and emphasis between legalism and nomism, as I have defined the terms, we cannot continue to allow the one characterization to apply to both orientations. It is incumbent upon us to consider the religion and piety of a nomist, allowing the usual characterization to remain valid for that of the legalist.

The analogy of Qumran. Two common misrepresentations of a legal religion such as Judaism are (1) that fidelity to Law is necessarily to be equated with legalism, as I am using the term;[68] and (2) that a religion which stresses fidelity to Law is necessarily egocentric and not theocentric.[69] But both of these accusations are refuted by the analogous evidence to Pharisaism found at Qumran; if not by some of the previously known noncanonical writings and the Talmudic literature itself.

That the Qumran community, an Essene group,[70] was more detailed in its legislation and more rigid in its observance than Pharisaic Judaism is beyond doubt. Josephus long ago informed us of this fact,[71] and now it is evident in their own literature. Yet one of the most striking aspects of the evidence from Qumran is that of the coincidence of nomism and a prophetic spirit. There is a scrupulous concern for ritual purity, but there is no indication of a merely mechanical and external observance. The emphasis is rather upon God's *hesed,* and from this basis spring true righteousness, true motivation, and true strength to be pleasing unto Him in obedience to His commandments.[72] A mere formalistic piety is strongly condemned.[73] Though

[68] E.g., W. H. P. Hatch: "Indeed, fidelity to the divine law was the fundamental principle of Jewish religion, and hence Judaism stands forth as a leading representative of the legalistic type of religion" (*Pauline Idea of Faith,* p. 14).

[69] E.g., Dodd: "A legal religion lays all the emphasis on what a man does, or wills to do. The power of the will, the self-assertive element in us, is brought into the foreground. In direct contrast to this is the religion which says that not what we do, but what God does, is the root of the matter" (*Meaning of Paul,* p. 122).

[70] As Cross rather ironically says: "If the people of the scrolls were not the Essenes, they were a similar sect, living in the same center, in the same era" (*Ancient Library of Qumran,* p. 42).

[71] War II. 8. 9: "They are stricter than any other of the Jews."

[72] 1QH and the closing psalm (columns 10 and 11) of 1QS are especially full of this theme; but traces are also found in other parts of the literature, the most obvious examples being 1QH 10.16, 11.18-19, 1QS 11.2-5, 13b-15, 17.

[73] Cf. 1QS 3.4-12, where the prerequisites to walking blamelessly in the com-

they possessed a great assurance of their own election and were convinced that the true revelation of the meaning of the Law and the Prophets had been given them, the Essenes were also acutely aware of their own sinfulness and possessed a real humility.[74] Theirs was the need to depend upon God alone for righteousness, wisdom, and strength; and theirs was to be that attitude of seeking God "with all their heart and with all their soul."[75] To judge from the merely external criterion of the proportion of legal to prophetic biblical writings found to date at Qumran, the study and reading of the Essenes seems to have been fairly balanced.[76] W. D. Davies has well summed it up in saying: "The community is aware of itself as under 'the Law' and yet as a 'household of the spirit'; it reveals no sense of an essential incompatibility or essential tension between life under 'the Law' and life under 'the Spirit.' "[77]

The significance of this evidence from Qumran for Pharisaism is not so much that here was a nomistic group with the spirit of

---

mandments (10-11), being acceptable before God (11), and becoming accepted by the sect (12), are not "by mere ceremonies of atonement" or washings, sanctifications, or purifications, but rather a spiritual apprehension of God's truth (6-7), the working of God's Holy Spirit (6-7), and an attitude of uprightness, humility, and submission (8). Likewise, 1QS 5.13 insists that ritual washings will not gain one the purity of a holy man, "for men cannot be purified except they repent their evil." The whole attitude of the Essenes toward the polluted sacrifices at Jerusalem and the relation of sacrifice to the spiritual life is further evidence at this point; cf. J. M. Baumgarten, "Sacrifice and Worship Among the Jewish Sectarians of the Dead Sea (Qumran) Scrolls," *H. T. R.*, Vol. XLVI, No. 3 (July, 1953), pp. 141-59, and Cross, *Ancient Library of Qumran*, pp. 74-77.

[74] J. T. Milik says: "They realized . . . man's congenital inability to carry out his part in God's plan of salvation" (*Ten Years of Discovery*, p. 120). Cf. M. Burrows, *Dead Sea Scrolls*, pp. 263-64.

[75] In the opening words of 1QS (1.2), and before the command to obedience, there are the words "to seek God," followed by a lacuna. The command to seek God is undoubtedly taken from II Chron. 15:12 (cf. W. H. Brownlee, "The Dead Sea Manual of Discipline," *B.A.S.O.R.—S.S.*, Nos. 10-12 [New Haven, Conn.: American Schools of Oriental Research, 1951], p. 7, n. 5), where, likewise, a covenant is entered into. Thus the text of the lacuna probably read "to seek God with all their heart and with all their soul."

[76] "The most popular books among the sectarians, to judge from the number of copies preserved in Cave IV, are Deuteronomy, 14 MSS.; Isaiah, 12 MSS.; and Psalms, 10 MSS. There are also eight copies of the Book of the Twelve Prophets. None is complete" (Cross, *Ancient Library of Qumran*, p. 34).

[77] W. D. Davies, "Paul and the Dead Sea Scrolls: Flesh and Spirit," *Scrolls and the N. T.*, ed. Stendahl, pp. 180-81.

prophecy which influenced Pharisaism for the better—though that is not out of the question.[78] But rather:

1. The Qumran literature shows that fidelity to the divine law does not necessarily imply for a Jewish group a legalistic and egocentric piety.

2. The men of Qumran and the men of Pharisaism probably had their roots in a common subsoil, that of the Maccabean Hasidim;[79] and thus the basic elements of the one community would probably be more or less common to the other.

This new evidence from the caves of the "separating" Hasidim necessitates that we revise many previous opinions regarding the spirituality of the nomistic element within the "continuing" Hasidim.

Nomistic Pharisaism. With the somewhat parallel evidence from Qumran, it now seems more probable than ever before that the religion of a nomistic Pharisee was truly spiritual and noble. While he insisted that faith was wholehearted trust in God *and* fidelity to His instruction, his emphasis, as opposed to the legalist, was upon God and trust in Him. He agreed that "God demands obedience," but likewise insisted that such was "only as the proof and expression of something else; the intimate personal attitude of trust and love."[80] Yet he did not forget for a moment that such faith "is of value only in so

[78] The extent of Essene influence in Palestine is very uncertain (cf. A. Dupont-Sommer, *Jewish Sect of Qumran and the Essenes,* pp. 147-48, for the extreme view that they had considerable influence upon contemporary Jewish thought, and T. H. Gaster, *The Scriptures of the Dead Sea Sect* [London: Secker & Warburg, 1957], pp. 44 and 110, n. 25, for an expression of a more moderate opinion). At any rate, Josephus clearly tells us that they were dispersed into every city (War II. 8. 4), and CDC provides for such urban members in 12.19-22 (15.1-3). The fact that there were laws designated for the camps implies that there were Essenes not living in camps; cf. CDC 7.6 (9.1), 12.22 (15.4), 13.20 (16.9), 14.3 (17.1). There is even the intriguing suggestion of Glatzer that there was personal contact between Hillel and the Essenes, a contact established through Hillel's continued friendship with Menahem, who preceded Shammai as a leading Pharisaic teacher but who later separated to become (possibly) the Essene Menahem ("Hillel the Elder in the Light of the Dead Sea Scrolls," *op. cit.,* pp. 242-43).

[79] H. Lietzmann spoke of the Pharisees and the Essenes as two shoots from the same Hasidic root (*The Beginnings of the Christian Church,* trans. B. L. Woolf [London: Nicholson & Watson, 1937], pp. 36-41). Cf. also Milik, *Ten Years of Discovery,* pp. 59, 80-81, 87-90; Cross, *Ancient Library of Qumran,* p. 107, n. 66; Dodd, *History and the Gospel,* pp. 117-18.

[80] W. F. Lofthouse, "The Old Testament and Christianity," *Record and Revelation,* ed. H. W. Robinson, pp. 473-74.

far as it is productive of faithful action."[81] Thus *emunah* was both "trust in" and "fidelity to"; reliance and faithfulness.[82] The emphasis must always be upon the former, though without negating the importance of the latter. In this he was a true child of Old Testament piety. Through his endeavor "to make a hedge about the Torah," to create as it were "applied prophecy" so that a man might be saved from transgression before it was too late,[83] the nomistic spirituality was probably often hidden under a mass of legislation. From our Christian viewpoint, we cannot but disagree with his methods and means. The taut and precise ordinances still first met the eye of the worshiper. But behind the chancel rails glowed the Shekinah. We see it in comparing the legislative writings with the psalms and hymns at Qumran, and there is no reason to doubt a similar phenomenon in Pharisaism.

THE ESSENTIAL TENSION OF JUDAISM

For most Christians who take up the study of predestruction Judaism the general objective is the determination of the differences between the Christian and the Jewish faiths, with particular reference to why Paul left Judaism for Christianity. The question usually revolves around the quest for the unresolved tension in the Jewish religion and the experience of Paul which the Apostle found resolved in his Christian experience; i.e., the search for the inadequacy of the former system which finds satisfaction in Jesus Christ. The Jews, of course, argue that there is no such tension and inadequacy in Judaism. Whatever tension Paul felt in his early religious experience

[81] I. Epstein's words, *Babylonian Talmud* (Soncino), Seder Zere'im I, p. xv.

[82] Cf. 1QHab. 2.4, where the Essene definition of faith is to fear God and do His will, and the adjunct to 1QS (Gaster's "A Formulary of Blessings"), where the definition of a righteous man is one who fears God and does His will. Acceptance in the community meant trust in the mission and message of the teacher and fidelity to his instruction.

[83] Herford is quite correct in emphasizing this motivation for nomistic Pharisaism (*Pharisaism,* pp. 26-27, 64-65; "The Law and Pharisaism," *Judaism and Christianity,* Vol. III, ed. E. I. J. Rosenthal [London: Sheldon Press, 1938], pp. 108-109); though it is not entirely correct for legalistic Pharisaism. Cf. the Letter of Aristeas, 240: "If you know that God put the thoughts in the mind of the lawgivers for the sake of preserving the lives of men you will become a follower of them."

was his alone, and does not reflect upon real Judaism. It was the product of his unorthodox background, his pernicious state of mind, or both. Christians insist that there is a real tension in Judaism; though a major number have implied that the tension exists in the relation between externalism and inward piety, between mere formalism and a prophetic spirit.

It is the thesis of this section of my study that the essential tension of predestruction Hebraic Judaism—especially of the nomistic element—was not primarily that of legalism versus love, or externalism versus inwardness, but fundamentally that of promise and fulfillment. Early Judaism in its principles and noble representatives need not be viewed as entirely legalistic; at least not in the connotative use of that term. I have made a distinction between the words "legalism" and "nomism," and suggest that the latter and not the former best fits a certain element in predestruction Pharisaism. It remains to identify the particular religious orientation of Paul in his Judaistic days, as I shall attempt in the following chapter. Suffice it here to insist that the change which took place in the conversion experience of at least many early Jewish Christians was not necessarily in the abandonment of an acting religion for a reacting faith; not necessarily the change from outward to inward piety and motivation. The primary tension of Judaism, which dominates all Old Testament and Jewish thought, is that of promise and fulfillment. And this was what the earliest Christians found resolved in Christ.

From the "Prayer for the Coming of the Messiah" in the Shemoneh Esreh[84] through the whole body of Talmudic literature,[85] the theme of recalled promise and anticipation is present. The cry "What delays it?" is neither accidental nor incidental in the Talmud.[86] The Targums[87] and noncanonical literature[88] only underline the longing of

[84] Benedictions Nos. 14 and 15.

[85] See *Str.-Bil.,* Vol. I, pp. 6-11, on Matt. 1:1b, "Christus," and Vol. IV, "Exkurs 29," pp. 799-976. Also K. Kohler, "Eschatology," *J. E.,* Vol. V, pp. 209-18; M. Buttenwieser, "Messiah," *J. E.,* Vol. VIII, pp. 510-11; J. Klausner, *Messianic Idea in Israel,* p. 396.

[86] See *Str.-Bil.,* Vol. II, p. 589 on Acts 1:7.

[87] See S. Mowinckel, *He That Cometh,* pp. 282-84, which section begins: "In particular, the Targums provide evidence of the important place given to the Messianic idea in leading religious circles," and then goes on to cite many references.

[88] See Buttenweiser, "Messiah," *op. cit.,* p. 508, for extensive citation.

Judaism. And the Qumran community lived solely for the Messianic consummation.[89] Here was the real tension of predestruction Hebraic Judaism.

W. F. Lofthouse has well characterized nomistic Judaism as well as the religion of Israel in saying: "The religion of every part of the Old Testament is the religion of promise. . . . When the Hebrew . . . looks within his own heart he knows the blessedness of trust in Jahweh; but fightings are without as fears are within; it is when he awakes that he will be satisfied."[90] Paul had awakened to life in Chirst Jesus.

[89] K. Stendahl says quite simply: "The sect is an anticipation" ("Introduction and Perspective," *Scrolls and the N. T.*, ed. Stendahl, p. 10).
[90] Lofthouse, "O. T. and Christianity," *op. cit.*, p. 460.

IV

Saul and the Law

THE SPIRITUALITY OF Paul's preconversion religious experience must be considered in light of the opposing orientations of "legalism" and "nomism" within Hebraic Pharisaism. It can only be determined, however, by reference to the reminiscences in his writings of life in Judaism. Admittedly the endeavor to understand Paul's Judaistic theology and attitude toward the Law is fraught with difficulties and uncertainties. But it is not at all lost labor.[1] The greatest difficulty in the investigation is that the view in retrospect always is based upon the criteria of the present; i.e., the Apostle's reminiscences are colored by his Christian perspective. And this means, in Paul's case, that his Christian convictions can hardly be expected to heighten his appreciation of the former life. If anything, they would lessen it. But keeping this factor in mind, the implications of his references to a former day may lead to valid information. While they may never produce decisive answers, they can point the way toward an understanding of Paul's relation to and attitude toward the Law in his Judaistic days—an understanding of "Saul and the Law."

THE TESTIMONY OF ROMANS 7

From earliest times, debate regarding the nature of Paul's religious experience in Judaism has centered in Romans 7:7-25. Origen and most of the Greek Fathers viewed this passage as a reminiscence of life under the Law, and they have been followed by such scholars

[1] As P. Wernle insisted, arguing that "we are completely ignorant" regarding Paul's Judaistic thought (*The Beginnings of Christianity,* trans. G. A. Bienemann [London: Williams & Norgate, 1903], Vol. I, p. 225).

as John Wesley, A. Deissmann, H. St. John Thackeray, A. S. Peake, J. S. Stewart, and C. H. Dodd. In opposition, Augustine and the Latin Fathers interpreted the passage as reflecting the writer's postconversion experience, which finds analogy in the inner conflicts of every true Christian. And agreement with this latter position has been voiced by Martin Luther, John Calvin, Calvinistic theology, and lately by Anders Nygren.[2] A third type of interpretation has arisen in denial of the biographical implications of both the pre- and the postconversion views. Such men as H. Lietzmann, H. Windisch, W. G. Kümmel, G. Bornkamm, M. Dibelius, and C. L. Mitton are representative figures. Most of those who oppose the biographical interpretation view the passage as depicting mankind in the general sense. Some insist that it is mankind in general because it is mankind in Adam; while the Barthians prefer to speak of mankind in its nonhistorical and primal existent present.

The issue concerns the subject and the temporal reference of the early section of the chapter, Romans 7:7-13. Verses 14 to 25 are important for the Pauline teaching and must be considered later; we need not be detained now in their interpretation. The question here is: does Romans 7:7-13 portray a preconversion experience of the Apostle Paul?

The subject of Romans 7:7-13. The question regarding the subject in this passage has traditionally appeared to be the more easily answered of the problems involved. The *prima facie* evidence of the constant repetition of *egō,* and the analogy of experience as revealed in both biography and the soul of the interpreter, have led most commentators to view the subject as quite obviously Paul himself.

But there is evidence that Judaism did not always use the first person singular in a strictly biographical fashion. Kümmel cites three Talmudic passages where "I" is used as a stylistic form, a *Stilform*:[3] Mish. Ber. 1.3, where R. Tarphon relates his dangerous experience of reciting the Shema lying down in the presence of robbers; Mish. Aboth 6.9, where R. Jose b. Kisma describes an encounter with a Gentile while out walking; and b. Ber. 3a, where R. Jose recounts a

[2] For the positions of the Fathers, the Reformers, and German scholarship to 1929, see W. G. Kümmel, *Römer 7 und die Bekehrung des Paulus* (Leipzig: Hinrichs, 1929), pp. 74-109.

[3] *Ibid.,* pp. 128-32.

conversation with an appearance of Elijah. These passages present general teaching in the form of the first person, and are not meant to be taken autobiographically. Yet their value as illustrating a gnomic and general Pauline usage of "I" in Romans 7 is lessened by two factors: (1) their confessedly late date, all being from the third generation Tannaitic dating approximately A.D. 120-140; and (2) their imaginative and conjured character. A more significant example of the *Stilform* use is Philo's change from the first person plural to the first person singular in De Somn. i. 177. The context concerns the relationship of mind and body; and in that short section, without the general nature of the thought changing, the first person singular in the dative (locative) and the accusative is used.

New evidence has come from Qumran on this question. And it is here that we have the most significant outside aid to the understanding of Romans 7. In columns 10 and 11 of lQS there is a recitation of the eternal possessions and privileges of those whom God has chosen. In the midst of this description of the gifts of salvation—knowledge, righteousness, strength, and glory—there is the sudden cry: "But I belong to wicked humanity and to the assembly of perverse flesh. My iniquities, my transgression, my sin (together with the perversities of my heart) belong to the assembly of worms and of things that move in darkness."[4] In the dualism of Qumran, such a passage might easily be attributed to those who are of wickedness and darkness. And Gaster's caption to columns 10 and 11, "The Hymn of the Initiants," might lead one to believe that these are the words of the initiant *before* his admittance into "the elect of God." But the context of the passage and the frequent cases of similar utterance in the hymns and psalms of the community[5] demand that we view these words as the expression of the believer fully conscious of his election by God and his acceptance in the community. The significance of this passage for Romans 7 is well summarized by Kuhn:

> We have in this text the same "I" as in Rom. 7; it is the same "I" not only in regard to style, but especially in regard to theological connotations: "I" is here, just as in Rom. 7, not meant individually or biographically; it is

[4] 1QS 11.9-10a, trans. W. H. Brownlee, "The Dead Sea Manual of Discipline," *B.A.S.O.R.—S.S.*, Nos. 10-12, 1951.
[5] Eg., 1QH 1.21-23, 3.24-36.

gnomic, descriptive of human existence. The "I" in this Qumran passage, as in Rom. 7, signifies the existence of mankind, which is flesh.[6]

But we need not resort entirely to outside analogous writings. Despite the assertions of the opposite and the volume of passages where Paul's reference is clearly to himself,[7] within the Pauline letters there are instances where the Apostle's use of the first person singular is clearly gnomic and general.[8] Romans 3:7 is an example: "But if the truth of God through my lie (*en tō emō pseusmati*) abounded to his glory, why am I also still (*ti eti kagō*) judged as a sinner?" In context, Paul definitely renounces this as his teaching, much less his personal practice; though, of course, the abounding grace of God amidst human deceit is the experience of all who know God—Paul included. I Corinthians 13:1-3 may also be cited. The inadequacy of all without love, as portrayed in these verses, is meant neither as a strictly personal experience nor as a strictly personal realization. It is gnomic, aphoristic, meant to be taken as a general truth; though certainly Paul would insist that the general truth has been experienced and realized in his own life. True, his awareness of this general truth came through personal experience and personal realization. But his experience and realization are but aspects of the general situation. And it is of this general truth and situation, and not of a strictly biographical circumstance or situation, that he speaks. So also the rhetorical question of I Corinthians 6:15, "Shall I make (*poiēsō*) the members of Christ the members of a harlot," with its emphatic negative *mē genoito,* is to be taken as a general maxim couched in

[6] K. G. Kuhn, "New Light on Temptation, Sin, and Flesh in the New Testament," *Scrolls and the N. T.,* ed. K. Stendahl, p. 102.

[7] C. H. Dodd has said: "It will in fact be found on examination that Paul rarely, if ever, says 'I' unless he is really speaking of himself personally, even if he means to generalize from the particular instance. Certainly, when he is describing religious experience, his 'I' passages bear the unmistakeable note of autobiography" (*Romans,* M.N.T.C., p. 107). Such an insistence is based only upon those passages where the pronoun itself is used, excluding instances where the person is designated in the verb. But it is doubtful whether such an assertion can be upheld even then. In the examples I cite in this section, Mish. Ber. 1.3, Mish. Aboth 6.9, 1QS 11.9-10a, Rom. 3:7, and Gal. 2:18-21 use the pronoun in the nominative; I Cor. 13:1-3 and I Cor. 14:14-15 use it as a possessive genitive; De Somn. i.177 and Rom. 3:7 use it in the dative; and De Somn. i. 177 has it also in the accusative.

[8] Cf. Kümmel, *Römer 7 und die Bekehrung des Paulus,* pp. 121-23.

the dramatic first person singular. Probably I Corinthians 14:11, 14, and 15, and possibly Galatians 2:18-21, are similar cases. The indefinite "one" (*tis*) could as easily have been used in all these cases; though with considerable loss to the power and graphic character of the passage.

With the analogies from Qumran and these examples of Pauline usage, there is the increased possibility that the "I" of Romans 7 is used in a gnomic and general sense. Whether this possibility is an actuality, or at least a probability, depends upon the further question of the temporal reference in the passage.

The temporal reference of Romans. 7:7-13.—To some, the fact of Paul's reference to the Tenth Commandment is evidence not only that he is speaking biographically but also that he is referring to his adolescent life, when sexual passions began to assert themselves. And so it is argued that it was in this area and at this time that "the shoe pinched for Paul."[9] But this is not a necessary inference from the Apostle's reference. That one is "never safe from the snares of specially sexual temptation" is a theme of many rabbis;[10] and preaching on this most inward prohibition, "thou shalt not covet" as the essence of the negative commands of the Decalogue, is not uncommon to either the ancient or the modern preacher.[11] The temporal reference must be determined on other grounds than Paul's reference to *ouk epithumēseis,* for that term "includes every kind of illicit desire."[12]

The vital issues and expressions relating to the temporal reference of Roman 7:7-13 are in verses 9 to 11. We cannot go further until we understand Paul's meaning in the phrases "I was alive" (*egō ezōn*), "formerly without law" (*chōris nomou pote*), "the commandment" (*hē entolē*), and "I died" (*egō apethanon*); and his allusion in the use of "it deceived me" (*exēpatēsen me*). These expressions

[9] Dodd, *Romans,* p. 110.

[10] Cf. C. G. Montefiore and H. Loewe *Rabbinic Anthology,* p. xxxv.

[11] E.g., IV Macc. 2:1 ff. and M. Luther, "A Treatise on Christian Liberty," *Works of Martin Luther,* Vol. II trans. W. A. Lambert (Philadelphia: Holman, 1916), p. 317. In speaking of the Commandments as teaching "a man to know himself, that through them he may recognize his inability to do good and may despair of his powers," Luther says: "For example: 'Thou shalt not covet' is a command which convicts us all of being sinners, . . . And as we fare with this one command, so we fare with all."

[12] W. Sanday and A. C. Headlam, *Romans,* I.C.C., p. 179 on Rom. 7:7.

have been variously approached from the viewpoint of Greek philosophy, modern psychology,[13] and Talmudic age requirements.[14] Thus, Paul's use of "I was alive" is considered "a vivid figurative expression, not of course with the full richness of meaning which he sometimes gives to it."[15] The former time of being "without law," and of "not knowing" as in verse 7, is referred to his days of childhood innocence—that *Unschuldsparadise seiner Kindheit*. The "commandment" is that portion of the Torah, a negative precept, which first arrested his freedom and brought him to consciousness of sin. His use of "I died" is again figurative for the awful consciousness of guilt which he felt as a result of the work of the Law in bringing home to him the consciousness of sin. The passage is therefore an autobiographical portion of religion under the Law.[16]

Nevertheless, there are weighty considerations against such an interpretation. Paul's use of "life" and "death," while not designating physical life and death, certainly cannot easily be weakened to mean only untroubled childhood and a consciousness of guilt. His usual exalted use of "life" and ominous reference to "death" must cause at least some hesitation in assigning such mild definitions to these terms in Romans 7 as the biographical interpretation necessitates. It is also very difficult to speak of a Jewish childhood as being lived apart from the demands of the Law. Indeed, Philo spoke of a child's first seven years as being without the conceptions of good or evil, and he could, as did Aristotle, divide man's life into four periods.[17] But his interest as this point was epistemology, not ethical theology; and his *tabula rasa* theory has nothing to do with the rabbinic doctrine of the two *yetzers* in man. His debt is clearly to Grecian thought, and

[13] Cf. Dodd, *Romans,* pp. 105-11, for a skilled blending of philosophy and psychology.

[14] E.g., A. Deissmann, *Paul,* pp. 92-93, and *Religion of Jesus and the Faith of Paul,* pp. 231-32; W. D. Davies, *Paul and Rabbinic Judaism,* pp. 25-26.

[15] Sanday and Headlam, *Romans,* p. 180 on Rom. 7:9.

[16] Cf. C. H. Dodd, *Mind of Paul: A Psychological Approach,* pp. 10-13; *Romans,* pp. 105-11; A. S. Peake, *The Quintessence of Paulinism* (Manchester: John Rylands Library, 1918), pp. 16-17; Sanday and Headlam, *Romans,* pp. 179-89; W. L. Knox, *St. Paul,* p. 28; *St. Paul and the Church of the Gentiles,* p. 98; *St. Paul and the Church of Jerusalem,* pp. 108-10, n. 9. Also Davies, *Paul and Rabbinic Judaism,* pp. 25-26, and F. V. Filson, *St. Paul's Conception of Recompense,* p. 8, to name only a few of the many English-speaking scholars and thus more fully round out Kümmel's listing at this point.

[17] Quis Rer. Div. Heres 293-99.

such a philosophically orientated fourfold division in man seems to have made no impression on Palestinian Pharisaism. It is true that at thirteen the Hebrew boy became a *bar mizvah*, a son of the Commandments, and as such was obligated to their performance. Yet many of the same Talmudic passages that recount the age for the *bar mizvah* also insist that at five years the boy is ready for the study of the Scriptures, and at ten for the Mishnah.[18] He is not without instruction in his early years, and it seems hard to imagine the disjunction of instruction and obedience at any stage in Jewish society.[19] Such a proposed separation between knowing the Law and doing the Law on the part of the Jewish boy has indeed appeared incongruous to many interpreters.[20]

In view of the difficulties of the usual biographical presentation, it is not presumptuous to suggest a different approach. The need is for an exegesis which does not necessitate either (1) toning down expressions and terms to make the presentation coherent, or (2) a primary dependence upon Greek philosophy, Christian biography, and/or modern psychology. Such an all-purpose remedy seems too much to hope for. Yet there is such a solution and basis of interpretation, and this is found in the strictly Hebrew concepts of "identification" and "corporate community." While such concepts have long been recognized, they have not received their due recognition for the passage at hand.

Using this approach, Romans 7:7-13 presents a personal identification with the Genesis account of the Fall. Significant is the parallel of terminology between Romans 7 and Genesis 3 in the LXX:

Genesis 3:13. The serpent deceived me (*ho ophis ēpatēsen me*).

[18] E.g., Mish. Aboth 5.21.

[19] In like manner b. Kid. 40b speaks of the Torah as given to Israel at Sinai, "whereas liability to 'hallah' came into force forty years later, when they entered Palestine" (I. Epstein, footnote 9 to b. Kiddushin 40b). Yet it is contrary to the records to insist that no obedience was demanded until full liability was reached.

[20] So much so to H. Lietzmann that he translated Rom. 7:9 as "Ich aber war lebendig einst, als kein Gesetz da war," instead of the usual "ohne Gesetz" (*Römerbrief*, H. N. T. [Tübingen: Mohr, 1906], p. 35). Cf Kümmel's excellent treatment of "without law" in *Römer 7 und die Bekehrung des Paulus*, pp. 89-94. Wm. Manson has said: "But was there ever an actual time when Paul lived *chōris nomou*?" ("Notes on the Argument of Romans," *New Testament Essays*, ed. A. J. B. Higgins [Manchester: Manchester University Press, 1959], p. 161).

Romans 7:11. Sin . . . deceived me (*hē hamartia . . . exēpatēsen me.*)

And this parallel use of (*ex*)*apataō* is not accidental, for Paul uses the same term in connection with the Fall in II Corinthians 11:3 and I Timothy 2:14. Whereas in Genesis it is the serpent as the instrument of sin which deceived through the appeal to the flesh, in Romans it is sin which deceives, using the flesh as its seat of operations and the Law as an instrument. The expressions vary slightly, but the thought is basically the same. Here, then, is the first half of that contrast between Adam and Christ portrayed in Romans 5:12-21. Romans 7, with 8, carries on the contrast between man's condition in Adam and his state in Christ.[21] Here, in the cry "Sin deceived me," we have the Adam of Romans 5 finding his voice.[22] But it is not just Adam. By the concept of identification and the realization of corporate community, it is humanity in Adam—and thus true of Paul as well. The Apostle is not allegorizing;[23] he is identifying. For him the experience of Adam was an historical reality. And since he is identified with Adam, even though as a Christian also identified with Christ, the history of Adam is his irrevocable history. When Adam lived, I lived; when Adam coveted, I coveted; when Adam was deceived, I was deceived; when Adam died, I died. As Wm. Manson

[21] Note also the continuance of this contrast in Phil. 2:6-11, where "the noteworthy expression, 'did not snatch at equality with God,' contains a reminiscence of the First Adam, who, in disobedience to the Almighty, yielded to the temptation to 'be as God' (Gen. iii.5)" (H. A. A. Kennedy, *Theology of the Epistles,* p. 159).

[22] G. Bornkamm: "In dem *egō* von Röm. 7.7 ff. bekommt Adam von Röm. 5.12 ff. seinen Mund" (*Das Ende des Gesetzes* [München: Kaiser, 1952], p. 59).

[23] Dodd has argued that we must not assume that Paul considered the Fall as a literal event. "The subtler minds of his age (like Philo of Alexandria, and the Egyptian Greek who wrote the Hermetic tract Poimandres) treated it as a symbolic allegory, and Paul's too was a subtle mind" (*Romans,* p. 80; cf. pp. 105-106). But while it is true that Paul's emphasis is not upon origins but upon the grace of God, this is not, as Dodd has conjectured, because he viewed origins and the historicity of the Genesis account as unimportant. Rather, as A. Marmorstein has pointed out in regard to Rom. 5:12-21, "Paulus folgte hier einem Prinzip, welches sehr häufig in der altpalästinensischen Haggada angewandt worden ist" ("Paulus und die Rabbinen," *Z. N. W.,* Vol. XXX, Heft 3/4 (1931), p. 271). That principle is regarding the interpreter's primary interest: "Es ist bei der Gabe der Gnade nicht so wie beim Fall" (*ibid.,* p. 277). See also *Str.-Bil.,* Vol. II, p. 230. There is no evidence that a Palestinian Pharisee would so allegorize the Genesis account of the Fall. Dodd has been led astray by Philo.

has said: ". . . here the Apostle is not speaking historically of himself, but theologically. He is seeing all human life, his own included, against the background of Gen. 3."[24]

Such an interpretation of Romans 7:7-13 has several factors in its favor: (1) the past tenses of the verbs in the passage continue to be meaningful; (2) the full force of the expressions "I was alive," "formerly without law," and "I died" is retained; (3) the connection of thought between Romans 5:12-21 and Romans 7-8 is maintained; (4) the parallel usage of *(ex)apataō* in Genesis 3:13 and Romans 7:11 is given its proper significance; and (5) the gnomic import of the passage is not relegated to the secondary sense of application.

The major objection to this "identification-gnomic" interpretation is that it causes "the commandment" of Romans 7:8-13 to refer to a pre-Mosaic law, while "the law" refers elsewhere in the chapter to the Mosaic Law. To designate "the commandment" as that of Genesis 2:16-17 and "the law" as the Mosaic Law breaks the connection between the two and leaves the passage jumbled. But to identify both with the Mosaic Law, as is common to the usual biographical view, is also difficut. For the position argued here it presents an anachronism, which could possibly be excused in the rush of the passage's fervent expression but is nonetheless a problem. For the biographical interpretation it involves the mitigating of some pregnant Pauline expressions. There is, however, the real possibility that Paul is here thinking of "the law," in accordance with at least some rabbinic thought, as that body of instruction (Torah) which was given to man from the first and which was later reiterated, amplified, and clarified through Moses.[25] Not that he felt the Law to be eternal, but that in its basic standards and directions it had existed from the beginning of human history; i.e., the instruction of God which was given when

[24] Manson, "Notes on the Argument of Romans," *op. cit.*, p. 161.

[25] See G. F. Moore, *Judaism,* Vol. I, pp. 262-77, regarding the Jewish doctrine of pre-Mosaic Torah. What is pertinent here is the fact that "the Jews could no more conceive a world in the past without a revelation of God's will for man's life than in the present or the future. Accordingly they believed that certain laws for all mankind were given to Adam" (*ibid.*, p. 274). Since religion was viewed as in no way an afterthought of God, it was impossible to conceive of man at any time without the instruction of God. This basic outlook served as the foundation for the later Talmudic doctrine of the pre-existence and eternality of both the written and the oral Law.

man first had need of such instruction.[26] His reference to it must of necessity be in terms of what he knew, i.e., the glorious revelation through Moses. But his thought could still be that God's Torah in a pre-Mosaic prototype was from the beginning; a prototype of basic instruction minus the particular national and ceremonial features. In fact, is this not what he implies in Romans 5:13-14a? Here he says that sin is not counted—i.e., actions, thoughts, etc., are not reckoned sinful—in the absence of law, and yet insists that the judgment of sin came upon all men even from the beginning: "death reigned from Adam to Moses." To a Jewish monotheist of the first century who viewed history as the activity of God, no time could be without the instruction of God.[27]

The other objections to this interpretation are relatively minor. That (1) the name of Adam is not mentioned, or (2) the passage represents man as in a world in which sin has already found entrance, are not arguments necessarily disastrous for a Pauline reference to the Genesis account. The story of the Fall is so prominent in Jewish literature that the recital of its characters is not absolutely necessary in every reference to it. Such an omission would most likely occur when writing to a church with a sizable Jewish contingent and/or in impassioned address—both of which are highly probable here. Nor can the presence of sin already in the world be a major objection, for the Genesis account itself assumes the presence of dormant evil even before the command of Genesis 2:17. The Devil was not invented to test the commandment, but the commandment was given in the presence of lurking evil. The very presence of law presupposes lawlessness and the possibility of sin.

We many conclude, therefore, that Romans 7:7-13 is neither

[26] Gal. 3:17 does not oppose this. There need be no conflict in accepting the basic standards and directions of God as given at the beginning of human history and the amplifications of that law, with its particular national and ceremonial stress, given through Moses. R. Jose accepted the eternality of the Torah while still dating it at the time of Moses (b. Kid. 40b).

[27] R. Bultmann insists that "verse 13 is completely unintelligible: 'sin indeed was in the world before the law was given, but sin is not counted where there is no law.' What sort of sin was it if it did not originate as contradiction of the Law? And how can it have brought death after it if it was not 'counted'? These questions cannot be answered" (*Theology of the N. T.*, Vol. I, p. 252). But the difficulty of both Rom. 5:13-14a and 7:7-13 is cleared up if we interpret Paul as viewing the history of man as at no time without the law of God.

strictly autobiographical nor strictly gnomic. The temporal reference of the passage is neither to Paul's youth, nor to be taken in the non-specific sense of humanity in general. It is not just Paul, nor is it just humanity. Both these positions have hold of aspects of the truth, yet both fall short in representing Paul's meaning. It is both Paul and humanity, but only as and because it is humanity in Adam.[28]

The significance of Romans 7 for Paul's background. I shall leave the development of verses 14 to 25 to the following chapter in this study. Yet it is necessary to say here that I do not believe any of Romans 7 to be strictly biographical. In 7:7-13 Paul is identifying himself and humanity with Adam; 7:14-25 is his realization of that relationship in his experience. In harmony with his presentation of human estrangement from God as resulting from both the Fall[29] and human perversity,[30] man's inability to serve God stems from the interrelated facts that "I am in Adam" and "Adam is in me." The reference is not to a specific pre- or postconversion instance of failure, but an abiding realization of the futility of human effort in itself. It is a general realization, but one that takes specific form in the life of even the most earnest and pious—the great human cry of especially the earnest and pious. It is the realization that "I of myself," the *autos egō* of Romans 7:25b, am unable truly to serve God.

Without doubt Romans 7 is a Christian utterance. But it need not be viewed as an exclusively Christian conviction. Many pre-Christian passages view man's predicament as resulting from both the Fall and personal wickedness.[31] The Talmud speaks of a man's will desiring to do God's will, but "the yeast in the dough" (i.e., the evil impulse) preventing him from performing that which he desires.[32] Qumran parallels Romans 7 and 8 in piety, though not in theology.

[28] Cf. Lietzmann: "Ich" is "die Menschheit in Adam, *pote* ist die Zeit der paradisischen Unschuld und die *entolē eis zōēn* ist Gen. 2.16-17" (*Römerbrief*, p. 35 on Rom. 7:9 ff.).

[29] Rom. 5:12-21.

[30] Rom. 1:18—3:23.

[31] Cf. Marmorstein, "Paulus und die Rabbinen," *op. cit.*, pp. 278-85, where many Talmudic passages and implications regarding original sin and the continued sinfulness of man are brought together and shown to be the basis of Paul's teaching. Christianity's emphasis on the Fall probably did lead to "a tendency to minimise it in rabbinical Judaism" (W. L. Knox, *St. Paul and the Church of the Gentiles*, pp. 94-95). Yet both factors are still present in the Talmud. Cf. IV Ezra 7.118, Wisdom 2.23, and II Baruch 54.15, 19.

[32] B. Ber. 17a, attributed to R. Alexandri. Cf. IV Ezra 7.72.

The contrast at the end of column 4 in 1QH is of that awful condition "when I called to mind all my guilty deeds and the perfidy of my sires" and the blessed realization "when I remembered the strength of Thy hand and Thy multitudinous mercies."

Romans 7 was written by the Christian Apostle. Except for the Christological emphasis of verse 25, it could also have been composed by a Jewish reacting nomist. It was Paul's Christian conviction. To an extent, it could also have been his realization in Judaism.[33] But there is no evidence that it is a personal reflection of a life of legalism.

BLAMELESS ACCORDING TO THE LAW

Also of significance here are the biographical statements of Galatians 1:14, Philippians 3:4-6, Acts 22:3, and Acts 26:5, in which Paul's religious life in Judaism is described as having been "blameless" (*amemptos*) and "strict" (*akribeia, akribēs*). In the psychological schools of Pauline interpretation, these claims are taken to indicate a realization on the part of the Apostle of his previous legalistic pride.[34] And some further assert that "his constant emphasis in the earlier letters that he had no boast save in Christ indicates that this sort of pride was for him a realized danger."[35]

Yet being "strict" and "blameless according to the righteousness in the law" need not imply legalism in the sense in which I have defined that term. We now know of a nomistic, even antilegalistic, piety which existed amidst the strictness of Qumran. And the Dead Sea Scrolls often speak expressly of being "blameless" or "free from fault" in the keeping of the commandments of the Lord,[36] yet without that blamelessness being viewed as a legalism or mere externalism.[37] For the men of Qumran it was only through a spiritual apprehension of God's truth, the working of His Holy Spirit, and an attitude of uprightness, humility, and submission that one could acceptably keep God's commandments and thus be accounted before Him as blameless.[38]

[33] See *infra.*, chap. V, esp. pp. 114-16.
[34] E.g., Filson, *St. Paul's Conception of Recompense,* p. 12.
[35] A. D. Nock, *St. Paul,* p. 29.
[36] E.g., 1QS 1.9, 3.9-10; CDC 2.15 f., 3.2.
[37] 1QS 3.4-6, 5.13.
[38] 1QS 3.6-12.

Paul's designation of his religion as strict and of his life as blameless, therefore, need carry no legalistic implications. Abraham, his favorite example of a man of faith, was commanded to be "blameless";[39] and the Apostle interpreted his blamelessness as resulting from a faith which engendered obedience. Likewise, Paul exhorted his Christian converts to be blameless (*amemptoi*),[40] prayed that God would establish their hearts unblamable (*amemptous*) in holiness,[41] and spoke of his own conduct towards them as being blameless (*amemptōs*).[42] To interpret his Judaistic experience as legalistic because he spoke of it as being blameless is to attribute the same to his Christian life and preaching, and for the same reason. Indeed, his life was strict within Judaism. But this might have resulted from a nomistic faith as well as a legalism.

KICKING AGAINST THE GOADS

The phrase which most naturally suggests mental and spiritual struggle of the type indicated by the psychological interpreters of Paul's preconversion experience is that of Acts 26:14: "It is hard for you to kick against the goads" (*sklēron soi pros kentra laktizein*). By most it is taken to refer to his inner spiritual warfare in having to repress "all humaner tendencies in the interests of his legal absolutism,"[43] his "sheer revulsion from his task" of persecuting,[44] and his perplexity regarding Christianity[45] Some view it as expressive of his early dissatisfaction within a basically satisfying Judaism;[46] others assign it only to his qualms in persecuting.[47] A recent entry into the field of suggestions is Johannes Munck's view of this as the natural

[39] Gen. 17:1.
[40] Phil. 2:15.
[41] I Thess. 3:13.
[42] I Thess. 2:10.
[43] C. H. Dodd, *The Mind of Paul: Change and Development* (Manchester: John Rylands Library, 1934), p. 36.
[44] Dodd, *Mind of Paul: A Psychological Approach*, pp. 12-13.
[45] E.g., J. S. Stewart, *Man in Christ*, pp. 119-22; W. L. Knox, *St. Paul*, pp. 36-37.
[46] E.g., C. G. Montefiore, *Judaism and St. Paul*, pp. 117-18; J. Parkes, *Judaism and Christianity* (London: Gallancy, 1948), p. 75.
[47] A. Lukyn Williams, *Talmudic Judaism and Christianity*, p. 61.

Jewish revulsion to the inevitable Gentile mission.[48] Our problem thus centers in the question of how much this phrase implies a spiritual struggle in Paul's earlier experience.

It is well-known that "to kick against the goads" was common in the Greek world as a circumlocution for opposition to deity.[49] Euripides' *pros kentra laktizoimi*[50] and Aeschylus' *pros kentra kōlon ekteneis*[51] are the chief examples of the phrase as being synonymous with "set against God." In Euripides' use, it was a conscious opposition to Dionysus' son in refusing to recognize his divinity. In Aeschylus, Prometheus consciously opposed the unjust Zeus, believing that he must do that which was required even though it meant the displeasure of the tyrannical god and would thus result in his own discomfort. In both cases, the opposition was determined and the ones in opposition had no qualms or misgivings regarding their actions. In the one case, it was a conscious opposition to false claims of deity; in the other, to an unjust deity. But in all likelihood the precise context of the Greek usage is irrelevant. It was probably known by Paul as no more than a catch phrase, a *Sprichwort*, a saying.

Assuming the Apostle to have been correctly quoted,[52] it is of importance in the understanding of the expression to notice: (1) where it was used, and (2) how it was used. It is significant that it is only employed in the conversation with Agrippa in Acts 26. The general account of Paul's Conversion in Acts 9 and the defense before the Jewish crowd in Acts 22 are devoid of the phrase.[53] Since Paul spoke Greek to Hellenists and Aramaic to Palestinian Jews,[54] it seems probable that his words to Agrippa were in Greek. Undoubtedly Agrippa had some knowledge of Aramaic, but his native tongue

[48] J. Munck, *Paulus und die Heilsgeschichte* (Copenhagen: Munksgaard, 1954), pp. 15 ff.

[49] Cf. Kümmel, *Römer 7 und die Bekehrung des Paulus,* pp. 155-57, and Munck, *Paulus und die Heilsgeschichte,* pp. 10-14.

[50] Euripides, Bacchanals, lines 794-95.

[51] Aeschylus, Prometheus, lines 324-25.

[52] If we assume otherwise, the expression is no longer a problem in the understanding of Paul.

[53] Though it appears also in Acts 9 in the eighth-century E and some lesser texts.

[54] Cf. Acts 21:37 ff., where the tribune is addressed in Greek and the native crowd in Aramaic.

was Greek. It need not be assumed that the expression had become common in Palestine or translated into Aramaic, as Munck has theorized.[55] Seldom are such idioms meaningful in another language. The Apostle certainly had time and opportunity to pick it up outside of Palestine, either in his boyhood or in his travels. It is also significant that the phrase is used in the context of an evangelistic sermon. The speech in Acts 26 is not strictly a defense, for Paul's destination had been already determined.[56] It seems, therefore, that he considered Agrippa's desire to hear his message to stem from more than a judiciary interest, and that he accepted this occasion as an opportunity for judicious proselytizing. With the hope of Agrippa's conversion, the sermon crescendoes to the pitch of fervent expectancy. It is in this context that the expression in question must be considered.

In view of the above, it is not unreasonable to picture Paul as here giving a slight twist and extension to the narration of his conversion experience for the purpose of evangelization. Not that he is prevaricating for God's glory. He has earlier renounced this as a proper methodolgy.[57] But he is making explicit to Agrippa what was implicit in the words "Saul, Saul, why are you persecuting me?" And he is doing it judiciously by a phrase he knows Agrippa will understand and appreciate. Lest he be misunderstood to have been opposing—and now proclaiming—only a Galilean prophet, he points out what would be obvious to any Jew: that a correction by a voice from heaven meant opposition to God Himself. This may have been Paul's usual technique before other Gentile audiences. At least it seems to be the import of his usage before a reasonably well-informed Roman official, after extensive travels in the Greek world.

One may therefore conclude that the expression "It is hard for you to kick against the goads," when viewed as containing a Greek idiom and in the context of Acts 26, does not in itself carry the implication of either a conscious or an unconscious internal spiritual conflict. It was indeed "hard" for him to persecute, especially so if he were a sensitive nomistic Pharisee. But there is no necessary indication in the phrase "to kick against the goads" that he had the slightest

[55] Munck, *Paulus und die Heilsgeschichte,* p. 11. The use of a Greek idiom in a passage designated as being "in the Hebrew language" is not contradictory when viewed in the light of the explanation here given.

[56] Cf. Acts 25:12, 26:32.

[57] Rom. 3:7-8.

consciousness of being in opposition to the will of God. When approached from the perspective of the *Sitz im Leben*, the inclusion of this phrase in the Acts 26 account and its exclusion in Acts 9 and 22 are perfectly understandable. In the situation of Acts 22, and probably Acts 9 as well, the implication of the words in the vision would be quickly grasped. But in that of Acts 26 there was need for the implication to be drawn out. Paul is no pedantic literalist. Words are tools to convey meaning, not just gems to be treasured. His task is to transmit and interpret the revelation he has received, in both its explicit form and its implications. Thus he makes explicit to Agrippa what was implicit to him in the Aramaic words: "Saul, Saul, why are you persecuting me?" And he does this through a Greek idiom.

ZEALOUSLY PERSECUTING

Zeal as such cannot be restricted to either a nomistic or a legalistic piety. But the association of zeal with persecution, as in all the chief biographical passages,[58] has seemed conclusive to many that a preconversion legalism and dissatisfaction is being portrayed. C. H. Dodd is most expressive at this point:

> Now when a severe conflict exists within the self, one way of relief is to externalize the conflict by identifying that which one detests in oneself with some other person or body of persons. . . . Now Paul found relief in persecuting the Nazarenes. In doing so, he was gratifying his desire to excell in the service of the Law. . . . We may be sure that the principal reason why he could embrace this grim task was that here were enemies of the Law whom he could smite as he was failing to smite the enemies of the Law in his own breast. . . . The repressed passions of his nature found a consecrated outlet here: the "threatenings and slaughter" which he breathed out promised to cleanse his bosom of much perilous stuff.[59]

Dodd goes on to point out that in the Psalms of the canonical Psalter and the noncanonical Solomon we find a similar attitude of both loving God's law and hating them that hate Him, and he implies that in these passages there is a similar psychological unrest and dissatisfaction.

Is it not, however, just as possible to explain Paul's early reactions

[58] Acts 22:3-4, 26:4-12; Gal. 1:13-14; Phil. 3:6.
[59] Dodd, *Mind of Paul: A Psychological Approach*, p. 12.

by a nomistic interpretation of the Psalms as to explain the Psalms by a psychological interpretation of Paul's references to his former life? Paul certainly could validate his action by such nomistic precedents as: (1) Moses' slaying of the immoral Israelites at Baal-peor,[60] (2) Phinehas' slaying of the Israelite man and Midianite woman in the plains of Moab,[61] and (3) the actions of Mattathias and the Hasidim in rooting out apostasy among their own people.[62] The divine commendation of Phinehas' action in Numbers 25:11-13 is significant:

> Phinehas, the son of Eleazar, the son of Aaron the priest, hath turned away my wrath from the children of Israel, while he was zealous for my sake among them; therefore I consumed not the children of Israel in my jealousy. Wherefore, say [unto him]: Behold, I give unto him my covenant of peace, and he shall have it and his seed after him, even the covenant of an everlasting priesthood; because he was zealous for his God, and made an atonement for the children of Israel.

Similarly, the exhortation of II Maccabees 6:13 should be noted: "For indeed it is a mark of great kindness when the impious are not let alone for a long time, but punished at once." Such precedents, coupled with the rising Jewish Messianic expectancy,[63] could have been sufficient motivation for Paul's action.

That a nomistic reacting piety could be blended with a zeal for holy war is again illustrated by the Qumran texts. That of 1QM assuredly emphasizes the latter aspect, but does not neglect the former;[64] 1QS 9.22 defines the righteous man as one who "is to bear unremitting hatred towards all men of ill repute." And the two separate columns which probably formed the introduction to 1QS mention holy war against the Gentiles. The fourteenth column of the hymns of the community significantly associates zeal for holy war with a reacting nomistic piety:

[60] Num. 25:1-5.

[61] Num. 25:6-15.

[62] I Macc. 2:23-28, 42-48.

[63] See J. Klausner, *Messianic Idea in Israel*, pp. 427-29, where three pre-Hadrian Talmudic passages are discussed (b. Sanh. 97b-98a, b. Bab. Bath. 10a, and b. Yom. 86b) dealing with the idea of repentance and the keeping of the Law as prerequisite to the Messianic Age.

[64] Note 1QM 11.1-6.

The nearer I draw to Thee, the more am I filled with zeal against all that do wickedness and against all men of deceit. For they that draw near to Thee cannot see Thy commandments defied, and they that have knowledge of Thee can brook no change of Thy words, seeing that Thou art the essence of right, and all Thine elect are the proof of Thy truth.[65]

Paul's attitude could have been very similar to that of the Essenes. He may also have felt that in the light of the Messianic expectations the nation must be found faithful in its obedience[66] and kept from going astray.[67] So, too, the grisly task of uprooting apostasy could not be left or delegated to the insensitive, but must be undertaken by a blameless one whom God stirred up.[68] And in his task, he may have expected to realize the divine presence and blessing.[69] Much as we may recoil at the thought of so-called "righteous crusades" and "holy wars," we cannot deny that Judaism has many examples of zeal for a holy war within a nomistic piety.

Zeal in the carrying out of persecution is of itself an indication neither of legalism nor of nomism. The motivation is important. And the only inward glimpse we have into Paul's early persecution is contained in the words "I acted ignorantly" (*agnoōn epoiēsa*).[70] We must therefore conclude that, while Paul's persecution could have been the result of his inner turmoil over and dissatisfaction with the Law, it could have been, with at least as much plausibility, the result of his supreme satisfaction with and solid commitment to the splendor that came through Moses.

THE OLD COVENANT IN RETROSPECT

It is significant that in II Corinthians 3:7-18, Paul's contrast between the Old and the New Covenant is not that of a crushing legalism and a new prophetism. Rather, it is between what was "glorious"

[65] 1QH 14.13-15.

[66] Cf. 1QS 9.20-21.

[67] 1QS 9.3-4 speaks of unswerving allegiance to God and His ordinances as providing a sound foundation for the Holy Spirit, truth, and Israel's hope.

[68] 1QM 7.5: "They shall all be volunteers for war, blameless in spirit and flesh." 1QM 10.5 again speaks of "willing volunteers." This same idea crops up in Gal. 6:1, where Paul speaks of *hoi pneumatikoi* who are to restore the wayward from apostasy.

[69] 1QM 10.2-5 promises God's presence and blessing upon those willing and blameless volunteers for holy war, using the words of Deut. 20:3-4.

[70] I Tim. 1:13.

(*doxa*) and what is "of exceeding glory" (*tēs huperballousēs doxē*).[71] It is true that he speaks of the Old Covenant as "the ministration of death" (*hē diakonia tou thanatou*)[72] and "the ministration of condemnation" (*hē diakonia tēs katakriseōs*),[73] but he also insists that "it was brought forth in glory" (*egenēthē en doxē*)[74] and "through glory" (*dia doxēs*)[75] by the same God of the New Covenant[76] and that men found life through faith under it.[77] It was indeed a bondage[78] and a slavery,[79] but this is only presented in its relation to the liberty that is found in Christ Jesus. And even then the bondage of the Old Covenant is not necessarily equated with a crushing legalism,[80] though it was certainly that to a legalist. A God-ordained and supervising nomism is all that need be implied.

We need not visualize every Jew under the Old Covenant as feeling frustrated, oppressed, and dissatisfied with his lot, even as we need not suppose that every minor or servant is chafing at the bit under the rule and supervision of superiors. There is such a thing as a loving and rejoicing nomism as well as a burdened and biting legalism; a willing and loving subjection as well as an enforced slavery. And strange as it may seem, in the sphere of family relations the attitude of the minor, and even of the servant, takes on the former character in direct relation as the authority over him is viewed as loving, benevolent, just, and trustworthy. It is usually the more noble and discerning who respond in willing obedience to their elders and trusted superiors in the family relationship, while the blunt of perception feel the awful burden of resentment. Yet both the loving son and the resentful offspring await the day when each shall stand on his own in full legal and—it is to be hoped—emotional maturity.

[71] II Cor. 3:10-11.
[72] II Cor. 3:7.
[73] II Cor. 3:9.
[74] II Cor. 3:7.
[75] II Cor. 3:11.
[76] Acts 24:14.
[77] The Patriarch Abraham certainly did not exhaust Paul's list of the men of faith in the Old Covenant.
[78] Gal. 4:1-7.
[79] Gal. 4:21-31.
[80] J. Weiss was certainly wrong in insisting that "all his previous life must have seemed to him a hideous mistake" (*Primitive Christianity,* Vol. I, p. 194; cf. also p. 185, and Wernle, *Beginnings of Christianity,* Vol. I, p. 225).

In view of the lack of evidence for his dissatisfaction within Judaism, his hesitation to associate the Jewish religion before the coming of Christ with legalism, and his insistence that the Old Covenant was of God, need we assume any less for Paul? His could have been a longing for the realization of the hope of Israel, and yet a thrill to the present revelation of God and a reacting obedience to it. One must insist again, as earlier, that the essential tension of pre-destruction Hebraic Judaism—especially of the nomistic element *and* probably of Paul himself—was not primarily that of legalism versus love, or externalism versus inwardness, but fundamentally that of promise and fulfillment. It was the Person and work of Jesus Christ as the fulfillment of Israel's hopes, and not an early dissatisfaction with the Law, that made all the difference; thereby transforming the zealous Rabbi Saul into the zealous Apostle Paul.

Teaching

V

Legality and Law

IT IS THE HOPE of every interpreter of Paul "to find the proper way to a theological understanding of the apostle's teaching about the law, which, in spite of much labour, has not yet been adequately dealt with."[1] And it is mine as well. But in so doing, the related question of legality must be considered also; for only in the consideration of both "legality" and "law" in the Apostle's thought can we come to the heart of the matter.

ROMANS 7 AND HUMAN INABILITY

Since Paul's teaching is that the Law "was weak through the flesh,"[2] it is best to begin our study on the lines of Pauline anthropology before moving on to those of soteriology. And while scattered references and inferences regarding the nature of man abound in the Apostle's letters, there is one fairly long passage where the dominant theme is that of man as he is in himself before God. That passage is Romans 7:7-25. It is here we must start if we are to understand Paul's teaching regarding legality and law.

The problem of Romans 7:7-25. As noted in the previous chapter, interpreters of the passage have taken their stand in one or the other of two schools of thought. To the one, the passage has primary reference to Paul's preconversion days under the Law. To the other, the Apostle is describing that struggle which goes on within the dual nature of every Christian, between what he was and is in Adam and what he is and shall become in Christ. The arguments for each posi-

[1] E. Stauffer, *N. T. Theology*, p. 90.
[2] Rom. 8:3.

tion are almost equally convincing. The preconversion view stresses (1) the past tense of the verbs in verses 7-13; (2) the definite contrast between chapters 7 and 8, as signaled in the emphatic "now" of 8:1, the absence of Christian expressions in chapter 7 until verse 25, and the abundant references in chapter 8 to Christ Jesus, the Spirit, and the Christian life; (3) the expressions of chapter 7 which are definitely contrary to Paul's presentation of the Christian life, e.g., "sold under sin" in verse 14 and "wretched man" in verse 24; (4) the logical argument that redemption by Christ is no redemption at all if this is a picture of the Christian life; (5) the experiential argument that such a preconversion struggle has been not uncommon to many in either past or present day; and (6) the pragmatic argument that a threefold division of the Apostle's life—i.e., childhood innocence, struggle under the Law, freedom in Christ—"fits like a glove" what we know of Judaism, Paul's life, and this passage. On the other hand, the postconversion interpretation emphasizes: (1) the present tense of the verbs in verses 14-24; (2) the fact that Romans 7 is set in the context of Romans 5, 6, and 8, which speak of the Christian life; (3) that a preconversion interpretation is inconsistent with what Paul later says of his former life in Philippians 3:6; (4) that an interpretation of the passage as the tension that exists in the life of the Christian between the old and the new creations is consistent with the similar tension presented in Romans 8:23 and Galatians 5:17; and (5) that such an interpretation is consistent with what we know of the Christian life in the past and present day as it is lived between the old and the new aeons. Judging from the near balance of arguments pro and con, it would seem that the interpretation of Romans 7 has arrived at a stalemate. Yet perhaps the answer "may be found to lie, where so often it does, at the very point where the problem appears most intractable."[3]

The key to Romans 7:7-25. The great textual problem for every interpreter of whatever persuasion is that presented in verse 25b. Whether the deliverance pictured in Romans 7 is seen as that from Law to Christ in the conversion experience or that from the old man to the new in the daily experience of the Christian, most commentators agree that "it is scarcely conceivable that, after giving thanks

[3] C. L. Mitton, "Romans vii. Reconsidered—III," *E. T.*, Vol. LXV, No. 5 (Feb., 1954), p. 133.

to God for deliverance, Paul should describe himself as being in exactly the same position as before."[4] Thus, though manuscript evidence is unanimous in locating this portion immediately after verse 25a, the majority of interpreters of whatever view insist that verse 25b is logically out of position. James Moffatt and C. H. Dodd, who see in Romans 7 Paul's reminiscence of his conscious inward conflict under the Law, locate this portion immediately before verses 24-25a and attribute its displacement to a scribal insertion of a marginal note or a confusion on the part of Paul's amanuensis.[5] They argue that "we do seem to have here one of the cases . . . where a primitive corruption of the text has affected all our surviving MSS., and we cannot avoid trusting our own judgment against their evidence."[6] Rudolf Bultmann, in basic agreement with the preconversion position though insisting that such was known and presented "only from the standpoint of faith,"[7] says of verse 25b: "This sentence is very likely a gloss, which, in addition, has landed in the text at the wrong place; it belongs to vs. 23."[8] Likewise, the postconversion advocates either transpose the verse to an earlier position or omit any serious consideration of it. Anders Nygren, for example, says after treating verse 25a, "Paul has reached the conclusion of his discussion."[9] Even many who see in the chapter more of a general situation are prepared to argue, as does Lietzmann, that verse 25b is an interpolation or an error through dictation.[10] Some go a step further and suggest that not only is verse 25b only rightly placed when it precedes verses 24-25a, but that Romans 8:2 must also be transposed to follow immediately after Romans 7:25a.[11]

But in 1954 C. L. Mitton asked whether, in disregarding the position of Romans 7:25b and the import of the pronouns *autos egō*, we are not in reality setting aside the key to the passage; and he

[4] C. H. Dodd, *Romans,* M.N.T.C., pp. 114-15.
[5] *Ibid.*; J. Moffatt, *Intro. to the Literature of the N. T.*, p. 143.
[6] Dodd, *Romans,* p. 115.
[7] R. Bultmann, "Christ the End of the Law," *Essays,* trans. J. C. G. Greig (London: S. C. M. Press, 1955), p. 40.
[8] Bultmann, *Theology of the N. T.,* Vol. I, p. 212, n.
[9] A. Nygren, *Commentary on Romans,* trans. C. C. Rasmussen (London: S. C. M. Press, 1952), p. 302.
[10] Cf. H. Lietzmann, *Römerbrief,* p. 39.
[11] E.g., F. Müller, "Zwei Marginalien im Brief Paulus an die Römer," *Z. N. W.,* Vol. XL (1941), pp. 249-54.

answered in the affimative.[12] He pointed out that the pronouns are "exceedingly emphatic" and argued that they were used to sum up in an emphatic manner all the previous occurrences of *egō* in the chapter. Thus he insisted that verse 25b is not out of place but is to be regarded as the summary of the whole chapter, and that the true contrast between chapters 7 and 8 is to be found in that of the *autos egō* of 7:25b and the *en Christō Iēsou* of 8:1.

It is certainly true that the expression *autos egō* carries more of an emphasis than is indicated by Luther's "Ich" or the "I myself" of the Authorized Version. Moffatt's "left to myself" and Phillips' "in my own nature" more faithfully render the expression, though perhaps with the implication to some of a hypothetical deism. Probably the best translation is the "I of myself" of the American Standard Version and the Revised Standard Version, understood as "I of my own resources." Mitton's observation concerning the centrality of this neglected verse has much to commend it.

When *autos egō* is used as the key to the passage, what do we find? First, as was pointed out in chapter IV, we discover that this "I" has its irrevocable history in Adam and has suffered the consequences. The sentiment of IV Ezra 7:118 is Paul's as well: "O thou Adam, what hast thou done! For though it was thou that sinned, the fall was not thine alone, but ours also who are thy descendants!"[13] The passage thus begins in verses 7-13 by asserting that when we speak of what "I of myself" am, we must remember that our history begins with the fact that "I am in Adam." Secondly, we find the passage pointing out the dreadful realization that "I of myself" am unable to attain to the law of God which I know to be right and which I desire. Certainly the Law is prominent in the chapter, and true it is that the conclusion to the matter is only to be found "in Christ Jesus," but the dominant theme of verses 14-24 is neither law nor victory but the recognition that "I of myself" am unable to measure up to that law of God or gain victory. And so the terrible truths strike home:

1. "I am carnal" (vs. 14).
2. "I am . . . sold under sin" (vs. 14).

[12] Mitton, "Romans vii," *op. cit.*, pp. 132-35.

[13] Cf. also 3:7 and II Baruch 48:42-43: "O Adam, what hast thou done to all those who are born of thee?" Also see *Str.-Bil.*, Vol. III, pp. 227-29, for Talmudic expressions regarding Adam's sin.

3. "I do not understand my own actions" (vs. 15).
4. "I do not do what I want, but I do the very thing I hate" (vs. 15).
5. "I know that nothing good dwells within me, that is, in my flesh" (vs. 18).
6. "I do not do the good I want, but the evil I do not want is what I do" (vss. 18-19).
7. "I am so completely under the thralldom of sin that I sin against my wish" (vs. 17, 20).[14]

Thus Paul concludes this second section of Romans 7 with the confession of all humanity: "I find then this law: that when I would do good, evil is present with me" (vs. 21); and with the universal cry of man as he is in himself: "Wretched man that I am!" (vs. 24). It is not only that "I am in Adam," but I find that "Adam is in me." Third, the expression of verse 25a, "I thank God through Jesus Christ our Lord," must be considered an anticipatory exclamation arising out of the cry of despair. The Apostle cannot think of the inability of man without immediately rejoicing in the ability of God through Christ. But these words are not the main theme at this point, and must be taken as an interjected parenthesis. Fourth, he concludes the whole treatment by saying in verse 25b: "So then, I of myself—with my mind I serve the law of God, but with my flesh the law of sin." Mitton has paraphrased vs. 25b thus:

This then is the conclusion to which I have been leading: when I rely on my own resources, and cease to depend on God, then this is what happens —I continue to acknowledge with my judgment the authority of God's commands, but in my thoughts and actions it is the authority of sin which holds sway.[15]

Sanday and Headlam have phrased it as follows:

Without His intervention—so long as I am left to my own unaided self— the state that I have been describing may be briefly summarized: In this twofold capacity of mine I serve two masters: with my conscience I serve the Law of God; with my bodily organism the Law of Sin.[16]

[14] C. H. Dodd's words are pertinent in the interpretation of vss. 17 and 20: "Paul is not meaning to shuffle out of responsibility for his actions by ascribing them to the alien power. What he wishes to show is how completely he is under 'the thraldom of sin'—so completely that he sins against his wish" (*Romans,* p. 114).

[15] Mitton, "Romans vii," *op. cit.,* p. 134.

[16] W. Sanday and A. C. Headlam, *Romans,* I.C.C., p. 178.

Or, in other words, I of myself am unable before God. The passage is therefore composed of four elements: (1) historically, "I am in Adam," verses 7-13; (2) existentially, "Adam is in me," verses 14-24; (3) an anticipatory interjection of God's ability, verse 25a; and (4) the summary and conclusion of the matter, "I of myself" am unable before God.

Thus Romans 7:7-25 is not specifically either Paul's or mankind's preconversion state or postconversion experience. Nor is it the cry of only "the man under the law" or "the Christian who slips back into a legalistic attitude to God."[17] It is Paul uttering mankind's great cry of its own inability. It is Paul's and humanity's realization that in our history and experience we have become so bound up by sin that there can be deliverance and victory only through God. This is not the recognition of the legalist. Rather, it is the abiding realization of the sensitive and is felt most by those who are the closest to God.

Here, then, is the Apostle's answer to those who would gain righteousness via a legalistic endeavor; the same answer as given in Galatians 5:17: we are so bound by what is antagonistic to God that we are unable to do His will.[18] Thus, "it depends not upon man's will or exertion but upon God's mercy."[19] Windisch is right in noting that Romans 7 is the expression of man's inability to obey the will of God, but he is wrong in claiming it to be unique in the New Testament.[20] It is unique only in that it is the longest explicit passage to this effect.

The character of this recognition. At least one further matter needs to be treated in the interpretation of Romans 7. I have said that this recognition of humanity's inability before God "is the abiding realization of the sensitive and is felt most by those who are the closest

[17] As A. M. Hunter asserts in *The Epistle to the Romans* (London: S. C. M. Press, 1955), p. 74. Both Hunter and Wm. Manson recognize the significance of the pronouns *autos egō* as the summary of Rom. 7:7 ff., but they still speak of the dominant theme in the passage as being that of man under law rather than that of man unable of himself because of sin (cf. Hunter, *ibid.*, and Manson, "Notes on the Argument of Romans," *op. cit.*, p. 162).

[18] Cf. also Rom. 8:6-8.

[19] Rom. 9:16. Note also 9:11.

[20] H. Windisch, *The Meaning of the Sermon on the Mount*, trans. S. M. Gilmour (Philadelphia: Westminster, 1951), p. 122.

to God." Does this mean that it is only realized by the Christian? Bultmann argues that the presentation in Romans 7 is what is apparent "only from the standpoint of faith, and which the Jew himself does not perceive at all."[21] The cry of Romans 7 is put "into the mouth of the Jew and thereby exposes the situation of the Jew which is not visible to himself";[22] "the man without Christ is not described as he sees himself, but as he is seen from the standpoint of faith."[23] "The Christian is aware of a split in himself which the Jew had not as yet known."[24] Similarly A. Nygren, though differing with Bultmann on the interpretation of the passage, agrees that this is solely the realization of the Christian.[25]

Now it is true that the Christian, knowing God's ability more intimately and personally than any could have known under the Old Covenant, is in a position to realize his own inability to a greater measure than could any under the Old Covenant. But that does not mean that a spiritually sensitive Jew in the Old Covenant could not have been at least aware of his own inability before God. It is true that Romans 7 presents in an anticipatory ejaculation, and Romans 8 in a connected development, the Christian answer; i.e., that mankind's inability is met by God's ability "through Jesus Christ our Lord" and "in Christ Jesus." But that does not mean that human inability was never met by divine ability—and realized so by men—in the Old Covenant. Paul is writing approximately a quarter-century after his conversion, and all his words bear the Christian stamp. But this does not require us to view all his expressions as exclusively Christian. The great insistence in the Qumran literature on the inability of all flesh of itself before God[26] strikingly reveals that "the point at which the very roots of Paul's theology and that of the Dead Sea Scrolls are intertwined is the experience of moral frustration, with the resulting conviction of man's hopeless sinfulness."[27] The writer of IV Ezra shares this same conviction of the total inadequacy of mankind in

[21] Bultmann, "Christ the End of the Law," *op. cit.*, p. 40.
[22] Bultmann, *Theology of the N. T.*, Vol. I, p. 266.
[23] Bultmann, "Christ the End of the Law," *op. cit.*, p. 50.
[24] *Ibid.*, p. 53.
[25] Nygren, *Romans*, pp. 292-303.
[26] Esp. 1QH 1.21-23, 3.24-36, 4.5-40, and 1QS 11.9-10.
[27] M. Burrows, *More Light on the Dead Sea Scrolls*, p. 119.

itself before God,[28] though his solution differs from that of Paul's.

Romans 7, therefore, cannot be considered an exclusively Christian conviction. It is the human cry, drawn from mankind's history and experience, of the spiritually sensitive. Though Paul's intimate and personal knowledge of the power of God as it is in Jesus Christ has resulted in a more intense realization and expression of this inability, we cannot assume that he was entirely unaware of that inadequacy in his Judaistic days. Qumran stands as a warning against such an assumption. What can be said of "legalistic" Pharisaism cannot necessarily be attributed to "nomistic" Pharisaism. It may be that Paul's Christian presentation in Romans 7 differs from his preconversion position only in the intensity of his realization and expression.

THE "ETHICAL ABILITY" INTERPRETATION

Another passage in this same letter to the Romans has often been claimed to be diametrically opposed to any thought in Paul of the moral inability of man, and to be the true basis for all the Pauline doctrine. That passage is Romans 2:6 ff. The following four clauses in this section have been cited as specifically indicating that man is able of himself to "work" and "do" that which is well-pleasing before God, and that God responds on the basis of such action:

Vs. 6. "God . . . will render to every man according to his works."

Vs. 7. "To those who by patient continuance of good work, eternal life."

Vs. 10. "But glory and honor and peace to everyone that works the good, to the Jew first and also to the Greek."

Vs. 13b. "The doers of the law shall be justified."

On the basis of these statements, many commentators have insisted that while Paul rejected a righteousness consisting of statutory rules he did accept and teach that true righteousness before God is to be attained through the following of true ethical principles.

Representative of older commentators taking this position are H. P. Liddon and Charles Gore. Liddon interpreted Romans 2:6 as teaching that "God's award to every man hereafter will be in accordance with his conduct, and not, as the Jews thought, with his theocratic

[28] Esp. IV Ezra 8:31-36.

position."[29] Gore insisted that Paul was presenting in these verses a "natural religion," i.e., "the religion that appeals straight off to the conscience of almost all honest and civilized men," in the belief "that God will judge men with absolute power and insight and impartiality according to their conduct and their characters."[30] According to this position, it is conduct and character that the Apostle makes basic, "and whatever is true about free grace and justification by faith only, is true because, and only because, this free grace and this justifying faith are necessary means or steps towards the realization of actual righteousness."[31] Thackeray also viewed Romans 2 as teaching "the possibility and merit" of man fulfilling "the ethical side" of the Law.[32] He recognized an inconsistency between such an interpretation and the argument of Galatians, but he explained it as due to the exaggerated depreciation of the Law and human ability in Galatians, which is naturally to be expected "in the heat of the controversy for Gentile liberty."[33] In more recent times, E. Burton, E. F. Scott, and a host of others have been advocates of this position,[34] viewing man's ability to follow ethical principles as the fundamental prerequisite of true religion. Even some who view Paul as opposed to the doctrine of the moral ability of man have said of Romans 2:6 ff. that "the passage is somewhat inconsistent with the main trend of St. Paul's teaching, since it implies that both Jews and Gentiles could really attain to righteousness by following the light of conscience and obeying the essential principles of morality contained in the Law."[35]

Difficulties of the "ethical ability" interpretation. The exegetical difficulties of such an interpretation are at least three. Basic to this view are two distinctions and an omission: (1) the distinction between

[29] H. P. Liddon, *St. Paul's Epistle to the Romans* (London: Longmans, Green, 1893), p. 43.

[30] C. Gore, *St. Paul's Epistle to the Romans* (London: Murray, 1900), Vol. I, p. 106.

[31] *Ibid.*, p. 107.

[32] H. St. J. Thackeray, *Relation of St. Paul to Contemporary Jewish Thought*, pp. 59, 78.

[33] *Ibid.*, p. 78.

[34] E. Burton, *Galatians*, I.C.C., pp. 451-54; E. F. Scott, *Romans* (London: S. C. M. Press, 1947), p. 35. Cf. also W. M. MacGregor, *Christian Freedom* (London: Hodder & Stoughton, 1914), and F. V. Filson, *St. Paul's Conception of Recompense*.

[35] W. L. Knox, *St. Paul and the Church of Jerusalem*, p. 351, n. 10.

ho nomos (the Mosaic Law) and *nomos* (law in general); (2) the distinction between the ceremonial and the ethical portions of the Mosaic Law, with each of separate validity; and (3) the failure to consider seriously the context of Romans 2:6 ff.

In the latter half of the nineteenth century, Lightfoot and Gifford in Britain and Volkmar and Holsten on the Continent argued that Paul used "the Law" with the individualizing force of "the Law of Moses" but that when he used "law" without the article he had in mind the qualitative idea of law—exemplified often in the Mosaic Law but much wider than that in its application.[36] And this distinction serves as the basis for most of the ethical ability interpretation of Romans 2, which views "the Law" as finished in Christ but "law" as remaining the way of man's approach to God.[37] In 1893, however, Eduard Grafe, in his small work *Die paulinische Lehre vom Gesetz*, took this position to task. He pointed out that in the over 110 uses of *ho nomos* and *nomos* in the *Hauptbriefe* (primarily in Romans and Galatians), such a distinction was just not present in the Apostle's use of the term.[38] Grafe certainly went too far in asserting that Paul never distinguished between the law of God in general and in terms of the Mosaic Law, for the discussions of the Gentile and the divine law in Romans 1:18-32 and 2:14-16 point out just such a distinction.[39] But his main point that *ho nomos* and *nomos* are not used to signal such a distinction is well taken. Of significance in his evidence is Paul's statement in Galatians 3:23 that before Christ "we were kept under law" (*hupo nomou*); which state he speaks of further in verse 24, beginning with the words "so then the law (*hōste ho nomos*) was our pedagogue unto Christ"—thus equating *ho nomos* and *nomos*. The terms are likewise interchanged in Romans 2:23-27, even to the ascribing of *ho nomos* to Gentile observance and *nomos* to that which was broken by the Jew. Thus Paul spoke of Christ as the end of "law" (*nomou*) in Romans 10:4, not just of "the Law," and of love as the fulfilling of "law" (*nomou*) in Romans 13:10. It

[36] J. B. Lightfoot, *Galatians*, p. 118 on Gal. 2:19; E. H. Gifford, *The Epistle of St. Paul to the Romans* (London: Murray, 1886), pp. 41-48.

[37] Cf. esp. Burton's treatment, *Galatians*, pp. 449-60.

[38] E. Grafe, *Die paulinische Lehre vom Gesetz* (Leipzig: Mohr, 1893), pp. 2-11.

[39] Grafe has likewise gone beyond the evidence in his conclusion as to the positive content of Paul's message.

is not sufficient to argue, as some have, that the Apostle really did make a distinction between "the Law" and "law," but that in some cases "the distinction has been somewhat carelessly applied by Paul or his amanuenses."[40] When there are clear cases of equating and even interchanging the terms, it seems best to admit that he did not make any real distinction in his use of *nomos* with or without the article.[41]

Often associated with the question of "the Law" and "law," though not necessarily so, is the distinction many believe Paul to be making between the ceremonial and the ethical aspects of the Law; or, to put it more bluntly, between the ethical kernel and the ceremonial husk. The position is taken that in Galatians he spoke of Christ as the end of the ceremonial law, while in Romans 2 he reasserted that the general moral requirements of the Law are still the basis for righteousness. And in this assertion, substance is given to the Jewish charge that "Paul, who ought to have known better, perpetuated the same mischievous error" of the LXX in narrowing the Jewish concept of the Torah down to the narrowly legalistic and ritualistic.[42] But there is no real reason for believing that Paul differed from contemporary Judaism in its insistence that the ethical and ceremonial aspects of the Law together make up one indivisible whole.[43] To those who insist that his substitution of *nomos* for "Torah" indicates a narrower concept of the Mosaic Law and served as the point of departure for such a cleavage between ceremonial and ethical aspects, we can only repeat T. R. Glover's fitting reply: "Such purism is hard to understand; whatever 'Torah' and *nomos* first meant, two hundred years of equation is not irrelevant in the history of words."[44] To those who argue that such a distinction was present in his mind from the fact that he stressed with disapproval the ceremonial aspects of the Law in Galatians but spoke with approval of the ethical standard of God in Romans 2, we must point out that there is a vast difference

[40] MacGregor, *Christian Freedom,* p. 248, n. 1.

[41] Cf. Sanday and Headlam, *Romans,* p. 80, where this distinction is called in question; and P. P. Bläser, *Gesetz bei Paulus,* pp. 1-30, where Grafe's argument is reproduced.

[42] R. T. Herford, *Pharisees,* p. 54. Cf. S. Schechter, *Aspects of Rabbinic Theology,* p. 117; G. F. Moore, *Judaism,* Vol. I, p. 263; H. J. Schoeps, *Paul,* p. 29.

[43] Cf. Grafe, *Paulinische Lehre,* pp. 11-25; Bläser, *Gesetz bei Paulus,* pp. 38-44, 63-71.

[44] T. R. Glover, *Paul of Tarsus,* p. 35, n. 1.

between stressing one aspect or another of an indivisible law—also in using "law" somewhat figuratively[45]—and separating that law into two unequally valid parts. Further, as will be pointed out later, Paul spoke of the ceremonial aspect of the Law in Galatians and the ethical aspect in Romans 2 in two different contexts. His disapproval in one case and approval in the other cannot simply be contrasted. This whole question of the significance of the Mosaic Law, its extent, and the degree to which it has been fulfilled and abrogated by Christ, are to be treated in the following pages of this chapter and the next. Positive evidence for Paul's view of the indivisibility of the Mosaic Law is therefore better left for those more pertinent sections. But it should at least be noted here that his insistence, in Galatians 3:10 and 5:3, that anyone who takes upon himself the outward physical sign of obligation to the Law with the intention of bringing upon himself the benefits of it is under obligation to the *whole* Law, is in conformity with Jewish thought[46] and stands as a warning to those who would see Paul narrowly defining the Mosaic Law or separating it into unequally valid parts.

It must also be pointed out that the advocates of this position have failed to consider seriously the context in which these verses are set. The section begins with a strong declaration of the wrath of God upon the Gentile, goes on to proclaim that this same wrath stands over the Jew, and concludes by stating that no human being will be justified before God "by the works of the law" (*ex ergōn nomou*).[47] In opposition to the optimistic view of human ability as proposed by some commentators, the résumé of this section declares that "all have sinned and come short of the glory of God."[48] In declaring that mankind has proved itself unable, the passage is in full agreement with the assertion in Galatians 2:16 and 3:11 that man is not justified before God *ex ergōn nomou* or *en nomō*. Whatever the import of Romans 2:6 ff., it does not seem to be that of the ethical ability of man before God.

[45] E.g., Rom. 3:27, 7:21, 23, 25b, 8:2.

[46] Cf. Tos. Dem. 2.3-5, where an *am haarez* who has imposed upon himself the obligations of a *haber* and a proselyte who has imposed upon himself the obligations of the Law are not accepted unless they perform all the Law without exception.

[47] Rom. 3:20.

[48] Rom. 3:23.

The two strands of Law and Gospel. But in declaring the "ethical ability" interpretation of Romans 2:6 ff. to be in error, we are still left with the problem of the proper exegesis of the passage. And some of the other treatments of the passage proposed are just as unreliable exegetically as that just denied; e.g., the view that Romans 2:6 ff. refers to works that *follow* justification. Calvin advocated this position, arguing that these are the good works of the elect and faithful who aspire to their Lord;[49] while others compare them to the "fruits of the Spirit."[50] But surely the context of Romans 2 rules out such an interpretation. Paul is certainly not exhorting Christians to express their faith in good works in this passage.

The interpretation of Hans Lietzmann approaches the Pauline point of view. He argues that here "stellt Paulus hypothetisch das Princip des Endgerichtes dar, wie es kommen würde wenn 1) das Evangelium nicht da wäre und 2) es möglich wäre, das Gesetz zu erfüllen."[51] But his emphasis upon the hypothetical nature of Paul's words is misleading. The Apostle is not presenting what would be if the Gospel were not present, but the command of God as contemporaneous with the Gospel. He saw two strands running throughout the Old Testament and the New: (1) the law of God, which promised life but because of man's sin and inability brought only judgment and death, and (2) righteousness based on faith.[52] These two are both viewed as of God, both are according to His purpose, and both have run and will continue to run in adjoining paths throughout the course of human history. Martin Luther probably best understood and most adequately represents Paul's emphasis at this point in saying: "All the Scriptures of God are divided into two parts—commands and promises."[53] We must deal with the relationship of the two parts in the following section. Suffice it here to say that the contrast we see between Romans 2:6 ff. and 3:21 ff. is the same as that between Law and Gospel.[54] In Romans 2:6 ff. the Apostle cites the Law,[55] which

[49] J. Calvin, *Commentary on the Epistle to the Romans,* trans. F. Sibson (London: Seeley & Sons, 1834), on Rom. 2.

[50] E.g., Hunter, *Romans,* p. 36.

[51] Lietzmann, *Römerbrief,* p. 13.

[52] Note esp. the contrasts in Gal. 3:11-12 and Rom. 10:5 ff.

[53] M. Luther, "A Treatise on Christian Liberty," *Works of Martin Luther,* Vol. II, trans. W. A. Lambert, p. 317.

[54] Cf. E. Gaugler, *Der Römerbrief* (Zürich: Zwingli, 1945), Vol. I, pp. 61-62.

[55] Vs. 6 is a word for word quotation of Ps. 62:12 (cf. Prov. 24:12 and Jer.

promises life and would bring life *if* the factors of human sin and inability were not present. But the point is that it is still valid as the standard and judgment of God in spite of the "if."[56] Thus Paul, in accordance with the principle that "all who have sinned under the law will be judged by the law,"[57] cites that law in order to point out the judgment the Jew is under.[58] And rather than argue for the ethical ability of man, he is presenting the valid standard of God in order to show how far man has gone in proving himself unable.

THE LAW IN THE OLD COVENANT

The question as to Paul's teaching regarding the purpose of the Law in the Old Covenant has been anticipated in the previous chapter and in the earlier sections of this chapter, and at times a partial answer has been proposed. But it is not without profit at this point to bring together the Apostle's scattered hints and statements in order to form some type of organized presentation. We need to understand Paul on this issue, for here he undoubtedly differed from a vast number of his brethren "according to the flesh." But it is also essen-

---

32:19). Vs. 13 has a significant parallel in Mish. Aboth 1.17, attributed to the Simeon who was either the father or the son of Gamaliel I, Paul's teacher: "Not the expounding [of the law] is the chief thing but the doing [of it]." Parallels to vs. 13 are also found in Jas. 1:22 and Matt. 7:24, 26. It seems that Judaism of Paul's day considered this saying to be an explicit expression of what was implied in the written Torah.

[56] Lietzmann has correctly seen the hypothetical life-giving character of the Law in its contractual aspect, but has also implied a similar hypothetical character for the Law as the standard and judgment of God. In this latter case he is misleading.

[57] Rom. 2:12.

[58] Wm. Manson has pertinently remarked: "If in the preceding section [i.e., Rom. 1:18-32] the Apostle had Wisdom 13 in mind, here he is thinking of Wisdom 15 where the Jewish writer turns from the heathen with the comforting reflection: 'But Thou, our God, art gracious, true, long-suffering. . . . Even if we sin, we are Thine, etc.' This delusion of the Jew lies behind the Apostle's taunt in 2:3-4. While acknowledging the magnificent privilege of the Diaspora Jew (2:17-20), he presses the rigour of God's ethical demand. The Jew has in the Law 'the very embodiment of religious knowledge and divine truth,' but the Gentile also has an inward law, the sanctions of which he recognizes in conscience, philosophy, and life. Thus Jew and Gentile stand alike before the one tribunal of God's inexorable holiness, and this, according to the Apostle's gospel, is the judgment-seat of Christ (2:16)" ("Notes on the Argument of Romans," *op. cit.*, p. 155).

tial to understand rightly his thought here if we are to appreciate his teaching regarding the work of Christ in relation to the Law and regarding righteousness in the New Covenant.

Law as the standard and judgment of God. To those Jews who argued that the Law was given to Israel as *the* means for righteousness before God, Paul answered that though it promised life[59] it could never give life because of man's sin and inability.[60] In fact, it was never meant to supersede the divinely ordered plan of righteousness by faith.[61] Thus, since (1) the Scriptures declare plainly that the righteous shall live *ek pisteōs*,[62] (2) the promises were made "four hundred and thirty years" before the Mosaic Law,[63] and (3) "no one annuls even a man's will, or adds to it, once it has been ratified,"[64] "if it is the adherents of the law who are to be the heirs, faith is null and the promise is void."[65]

But though the Law is contrary to faith and the promises when taken as *the* means for righteousness, it is not contrary to either when considered rightly—not at all, *mē genoito*.[66] "The law is good, if one makes use of it rightly (*nomimōs*)."[67] And one major aspect of its purpose was and is to bring to consciousness in sin-deadened humanity[68] the realization of the judgment of God, by (1) showing

[59] Rom. 7:10.
[60] Gal. 5:17; Rom. 7:7-25, 8:3, 8.
[61] Rom. 4; Gal. 3:15-22.
[62] Hab. 2:4; cf. Rom. 1:17; Gal. 3:11. The context of Gal. 3:11 indicates that Paul interpreted Hab. 2:4 as human trust and reliance, not as human faithfulness or even the divine faithfulness of the LXX rendering *ek pisteōs mou*.
[63] Gal. 3:16-17. This type of argument was respected in rabbinic circles; cf. b. Kid. 40b, where R. Jose is reported as saying: "Great is learning, since it preceded 'hallah' by forty years, 'terumoth' and tithes by fifty-four years, 'shemittin' by sixty-one, and jubilees by one hundred and three." I.e., since the Torah was given and studied forty years before its precepts for the land of Palestine could be carried out, etc., the study and learning of Torah is greater than the actual practice. Such an injunction to value study over practice was not typical of the Judaism of Paul's day. This emphasis was only felt to be necessary in the postdestruction period when much of the performance of the Law in its details was no longer possible but when the study of the Law was viewed as essential to the national survival. But the temporal argument seems to have been an accepted rabbinic method.
[64] Gal. 3:15-18.
[65] Rom. 4:14.
[66] Gal. 3:21.
[67] I Tim. 1:8.
[68] Rom. 7:15: "I know not my own actions."

sin to be what it is before God and (2) revealing the depths of rebellion in the human heart. Not only does the Law reveal sin and sinful action to be "exceeding sinful,"[69] but, on the principle that forbidden fruits are sweetest, it provokes within man a reaction against its prohibitions. And, by thus increasing trespasses, it increases man's understanding of the extent of his own rebellion against God.[70] Paul saw both these facets of its purpose as divinely ordained; i.e., as the standard and judgment of God it was given "in order that sin through the commandment might become exceeding sinful" *and* "in order that the trespass might abound."[71] Thus he speaks of the Law as given to "the lawless and disobedient"[72] "because of transgressions"[73] in order to quicken the consciousness and activity of sin[74] to the end that man might "through law" come to death, and out of death find life by faith in God.[75] It truly "brings wrath,"[76] and all who are submissive to no higher allegiance are "under a curse."[77] It can be spoken of as "the dispensation of death,"[78] "the dispensation of condemnation,"[79] and "the strength of sin."[80] But Paul never taught that the Law was "a dismal failure"[81] or "was all very bad and did exceedingly ill."[82] Rather, though the promise of life in the Law was brought to nought by man's sin, it is still God's grace and plan that the Law leads "to death," because by this route man is led to God, the God who gives life to the dead. Though it is God's "strange work" as compared to His "proper work," it is never to be disassociated from that proper work in either ultimate origin or ultimate purpose.

[69] Rom. 7:13; cf. Rom. 3:19-20.
[70] Rom. 5:20; cf. Rom. 7:5, 7 ff. Augustine's experience is the classic example (Confessions II. 4-6), but our own hearts yield primary confirmation of the validity of this principle.
[71] Rom. 7:13 and 5:20.
[72] I Tim. 1:8.
[73] Gal. 3:19.
[74] Rom. 5:20, 7:7 ff.
[75] Gal. 2:19; Rom. 7:5, 3:19.
[76] Rom. 4:15.
[77] Gal. 3:10, 13.
[78] II Cor. 3:7.
[79] II Cor. 3:9.
[80] I Cor. 15:56.
[81] As W. H. P. Hatch characterizes the Apostle's thought regarding the Law in *The Pauline Idea of Faith,* p. 59.
[82] As C. G. Montefiore asserts Paul to be saying, *Judaism and St. Paul,* p. 106.

Law as contractual obligation. But there is another aspect to the purpose of the Law in the Old Covenant. I have argued in chapter III that in the Old Testament and Judaism the concept of faith carried the twofold designation of "trust in" and "fidelity to"; reliance upon and faithfulness. And I proposed that the distinction between a "reacting nomist" and an "acting legalist" is that of the starting point and emphasis of each in this two-element conception. In other words, whereas the nomist began with what God has done and does, and thereby laid emphasis upon trust in God, the legalist began with what he himself was able to do and had done, and stressed personal fidelity. But it must be emphasized that both viewpoints recognized that there was the element of contractual obligation in their relationship with God. Both recognized a prescribed form of religious expression and ethical guidance which was to be faithfully followed by man in fulfillment of the contract. The canonical prophets and postcanonical pneumatics of Judaism never attempted to destroy this sense of contractual obligation.[83] Theirs was not to annul the required fidelity, but to insist that trust must precede any acceptable faithfulness and that a loving response must be the basis for it.

In the letters of Paul, this aspect of the Law is assumed. He says that "before the coming of the faith (*tēn pistin*) we were kept under law (*hupo nomon*)";[84] and he goes on to compare this aspect of the Law's purpose to the function of a pedagogue in relation to a child.[85]

[83] K. Lake is one of many who have grossly misrepresented the prophets in claiming that they made "a fundamental attack" on "the whole sacrificial system" (*Paul: His Heritage and Legacy,* p. 27). His insistence is that their message "was wholly different" from that of any of their predecessors. "God, they said, does not care for presents or compliments. He merely wishes men to behave well to one another" (*ibid.,* p. 25). Thus Lake asserts that "the logical end of their teachings would be the abolition of all cultus" (*ibid.,* p. 26). H. H. Rowley, however, has convincingly reminded us that while the prophets undoubtedly differed from the mere ceremonialists, theirs was not a fundamental conflict with the priests as such but only a difference of emphasis. The prophets did not condemn the ritual as such, but its abuse in mere externalism ("The Unity of the Old Testament," *Bulletin of the John Rylands Library,* Vol. XXIX [1945-46], pp. 326-58).

[84] Gal. 3:23. Not before the coming of "faith," for Paul has just previously argued that faith was before "contractual obligation," or the "covenant of works"; but "faith" in the New Covenant sense of the term—Christian faith, *the* faith of which he has been speaking.

[85] Gal. 3:24 ff. In Plato's Lysis, 208-10, there is a good description of what Paul probably had in mind in the use of this term. Here the boy Lysis is held

It is this concept of contract in the Old Covenant which seems to lie in the background of his thought in Galatians 3:20: "Now a mediator implies more than one; but God is one." The verse is truly "one of notorious difficulty,"[86] but Lightfoot's exposition probably best brings out the contrast in the Apostle's mind:

> The very idea of mediation supposes two persons at least, between whom the mediation is carried on. The law then is of the nature of a contract between two parties, God on the one hand, and the Jewish people on the other. . . . Unlike the law, the promise is absolute and unconditional. It depends on the sole decree of God. There are not two contracting parties.[87]

The contractual aspect of the Law is also implied in Paul's continued use of "under law" (*hupo nomon*) in reference to the piety of the Old Covenant.[88] And his reference to New Covenant piety as being "apart from law" or "without law" (*chōris nomou*) implies that formerly piety was associated in some manner with law.[89]

Again at this point great care must be taken; for not only does the association of law with piety in the Old Covenant not necessitate legalism in the sense in which we are using that expression, but it also does not necessarily imply that law is equal with faith in the quest for righteousness. Paul might recognize that fidelity to the Law was associated with righteousness in the Old Covenant, but he insisted that it was never *the* basis for righteousness or even equal with trust in God as a basis of righteousness. His statements imply that he regarded the Law in the Old Covenant as the prescribed expression of a more basic and vital relationship with God, and never more than that; "das

---

in restraint by a superior slave; and when he is asked by Socrates who it is that rules him, he answers: "My pedagogue." There is much he would like to do, but his father keeps him in check until he is ready for manhood. Cf. Lightfoot, *Galatians,* pp. 148-49; H. A. A. Kennedy, *The Theology of the Epistles,* pp. 43-44.

[86] Thackeray, *Relation of St. Paul to Contemporary Jewish Thought,* p. 67.

[87] Lightfoot, *Galatians,* pp. 146-47.

[88] I. Cor. 9:20; Gal. 4:21, 5:18. Even Christ is spoken of as being "born 'under law' in order to redeem those who were 'under law' " (Gal. 4:4-5). Similarly Josephus speaks of Moses' institution of the Law as the standard and rule *hina hōsper hupo patri toutō kai despotēs zōntes* (Contra Apion II. 17). Cf. also b. Sanh. 97a and b (and with a few differences b. Ab. Zar. 9a) where the history of the world is divided into three periods by the post-Hadrian "school of Elijah": Chaos, under the Law, and the Messianic Age.

[89] Rom. 3:21, 28.

formale Kriterium des Gerichtes,"[90] but not the fundamental factor. As such it remained secondary, though of course essential under the terms of contract. And in this recognition of the essential yet secondary nature of the Law in the Old Covenant, Paul was in agreement with Jewish reacting nomism as portrayed in the last chapter.

[90] Bläser, *Gesetz bei Paulus,* p. 72.

VI

The End of Nomism

WHILE MANY SIMILARITIES between Paul's thought and that of Jewish nomism have been previously noted, we now come to the place where all possible agreement between the two ends. At the heart of the Apostle's teaching is his conviction that the Law in its contractual aspect—and that means especially Jewish nomism—has come to its full completion and terminus in Christ. We must not suppose, as have many, that "St. Paul's arguments are only thought out in order to justify a step to which he was irrevocably committed."[1] His thought has a vital core other than just that of necessity and the practicable; and it is from this core that his teaching regarding the Law, legality, and nomism stems. But before dealing with his statements it is well to note the factors that went into the formation of his thought.

FORMATIVE FACTORS

In evaluating the influences that were at work in the formulation of the Pauline doctrine of law, four areas must be considered: (1) Judaism's expectation regarding the status of the Law in the future, (2) the early Church's impact upon Paul, (3) Jesus' attitude toward the Law, and (4) Paul's own conversion experience.

The expectation of Judaism. It must be realized in taking up a survey of the Jewish expectation as to the status of the Law in the Messianic Age and/or the Age to Come that the two concepts of the "abrogation of the Law" and the "establishment of a new law" are not necessarily mutually dependent. It is often supposed that to

[1] As W. L. Knox insists, *St. Paul and the Church of Jerusalem,* p. 28, n. 65.

demonstrate that Judaism expected some type of new lawgiver and law in the time to come is to make it *a priori* certain that the old Law was expected to be nullified; and, conversely, that to note scattered references in the Jewish literature which indicate an expected cessation of certain laws is necessarily to view Judaism as expecting a new law and lawgiver. Such argumentation is fallacious. While the two questions lie tangent to one another and often complement each other, they are not so necessarily interrelated that such deductions can be made. We must therefore treat them as separate questions; this section will deal with Judaism's expectation of the Law's duration, with the further question of a new lawgiver and Torah considered in a later chapter.[2]

The major Jewish objection to Paul's teaching regarding the abrogation of the Law is that "the Law gives no indication of its own transitoriness. Its enactments are to be 'statutes for ever throughout your generations.' "[3] Some have attempted to answer this objection by insisting that Paul viewed this "for ever" as an enigmatic presentation meant to obscure the Law's real transitoriness lest the people should become self-assertive, discouraged, or even forgetful.[4] Others argue that "for ever" must be taken in the sense of I Maccabees 14:41: "And the Jews and the priests were well pleased that Simon should be their leader and high-priest *for ever, until* [emphasis supplied] a faithful prophet should arise" (*eis ton aiōna, heōs tou anastēnai prophētēn piston*). But both Strack-Billerbeck[5] and G. F. Moore[6] have made it clear that at least postdestruction Judaism expected that "the law should not only be in force in the messianic age, but should be better studied and better observed than ever before; and this was indubitably the common belief."[7] Even the individual commandments were claimed to be eternal.[8] In fact, "das rabbin. Schrifttum setzt die ewige Gültigkeit der Tora als selbstverständlich überall voraus."[9] That

[2] *Infra*, pp. 184-86.

[3] C. G. Montefiore, *Judaism and St. Paul*, p. 170.

[4] E.g., A. Nissiotis, "Paul as Interpreter of the Old Testament," *Paulus-Hellas-Oikumene* (Athens: Student Christian Association of Greece, 1951), pp. 156-57.

[5] Vol. I, pp. 244-49, and Vol. IV, Exkurs, 29.

[6] *Judaism*, Vol. I, pp. 269 ff.

[7] *Ibid.*, p. 271.

[8] Cf. *Str.-Bil.*, Vol. I, pp. 244-49.

[9] *Ibid.*, p. 245.

there is polemic intention in at least two Talmudic passages regarding the kindred subject of a new Torah is evident,[10] and the possibility remains that such an interest was the motivation for some of the passages cited by Strack-Billerbeck and Moore. Yet the fact that Philo,[11] Josephus,[12] some of the apocryphal works,[13] and portions of the sectarian literature[14] are in basic agreement with the later Talmudists at this point indicates that belief in the continuance of the Law was characteristic even of predestruction Judaism.[15]

But there is another aspect to this question. In a well-balanced presentation W. D. Davies has shown that "despite the 'doctrine' of the immutability of Torah, there were also occasional expressions of expectations that Torah would suffer modification in the Messianic Age. There were some *Halakoth* which would cease to be applicable in that Age; others, by contrast, would acquire a new relevance."[16] Among the passages pointed out by Davies, the following are significant: Lev. R. 9.7, which, though of late date, speaks of all sacrifices being annulled but that of Thanksgiving in "the time to come";[17] Yalqut on Proverbs 9.2, which, dated c. A.D. 80-120, speaks of all the festivals but Purim ceasing (R. Eleazar adding also the Day of Atonement); Midrash Tehillim 146.7, where distinctions between clean and unclean animals are spoken of as abrogated in the Messianic Age; b. Shab. 151b, where R. Simeon b. Eleazar (A.D. 165-200) argues that "the Torah no longer holds in the Messianic Age, so that questions of reward for observing it and guilt or punish-

[10] Deut. R. 8.6 and b. Shab. 104a; see *infra,* p. 185 *n.*

[11] De Vita Mos. 11.44: In the Messianic Age "each nation would abandon its peculiar ways and throwing overboard their ancestral customs, turn to honouring our laws alone."

[12] Contra Apion II. 39: "Though we be deprived of our wealth, of our cities, or of the other advantages we have, our law continues immortal."

[13] Baruch 4.1, IV Ezra 9.37, and possibly Wisdom 18.4. Cf. R. Marcus, *Law in the Apocrypha,* p. 53.

[14] Qumran's "A Formulary of Blessings" twice presents this idea, as also probably Apoc. of Baruch 48.47 and 77.15.

[15] Matt. 5:17 ff. offers further evidence to this first-century Jewish expectation both in the need for Jesus to allay the fears of His audience and in His words.

[16] W. D. Davies, *Torah in the Messianic Age and/or the Age to Come* (Philadelphia: Society of Biblical Literature, 1952), p. 66.

[17] While "the time to come" has a rather flexible meaning, Davies has pointed out that in view of the context of this passage its meaning here is to be equated with "the Messianic Age" (*ibid.,* p. 55).

ment for refusing to do so do not arise";[18] and possibly b. Nid. 61b, where freedom from ceremonial laws is noted as a characteristic of "the time to come." Especially pertinent is the passage found in both b. Sanh. 97b and b. Ab. Zar. 9b: "The Tanna debe Eliyyahy taught: The world is to exist six thousand years: the first two thousand years are to be void; the next two thousand years are the period of the Torah; and the following two thousand years are the period of the Messiah." Freedman is quite right in pointing out that the passage "does not mean that the Torah shall cease" in the third period,[19] but it does imply that the period of the Messiah was not expected to be characterized or dominated by the Torah but by the Messiah.

Klausner has acknowledged that there are passages which seem to argue against his presentation that Judaism expected the absolute eternal validity and dominance of the Law. But he argues that these contradictions are all of late date, have been influenced by Christian thought, and thus are of no importance in understanding real Judaism of the first century.[20] Lateness of date, however, is not determinative if there is no evidence of outside influence. And it is hard to imagine that Judaism would so easily agree with such a prominent and vexing doctrine of its main religious adversary if that doctrine had not already been a part of its heritage. Moore accepts these expressions as truly reflecting first-century Jewish thought and as teaching that "the greater part of the laws in the Pentateuch would have no application or relation to anything actual,"[21] but he insists that the period of time in mind was not that of the Messianic Age but of the Age to Come.[22] But such a definite distinction between the two ages on the part of the Jewish teachers is difficult to maintain. It is probable that these terms were both used to designate "the ideal future of Jewish expectation"[23] and were not so sharply differentiated in the predestruction period as they were by the later rabbis.[24] Even Klausner, while arguing that the

[18] Davies' free interpretive paraphrase (*ibid.*, p. 65).

[19] *The Babylonian Talmud* (Soncino), Tractate Sanhedrin, Vol. II, p. 657, n. 9.

[20] Klausner, *Messianic Idea in Israel,* pp. 446-49.

[21] Moore, *Judaism,* Vol. I, p. 272.

[22] *Ibid.,* pp. 269-74.

[23] Davies, *Torah in the Messianic Age,* p. 1, n. 1.

[24] Cf. *Str.-Bil.,* Vol. IV, Exkurs, 29, pp. 815 ff. L. Finkelstein says that the ages were only separated in R. Akiba's time (*Akiba* [Philadelphia: Jewish Publication Society of America, 1962], p. 220).

ideas of the two ages were always differentiated in the minds of the rabbis, admits that the terms were often interchanged in their writings.[25] It seems that the future was not so definitely bisected by the earlier rabbis as some would ask us to believe. Nor was it accepted by early Christianity as so neatly departmentalized. Many investigators of early Jewish thought have accepted these Talmudic statements as expressions of a facet of Judaism's Messianic expectations, which expectations Jesus and Christianity capitalized upon.[26] Further evidence as to this Jewish expectation has come from Qumran, for that literature speaks frankly of enacting laws which were to be in force only until the coming of the Messiah(s).[27]

It therefore seems best to agree with W. D. Davies and Jakob Jocz[28] that while Judaism expected the Law to continue in the days of the Messiah as the expression of the eternal will of God, it also realized that some abrogation and/or alteration would take place within that law as a result of the Messiah's presence. Strack-Billerbeck "probably errs on the side of caution"[29] in stressing the Law's immutability and only mentioning the thought of some type of change. It seems that both elements are present: the affirmation of the Torah on one level and the recognition of some type of abrogation and modification on another.

The impact of the early Church. While we must consider more fully the interaction between Paul and the early Jerusalem church later,[30] one point of that relationship is pertinent here: the impact of the early Church on the formation of the Apostle's thought regarding the abrogation of the Law.

There have been many who have seen the seeds for Paul's teaching

[25] Klausner, *Messianic Idea in Israel,* pp. 408-19.

[26] E.g., H. Loewe, "Pharisaism," *Judaism and Christianity,* Vol. I, ed. W. O. E. Oesterley, pp. 175-77; K. Kohler, "Nomism," *J. E.,* Vol. IX, p. 326.

[27] E.g., 1QS 2.19, 8.9, 9.10-11; CDC 14.18-19. J. T. Milik says regarding the community's thought concerning "the End of Days," which they believed began with the Teacher of Righteousness: "During this period which precedes the End of Times, the laws observed have only a provisional and temporary value (1QS IX. 10f.; CDC XIV. 18f.). Later on, they will be replaced by a new and final Law, proclaimed by the eschatological figure called 'the Interpreter of the Law' " (*Ten Years of Discovery,* p. 114; cf. pp. 126-27).

[28] J. Jocz, *The Jewish People and Jesus Christ* (London: S.P.C.K., 1949), pp. 155-56.

[29] Davies, *Torah in the Messianic Age,* p. 85.

[30] *Infra,* pp. 211-29.

regarding the Law lying in the subsoil of the early Church. Some have insisted that the conviction of the nonessential character of the Law for righteousness was implanted within his soul even in his Judaistic days through "the logical force"[31] of the Christian apologetic and/or the tranquility of the early Christian martyrs.[32] Yet it is probable that Paul had taken up his task of persecution with full knowledge of both the stamina of the martyr and the agony he would necessarily inflict. Fanaticism was not so foreign to the Palestine of his day as to permit him to be unaware of these factors, and it is quite possible that he was prepared for the emotional strain involved in persecuting those he believed to be misguided but dangerous foes. Nor need we suppose that the logic of the Christian preachers greatly affected him.[33] His later references to the scandal of the cross indicate that this was the great stumbling-block for him, which no amount of logic or verbal proof could remove.[34] Only the Damascus experience was powerful enough

[31] G. J. Inglis, "The Problem of St. Paul's Conversion," *E. T.*, Vol. XL, No. 5 (Feb., 1929), p. 229.

[32] E.g., J. Weiss, *Paul and Jesus,* trans. H. J. Chaytor (New York: Harper & Brothers, 1909), pp. 32-37, and *Primitive Christianity,* Vol. I, p. 189; A. S. Peake, *Quintessence of Paulinism,* pp. 16-17; T. R. Glover, *Paul of Tarsus,* pp. 59-60.

[33] Stephen has often been viewed as anticipating the Pauline position and even going beyond it. Such scholars as F. C. Baur (*Paul,* Vol. I, pp. 47-49, 59-60) and W. L. Knox (*St. Paul and the Church of Jerusalem,* pp. 39-47 and 54, n. 24) have portrayed him as almost a pre-Marcionite; while on the other hand H. J. Schoeps (*Theologie und Geschichte des Judenchristentums* [Tübingen: Mohr, 1949], pp. 233-42, though Schoeps takes "Stephen" to be only "eine Deckfigur des Lukas für Jakobus") and M. Simon (*St. Stephen and the Hellenists* [New York: Longmans, Green, 1958] esp. pp. 113-16) interpret him as the predecessor of the Ebionites. But both interpretations seem extreme. While Stephen is more outspoken than the early disciples, is more ready to attribute Israel's rejection of the Christ to a perpetual callousness of heart (whereas Peter and Paul credit it to ignorance), and is ready to give up the strict observance of the Law (see *infra*, pp. 272-76, it seems that his desire was to raise a prophetic voice *within* a Jewish Christianity that still held to the basic observance of the national customs rather than to proclaim a law-free Gospel. Harnack is probably right in saying that "when Stephen was stoned, he died, like Huss, for a cause whose issues he probably did not foresee" (*The Mission and Expansion of Christianity in the First Three Centuries* trans. J. Moffatt [London: Williams & Norgate, 1908], Vol. I, p. 50).

[34] I Cor. 1:23, Gal. 5:11. Note Justin's Dialogue with Trypho, 32 and 89, for a Hebraic Jew's reaction to a death on the cross. A Hellenistic Jew might not have been so offended by such a death, judging from Philo's interpretation of Deut. 21:23: "Cursed is the man who clings to corruptible matter instead of to God" (De Post. Cain. 8 and 17). Klausner's view of the teaching and

to cause him to reconsider the death of Christ. Humanly speaking, he was "immune to the Gospel."[35] Nor can we assume that Paul's thought at this point was greatly influenced by the early Church after his conversion. While it is certain that he learned and adopted much from his Christian predecessors,[36] his strong denial that his *distinctive* message was gained from them[37]—coupled with the early uncertainty of the leaders of both the Jerusalem and the Antioch churches on this matter[38]—indicates that he was not in their debt for his treatment of the Law.

Cullmann has raised a pertinent point in suggesting that possibly the Hellenists of Acts 6:1 and 9:29 (and in some texts 11:20) were "in some way in contact with the kind of Judaism we find in the Qumran texts"—not that they were former Essenes "but that they come from a kind of Judaism close to this group"—and that through them Paul had been influenced by an Essene type of mentality.[39] He goes further in asking whether Paul might even have met and been influenced by members of the Qumran community itself while he and they were residing in Damascus. To this latter question of direct contact, as Cullmann himself acknowledges, a factual answer is impossible; not only because we are uncertain when the Essenes were at Damascus, but also because "we do not know, as a matter of fact, that they were ever at Damascus."[40] To the former suggestion of

---

attitude of Jesus as undermining the national existence and thus frustrating the basis for a Messianic hope is probably a modern example of Rabbi Saul's reaction to the message of Jesus and the apologetic of His followers (cf. *Jesus of Nazareth,* trans. H. Danby [London: Allen & Unwin, 1925], p. 390).

[35] J. Munck, *Paulus und die Heilsgeschichte,* p. 5.

[36] Cf. A. M. Hunter, *Paul and His Predecessors* (London: Nicholson & Watson, 1940).

[37] Gal. 1:11-12; cf. Eph. 3:3.

[38] Gal. 2:11-13.

[39] O. Cullmann, "The Significance of the Qumran Texts for Research into the Beginnings of Christianity," *Scrolls and the N. T.,* ed. K. Stendahl, pp. 18-32.

[40] M. Burrows, *More Light on the Dead Sea Scrolls,* p. 119. On pp. 219-27, Burrows gives a summary of the four views possible regarding the passages in CDC which suggest a migration to "the land of Damascus": (1) that the passages refer to the exiles of Israel in Assyria and Babylonia; (2) that they refer to an actual migration to Damascus; (3) that there was an actual migration to "the land of Damascus," by which is meant the Nabatean kingdom of which Wadi Qumran was a part; and (4) that "the land of Damascus" was the prophetic name for the Qumran retreat. He concludes by saying: "I am still more attracted to the view that what is meant by the migration to the land of

indirect contact and influence, one must, while recognizing the possibility of such influence along other lines, insist that this Essene type of influence upon Paul's doctrine of the Law was at best negligible. And we must judge it so for two reasons.

1. Because "whatever formal elements the Church may or may not have derived from the Qumran sect, if any, it is abundantly clear that they were made subservient to a new and quite different faith, in which Christ had a supreme, unique place to which nothing in the Judaism of Qumran is comparable."[41]

2. Because however much the Qumran group opposed the defilement of the Temple and considered its own "more pure lustrations" more acceptable, it was not in principle opposed to the sacrifices or the worship of the Temple.[42] It was, in fact, much more insistent upon the rigorous observance of the Law than were even the Pharisees. Cullman has been misled by Philo, and he misleads in saying that the "essential and characteristic point common simultaneously to the Qumran sect, the Hellenists, and the Fourth Gospel" is that of "the opposition to Temple worship."[43] The fact that Paul opposed such a mentality as that of Qumran's in his Colossian letter[44] speaks volumes against any positive Essene influence, even though indirect, in the formulation of his doctrine. For while Qumran indeed viewed the keeping of the forms of the Law to be secondary to the inward

---

Damascus is the movement of the group to Qumran itself" (*ibid.*, p. 227); thus agreeing with T. H. Gaster, as does F. M. Cross, Jr., in his revised opinion (*Ancient Library of Qumran*, pp. 59-60).

[41] Burrows, *More Light on the Dead Sea Scrolls*, p. 118.

[42] Note J. M. Baumgarten, "Sacrifice and Worship Among the Jewish Sectarians of the Dead Sea (Qumran) Scrolls," *H. T. R.*, Vol. XLVI, No. 3 (July, 1953), pp. 141-59; F. M. Cross, Jr., *Ancient Library of Qumran*, pp. 74-77; and R. H. Charles, *Ap. and Ps.*, Vol. II, p. 799, n. 3.

[43] Cullmann, "Significance of Qumran Texts," *op cit.*, pp. 27-28. H. Lietzmann has also relied too heavily upon Philo in characterizing the Essene attitude toward sacrifice, *Beginnings of the Christian Church*, p. 42.

[44] The Colossian heresy, this "obscure theosophy" (H. A. A. Kennedy, *Theology of the Epistles*, p. 153) and "hybrid blend of doctrines" (*ibid.*, pp. 155-56), has been seen of late, with the knowledge from Qumran available, to be more compatible to an Essene type of mentality than to any other. Older commentators were just at a disadvantage in not possessing this newer material from the Dead Sea; yet some did recognize the Essene flavor of the heresy at Colosse even then, e.g. Kennedy, *ibid.*, p. 156, and especially J. B. Lightfoot, *Epistle to the Colossians* (London: Macmillan, 1900), pp. 73 ff., and *Galatians*, pp. 326-27.

orientation, the community still considered prescribed performance of the Law as essential for righteousness. And it was at this point that the Apostle differed from the best of Jewish nomism—including Qumran.

There are also three incidents in the life of the Jerusalem church which could be cited as possible precedents to the Pauline teaching: (1) the conversion of Cornelius and its reception among the Jewish Christians;[45] (2) the ministry to the Samaritans, with its possible omission of reference to the temple worship of either Jerusalem or Gerizim;[46] and (3) the official acceptance by the Jerusalem church of their more liberal brethren in the church at Antioch.[47] But, in view of our lack of information regarding their early impact upon Paul and the Apostle's own assertions of independence, one must go beyond the evidence to view these as anything more than confirmatory of the Pauline teaching. It would be perilous to consider them the basis of that thought.

Christ and the Law. The question of Jesus and the Law is of no significance to the study of Pauline thought only if we assume that Paul knew little and cared less regarding the attitude of Jesus toward the Law.[48] But such was not the case. It has been shown quite conclusively that the Apostle knew much concerning the teaching, activity, and Person of the historical Jesus[49]—even to those areas wherein the Lord had not expressed Himself.[50] Whether or not he had ever seen Jesus in His earthly ministry must always remain a question.[51] Certainly he had a vivid impression of Jesus' character and

[45] Acts 10:1—11:18.

[46] Acts 8:4-25.

[47] Acts 11:20 ff.

[48] As, e.g., W. Wrede, *Paulus,* trans. E. Lummis (London: Green, 1907); A. Schweitzer, *Paul and His Interpreters*; D. K. F. Nösgen, *Deissmann's "Paulus" für Theologen und Laien beleuchtet* (Leipzig: Deichert, 1912).

[49] Cf., e.g., Baur, *Paul,* Vol. I, p. 91; Weiss, *Paul and Jesus,* pp. 18-22; Kennedy, *Theology of the Epistles,* pp. 102 ff.; J. S. Stewart, *Man in Christ,* pp. 286-91; A. M. Hunter, *Interpreting Paul's Gospel,* (London: S. C. M. Press, 1954), pp. 56-58, and *Paul and His Predecessors,* pp. 9-12, *passim;* and C. F. D. Moule, "The Use of Parables and Sayings as Illustrative Material in Early Christian Catechesis," *J. T. S.,* Vol. III, Pt. I (Apr., 1952), pp. 75-79.

[50] I Cor. 7:25.

[51] Scholarship has been almost equally divided on the significance of II Cor. 5:16 as evidence that Paul had seen and possibly heard Jesus during one of His visits to Jerusalem. In the affirmative have been such scholars as Weiss (*Paul and Jesus,* pp. 40-56), H. Lietzmann (*II Corinthians,* H.N.T. [Tübingen:

claims even before his conversion, as gathered from Jewish reports and Christian witnesses and as seen through Pharisaic eyes. But without doubt the greatest amount of information regarding the historical Jesus came to him through the testimony of his Christian predecessors. The firsthand accounts of men like Peter and John Mark, the information of Ananias and Barnabas,[52] and the investigations of Luke were all at his disposal. And indeed,

> why should the risen Christ give to His apostle detailed information which could be obtained perfectly well by ordinary inquiry from the eyewitnesses? Such revelation would be unlike the other miracles of the Bible. God does not rend the heaven to reveal what can be learned just as well by ordinary word of mouth.[53]

Nor is it impossible for Paul to have had in hand a *Logia,* i.e., a written "Sayings of Jesus" book.[54] Though he longed to know the power,

---

Mohr, 1923], p. 125), and C. A. A. Scott (*Christianity According to St. Paul,* pp. 11-12). In the negative, Kennedy (*Theology of the Epistles,* p. 49) and A. Deissmann (*Religion of Jesus and the Faith of Paul,* pp. 186-87) are representative. The issue is over the interpretation of *kata sarka*; does it refer to a fleshly kind of Christ or a fleshly kind of knowledge? Deissmann's argument seems to carry conviction and give the preference to the latter view: "If we would refer the words to personal acquaintance with the historical Jesus, the following conclusion, 'now we know Him no more,' would be trivial" (*ibid.,* p. 187). Of course to interpret this passage as having no real relevance to the question at hand does not settle the main issue of whether Paul had ever seen Jesus in His earthly ministry. It still would certainly have been possible regardless of how we interpret II Cor. 5:16. Yet it would also have been possible for both to be in the city without ever meeting. Christ's visits were few, and, except for the last, somewhat unspectacular. And an earnest Rabbi in the time of "Messianic travail" preceding the advent of the Messiah (b. Shab. 118a, b. Sanh. 98b, 1QH 3.3-18) was solely to "engage in study and benevolence" (b. Sanh. 98b; cf. 1QS 9.3-4).

[52] Barnabas too may have been an eyewitness; cf. W. L. Knox, *St. Paul and the Church of Jerusalem,* p. 20, n. 37 and pp. 363-71.

[53] J. G. Machen, *Origin of Paul's Religion,* p. 148; cf. also pp. 71, 76 and 137-48.

[54] The great problem with Rendel Harris' thesis, that there existed "two lost documents of the early Christian propaganda, . . . the first is the 'Collection of the Sayings of Jesus' (Book of Sayings), the second is the 'Book of Testimonies' from the Old Testament" (*Testimonies,* [Cambridge, Eng.: The Univeristy Press, 1916], p. 54), is that of methodology. In his approach there is "das falsche Zurücktragen späterer Verhältnisse in frühere Zeiten" (O. Michel, *Paulus und seine Bibel,* p. 52); i.e., all his evidence necessarily comes from subapostolic and patristic writers, and the results are made valid for the earlier apostolic era. Thus his evidence cannot really support his conclusions. Yet his conclusions are none the less possible. There is no real reason why there could not have been at least a written "Sayings of Jesus" document antedating the

presence and Person of the resurrected Christ,[55] he was not uninterested in His earthly ministry and work. Or, to put it in more modern terminology, while he thrilled to the existential, he did not depreciate the historical. James S. Stewart's words regarding the early Christians are true of Paul as well:

> If they were not always looking towards the past or dwelling in the memory of the Galilean and Judean days, it was not because the earthly ministry of Jesus meant little to them: it was because He had become a vivid and abiding presence. . . . But this does not mean that the knowledge of the historic facts ceased to be a treasured possession.[56]

Paul undoubtedly learned much regarding Jesus and the Law through the witness of the early Church—the same Church which was the source for our present Gospels. And four factors regarding this relation are pertinent here.

First, *Jesus came not to abolish the Law but to establish it.* Some have asserted that Matthew 5:17-19 is a later expression of the followers of James desiring to discount the position of Paul by inventing or misquoting words of Jesus in support of their position.[57] But the fact that Matthew 5:17 has no parallel in the other Synoptics is no necessary indication of its strictly Judaic character. The agreement of Luke 16:17 with Matthew 5:18 regarding the immutibility of the Law shows that this thought need not be assigned only to a record which has been "Judaistically influenced." And the agreement of Matthew 11:13 with Luke 16:16 that the Law and the Prophets were until John indicates that this so-called Jewish gospel is not quite so permeated with such a Judaic intention as has been supposed.[58] Thus,

---

Gospels. Oriental and rabbinically trained memories were indeed retentive, and yet that same type of mind at Qumran found the need to write down the particular interpretations of the community's (possible) historical originator and teacher. The early Church possessed men in the "great company of priests" (Essenes?) and the "Pharisees who believed" whose interests and abilities would lie in just such a collection. And Paul's expectation that his reference to the commands of the Lord regarding marriage (I Cor. 7:10-11) and material support for Christian preachers (I Cor. 9:14) would settle the matters in question seems to imply that even the Corinthians were quite knowledgeable regarding the content of Christ's teaching.

[55] Phil. 3:10.

[56] J. S. Stewart, *Man in Christ*, p. 284.

[57] E.g., A. S. Peake, "Law," *H.D.C.G.*, Vol. II, p. 15; B. H. Streeter, *The Four Gospels* (London: Macmillan, 1924), pp. 254-57.

[58] Cf. Jocz, *Jewish People and Jesus Christ*, p. 25.

though anticipating a later discussion, one must insist that the expression of these verses is not in reality opposed to the Pauline teaching at all.[59] In Matthew 5:17-19, Jesus begins by allaying any fears that His purpose is to abolish the Law. And throughout the couplets presented He is seeking to establish that law by sweeping away such notions as may have been heard and by bringing His hearers back to what was really meant in the ancient expression of the will of God. Many have pointed out that Christ's words were not new in Jewish thought;[60] and indeed, despite Windisch's insistence to the contrary,[61] we need not suppose that either Jesus or Matthew thought they were. What Christ is saying in Matthew 5 is this: Amidst the welter of conflicting interpretations of the Law which you have heard, I, authoritatively, say unto you that this is the correct meaning and interpretation of the will of God.[62] Part of His intention was to bring the Law out of the realm of externalism and casuistry, and thereby to establish its true meaning. And in this it is probable that some of the Pharisees could have commended Him, at least in principle.[63]

Second, *Jesus came to fulfill the Law*. The witness of all the Gospels (not only Matthew's), and of the earliest Christian preaching[64] is that Jesus fulfilled the Torah of God in its broadest definition. And there is no reason to doubt that this was the position of the Church from the earliest times. The Gospels present Jesus Himself as instigating this conviction: He spoke of His own presence,[65] ministry,[66] passion, and

[59] In opposition to the assertion of F. J. Foakes-Jackson and K. Lake that Matt. 5:17-20 "cannot be reconciled with the teaching of Paul" (*Beginnings,* Vol. I, p. 316).

[60] E.g., R. Bultmann, *Jesus and the Word,* trans. L. P. Smith and E. Huntress (London: Nicholson & Watson, 1935), p. 89.

[61] H. Windisch, *Meaning of the Sermon on the Mount,* p. 54.

[62] Cf. W. G. Kümmel, "Jesus und der jüdische Traditionsgedanke," *Z. N. W.*, Vol. XXXIII, Heft 2/3 (1934), pp. 105-30; D. Daube, *N. T. and Rabbinic Judaism,* pp. 55-62.

[63] A Gemara tells of Moses himself being unable to follow an interpretation of his own law in R. Akiba's school, so remote was it from Moses' intent (b. Men. 29b); and R. Joshua b. Hananiah (late first century A.D.) exclaims on a ruling regarding the ceremonial cleanliness of tools: "The Scribes have invented a new thing, and I cannot make answer" (Mish. Kel. 13.7, Mish. Teb. Yom. 4.6).

[64] E.g., Acts 3:18.

[65] Luke 4:21.

[66] Mark 1:15, Luke 24:44.

death[67] as the fulfillment of the Scriptures; He considered it needful to "fulfill all righteousness";[68] and He declared that His purpose in coming was to fulfill the Law.[69] Matthew 5:17 is the most pertinent single passage at this point. Strack-Billerbeck tell us that "Jesus wird statt *plēroun, ḳayyem* gesagt haben."[70] And Jakob Jocz agrees, adding that "*ḳayyem* was and still is in universal usage, and always associated with the fulfilment of the *mizwot*."[71] Then, significantly, Jocz adds: "But if this be the case, then the attitude of Jesus towards the Law is that of humble submission."[72] And that is just the witness of the earliest Christians: "He humbled himself and became obedient unto death, even the death of the cross."[73] He came to fulfill the Law in humble submission.

Yet, thirdly, while the Gospels present Jesus as establishing and fulfilling the Law, they also insist that *He set Himself and His purpose as being of more importance than the Law.* He recognized the legitimate authority of the rabbinic succession,[74] yet He did not seek rabbinic ordination for His ministry but claimed to have a higher authority than that contained in the Law—namely "from heaven."[75] While He violated no specific precept of the written Torah, He refused to allow the Pharisaic principle of separation or the scribal interpretations of ceremonial defilement and the eating of untithed foods to impede His ministry to sinners and Samaritans.[76] And on the principle

[67] Matt. 26:54, Mark 14:49.
[68] Matt. 3:15.
[69] Matt. 5:17.
[70] *Str.-Bil.*, Vol. I, p. 241; cf. Daube, *N. T. and Rabbinic Judaism*, pp. 60-61.
[71] Jocz, *Jewish People and Jesus Christ*, p. 26.
[72] *Ibid.*
[73] Phil. 2:8. Phil. 2:6-11 is probably "one of the first confessions of faith composed for the worship of the primitive community" and was taken over by Paul from the community (O. Cullmann, *The Earliest Christian Confessions*, trans. J. K. S. Reid [London: Lutterworth, 1949], p. 22).
[74] Matt. 23:2-3a. In this, Jesus was in accordance with the Law (cf. Deut. 17:8-13). Cf. the idea of rabbinic succession in Mish. Aboth 1.1.
[75] Matt. 21:23-27, Mark 11:27-33, Luke 20:1-8. Cf. Daube, *N. T. and Rabbinic Judaism*, pp. 217-19, for a treatment of rabbinic ordination and Jesus' claims.
[76] Note Jesus' ministry to those at Levi's feast (Mark 2:15, par.), to the sinful woman who shocked the Pharisaic sense of ceremonial propriety in her anointing of Jesus (Luke 7:37 ff.), to the tax collectors and sinners who drew near to Jesus and possibly ate with Him (Luke 15:1), to Zacchaeus (Luke 19:5 ff.), and to the Samaritans (John 5). Such actions quite naturally raised

that the more important obligation sets aside the demands of the lesser,[77] He asserted that His presence and ministry overrode the sabbatical laws[78] and the fasts.[79] As T. W. Manson says:

For Jesus the thing of first importance, the only thing of *any* importance, is His own Ministry, . . . For Him that is the only thing in the world that comes with an absolute and unqualified claim. Not even the Law can compare with this supreme obligation. That is not to say that Jesus rejected the Law or that He lightly disregarded any of its commands and prohibitions. It does mean that He did not hesitate to break through its restrictions in the interest of His own task.[80]

Still there is a fourth point to be noted, for in setting Himself over the Law *Jesus anticipated its change*. While His interest and action in reaching the sinner hinted at some type of alteration, His speech likewise foreshadowed a change. Mark 7:14-23 is the clearest example of an enigmatic statement that was only later understood. Here Jesus is recorded as saying: "There is nothing from without the man that going into him can defile him; but the things which proceed out of the man are those that defile the man." The account then tells how

---

in Pharisaic minds the objection: He befriends the *am haarez*! (Mark 2:16, par.; Matt. 11:19, Luke 7:34; Luke 7:39; Luke 15:2; Luke 19:7). In all of these contacts "Jesus probably ate no prohibited foods—custom and ordinary courtesy to a great religious teacher would take care of that—but he did run the constant risk of ceremonial defilement and of eating untithed foods" (B. H. Branscomb, *Jesus and the Law of Moses* [London: Hodder & Stoughton, 1930], p. 135). Thus He ignored the Pharisaic principle that "one does not stay as guest with an *am haarez*" (Mish. Dem. 2.2-3. Tos. Dem. 2.2) and probably broke rabbinic rulings in (1) eating untithed food in the house of an *am haarez* (Tos. Dem. 2.2), (2) allowing His disciples to buy food in a Samaritan village (Mish. Dem. 2.3), and (3) talking with the Samaritan woman and actually drinking from her vessel (Mish. Kel. 1.1 ff.), since "the daughters of the Samaritans are menstruants from their cradle" (Mish. Nid. 4.1). Cf. Daube, *N. T. and Rabbinic Judaism*, pp. 373-74.

[77] E.g., the Sabbath may be broken for the rite of circumcision, "as the essence of the covenant lay in the performance of the ceremony on the eighth day" (Loewe, "Pharisaism," *op. cit.*, p. 169); and defensive warfare takes precedence over the observance of the Sabbath (Antiq. XII. 6. 2; XIII. 1. 3; XIV. 4. 2-3; War I. 7. 3).

[78] Note Jesus' healings on the Sabbath (Mark 3:1-6, par.; Luke 13:10-17; 14:1-6; John 5:1 ff., 7:23, 9:1 ff.) and the plucking of the grain (Mark 2:23-28, par.).

[79] Mark 2:18-20, par.

[80] T. W. Manson, "Jesus, Paul, and the Law," *Judaism and Christianity*, Vol. III, ed. E. I. J. Rosenthal, p. 129.

the disciples at the time were perplexed at such a saying. The fact that it was only later understood by the early Church and considered to be a strong anticipatory hint regarding the abrogation of the food laws is indicated by the interjection of the Gospel writer: *katharizōn panta ta brōmata*—"making clean all foods."[81] There is a spirit in Jesus' teaching which suggests something entirely new. "He bids men come to Him, learn of Him, listen to Him, obey Him, as if all other authority was at an end."[82] "He speaks of His own approaching death as if it had some strange and unique importance in the dealings of God with men."[83] He speaks of new cloth being quite incompatible with the old,[84] new wine as not to be contained by old skins,[85] "the law and the prophets" being until John the Baptist,[86] the new covenant in His blood,[87] "*my* yoke"[88] and "*my* words."[89] Thus, though He spoke of His purpose as being to establish the Law and to fulfill it, Jesus none the less considered His person and work to be of a more vital nature than that of the Law—and on this basis anticipated its alteration.

This, then, is what Paul learned of Jesus and the Law through the accounts mediated by the early Church: that Jesus established the Law, fulfilled it and—almost paradoxically, it might seem—anticipated its change.

The Damascus encounter. But it was not the Jewish expectation or any contemplation of the Jesus of history that was the vital and

[81] Mark 7:19. There is no real reason, apart from theological predisposition, for considering this exclamation a gloss or mistranslation. Cf. Branscomb, *Jesus and the Law of Moses,* p. 90, n. 36, for a sane evaluation of the problem.

[82] W. F. Lofthouse, "The Old Testament and Christianity," *Record and Revelation,* ed. H. W. Robinson, p. 467.

[83] *Ibid.*, p. 466.

[84] Mark 2:21, par.

[85] Mark 2:22, par. W. L. Knox says of these two verses: "The thought of the Gospel as a revolutionary novelty appears to belong to the earliest stratum of the N.T." (*St. Paul and the Church of the Gentiles,* p. 98).

[86] Matt. 11:13; Luke 16:16.

[87] Accepting the majority reading in Luke 22:20 and that of D and C in Matt. 26:28. Cf. Paul's understanding of Jesus' words at this point in I Cor. 11:25; also J. Denney's defence of the phrase "new covenant" as being on the lips of Jesus, *The Christian Doctrine of Reconciliation* (London: Hodder & Stoughton, 1917), p. 140.

[88] Matt. 11:29-30, thus implying "a special 'yoke' in contrast to that of the Law as understood" (A. D. Nock, *St. Paul,* p. 39, n. 1). See, e.g., Ps. Sol. 7.8 and Baruch 41.3 for the phrase "yoke of the law" in its Jewish context.

[89] Mark 13:31, par.

formative element in Paul's thought regarding the Law. The expectation of Judaism was indeed a pre-stage in his thought, and the anticipation of Jesus was instructive for it. But the conversion experience "was far and away the most vital and formative influence of Paul's life."[90] "Das paulinische Nein zum Gesetz entstammt seinem Ja zu dem in Jesus Christus Geschehenen, nicht einer rationalen Kritik oder missionarischen Taktik."[91] Like the first disciples, who began from their Easter experience and whose thought was both a recollection and an anticipation from the standpoint of that historical and existential occasion, Paul looked back on his former hopes and the ministry of Jesus in the light of the Christ-encounter. While it is true that portions of his thought have a rabbinic tone, a prophetic ring, and/or carry overtones of the teaching of Jesus and the early Church, yet the creative element of his doctrine was born beside the Damascus road. For him, "futuristic eschatology" had become to a large extent "realized eschatology"[92]—or, better yet, inaugurated eschatology. The straining of the ancient faith had suddenly given way to fulfillment; D-Day had arrived with its assured promise of V-Day.[93] While previous and received ideas helped him to clarify and express his thought, the vital element in his Christian thinking must be acknowledged to be "through revelation of Jesus Christ."[94]

Albert Schweitzer has accused those who take the Damascus encounter as formative in Paul's life and thought of claiming "a specially favourable position" and escaping the tasks of careful scholarship by retreating into an area "which of course eludes analysis."[95] Yet, whether we explain that experience as a purely psychological experience through which God worked[96] or a prophetic revelation comparable to that of the prophets of old,[97] we must acknowledge that

[90] J. S. Stewart, *Man in Christ,* p. 82.

[91] W. Gutbrod, "Nomos," *Theologisches Wörterbuch zum Neuen Testament,* ed. G. Kittel (Stuttgart: Kohlhammer, 1935), Vol. IV, p. 1067.

[92] C. H. Dodd's terminology; see *The Apostolic Preaching and Its Developments* (London: Hodder & Stoughton, 1936), p. 85 and *passim.*

[93] O. Cullman's analogy; see *Christ and Time,* trans. F. V. Filson (London: S. C. M. Press, 1951), pp. 84-85, *passim.*

[94] Gal. 1:12.

[95] Schweitzer, *Paul and His Interpreters,* p. 71.

[96] As, e.g., Weiss, *Paul and Jesus,* pp. 28-37; W. L. Knox, *St. Paul,* pp. 37-38.

[97] As, e.g., Machen, *Origin of Paul's Religion,* pp. 60-68; Munck, *Paulus und die Heilsgeschichte,* pp. 22-25.

Paul himself believed he had truly seen the Lord,[98] and believed this experience to have been the determinative factor in his whole life. If we are to understand the Apostle, we must at least seriously consider what he explicitly states was formative in his experience before we cast it aside for an alternative. While the thought of a revelational quality in the Damascus experience may irk our modern naturalistic orientation, the alternatives have lacked conviction.[99] We are brought back to the Apostle's assertion and must take it seriously if we are to understand his thought aright.

CHRIST THE END OF THE LAW

Paul's teaching regarding the Law is concisely expressed in Romans 10:4: "For Christ is the end of the law in its connection with righteousness to all who believe" (*telos gar nomou Christos eis dikaiosunēn panti tō pisteuonti*). In this statement, the Apostle is not thinking primarily of the general qualitative idea of law or even of the principle of legality; though, of course, such concepts are never unrelated to the main point of his thought. Rather, the context shows that here he is specifically considering the Mosaic Law and declaring that it has been completed and abrogated by Christ on a specific level. It is with that thought of the Law's completion and abrogation that we must deal in the following pages.

The abrogation of the Law "in its connection with righteousness." There is one phrase in the passage which has been grossly ignored. Since it has not fitted in with the common misconception that Paul made a distinction between the moral and the ceremonial aspects of the Law, viewing the latter as fulfilled and ended but the former as continuing, it has been treated as though it were of no real pertinence in the understanding of the Apostle's doctrine of law. But in reality the expression *eis dikaiosunēn* serves to unlock Paul's thought. While he

[98] I Cor. 9:1. Cf. G. G. Findlay, *I Corinthians,* E. G. T., ed. W. Robertson Nicoll (Grand Rapids: Eerdmans, 1952 repr.), Vol. II, p. 845, on the use of *heoraka.*

[99] In regard to the "psychological school," note W. G. Kümmel's insistence that in view of its inadequacies we must take Paul's statements seriously (*Römer 7 und die Bekehrung des Paulus,* pp. 139-60); regarding the "consistent eschatology" position, note the criticism of J. Weiss by Michel (*Paulus und seine Bibel,* pp. 31-33) and that of Schweitzer by Cullmann (*Christ and Time,* p. 85) and W. D. Davies (*Paul and Rabbinic Judaism,* p. 290).

could speak of the moral and ceremonial aspects of the Law separately, there is no suggestion that he viewed them as possessing separate validity or as being possible to separate. There is no reason to doubt that he viewed the Law, as did Judaism, as one indivisible whole. Yet there are many indications that he did distinguish between the two purposes of the Law in the Old Covenant; i.e., between "the Law as the standard and judgment of God" and "the Law as contractual obligation"—between "the standard of God" and "the covenant of works."[100] It is that latter purpose that the Apostle has in mind when he says: Christ is the end of the Law "unto righteousness" (ASV), "for righteousness" (AV), or "in its connection with righteousness."[101]

Paul makes much of the change that has taken place in the purpose of the Law with the coming of Christ in such contrasts as "before" (*pro de*) and "but now" (*nun de* or *nuni de*).[102] Before, Israel had been "kept under" the contractual obligation of the Law; "but now" we are discharged from that contractual obligation which held us captive.[103] Righteousness is "no longer" (*ouketi*) to be associated with works[104] in that God has done something new in manifesting His righteousness "apart from the law" (*chōris nomou*).[105] Formerly such righteousness had been kept hidden, "but now" it has been disclosed to His saints.[106] The Apostle pictures what was preparatory as completed by what was anticipated,[107] what was meant to be temporary

[100] C. A. A. Scott has noted this same distinction of purpose in Paul's view of the Law by the terms "the contents of the Law" and "the Law as a system" (*Christianity According to St. Paul,* p. 42), the latter being terminated in Christ. His opening words on this subject are pertinent: "It is . . . important to observe in what sense Paul understood that Christ was the end of the Law, and of law—in what sense it had ceased to function in the case of believers. It is mainly on a misapprehension of this that the charges of inconsistency rest which have been freely and frequently levelled at the Apostle" (*ibid.,* p. 41).

[101] Or, as Kennedy translated it, "with a view to righteousness" (*Theology of the Epistles,* p. 129). In shuffling this phrase to the end of the sentence, RSV and Moffatt's translation have broken the connection between *nomou* and *eis dikaiosunēn,* and have thus lost the significance of Paul's statement.

[102] E.g., Gal. 3:23; Rom. 3:21, 7:6, 16:26; Col. 1:26.

[103] Rom. 7:6.

[104] Rom. 11:6.

[105] Rom. 3:21.

[106] Rom. 16:26; Col. 1:26; Eph. 3:5.

[107] Gal. 3:24-25: "So then the law was our pedagogue to lead us unto Christ, . . . but with the coming of the faith we are no longer under a pedagogue." Cf. Gal. 4:1-7.

being set aside for what is lasting,[108] what was mediated as resolved into what is immediate.[109] The Law in its contractual obligation—i.e., "in its connection with righteousness" (*eis dikaiosunēn*)—has been abrogated. It has died,[110] been "torn down."[111] Not because it has evolved into something new,[112] but because God has established a new

[108] Gal. 3:19a: "It was *added until*" (*prosetethē, achris*). Note also Paul's contrast between the fading and the permanent in II Cor. 3:7-13.

[109] Gal. 3:19b: "Ordained through angels, in the hand of a mediator." In Deut. 33:2 (LXX), Ps. 68:17, Antiq. XV. 5. 3, Jubilees 1:27 ff., Acts 7:38, 53, Heb. 2:2, and many Talmudic passages, the presence of angels in the giving of the Law is regarded as an indication of the Law's excellence (cf. H. St. J. Thackeray, *Relation of St. Paul to Contemporary Jewish Thought,* pp. 161-63, Lightfoot, *Galations,* p. 145, *Str.-Bil.,* Vol. III, p. 556). But in the light of God's immediate revelation in Jesus Christ, Paul uses this tradition of angelic mediation to depreciate the Law; cf. Gal. 4:1-11 and Col. 2:8-23. Whatever opposition to the mediation of the Law by angels appears in the Talmud must be explained as a later reaction to this Pauline depreciation (cf. Daube, *N. T. and Rabbinic Judaism,* pp. 325-26; also W. D. Davies, "A Note on Josephus, Antiquities 15:136," *H. T. R.,* Vol. XLVII, No. 3 [July, 1954], p. 140, n.).

[110] Most commentators on Rom. 7:1-6 have argued that "the illustration is not happy, for the law does not die," but that Paul's general message of Christian freedom from the Law is clear in any case (Wm. Manson, "Notes on the Argument of Romans," *op. cit.,* pp. 160-61). The confusion has been attributed to the Apostle's lack of "the gift for sustained illustration of ideas through concrete images" (C. H. Dodd, *Romans,* M.N.T.C, p. 103) or a verbal confusion that has entered as a result of Paul's dictation (C. Gore, *Romans,* Vol. I, p. 240). Bo Reicke, however, has pointed out that instead of Paul having one idea in mind which he blunderingly expresses in two ways, "two different motifs become blended in the argument": the Law that has died to the Christian and the Christian who has died to the Law ("The Law and This World According to Paul," *J. B. L.,* Vol. LXX, Pt. IV [Dec., 1951] p. 267). Reicke adds: "When the Law in the first figure is said to be dead, it is, in the context of the history of redemption, precisely the same as that the sinful body is dead" (*ibid.*). Luther saw this dual emphasis in Paul, and exclaimed: "The law therefore is bound, dead and crucified unto me, and I again am bound, dead and crucified unto it" (*Galatians,* trans. P. S. Watson [London: Clarke, 1953], p. 167 on Gal. 2:20).

[111] Gal. 2:18. Luther said regarding the Mosaic Law: "For Christ, toward whom this law was directed, has clean abolished it by His Passion and Resurrection; He slew it and buried it forever, rent the veil of the Temple in twain, and then broke and destroyed Jerusalem, with priesthood, princedom, law, and everything" ("On the Councils and the Churches," *Works of Martin Luther,* Vol. V, trans. C. M. Jacobs [Philadelphia: Holman, 1916], p. 184).

[112] R. Bultmann: "The modern theory of evolution is far from his thoughts" ("Christ the End of the Law," *Essays,* p. 36). Harnack: For Paul, "no part of the law had been depreciated in value by any noiseless, disintegrating influence of time or circumstance; on the contrary, the law remained valid and operative in all its provisions. It could not be abrogated save by him who had ordained it—i.e., by God himself. Nor could even God abolish it save by affirming at the

covenant[113] wherein "commandments" and "ordinances" are ended[114] and the distinction between Israel under contract and the Gentiles outside the covenant is abrogated.[115] It is because Christ in His Person and work has terminated the contractual purpose of the Law that Paul expected his placarding of Christ Jesus to settle once and for all this question of whether righteousness in the New Covenant is "through the Law" or "in Christ."[116] "It is finished" is just as much a cry of Paul as of Christ.[117]

Yet we must be careful to note that in all of the Pauline expressions there is no hint that the Law as the standard and judgment of God is also ended. In fact, his use of the Law in that manner in Romans 2 argues against such a position. It is on a specific level, i.e., as the expression of the contractual obligation instituted in the Old Covenant and thus in its direct association with righteousness, that the Law had come to its complete fulfillment and terminus. This is not to say that it has ceased as the judgment of God to reveal sin and human rebellion to the ungodly and to the Christian who would presume upon his privileged position, nor that its obligations have been met and thus ended for any except Christ and those who are His. It is as Luther expressed it:

> Not that the law is utterly taken away: nay, it remaineth, liveth, and reigneth still in the wicked. But the godly man is dead unto the law like as he is dead unto sin, the devil, death, and hell: which notwithstanding do still remain, and the world with all the wicked shall still abide in them.[118]

The abrogation of the Law because fulfilled by Christ. Basic to Paul's teaching regarding the abrogation of the Law in its contractual aspect,

---

same time its rights—i.e., he must abolish it just by providing for its fulfillment. And this was what actually took place. By the death and resurrection of Jesus Christ, God's Son, upon the cross, the law was at once fulfilled and abolished" (*Mission and Expansion of Christianity,* Vol. I, p. 54).

[113] I Cor. 11:25; II Cor. 3:6.

[114] Eph. 2:15.

[115] Eph. 2:11-18.

[116] Gal. 3:1.

[117] John 19:30. Cf. John 4:34, 17:4; Rom. 10:4; Gal. 3:13.

[118] Luther, *Galatians,* p. 159 on Gal. 2:19. G. Bornkamm argues that as there is a new creation in Christ without the old passing away, so there is a new law in Christ freeing us from the old Law without the old passing away; thus, "wie es für die Schöpfung gilt, so auch für das Gesetz" (*Gesetz und Schöpfung im Neuen Testament* [Tübingen: Mohr, 1934], p. 26).

and thus in its association with righteousness, is his realization that the antagonism between God and man has been removed and the contractual obligation of the Law has been fulfilled by Christ. Jesus Christ in His death and in His life, in His sacrifice and in His obedience, has taken both the curse and the requirements of the Law unto Himself. And in so doing, He has abrogated both the curse and the contract in both His act and His life of faithfulness.

Certainly the sacrifice of Christ as redeeming from the curse of the Law and as reconciling to the Father is prominent in the Apostle's thought.[119] In Galatians, Christ came under (*hupo*) the Law[120] in order to redeem those who were under (*hupo*) the Law[121]—and thus under (*hupo*) a curse[122]—from (*ek*) the curse of the Law[123] by becoming a curse for (*huper*) us.[124] In Colossians, Christ has "cancelled the bond which stood against us . . . nailing it to the cross"[125] and has reconciled the believer to God "in the body of his flesh through death."[126] And the other Pauline letters contain similar expressions.[127] But the act of Calvary is not the whole story. Paul does not proclaim a salvation that only wipes out the curse of the Law, presenting the individual to God as neutral. He insists that Christ has also fulfilled the legal demands of the contractual obligation established in the Old Covenant, thus presenting before the Father a positive righteousness for all of those who are "in Him."

The thought of the obedience of Christ, while included in that of the sacrifice of Christ,[128] is not exhausted in the consideration of that act. The declared purpose of Jesus included a fulfilling of the Law, and Paul picks up that theme in Romans 5:18-19, contrasting the disobedience of Adam with the obedience of Christ. Not only was "one man's trespass" countered by "one man's act," but "one man's disobedience" was rectified by "one man's obedience." Christ stood in

[119] Cf. J. Denney, *The Death of Christ* (London: Hodder & Stoughton, 1903), *passim*; *Christian Doctrine of Reconciliation,* pp. 233-85.
[120] Gal. 4:4.
[121] Gal. 4:5.
[122] Gal. 3:10.
[123] Gal. 3:13.
[124] Gal. 3:13.
[125] Col. 2:14.
[126] Col. 1:22.
[127] E.g., Rom. 3:24, 4:25, 5:6-10; I Cor. 5:7; Eph. 1:7, 2:13.
[128] E.g., "obedient unto death, even the death of a cross" (Phil. 2:8).

the place of humble submission and complete obedience to the Law, as Adam and all his descendants had not done. "He was the only one who completely and genuinely stood in that place; He was *the* Jew."[129]

Likewise, Paul's thought seems to run along this line in his use of *pisteōs Iēsou Christou.* The phrase *dia pisteōs Iēsou Christou* has always been a thorn in the flesh for the interpreter. The generally accepted view is that it is an objective genitive, meaning "through faith in Jesus Christ."[130] A few have considered it a subjective genitive, "through the faith of Jesus Christ."[131] Others insist that it is impossible in this case to separate the objective from the subjective; that righteousness and justification must always be by both "the faith of Jesus Christ" and "faith in Jesus Christ." Thus Deissmann insisted that a new use of the genitive must be designated here: "the 'genitive of fellowship' or the 'Mystical genitive'."[132] But a fourth position has arisen of late. In the increasing consciousness that while the Apostle spoke and wrote Greek his words were always colored by their Hebrew association, exegetes are beginning to find Paul's use of *pistis* more influenced by the Hebrew *emunah* than was previously suspected. A. G. Hebert argues that just as *emunah* meant both "faithfulness" and "faith," so Paul used "the one word *pistis* for the two things, Divine faithfulness and human faith."[133] He points out that the Hebrew idea of faithfulness often emerges in the Septuagint's use of *pistis,*[134] and that there is no disagreement as to the fact that Paul and other New Testament writers used the word elsewhere in this Hebrew sense.[135] He also notes that in three passages where *dia pisteōs Iēsou*

[129] K. Barth, *Christ and Adam,* trans. T. A. Smail (Edinburgh: Oliver & Boyd, 1956), p. 33.

[130] E.g., W. Sanday and A. C. Headlam, *Romans,* I.C.C., p. 83.

[131] E.g., J Haussleiter, *Der Glaube Jesu Christi und der christliche Glaube* (Leipzig: Dörffling & Franke, 1891), and "Was versteht Paulus unter christlichen Glauben," *Theologische Abhandlungen Hermann Cremer dargebracht* (Gütersloh: Bertelsmann, 1895), pp. 159-81.

[132] A. Deissmann, *Paul,* pp. 162-63; *Religion of Jesus and Faith of Paul,* pp. 177-78. Cf. J. S. Stewart, *Man in Christ,* pp. 182-83.

[133] A. G. Hebert, " 'Faithfulness' and 'Faith'," *Theology,* Vol. LVIII, No. 424 (Oct., 1955), p. 376.

[134] E.g., Ps. 36:5-7; Isa. 28:16; Hab. 2:4.

[135] Rom. 3:3: "The *pistis* of God"; I Cor. 1:9, 10:13: "God is *pistis*"; I Thess. 5:24: "*Pistis* is the one who calls you"; II Thess. 3:3: "But the Lord is *pistis.*" Cf. Heb. 2:17, 3:2; I John 1:9; Rev. 1:5, 3:14, 19:11.

Christou is used, the following phrase "to all who believe" is simply redundant if the objective genitive interpretation of "through faith in Jesus Christ" is accepted.[136] Thus he suggests that this difficult expression *pisteōs Iēsou Christou* should be translated "the faithfulness of Jesus Christ," understanding that expression to mean "God's faithfulness revealed to him."[137] K. Barth and T. F. Torrance have likewise interpreted the expression as referring to divine faithfulness; Barth translating it "God's faithfulness in Jesus Christ"[138] and Torrance as "the faithfulness of Jesus Christ."[139] Considering Paul's background, his other uses of *pistis* in this sense, and the redundant nature of three passages if this position is not accepted, the translation "the faithfulness of Jesus Christ" for certain occurrences of this phrase is most convincing. There is no real reason for interpreting it as "God's faithfulness revealed to Jesus Christ" or "in Jesus Christ." The Christology of Paul makes the expression "the faithfulness of Jesus Christ" most natural.

That is not to say that in every Pauline use of *pistis* the idea of divine faithfulness is to be understood. Certainly *pistis* and *pisteuō* often carry the idea of human faith, trust, and committal.[140] But it is to advocate that in the following passages, at least, the expression *pisteōs Iēsou Christou* is best understood as "the faithfulness of Jesus Christ":

1. Romans 3:22. "The righteousness of God [is manifested] through the faithfulness of Jesus Christ (*dia pisteōs Iēsou Christou*) to all who believe."

2. Galatians 2:16. "Knowing that a man is not justified by the works of the law but by the faithfulness of Christ Jesus (*dia pisteōs Christou Iēsou*), even we have believed in Jesus Christ in order to be justified on the basis of the faithfulness of Christ (*ek pisteōs Christou*)."

[136] Rom. 3:22; Gal. 3:22; and Phil. 3:9.

[137] Hebert, " 'Faithfulness' and 'Faith'," *op. cit.*, p. 373.

[138] K. Barth, *The Epistle to the Romans,* trans. E. C. Hoskyns (London: Oxford University Press, 1933), p. 96.

[139] T. F. Torrance, "One Aspect of the Biblical Conception of Faith," *E. T.*, Vol. LXVIII, No. 4 (Jan., 1957), pp. 111-14.

[140] E.g., Rom. 4:14, 16; I Cor. 15:14, 17; II Cor. 1:24. The context of Gal. 3:11 indicates that Paul understood the *ek pisteōs* of Hab. 2:4 to refer to human trust and reliance, not human faithfulness or even the divine faithfulness implied in the LXX reading of *ek pisteōs mou.* The "through faith" of the RSV is an appropriate translation in Rom. 1:17 and Gal. 3:11.

3. Galatians 3:22. "The scripture has consigned all things under sin in order that the promise which is based upon the faithfulness of Jesus Christ (*ek pisteōs Iēsou Christou*) might be given to those who believe."

4. Philippians 3:9. ". . . not having my own righteousness which is of the law but that which is through the faithfulness of Christ (*dia pisteōs Christou*), the righteousness of God which depends upon faith."

5. Ephesians 3:12. The eternal purpose of God has been realized in Christ Jesus our Lord "in whom we have boldness and confidence of access through his faithfulness" (*dia tēs pisteōs autou*).

This may also be the idea behind the interjection of II Timothy 3:15: *dia pisteōs tēs en Christō Iēsou.*

Thus in II Corinthians 1:20 Paul presents Christ as not only the "Yes" from God, but also as our "Amen" to God. T. F. Torrance has well expressed it in saying: "Jesus Christ is thus not only the incarnation of the Divine *pistis,* but He is the embodiment and actualization of man's *pistis* in covenant with God. He is not only the Righteousness of God, but the embodiment and actualization of our human righteousness before God."[141] It is the faithfulness and obedience of Christ to the contractual obligation of the Law in His life and in His death, as well as His sacrifice in the incarnation and Calvary experience, that is proclaimed as perfectly executed in the triumphant cry "It is finished." It is through both the sacrifice and the obedience of Christ that reconciliation has been made possible; through both His death and His life.[142] To Him (and to His) have all the promises been made,[143] by Him have all the conditions been met, and in Him lies the fulfillment of the hopes and strivings of Israel—and of all men. In the faithfulness of Christ we find

[141] Torrance, "One Aspect," *op. cit.*, p. 113.

[142] Rom. 5:10: "If . . . we were reconciled to God through the death of his son, much more . . . shall we be saved in his life." "His life" certainly refers to His risen life (as Barth insists, *Christ and Adam,* p. 2), but we need not consider its reference to be exclusively such. Paul's statement seems broader, including (1) His earthly life of obedience, (2) His risen life of presenting that obedience to the Father on behalf of the believer, and (3) His risen life of making actual that obedience in the earthly life of every believer.

[143] The promises were made to Abraham's seed, i.e., to Christ (Gal. 3:16) and those that are Christ's (Gal. 3:29); cf. Gal. 3:22. Cf. C. A. A. Scott, *Christianity According to St. Paul,* pp. 154-55, regarding the application of the concept of solidarity at this point.

the supreme difference between the Old Testament and the New Testament. Like the Old Testament, the New Testament also lays emphasis upon the faithfulness of God, and requires from man a corresponding faithfulness. But in the gospel the steadfast faithfulness of God has achieved its end in righteousness and truth in Jesus Christ, for in Him it has been actualized as Truth, and is fulfilled in our midst.[144]

That which the contractual obligation of the Law demanded, Christ has provided. He stood for mankind in offering the perfect righteousness, so that all who stand in Him stand before the Father not in their own righteousness but as robed in His righteousness. "It is the voice of God, no less than that of the sinner, which says, 'Thou, O Christ, art all I want; more than all in Thee I find.' "[145] And it is because in His sacrifice He redeemed from the curse of the Law *and* in His perfect obedience He fulfilled the obligations of the Law that Paul can say, "Christ is the end of the law in its connection with righteousness." The sacrifice and the obedience of Christ are corollaries which can never truly be separated.

The abrogation of the Law "to all who believe." But there is yet another element in that key expression of Romans 10:4 which must be noted. Not only is the statement Christologically orientated, but Paul also asserts the element of conditional application. He speaks in Romans 3:22 of "the righteousness of God" which has been manifested "through the faithfulness of Jesus Christ," and adds, "unto all them that believe." In Galatians 3:22 "the promise which is based upon the faithfulness of Jesus Christ" is given "to those who believe." Philippians 3:9 speaks of "the righteousness of God" "which is through the faithfulness of Christ" and "which depends upon faith." And so Paul says in Romans 10:4 that "Christ is the end of the law in its connection with righteousness to all who believe" (*panti tō pisteuonti*). As James Denney said:

The mere existence of Christ does not constitute the new humanity. It is only constituted as men in faith freely identify themselves with Him.[146]

And again:

To emphasize the freeness of forgiveness is not to deny that it has other characteristics. It is not unconditional. God does not forgive the im-

[144] Torrance, "One Aspect," *op. cit.*, p. 113.
[145] Denney, *Christian Doctrine of Reconciliation*, pp. 162, 235, 301.
[146] *Ibid.*, p. 305.

penitent, who do not wish nor ask to be forgiven. He cannot do so, for forgiveness, like all spiritual things, cannot be given unless it is taken, and it can only be taken by a penitent and surrendered soul.[147]

Thus Romans 10:4 "must not be construed as an ordinary historical judgment, to the effect that the law ceased to function at a given point in time. The statement about the *telos* of the law applies only to those who have through Christ been made sharers in the righteousness of the law. Otherwise, outside of the realm of faith, the law still rules."[148]

RIGHTEOUSNESS IN THE NEW COVENANT

The thought of Paul goes beyond that of the canonical prophets, the noncanonical pneumatics, and even the explicit teaching of Jesus. But it is based upon, and in direct succession to, the prophetical spirit and the intention and work of Christ. While the prophets and pneumatics of the Old Covenant did advocate a reacting nomism, they also denounced a merely acting legalism—and anticipated a future time when God's relationship with man would take on a more intimate character. While Jesus' explicit utterances cannot be shown to go further than likewise denouncing a mere legalism and emphasizing the element of trust in the fulfillment of the contractual relationship, there is in His words and attitudes the veiled foreshadowing of—and in His sacrifice and obedience the basis for—the later decisive break with the Law.[149] The maxim *ex nihilo nihil fit* remains true, for, as Klausner insisted, "had not Jesus' teaching contained a kernel of opposition to Judaism, Paul could never *in the name of Jesus* have set aside the ceremonial laws, and broken through the barriers of national Judaism. There can be no doubt that in Jesus Paul found justifying support."[150] But, despite the importance of the note of anticipation in the manner and instruction of his Lord, it was the supreme act of sacrifice and obedience on the cross which "inevitably put the teaching into a

[147] *Ibid.*, pp. 132-33.

[148] A. Nygren, *Romans*, p. 380.

[149] Cf. J. S. Stewart, *Man in Christ*, pp. 291-93; J.-L. Leuba, "Law: N. T.," *Vocabulary of the Bible*, ed. J.-J. von Allmen, trans. Allcock *et al.* (London: Lutterworth, 1958), pp. 228-30.

[150] Klausner, *Jesus of Nazareth*, p. 369; cf. pp. 275-76, 369-71.

secondary place. The deed of Jesus was mightier than His word."[151] And in that "the finished work of Christ" was the foundation stone upon which the Apostle built his thought regarding righteousness in the New Covenant, the dictum is true: "St. Paul begins where the earthly life of Jesus ends."[152] It is in view of the person and work of Christ that Paul rejected nomism as well as legalism, both being now classed as forms of legality; "for in Christ Jesus neither circumcision nor uncircumcision is of any avail, but faith working through love."[153] It is "in Him" that "we have redemption"[154] and "have come to fullness of life."[155]

The believer in the New Covenant ceases to regard righteousness in terms of law at all. He is "neither condemned nor justified by it. He hopes for nothing from the law, and fears nothing. For him the law is completely eliminated, as far as righteousness and freedom, condemnation and the wrath of God are concerned."[156] He has found that "the gospel of Christ is *the very righteousness of God.*"[157] Or, as Luther has expressed it, he has found that "no external thing, whatsoever it be, has any influence whatever in producing Christian righteousness or liberty . . . One thing and one only is necessary for Christian life, righteousness and liberty. That one thing is the most holy Word of God, the Gospel of Christ."[158]

Since Christ has brought to an end the possibility of a valid nomistic piety, even Jewish nomism now is relegated to the position of one of "the elements (*ta stoicheia*) of the world."[159] Therefore any return to

[151] Peake, *Quintessence of Paulinism,* p. 12.

[152] Cf. W. Sanday, "Paul," *H.D.C.G.,* Vol. II, p. 891.

[153] Gal. 5:6. In the light of Christ's presence, "Paulus nennt auch den Kult der Juden einen Dienst der *sarx*" (Bornkamm, *Gesetz und Schöpfung,* p. 18).

[154] Eph. 1:7.

[155] Col. 2:10.

[156] Nygren, *Romans,* pp. 310-11.

[157] *Ibid.,* p. 303.

[158] M. Luther, "A Treatise on Christian Liberty," *Works of Martin Luther,* Vol. II, trans. W. A. Lambert, pp. 313-14.

[159] Whether *stoicheia* refers to (1) rudimentary instruction, (2) the physical elements of the earth, and, especially, the heavenly bodies, (3) the spirits over these physical elements and heavenly bodies, or (4) the angels that stood as executors of the Law, the intimate association of the Law with the *stoicheia* (note that both are likened to guardians, Gal. 3:24, cf. Gal. 4:2-3; both stand in contrast to Christ, Gal. 3:1 ff., cf. Col. 2:8; we have died to both, Rom. 7:4-6, cf. Col. 2:20; we were slaves to both, Gal. 4:21-31, cf. Gal. 4:3, 9)

the Law for either justification or, as in the case of the Galatians, for sanctification is a return to "the weak and beggarly elements"[160] and a renunciation of Christ.[161] It is to assert that the sacrifice and obedience of Christ are not sufficient, but are only the first step to or supplementary in the attainment of righteousness. But as righteousness in the New Covenant is not gained by the Law, neither is it aided or even necessarily to be expressed by the forms of the Law. The illustration of Luther at this point is entirely within the Pauline framework of thought: he who would gain righteousness by faith *and* works is as "the dog who runs along a stream with a piece of meat in his mouth, and, deceived by the reflection of the meat in the water, opens his mouth to snap at it, and so loses both the meat and the reflection."[162]

"suggests that Paul has placed both Judaism and paganism side by side among the elemental spirits" (Reicke, "Law and This World," *op. cit.*, p. 273).

[160] Gal. 4:9.

[161] Gal. 5:4.

[162] Luther, "Treatise on Christian Liberty," *op. cit.*, p. 325.

VII

Liberty in Christ

IT IS TRULY SAID that the term "liberty" is "so porous that there is little interpretation that it seems able to resist."[1] Moralists, religionists, and politicians throughout the course of human history have embraced the concept; and in the course of its wide usage, the idea has become encrusted with a varying assortment of associations and connotations. Thus it cannot be said that there is a standard definition which truly represents the term in all its contexts and which we can apply to it *a priori* in understanding Paul's thought. Nor may we assume that in comprehending the Apostle's teaching regarding legality we can merely reverse the affirmations of a nomistic position to their negatives and the negatives to positives, and by contrast thus understand his teaching regarding liberty. Paul does not so much balance the concepts of legality and liberty against each other as measure them both by Christ. His teaching regarding the abrogation of the Law and regarding Christian liberty are as two spokes radiating from a central hub. And as spokes in a wheel they are related and yet definitely stand apart—though not necessarily at an angle of 180 degrees to each other. It is thus incumbent upon us to study Paul's teaching regarding liberty as well if we are to understand his thought and action.

BACKGROUND AND PARALLELS

The Apostle's teaching concerning liberty not only has a context; it also has a background in his Jewish heritage and many parallels in Greek thought. It is to these factors that we must turn first.

[1] I. Berlin, *Two Concepts of Liberty* (Oxford: Clarendon Press, 1958), p. 6.

Jewish background. It is usually assumed that the concept of liberty arose on Greek soil, or at least is non-Semitic in origin.[2] Thus many treatments of the subject entirely omit any reference to its appearance in the Old Testament or Judaism.[3] But while it is true that the idea of liberty often became a consuming passion in the West, it is not entirely absent from Judaic thought.

In the Jewish literature there are few, if any, formal discussions of the subject; and where the thought occurs on a personal level it is always in a nomistic context.[4] Yet the Hebrews knew their God to be the God who sets His people free: He released them from bondage in Egypt that they might be in bondage to none but Himself;[5] He lifted foreign subjugations when the people turned to Him;[6] He delivered from Babylonian captivity;[7] He instituted the Jubilee (*apheseōs,* LXX), the period during which they were to "proclaim liberty [*aphesis,* LXX] throughout the land to all its inhabitants";[8] and He promised a day when His Servant would "proclaim liberty [*aphesis,* LXX] to the captives."[9] He is the God who forgives and frees. It was this conviction of true freedom as being theocentric which drove the nomistic extremists of Qumran into seclusion[10] and the nationalistic

[2] H. Schlier: "Freiheit ist eine abendländische Idee" ("Über das vollkommene Gesetz der Freiheit," *Festschrift Rudolf Bultmann,* ed. E. Wolf [Stuttgart: Kohlhammer, 1949], p. 190). Cf. also J. Weiss, *Christliche Freiheit* (Göttingen: Vandenhoeck & Ruprecht, 1902), pp. 7-11.

[3] E.g., Schlier, ibid., pp. 190-202; "Eleutheria," *Theologisches Wörterbuch zum Neuen Testament,* ed. G. Kittel, Vol. II, pp. 484-500.

[4] E.g., Ps. 119:44-45: "I will keep thy law continually, for ever and ever; and I shall walk at liberty, for I have sought thy precepts."

Mish. Aboth 6.2: "'And the tables were the work of God, and the writing was the writing of God, graven [*haruth*] upon the tables.' Read not *haruth* but *heruth* [freedom], for thou findest no freeman excepting him that occupies himself in the study of the Law; and he that occupies himself in the study of the Law shall be exalted."

B. Ber. 5a, where it is asserted that the study of the Torah protects from the influence of demons, releases one from suffering and gains forgiveness of sins.

[5] Lev. 25:39-46.

[6] Cf. the Book of Judges.

[7] Cf. Ezra 9:9; Hag. 2:4-5; Zech. 1:16-17.

[8] Lev. 25:10.

[9] Isa. 61:1. Paul uses *aphesis* to mean forgiveness; see Acts 13:38, 26:18; Eph. 1:7; Col. 1:14.

[10] A. Dupont-Sommer: "How eloquently the ideas of liberty, equality, and fraternity are proclaimed in this religious society" (*Jewish Sect of Qumran and the Essenes,* p. 79).

extremists of Zealotism into action.[11] And it is this realization that stands as bedrock to all of Paul's thought regarding Christian liberty. The Apostle simply could not conceive of a liberty which was not derived from God and which did not center in God. Whatever Christian convictions went into the foundation and structure of his thought, and whatever Greek terms and ideas embellish his theology, the Jewish conviction that freedom must be theocentric if it is to be freedom at all undergirds the whole.

Greek parallels. When we turn to the Greek thought of Paul's day, we find many points where the Apostle and Stoicism are in seeming agreement. Both spoke of liberty in the personal sense. Both taught that liberty was gained by surrender within a context of obedience, and that it had as its consequence a true self-realization and a real victory over circumstances—even death. Stoicism made this quest for liberty central. In fact, to judge from the available records, Epictetus, the leading advocate of freedom in Stoicism, used the word about four times as often as did Christianity's great advocate of freedom, Paul. W. A. Oldfather points out that "the words 'free' (adjective and verb) and 'freedom' appear some 130 times in Epictetus,"[12] while Paul used the noun *eleutheria*, with its adjective and verb, only 29 times.[13] Many are convinced because of the similarity of theme and treatment that the great emphasis upon liberty in the Pauline letters "was probably a part of Paul's debt to the Greek world."[14]

The comparisons, however, are largely superficial. Whether we view it as the result of merely natural social evolution or the product of divine activity within the human consciousness, there was in the spiritually sensitive of both Jewish and Gentile worlds of the first century "a truly pathetic longing as of tired men for a passive kind

[11] Josephus: The Zealots showed "an unconquerable love of liberty which did not allow them to acknowledge anyone except God as their Lord and master" (Antiq. XVIII. 1. 6).

[12] W. A. Oldfather, *Epictetus,* Loeb Classical Library (London: Heinemann, 1925), Vol. I, p. 218.

[13] I.e., with the inclusion of *apeleutheros* in I Cor. 7:22. The other instances are: *eleutheria*—Rom. 8:21; I Cor. 10:29; II Cor. 3:17; Gal. 2:4, 5:1, 5:13 (twice); *eleutheros*—Rom. 6:20, 7:3; I Cor. 7:21, 7:22, 7:39, 9:1, 9:19, 12:13; Gal. 3:28, 4:22, 4:23, 4:26, 4:30, 4:31; Eph. 6:8; Col. 3:11; *eleutheroō*—Rom. 6:18, 6:22, 8:2, 8:21; Gal. 5:1. In special cases *exagorazō* (Gal. 3:13, 4:5) and *exousia* (I Cor. 9:4, 5; Rom. 9:21) also carry the idea of liberty.

[14] W. M. MacGregor, *Christian Freedom,* p. 23.

of happiness."[15] And such an outlook would make the theme of liberty inevitable to any man who thought he saw a ray of light in the darkness. The Jewish community earnestly looked for the Messiah, while the Gentile world "stretched out its hands in longing for the other shore."[16] Just as Epictetus' theme of liberty is "not there as an effect of Christian teaching, but as a true reflection of the tone and temper of those social circles to which the Gospel made its powerful appeal,"[17] so Paul's insistence upon the same theme is not derived either directly or indirectly from the teaching of such men as Musonius Rufus, but is the expression of realized Messianic hopes. Similarly, Paul and the Stoics are quite independent of one another in their development of the theme. In fact, despite superficial resemblances, they are in the main in opposition. While for Paul freedom was based in the grace of God and charismatic in nature, it was grounded in philosophy and the result of education for the Stoics.[18] While Paul defined it as being "in Christ," the Stoics insisted that it was synonymous with educated moral autonomy. While Paul spoke of freedom from sin, the Stoics advocated freedom from fate. If Paul rejected Jewish legalism, which was theoretically theocentric but in practice received its impulse from man, how much more was he revolted by Stoicism, with both theory and practice centered in the human will. Never could the Apostle have defined freedom as "desire that is free from any hindrance,"[19] or claimed that the truly liberated man is he "who lives as he wills, who is subject neither to compulsion, nor hindrance, nor force" beyond that of his own educated moral intellect.[20] Neither is Paul's liberty an escape from creaturely fate. The "tolling bell"[21] of suicide as the ultimate liberty may resound throughout the Stoic writings,[22] but the Apostle can-

[15] Oldfather, *Epictetus* Vol. I, p. xxvii.

[16] Virgil, Aeneid, VI. 314, trans. H. R. Fairclough (Loeb Classical Library).

[17] Oldfather, *Epictetus,* Vol. I, p. xxvii.

[18] J. Weiss: "Paulus, ganz im Sinne des gesamten Urchristentums, fasst die Freiheit auf als eine wunderbare Wirkung Gottes, als etwas, das über die natürliche Ausstattung des Menschen hinaus liegt. Die Stoiker begründen ihren Begriff psychologisch. . . . Für Paulus ist die Freiheit ein Charisma, für sie ein Erziehungsprodukt" (*Christliche Freiheit,* p. 22).

[19] Epictetus, Dissertations, I. 19. 2.

[20] *Ibid.,* IV. 1. 175.

[21] Oldfather, *Epictetus,* Vol. I, p. xxv.

[22] E.g., Epictetus, Dissertations, III. 13. 14: "Now whenever He does not provide the necessities for existence, He sounds the recall; He has thrown open

not echo the strain; for it is not nothingness which is our friend and creatureliness our enemy, but redeemed creatureliness which is our purpose and nothingness an impossibility. At the very heart of the matter, Paul and Stoicism are in disagreement. Both speak of surrender and obedience, but to the one it is to Christ while to the other it is to the inner law of one's being. The one is theo- and Christo-centric; the other is anthropocentric. And in this aspect, Stoicism falls into the same category as Jewish legalism and nomism in view of Christ; i.e., legality.

Rather than Stoic thinking, probably the Jewish conviction of true liberty as being theocentric was more basic in the formulation of the Apostle's thought. The greatest contributions of the Greek world to Paul's doctrine were the terms *eleutheria, apeleutheros,* and *epi eleutheria,* and the moral and intellectual climate which gave to his message of freedom in Christ a willing ear. But in designating the Jewish conviction as the undergirding and Greek thought as the embellishment and vehicle of Paul's teaching, we have yet to note the heart and core of the matter.

IN CHRIST

It is at the foundation of his doctrine of liberty that Paul differs most radically from both Stoic and rabbi. To the Stoic glorying in his own educated moral intellect, claiming freedom from all influences except that of an enlightened self-desire, and advocating that the essence of true wisdom lay in the adage "know yourself," Paul answered: "But He [God] is the source of your life in Christ Jesus, whom God has made our wisdom, our righteousness and sanctification and redemption; that, as it is written, 'He that glorieth, let him glory in

---

the door and says to you, 'Go.' Where? To nothing you need fear, but back to that from which you came, to what is friendly and akin to you, to the physical elements."

Seneca, De Providentia, VI. 7: "Above all, I have taken pains that nothing should keep you here against your will; the way out lies open. If you do not choose to fight, you may run away. Therefore of all things I have deemed necessary for you, I have made nothing easier than dying."

Epictetus, Dissertations, II. 1. 19: "The poor flesh is subjected to rough treatment, and then again to smooth. If you do not find this profitable, the door stands open; if you do find it profitable, bear it."

the Lord'."[23] To the Jewish nomist claiming that righteousness and liberty can be gained only through subjection to law, Paul spoke of "our liberty which we have in Christ Jesus."[24] He centered his doctrine of liberty not in the law of God, which is "weak through the flesh," but in Christ. For, to be in Christ is to *have* righteousness and liberty. Educated moral intellect and guiding principles might be of aid in the exercise of the Christian's liberty, but neither knowledge nor law enters into the basis of that liberty. The Apostle proclaimed that the Christian is complete in Christ,[25] and that completeness includes the liberty of the Christian. It is this concept of being "in Christ" that dominates all Paul's thought regarding liberty, and thus we must look more closely at the phrase.

Interpretations of the phrase "in Christ." During the last century the expression "in Christ" has become the subject of much investigation and debate. The interpretations advanced fall easily into five basic categories, and these we must note.

In the flush of the realization that the Pauline letters could be paralleled at many points by what is known of the Hellenistic Mystery Religions, many investigators argued that Paul's "in Christ" was *a carry-over from the Mystery Religions*. Bousset and Reitzenstein,[26] as well as Lake and Loisy,[27] viewed the term as just one of the many items borrowed by Paul both in form and content directly from the Mysteries. Others, agreeing to the Hellenistic nature of the expression, insist that there was no need for Paul to borrow from a pagan source since the synagogues of Diaspora Judaism had themselves become homes for the Mysteries—as witness Philo.[28] Thus, it is argued, the Apostle's "in Christ" carries the connotations found in the Mysteries: sacramental initiation, absorption into divinity, mystic identity,

[23] I Cor. 1:30-31.

[24] Gal. 2:4.

[25] Col. 2:10.

[26] W. Bousset, *Kyrios Christos* (Göttingen: Vandenhoeck & Ruprecht 1934), pp. 104-20; R. Reitzenstein, *Hellenistischen Mysterienreligionen*, pp. 333-93.

[27] K. Lake and A. Loisy have gone further in claiming that "Christianity has not borrowed from the Mystery Religions, because [under the influence of Paul] it was always, at least in Europe, a Mystery Religion itself" (K. Lake, *Earlier Epistles of St. Paul* [London: Christophers, 1934], p. 215; cf. A. Loisy, "The Christian Mystery," *H. J.* Vol. X [Oct. 1911], pp. 50-64).

[28] E. R. Goodenough, *By Light, Light: The Mystic Gospel of Hellenistic Judaism* (New Haven: Yale University Press, 1935).

ecstatic experience, and all. But such a view has failed to carry conviction for both methodological and comparative reasons.

Methodologically, the question of Hellenistic influence upon Paul at this point can never be as decisively settled in the affirmative as this view claims, for the information concerning the Mysteries is both meager and of late date. The danger is to be more precise than the evidence allows[29] or to assume uncritically that the influence between the Mysteries and Christianity always moved in one direction.[30] Many today recognize that the question is not only how much was Christianity influenced by Greek thought and culture, but also how much are the Mysteries an abortion of Christianity. Comparatively, the differences between Paul's "in Christ" and the union with divinity of the Mysteries are most convincing against the view that Paul simply incorporated Hellenistic thought and form into Christianity at this point. In addition to the fact that he does not proclaim a sacramental initiation,[31] the Apostle does not advance the fundamental Mystery Religion concept of absorption into the divine. Similarly, while the Mysteries present a salvation that is solely individualistic, Paul's "in

[29] Edwyn Bevan has caustically commented: "Of course, if one writes an imaginary description of the Orphic mysteries, as Loisy, for instance, does, filling in the large gaps in the picture left by our data from the Christian eucharist, one produces something very impressive. On this plan, you first put in the Christian elements, and then are staggered to find them there" ("Mystery Religions and Christianity," *Contemporary Thinking about Paul, An Anthology*, ed. T. S. Kepler [New York: Abingdon-Cokesbury, 1950], p. 43).

[30] For an excellent discussion of such methodological considerations, see B. M. Metzger, "Considerations of Methodology in the Study of the Mystery Religions and Early Christianity," *H. T. R.*, Vol. XLVIII, No. 1 (Jan., 1955), pp. 1-20.

[31] A. Schweitzer (*The Mysticism of Paul the Apostle*, trans. W. Montgomery [London: A. & C. Black, 1931], pp. 16 ff., *passim*) and Lake (*Earlier Epistles*, pp. 384-90), among others, have followed P. Wernle in declaring that Paul viewed the sacraments as inherently efficacious and Christianity as "centrally sacramental" (*ibid.*, p. 389). Such an interpretation asserts that baptism was for Paul the essential initiatory rite into the relationship of "being-in-Christ." But, though the Apostle regarded baptism and the Lord's Supper as of real value for the quickening of faith, there is no evidence that he viewed either, or both, as necessary initiatory rites. His explicit subordination of baptism to the preaching of the Gospel in I Cor. 1:17 and his ethics indicate that he was no sacramentalist (cf. H. A. A. Kennedy, *Theology of the Epistles*, pp. 150-52; W. R. Inge, *Christian Ethics and Modern Problems* [London: Hodder & Stoughton, 1930], pp. 74-75).

Christ" is both personal and corporate.[32] While in Hellenism salvation is freedom from fate, Paul accepts creatureliness and announces a salvation from sin and its associates. While faith is intellectual acceptance in the Mysteries, it is personal and ethical commitment with the Apostle. While ecstatic rapture is the goal of the Mysteries, the ecstatic is only reluctantly spoken of by Paul and is not considered characteristic of the Christian life.[33] Even the form of the expression "in Christ," while certainly similar to that of the Mysteries, cannot with certainty be attributed to that milieu for its occurrence in Paul. The question must always be asked whether this phraseology is a true "genealogical" parallel, due to the borrowing of form or of thought, or merely an "analogical" parallel, to be regarded as arising from a more or less equal religious experience and temper.[34] Paul's Jewish background in the concept of identification, his Christian experience of personal fellowship with Christ, and his possible knowledge of the words of Jesus as recorded in John's Gospel[35] make it indeed probable

[32] W. D. Davies: "There is a social aspect to the Pauline concept of the being 'in Christ'; union with Christ however personal had meant incorporation into a community that could be described as one body. As far as we know, however, the mysteries were individualistic" (*Paul and Rabbinic Judaism,* p. 90).

[33] J. G. Machen has well stated the matter regarding the Pauline visions: "The fact should always be borne in mind that Paul distinguished the visions very sharply from the experience which he had near Damascus, when he saw the Lord. The visions are spoken of in 2 Corinthians apparently with reluctance, as something which concerned the apostle alone; the Damascus experience was part of the evidence for the resurrection of Christ, and had a fundamental place in the apostle's missionary preaching" (*Origin of Paul's Religion,* p. 59). Similarly, R. Bultmann: "Wohl kennt Paulus die Ekstase, aber sie ist für ihn ein besonderes Charisma, nicht die spezifisch christliche Lebensform (vgl. I Cor. 12-14)" ("Das Problem der Ethik bei Paulus," *Z. N. W.,* Vol. XXIII, Heft 1/2 [1924], p. 136). It is true that Paul highly regarded such experiences as recounted in II Cor. 12:1-5, but he valued them as prophetic revelations to an accredited apostle and not as something which should be considered an essential part of the Christian life.

[34] Note A. Deissmann, *Light from the Ancient East,* trans. L. R. M. Strachan (London: Hodder & Stoughton, 1910), p. 262, regarding this distinction; also Metzger, "Considerations of Methodology," *op. cit.,* pp. 9-10, for an illustrated discussion.

[35] While it would lead too far afield to enter into a discussion of the historic basis of the Johannine discourses, I believe that there is no valid reason to doubt that at least the phrase "Abide in me, and I in you" represents a real element in our Lord's teaching. Note: (1) the discourse on the bread of life in John 6:48-58, which draws to a close in the words "he who eats my flesh

that the latter situation is the true one. It will always remain a question just how Hellenistically orientated so-called Hellenistic Judaism was; but the position in question here, that of the Mystery interpretation of Paul's use of "in Christ," seems to have lost its case.

Adolf Deissmann argued that the phrase should be interpreted as *a literal local dative of personal existence in the pneumatic Christ.*[36] He asserted that Paul viewed the Spirit as a semiphysical and ethereal entity; and that by equating the personal resurrected Christ with the ethereal Spirit, he could quite easily think of Christ as permeating the Christian and the Christian as living in Christ. Deissmann's favorite analogy was that of air, of which it can be truly said that it is in us and we are in it. And his work on this phrase was a great advance in New Testament studies. Yet he left discussion open to two unwarranted allegations: (1) that since Paul could so closely equate the Spirit and Christ, what is true of the Spirit as semiphysical and nonpersonal existence must to some extent also be true of Christ; and (2) that in advocating the incorporation of man into the ethereal and semiphysical substance of the pneumatic Christ, Paul has shown himself to be a very primitive metaphysical thinker. Thus J. Weiss, agreeing in the main, argued that Deissmann did not go far enough; for while what is true of Christ is true of the Spirit, what is true of the Spirit is also true of Christ.[37] This association of Christ with the Spirit, insisted Weiss, is one place where "it cannot be denied that Paul's Christology is inclined, upon one side, to abandon the firm lines laid down by concrete ideas of a definite personality."[38] The Apostle here enters into "abstract speculation" and effects "the sublimation and dissolution of personality."[39] F. Büchsel, in opposition to Deissmann's literal local thesis,

---

and drinks my blood abides in me, and I in him"; (2) the analogy of the vine and the branches in John 15:1-11, where the "abide in me, and I in you" motif occurs repeatedly; (3) John 17:21: "that they also may be one in us"; (4) John 17:23 and 26: "I in them"; (5) John 14:20: "In that day you shall know that I am in my Father and you in me and I in you"; (6) John 16:33: "In me you may have peace. In the world you have tribulation"; (7) Matt. 18:20: "Where two or three are gathered in my name, there am I in the midst of them." Cf. also Matt. 25:40-45, where the concept is presented in embryonic form.

[36] A. Deissmann, *Die neutestamentliche Formel "in Christo Jesu"* (Marburg: Elwert, 1892).

[37] J. Weiss, *Primitive Christianity,* Vol. II, p. 464.

[38] J. Weiss, *Paul and Jesus,* p. 22.

[39] *Ibid.,* p. 24. Cf. *Primitive Christianity,* Vol. II, pp. 464-71.

both to the Pauline presentation of Christ, representing Him as "ein argued that to view Paul's "in Christ" as a local dative was degrading halb sachliches Fluidum,"[40] and to the person of Paul himself, portraying him as a "primitiver Denker."[41] And indeed, it is at these points that Deissmann's interpretation fails to do justice to the Apostle.

In reaction to the local interpretation, some have insisted that the expression must be viewed as *a dative of instrumentality, causality and/or source*. In a methodical piece of research, F. Büchsel concludes that "es ist instrumental, kausal, modal und im übertragenen Sinne lokal gebraucht."[42] He says that while the figurative sense is found at times, its primary meaning is more adequately expressed by applying the instrumental idea to "in Christ"[43] and the dynamic idea to "Christ in us."[44] Now it is evident that the position has the appearance of probability, for to take the phrase in this way often yields a perfectly intelligible and theologically sound meaning. None would disagree that, whatever the Apostle meant by the expression, he did not exclude the ideas of Christ as the source, cause, and power of the Christian's life. But the question which stands over all of Büchsel's work, and which he neglects to raise, is: Why then didn't Paul just use the terms *dia Christou* and *ek Christou* instead of also including *en Christō* if he desired to express only the idea of instrumentality? And further, why did he use all three expressions within a single presentation when, according to Büchsel, his thought was roughly singular?

Similarly in opposition to the local interpretation stands the view which sees the phrase as being *a metaphor of personal communion with Christ*. It is not that this position desires to minimize the personal element of intimate relation between the Christian and Christ contained in the expression, but it considers it "hazardous to press the 'local' significance of the formula."[45] It accepts the more general, but still profound, truth which Paul teaches of communion with Christ, but it shies away from trying to be more explicit in the exposition of

[40] F. Büchsel, " 'In Christus' bei Paulus," *Z. N. W.*, Vol. XLII (1949), p. 146.

[41] *Ibid.*, p. 152. H. Lietzmann refers to Paul's theory of being "in Christ" as "a plastically conceived mysticism" (*Beginnings of the Christian Church*, p. 183).

[42] Büchsel, " 'In Christus,' " *op. cit.*, p. 156.

[43] *Ibid.*, p. 146.

[44] *Ibid.*, p. 152.

[45] Kennedy, *Theology of the Epistles*, p. 121.

that union with Christ by an emphasis upon the form of the term. In its insistence that the metaphor stands for the believer's "supremely intimate relation of union with Christ,"[46] it has certainly caught the main theme of the Apostle's teaching. But—and here we must leave the argument for the following section—"the cumulative effect of all Paul's uses of the phrase 'in Christ' demands something even more than this."[47]

Of late there has risen to prominence a different type of objection to Deissmann's interpretation. This position agrees with the local emphasis, but interprets it as not primarily denoting individual and personal communion with Christ but as being *a locution for corporate communion in the Church.* Of course the Roman Church has always taken this position, asserting that to be in the living Christ was to be in "the Church with its centre in Rome."[48] But in the reaction to philosophic individualism and the rediscovery of the thought of corporate personality in the Scriptures, many non-Romanists have also viewed the phrase as speaking primarily of corporate life in the Body of Christ—i.e., the organic Church. Albert Schweitzer argued that " 'being-in-Christ' is the prime enigma of the Pauline teaching"[49] if we view it as "an individual and subjective experience" rather than "a collective and objective event."[50] Thus he insisted that "the expression 'being-in-Christ' is merely a brachyology for being partakers in the Mystical Body of Christ."[51] And while it is the commonest, it is

> not the most appropriate expression for union with Christ. It becomes the most usual, not only because of its shortness but because of the facility which it offers for forming antitheses with the analogous expressions "in the body," "in the flesh," "in sin," and "in the spirit," and thus providing the mystical theory with a series of neat equations.[52]

Similarly, Rudolf Bultmann states that " 'in Christ,' far from being a formula for mystic union, is primarly an ecclesiological formula"; and thus "to belong to the Christian Church is to be 'in Christ' or 'in

[46] *Ibid.,* p. 124.
[47] W. Barclay, *Mind of St. Paul,* p. 128.
[48] As is C. Cary-Elwes' conclusion, *Law, Liberty and Love* (London: Hodder & Stoughton, 1949), p. 247.
[49] Schweitzer, *Mysticism of Paul,* p. 3.
[50] *Ibid.,* p. 123.
[51] *Ibid.,* pp. 122-23.
[52] *Ibid.,* p. 123.

the Lord.' "[53] And in Britain this position is strongly advanced by J. A. T. Robinson and L. S. Thornton as a corollary to their insistence that "the Church as literally now the resurrection 'body' of Christ" was dominant in the thought of Paul.[54] To this renewed emphasis must be given credit for reminding the Church of a vital element in Pauline theology, for the Apostle could never envisage a Christian who could rejoice in the personal aspect of being "in Christ" without likewise accepting the corporate and social nature of that relationship. But while it is right in what it affirms, it errs in its emphasis and in what it denies.

Significance of being "in Christ." Endless debate will probably continue to gather around Paul's expression "in Christ," for it signifies that central aspect of the Christian life which is much better experienced than explained. Indeed, the more confident we are that we have reduced the expression to the cold prose of the psychologist's laboratory the more assured we can be that we have lost its central significance. The inexplicable must always remain in the truly personal relationship. Yet that relationship can be intellectually understood and expressed up to a point. It is to that point—and I trust only to that point—that I would seek to go in understanding the Apostle's thought here.

It is true that in many places the expression can be viewed as merely synonymous with the adjective and noun "Christian." For example, in his greetings to the churches, by "to all the saints in Christ Jesus" Paul could mean simply "to all the Christians";[55] in his reference to "the dead in Christ," he need mean no more than "the Christian dead";[56] and in his mention of certain individuals who were "in the Lord" or "in Christ," the use of the phrase could be only in order to identify them as Christians.[57] Similarly there are a host of passages where *dia Christou* or *ek Christou* could be read just as well as *en Christō,* and a perfectly intelligible meaning would emerge. The most prominent examples are II Corinthians 3:14, where

[53] R. Bultmann, *Theology of the N. T.,* Vol. I, p. 311.

[54] J. A. T. Robinson, *The Body* (London: S. C. M. Press, 1957), p. 51; cf. L. S. Thornton, *The Common Life in the Body of Christ* (London: Dacre Press, 1941).

[55] Phil. 1:1; cf. Eph. 1:1, Col. 1:2.

[56] I Thess. 4:16; cf. 1 Cor. 15:18.

[57] E.g., Rom. 16:7, 11.

the Apostle speaks of the veil that "is done away *en Christō*" (RSV, "through Christ"); Romans 5:10, which speaks of being "saved *en tō zōe autou*" (AV, ASV, RSV, "by his life"); Romans 14:14, where he says "I know and am persuaded *en kuriō Iēsou* that nothing is unclean of itself" (AV, "by the Lord Jesus"); and Philippians 4:13, where Paul asserts that he "can do all things *en* him who strengthens me" (AV, "through him"). But the fact that in the following passages Paul distinguishes *en* from *dia* and *ek* in regard to Christ suggests that he used the prepositions a little more exactly than some have thought in the past:

II Corinthians 1:20. "For all the promises of God have their 'Yes' *en autō*. Wherefore also we utter the 'Amen' *dia autou* to the glory of God."

II Corinthians 2:17. ". . . but as *ek theou* in the presence of God we speak *en Christō*."

Colossians 1:16. "*en autō* were all things created, ... All things were created *dia autou* and *eis auton*."

Colossians 1:19-20. "*en autō* it was considered proper for all the fullness of God to dwell, and *dia autou* to reconcile all things to himself."

Moreover, in most of the passages where it is possible that Paul meant only Christian by the term, or where it is asserted that the instrumental, causal, source, or dynamic idea is uppermost in his thought, the local designation, if it were not for the revulsion of the interpreter to the seeming crudity of the idea, can just as easily be seen. Certainly the following savor strongly of the local flavor:

Philippians 3:9. ". . . that I might gain Christ and be found *en autō*."

Romans 8:1. "There is therefore now no condemnation to those *en Christō Iēsou*."

II Corinthians 5:17. "If any one is *en Christō*, he is a new creation."

II Corinthians 5:19. "God was *en Christō* reconciling the world to himself."

Ephesians 1:20. God's working was accomplished "*en tō Christō* when he raised him from the dead."

Thus, while not assenting to all of Deissmann's positions, nor insisting that there be a unitary exegesis of the phrase, it seems one must assert that Paul's "in Christ" carries a quite definitely local flavor.[58] It is not just a bit of "verbal ingenuity"[59] or one of many metaphors subservient to the controlling concept of "the Body of Christ,"[60] but it is the dominant expression of the Apostle's thought for the relationship of the believer to Christ. While certainly the phrase has corporate overtones and social implications, it is used so often[61] and in such individualistic settings[62] that it must be viewed as much more than just an extension of meaning from a more fundamental concept of corporeity. Of two recent works on the subject, Best's title and treatment of *One Body in Christ* is much more representative of the Pauline emphasis than is Robinson's *The Body;* for Best recognizes the personal emphasis contained in the expression "in Christ" while also stressing the corporate nature of the Christian life as contained in the metaphor "the Body," whereas Robinson subdues all to the corporate idea.

But the question that arises when we insist upon a quite definite local and personal flavor for the phrase is the same one Deissmann wrestled with so valiantly: How can we speak of the intermingling of two personalities in local terminology? Deissmann argued along the lines of an ethereal Spirit and pneumatic Christ, in which the believer lived as in a sort of rarified air and which could, as can air, also indwell the believer. But such an analogy is not Pauline. Paul spoke of Christ more as the "Universal Personality"[63] than as ethereal or pneumatic. "In him all things were created in heaven and upon earth, things visible and invisible";[64] "in him all things consist";[65] "in him it was considered proper for all the fullness of God to dwell";[66] and "in him" God's plan for the fullness of time will be brought to completion in "bringing to summation all things in Christ, things in

[58] As E. Best, *One Body in Christ* (London: S.P.C.K., 1955), *passim.*

[59] As Schweitzer, *Mysticism of Paul,* p. 117.

[60] As J. A. T. Robinson, *The Body,* esp. pp. 58-67.

[61] One hundred and sixty-four times in ten Pauline letters, minus the Pastorals, according to Deissmann, *Die neutestamentliche Formel "in Christo Jesu,"* pp. 1-2, 118-23.

[62] E.g., Phil. 3:9; II Cor. 5:17.

[63] A. Oepke: "Grundlegend ist die Vorstellung von Christus als Universalpersönlichkeit" ("En," *Theologisches Wörterbuch zum N. T.,* ed. Kittel, Vol. II, p. 538).

[64] Col. 1:16.

[65] Col. 1:17.

[66] Col. 1:19.

heaven and upon earth."[67] As the Old Testament can say that Abraham "trusted *in* Jahweh"[68] (nine times out of eleven using the preposition *ba* rather than *la* with the hiphil form when its object is God[69]), and as Jesus is reported to have spoken of His relationship to the Father as being "*in* the Father,"[70] all without diminishing the concept of the real personality of God, so Paul, with his high Christology, can speak of being "in Christ" without that concept of person "in" person softening or dissolving the fixed outlines of personality for either Christ or the Christian. To have been forced to give a definite psychological analysis of this relationship would have left Paul speechless. But he was convinced that he had experienced just such an intimacy with Christ.

Of course in positing a local and personal flavor for the phrase "in Christ" one is admitting to a mysticism. But this need not be abhorred if we mean by the term mysticism "that contact between the human and the Divine which forms the core of the deepest religious experience, but which can only be felt as an immediate intuition of the highest reality and cannot be described in the language of psychology."[71] It is not the pagan mysticism of absorption, for the "I" and the "Thou" of the relation retain their identities. But it is the "I and Thou" communion at its highest.

Here, then, is the controlling concept for Paul's teaching regarding liberty. Christian liberty is constituted only "in Christ."

THE INDICATIVE OF LIBERTY

Liberty "in Christ" cannot, in actuality, be compartmentalized. The Apostle never conceived of a purely forensic or a purely inward freedom. Yet for purposes of analysis we may speak of his teaching as having relevance in three areas: (1) in the believer's relationship to his God, or the forensic aspect; (2) in the believer's ordering of his own inner life, or the personal aspect; and (3) in the believer's relationship to his fellow men, or the social aspect.

[67] Eph. 1:10.
[68] Gen. 15:6.
[69] Cf. Ps. 78:21 f.; Isa. 50:10; Zeph. 3:2; Jer. 17:5-7; Prov. 28:25 f.; Zeph. 3:12; Nah. 1:7; II Kings 18:5 f.
[70] John 10:38, 14:10, 11, 20, 17:21.
[71] Kennedy, *Theology of the Epistles,* p. 122.

Forensic liberty. The realization of having been set free by God to stand before Him as a free man in Christ was basic to Paul's Christian experience and thought. *Freedom from condemnation* was the initial realization; and it comes out strongly in the opening words of Romans 8, "There is therefore now no condemnation for those who are in Christ Jesus," and almost defiantly in verses 31-34 of the same chapter: "If God is for us, who is against us? . . . Who shall bring any charge against God's elect? It is God who justifies; who is to condemn? It is Christ Jesus who died, yea rather who was raised, who is on the right hand of God and who intercedes for us." The result of sin is that alienation from God which can rightly be called "death";[72] God justly pronouncing judgment upon "those who do such things."[73] Christ, however, "gave himself for our sins,"[74] and in so doing "redeemed us from the curse of the law."[75] And in this redemption the Father "has delivered us from the authority of darkness and transferred us to the kingdom of his beloved Son,"[76] thus giving to us the *freedom to live unto God* as a son and an heir;[77] a freedom which is real and yet not fully realized, for as yet there is a sense in which we still await full sonship.[78] This realization of forensic freedom was the cornerstone for Paul's doctrine of liberty.

Personal liberty. But while the Apostle speaks definitely of liberty in the forensic sense, he speaks at greatest length of that liberation which has taken place in the inward life of every believer. Of prime importance in this area is the *freedom from the compulsion of sin*. Paul argues from the Old Testament and general experience that "all men, both Jews and Greeks, are under the power of sin."[79] But he also asserts that as Christians we "died to sin" with Him[80] and were thus "set free from sin"[81]—"for he who has died is freed from sin."[82] This

[72] Rom. 6:16, 21, 23, 7:5; Gal. 6:8.
[73] Rom. 1:32; 2:8-9.
[74] Gal. 1:4.
[75] Gal. 3:13; cf. Col. 1:14.
[76] Col. 1:13.
[77] Rom. 8:14-17; Gal. 4:6-7, 22-31.
[78] Rom. 8:23.
[79] Rom. 3:9; cf. Rom. 1:18-3:20.
[80] Rom. 6:2-6.
[81] Rom. 6:18, 22, 8:2.
[82] Rom. 6:7.

freedom from sin is not presented as freedom from the possibility of sin, for the believer too must beware the tempter,[83] but as freedom from the inward power and authority of sin.[84] The Christian is under no compulsion to sin, but is for the first time given true freedom of choice and power "to walk in newness of life."[85] In close connection with this freedom is Paul's thought regarding the *freedom from the tyranny of self*. He saw man's condition as so dominated by sin, that when one would speak of what man is of himself he must speak of man as "sold under sin" and as controlled by his dead and deadening self.[86] It is this universal cry of the sin-controlled and deadened self that Paul utters in Romans 7:24: "Wretched man that I am! Who will deliver me from this body of death?" But he goes on in the next breath to praise God for deliverance from this tyranny,[87] "for the law of the Spirit of life in Christ Jesus has set me free from the law of sin and death."[88] C. H. Dodd has well caught the Apostle's thought at this point in characterizing his doctrine as that of "freedom from the tyranny of futile desires to follow what is really good."[89]

But not only is the man in Christ free from inner compulsion and tyranny; he has also *freedom from the domination of the Law*. Believers, who formerly were under the dominance of the Law as under a preparatory measure and until Christ,[90] have "died to the law" and in that death are "discharged from the law, dead to that which held us captive."[91] The Christian lives his life no longer under a detailed code which regulates each particular action, but "in the new life of the Spirit."[92] And thus he walks in liberty, "for where the Spirit of the Lord is, there is liberty."[93] He is "not under law but under

[83] I Thess. 3:5; I Cor. 7:5; II Cor. 2:11.

[84] Bultmann: "Freiheit von der Macht der Sünde" ("Das Problem der Ethik," *op. cit.*, p. 125).

[85] Rom. 6:4; cf. Col. 3:10.

[86] Rom. 7:14-23.

[87] Rom. 7:25a.

[88] Rom. 8:2.

[89] C. H. Dodd, *Meaning of Paul,* p. 150.

[90] Gal. 3:19 ff.

[91] Rom. 7:4-6.

[92] Rom. 7:6.

[93] II Cor. 3:17; cf. Gal. 5:18.

grace";[94] not that he might be uncontrolled but that he might belong to another.[95] And in close association with the abrogation of the external domination of the Law, Paul also speaks of *freedom from the power of unseen spiritual forces of evil.*[96] This factor of demonic forces external to man, an idea admittedly foreign to the modern mind, must be taken seriously in the understanding of Paul. For the Apostle, it was a real deliverance when Christ disarmed and triumphed over "the principalities and powers"; and it should not be too easily dismissed as an aspect in our own Christian liberty.[97]

Social liberty. Of our three categories mentioned above, that of liberty in its social aspect is least spoken of in the letters of Paul. Yet there are certainly undertones of the social implications of Christian liberty throughout. It is in this area that the widest divergence of opinion exists regarding what the Christian possesses. Certain sects have so emphasized liberty as to defy all human authority. Luther, on the other hand, tended to regard the justified man as free from all regulation "inwardly, in his spirit," but as not yet possessing freedom in the social area—and thus subject to all regulations and works in "the outward man."[98] Realizing that the Christian life is lived in the tension between a presently-effective and a yet-to-be-completed salvation, he tended to view the liberty of the Christian as only effective for the inner man at the present time and to relegate liberty for the outward man to "the last day, the day of the resurrection of the dead."[99] Yet while Luther closely approximated the Pauline conclusion, his argument is not quite that of Paul.

In its context the expression of Galatians 5:1, "Unto freedom Christ has freed us," need refer to no more than such an inward liberty. But the later words of Galatians 5:13, "For to freedom you were called, brethren," in the context of verses 13-15, certainly refer

[94] Rom. 6:14, 15.

[95] Rom. 7:4; cf. Paul's frequent reference to *doulos Iēsou Christou* (Rom. 1:1; I Cor. 7:22; Gal. 1:10; Eph. 6:6; Phil. 1:1; Col. 4:12).

[96] Col. 2:15; Eph. 6:10 ff.

[97] Cf. J. S. Stewart, "On a Neglected Emphasis in New Testament Theology," *S. J. T.*, Vol. IV (1951), pp. 292-301.

[98] M. Luther, "A Treatise on Christian Liberty," *Works of Martin Luther*, Vol. II, trans. W. A. Lambert, p. 328; cf. p. 312.

[99] *Ibid.*, p. 328.

to the outward man on the social side of liberty.[100] Similarly, the social side of Christian liberty is included in what is probably the strongest expression of freedom ever phrased, I Corinthians 3:21-22: "For all things are yours, . . . whether the world or life or death, whether the present or the future, all are yours." And in the exclamation of I Corinthians 9:1, "Am I not free?" and the agreement of the Apostle in I Corinthians 9:19 that "I am free from all men," Paul repeats this declaration of social liberty. His teaching was not that liberty was given only to the inner man. Rather, he taught that the gift of freedom is meaningful in man's outward actions as well—though other factors besides just the realization of liberty "in Christ" must enter into the exercise of that liberty. We must consider the "imperative" of liberty in the following section of this chapter and the "exercise" of liberty in the following chapter if we would understand Paul more fully at this point. Suffice it here to say that the very fact that Paul appeals to his readers to manifest their liberty in love[101] and speaks of voluntarily confining aspects of his liberty for sake of his purpose[102] indicates that he viewed social liberty as part of the indicative of the Gospel.

THE IMPERATIVE OF LIBERTY

But the indicative of Christian liberty does not stand alone in Paul's message. While he announces that God has worked and is at work in the life of every believer, he also exhorts his converts to work out their own salvation.[103] His teaching contains two sides: you are in Christ, "put on the Lord Jesus Christ";[104] you are dead to sin and alive to God, "consider yourself so to be";[105] "sin will have no dominion over you," so do not permit it to have dominion over

[100] See Deissmann, *Light from the Ancient East,* pp. 324-34, where it is pointed out that this phrase is probably adopted from the terms in the sacral manumission procedures and indicates a freedom to "do the things that he will" for "against all the world, especially his former master, he is a completely free man."

[101] Gal. 5:13-15.

[102] I Cor. 9:19-23.

[103] Phil. 2:12.

[104] Rom. 13:14.

[105] Rom. 6:11.

you;[106] you are set free from the dominance of the Law, so "stand fast";[107] you live by the Spirit, so "walk by the Spirit."[108] For Paul, the indicative and imperative of the Gospel are so inseparably connected that any attempt to stress the one without the other is a satanic parody.

Its essential nature. There are those who look upon the Apostle's reference to liberty's imperative as basically inconsistent with his teaching regarding its indicative, and only born of practical necessity. James Parkes, for instance, says that "the doctrine of works continually hurled through the front window of theological suppositions as often returned by the back door of practical necessity."[109] But Paul's insistence upon the imperative is not in itself a confession of a discrepancy between the theory and the practice of the faith he proclaimed, or an inconsistency born of necessity; though, of course, the fact that he must exhort his converts to recognize the imperative demand in the Gospel certainly indicates that such a disparity between theory and practice existed in many of their minds—and that he fully realized it. Rather than basing the imperative on practical necessity, he proclaimed that "the indicative bears at its heart an imperative."[110] It is part of the essential nature of the Gospel; "einer Notwendigkeit, die in dem, was von Gott her an uns geschehen ist, beschlossen liegt, also nicht nur aus der schmerzlichen Diskrepanz von Theorie und Praxis, Ideal und Wirklichheit erwächst, wie man immer wieder gemeint hat."[111]

Paul viewed the necessity of that apparently contradictory relation of indicative and imperative, *Gabe und Aufgabe,* as the result of "the present situation in redemptive history";[112] a situation in which, while the essence of the Gospel proclamation is fulfillment, there is still sounded a definite note of anticipation, and while the Christian legitimately rejoices in the "no longer," there is still a realization of the element of "not yet." Thus, while the old age has passed away,

[106] Rom. 6:12-14.
[107] Gal. 5:1.
[108] Gal. 5:25.
[109] J. Parkes, *Jesus, Paul and the Jews,* p. 130; cf. W. L. Knox, *St. Paul,* pp. 94-95.
[110] J. S. Stewart, *Man in Christ,* p. 199.
[111] G. Bornkamm, *Ende des Gesetzes,* p. 35.
[112] O. Cullmann, *Christ and Time,* p. 224.

the new has not been fully brought about; while the compulsion of sin is broken, sin is still present to tempt; while the tyranny of death is crushed,[113] the mortal body yet remains;[114] while the domination of the Law is ended, forms of legalism and our perverted desire to gain in divine favor still exist; while the supernatural antagonistic powers are disarmed and defeated, they are not destroyed.[115] Indeed, there is a sense in which those who have become righteous yet "wait for the hope of righteousness"[116] and those who have been raised to newness of life yet await "a resurrection."[117] This is that tension in redemptive history between the present and the future which Martin Luther said "no sophisters will admit, for they know not the true manner of justification,"[118] but which, as Oscar Cullmann argues, "contains the key to the understanding of the entire New Testament."[119] In this realization of a temporal tension inherent in the very nature of the Gospel itself, the Apostle grounds the necessity of liberty's imperative. And in the fact that the Gospel imperative is applicable to that time between "the new creation" of II Corinthians 5:17 and the final deliverance of I Corinthians 15:24-28, the Christian ethic is indeed an interim ethic; not in Schweitzer's sense of the term that it has no application for the generations following early Christianity, but that it is conditioned by the realization that "the present is in fact an interim in the redemptive history."[120] In this sense, all genuine Christian ethic is interim ethics.

The imperative of liberty must thus be declared an essential part of the Gospel message, not just an inconsistency in Paul's thought born of practical necessity. Whereas he argued that the keeping of imperatives is a matter of inconsequence before God when a man knows not the indicative of the Gospel nor the temporal tension involved in the Gospel, Paul also insisted that "just because he [the Christian] has been set free, what he does—previously a thing of no account—now really matters, and he can be exhorted."[121]

[113] Rom. 7:24.
[114] Rom. 6:12.
[115] Col. 2:15; Eph. 6:11 ff.; I Cor. 15:24 ff.
[116] Gal. 5:5.
[117] Rom. 6:5.
[118] M. Luther, *Galatians,* p. 226 on Gal. 3:6.
[119] Cullmann, *Christ and Time,* p. 199.
[120] *Ibid.,* p. 213.
[121] Bultmann, *Theology of the N. T.,* Vol. I, p. 321.

Its relation to the indicative. But a further question arises: In what sense does the imperative really matter in Paul's thought? What relation does it bear to the indicative in the Gospel message?

Many have viewed the indicative and the imperative of the Gospel proclamation as being of equal rank, equal function and equal intent—as though they stood shoulder to shoulder "so dass neben die Ethik des Wunders die Ethik des Willens tritt."[122] Windisch, for example, interprets Paul to be saying that while God makes us righteous by grace alone in the heavenly sphere (the indicative) we must make that righteousness truly applicable in the earthly sphere (the imperative), *and* that only as these two types of righteousness work together, the heavenly righteousness coupled with the earthly righteousness, is there bestowed the divine eschatological salvation.[123] He bases his position primarily on the Sermon on the Mount, but sees Paul saying the same thing in Romans 6:19b. Thus he gives only a slight twist to that view popularized by Harnack which sees the imperatives of the Gospel as determinatives on which "to hang heaven and hell."[124] Windisch interprets them as works which co-operate with the Gospel indicative in order to produce righteousness.

We must deal with the purpose of the ethical imperatives of the Sermon on the Mount in the following chapter. But while Windisch may believe that he has abundant material to prove his point from Matthew, chapters 5—7, his argument rests very precariously when

[122] Bultmann, (characterizing the position of P. Wernle), "Das Problem der Ethik," *op. cit.*, p. 126.

[123] H. Windisch, "Das Problem des paulinischen Imperativs," *Z. N. W.*, Vol. XXIII, Heft 3/4 (1924), esp. pp. 270-73. His words are: "Unzweifelhaft setzt auch er [i.e. Paul] die Erfüllung einer *dikaiosunē* in irgendeinem Sinne zum Ziel (vgl. Rom. 6.19b). Soweit nun die Rechtfertigungslehre die Voraussetzung des Imperativs ist, ist die Antinomie leicht aufzulösen. Sie besagt: was in der *nicht wahrnehmbaren* Sphäre des göttlichen Handelns Realität geworden, gilt es nun auch in der irdischen Sphäre *wahrnehmbar* zu realisieren. Auf die Erlösung von der Herrschaft der Sünde hat der Mensch mit rückhaltloser Unterwerfung unter den Willen seines Erlösers zu reagieren. Norm und Ziel dieser Anstrengung heisst, wie bei der Rechtfertigung, *dikaiosunē* Rom. 6.19 (II Cor. 5.21)" (p. 271). Cf. H. Windisch, *Meaning of the Sermon on the Mount,* pp. 27-29 and *passim.*

[124] A. Harnack, *What Is Christianity?* trans. T. B. Saunders (London: Williams & Norgate, 1901), p. 72; cf. E. F. Scott, *The Ethical Teaching of Jesus* (New York: Macmillan, 1924), pp. 38 ff.

he comes to Paul. It seems that Luther's translation of Romans 6:19b has too strongly influenced his exegesis: "Also begebet auch nun eure Glieder zum Dienst der Gerechtigkeit, *dass sie heilig werden.*" The verse reads literally: "Therefore now present your members (as) servants to righteousness unto sanctification" (*tē dikaiosunē eis hagiasmon*). Now while the idea of "in order that you become holy" can be read into the verse, it requires an extension of meaning for the preposition *eis* and a similar extension for *hagiasmos* in which it becomes equivalent to *hagiōsunē*.[125] Later, in Romans 12:1, Paul again urges his readers to present their bodies to God, without the idea that by so doing they gain a further degree of holiness; but rather, that they thereby but respond to the mercies of God.[126] This seems to weight the argument against Windisch's view that such a presentation is to be made as an element in the attainment of righteousness. While Windisch has certainly caught the note of urgency in the Apostle's letters regarding liberty's imperative, he has misconstrued the Pauline motive.

For Paul, the imperatives are *based in the fact of a new nature.* The Christian has become "a new creation," and in this capacity Christians are exhorted to present themselves "as those alive from the dead" (*hōsei ek nekrōn zōntas*).[127] In the context of Romans 6, the adverb *hōsei* carries the idea of actuality. Paul begins this passage with a declaration that the very fact of the believer's death to the old nature and his resurrection to the new ought to settle the question of his allegiance: "How can we who died to sin still live in it? Do you now know . . . ?"[128] Similarly, the contrast between the "works of the flesh" and the "fruits of the Spirit" in Galatians 5:19-24 points out this same emphasis of the changed nature as the basis for the acceptance and fulfillment of the Gospel imperatives. T. W. Manson has pointed out that "here the word 'fruit' seems to be chosen

[125] *Hagiasmos* properly refers to the process of sanctification, whereas Windisch would make the presentation referred to in the verse attain the result of that santification, i.e., *hagiōsunē*.

[126] Whatever *tēn logikēn latreian humōn* means ("spiritual worship," RSV; "spiritual service," ASV; "reasonable service," AV), it carries more the idea of response than of reward.

[127] Rom. 6:13.

[128] Rom. 6:2; cf. vss. 3-4.

deliberately in order to suggest that the good deeds of the believer are characterized by a certain spontaneity. They are the natural outcome of a transformed nature rather than the laborious attempt to conform to an external code."[129] We must thus agree with Kirsopp Lake when he says: "Paul's position is not really difficult to understand by any one who grasps his belief in regeneration, and the fact that to him the central point in life is what you are, not what you do, so that conduct necessarily follows nature."[130]

Also, the imperatives find their motivation in the indicative of the Gospel. Christian ethic is *motivated by love* and not impelled by a desire to gain righteousness. James Denney has well captured the essence of the Pauline motivation in saying:

> The child whom his father or mother pardons through pain cannot but be good while the sense of this forgiveness rests upon his heart, and it is this simple principle on which the whole New Testament rests. True forgiveness regenerates. Justification is the power which sanctifies. This truth, which we can verify in our forgiveness of one another daily, is the ultimate and fundamental truth of the gospel.[131]

Paul's position is the lover's position, as seen in his declaration that

> the love of Christ constrains us, as we realize this fact, that one died for all. Therefore all died. And he died for all in order that those who live might no longer live to themselves but for him who for their sake died and was raised.[132]

Christian ethic, therefore, has not the character of works which establish the relation of man to the beyond, but it *takes the form of obedience* to the One who has already established that relation for the believer. In Paul's proclamation, righteousness is already realized in Christ Jesus. Thus the ethic of the Gospel becomes a "therefore-wherefore" ethic. Even the oft-cited Philippians 2:12, which exhorts to "work out your own salvation," begins with the oft-neglected words: "As you have always obeyed, so do now"; thus assuming the works of the believer under the caption of "obedience."

[129] T. W. Manson, "Jesus, Paul and the Law," *Judaism and Christianity,* Vol. III, ed. E. I. J. Rosenthal, p. 139.
[130] K. Lake, *Paul: His Heritage and Legacy,* pp. 128-29.
[131] J. Denney, *Christian Doctrine of Reconciliation,* p. 137.
[132] II Cor. 5:14-15.

This distinction between works in order to gain righteousness and works taking the form of obedience on the basis of righteousness is the distinction Martin Luther was grasping for in declaring: "Our faith in Christ does not free us from works, but from false opinions concerning works."[133]

[133] Luther, "Treatise on Christian Liberty," *op. cit.*, p. 344.

VIII

The Exercise of Liberty

CHRISTIAN LIBERTY finds its basis in Christ and must be considered both a gift and a demand. But the discussion of Paul's doctrine cannot rest here, important as these considerations are. The further question arises: how is the demand of the Gospel to be known and carried out in the particular situation? Paul exhorted his converts to "put on the Lord Jesus Christ" and to "walk in the Spirit," but such exhortations are nebulous without some instruction as to how the Christian is to know the right and to actualize his freedom in the particular situation. Protestant theology has given varying answers to the problem, ranging from the exhortation to follow the teachings of the historical Jesus to the more modern emphasis upon the pneumatic guidance of the resurrected Christ as the only criterion of the Christian life. But perhaps it is best to listen once again to Paul, the Apostle of liberty, and give serious heed to his teaching.

THE MIND OF CHRIST

In I Corinthians, the epistle which deals most at length with the particular situation of liberty's exercise, the Apostle puts to the forefront of his discussion one major element of the Gospel which makes the Christian ethic different from all forms of legalism and stoicism: pneumatic direction. He argues that the Christian life is neither established nor guided by human wisdom,[1] but that as it has been "revealed to us through the Spirit"[2] so is it by the Spirit that we "under-

[1] I Cor. 1:18-2:5.
[2] I Cor. 2:10.

stand the things bestowed on us from God."[3] His contrast is between systems of ethics which consist "in words which human wisdom teaches" (*en didaktois anthrōpinēs sophias logois*) and the Christian life, which finds its direction "in the teaching of the Spirit" (*en didaktois pneumatos*).[4] And in that contrast there is an emphasis upon the immediate character of Christian guidance. This pneumatic element of direction he designates as "the mind of Christ" (*nous Christou*).[5]

Throughout Paul's discussions of liberty, this factor of the mind of Christ as applied by the Spirit reappears as the distinguishing feature in the direction of Christian liberty. Thus the Christian lives his life in the new life of the spirit, and not in the old of the letter;[6] and the Apostle is a minister of a new covenant which is not of the letter, but of the spirit.[7] Similarly, whereas it was the flesh that controlled and characterized the activity of the man outside of Christ, the spirit is the distinguishing feature in the believer's guidance and life.[8] The exact relation between Christ and the Spirit in this matter of immediate and direct guidance is not explicit in Paul's letters. It would probably be most true to his thought to say that the mind of Christ became operative in the life of the Christian through the activity of the Spirit, as is his emphasis in I Corinthians 2:6-16. In II Corinthians 3:17a, however, he appears to equate the two in saying "the Lord is the Spirit." But his conclusion is the significant aspect at this point: "Where the Spirit of the Lord is, there is liberty."[9] For Paul, there is no liberty at all without the pneumatic element present; liberty is a matter of immediate personal fellowship between Christ and the believer in its direction as well as in its basis. And in this immediacy the Apostle speaks of the spiritual Christian as having knowledge which no human wisdom can approximate or even test; knowledge of "the mind of the Lord"—for "we have the mind of Christ."[10]

[3] I Cor. 2:12.
[4] I Cor. 2:13.
[5] I Cor. 2:16.
[6] Rom. 7:6.
[7] II Cor. 3:6.
[8] Rom. 8:4-6; Gal. 5:16.
[9] II Cor. 3:17b.
[10] I Cor. 2:6-16.

Here indeed is that existential emphasis which has been so definitely and forcefully expressed by many modern theologians. And while it is explicitly stated in only a few places in Paul's letters, this emphasis lies implicit in his whole conception of the Christian life and of his own apostolic ministry. This is the realization that caused him to speak of the normal Christian as being a "spiritual man" and the Christian life as a "fellowship of the Spirit"[11] as well as a "fellowship of his Son Jesus Christ";[12] and which, when perverted, could lead to such pneumatic excess as found at Corinth.

THE LAW OF CHRIST

But does this emphasis upon pneumatic direction necessarily exclude any type of external criterion for the direction of the Christian life? Does Paul view the Christian life as entirely devoid of external guidance and ordered only according to the inner direction of the Spirit? Much of the modern interpretation of the Apostle answers Yes to this question. Emil Brunner, for instance, is most insistent in declaring that

> the Christian conception of the Good differs from every other conception of the Good at this very point: that it cannot be defined in terms of principle at all.
>
> Whatever can be defined in accordance with a principle—whether it be the principle of pleasure or the principle of duty—is legalistic. . . . The Christian moralist and the extreme individualist are at one in their emphatic rejection of legalistic conduct; they join hands, as it were, in the face of the whole host of legalistic moralists; they are convinced that conduct which is regulated by abstract principles can never be good.[13]

Thus, Brunner goes on to say, there can be no "predefinition" in Christian ethics, for "the particular decision is not anticipated"; externally, Christian ethics must be described as "opportunistic" and "lacking principles."[14] It is this interpretation of Paul as teach-

[11] Phil. 2:1.

[12] I Cor. 1:9.

[13] E. Brunner, *The Divine Imperative,* trans. O. Wyon (London: Lutterworth, 1937), pp. 82-83.

[14] *Ibid.,* p. 134. Brunner does not attack or repudiate biblical principles, but he views them as possessing validity only in that measure to which the Spirit validates them to the individual. He rejects the idea of externally valid "propo-

ing "a morality beyond rules," dependent *solely* upon the inward guidance of the Spirit, which has gained the ascendancy in the theological thought of the day.[15] Yet serious exegetical objections have been raised by such men as C. H. Dodd, W. D. Davies, and O. Cullmann against interpreting Paul's thought so one-sidedly.

The new lawgiver and Torah in the Messianic thought of Paul's background. In a careful and well-substantiated piece of research into the Jewish expectation of a new Torah, W. D. Davies argues that, while Edersheim and Dalman have overstated the case, the evidence for such an expectation within Judaism is not "inconsiderable and questionable enough for us to dismiss it, as does Klausner, as merely a late development in a Judaism influenced by Christianity."[16] Many points in Davies' investigation are pertinent to our discussion here. He points out that while Jeremiah 31:31-34 speaks of a new covenant wherein God's law would be written on the heart, the passage does not automatically exclude the thought of an external type of direction as well. Certainly the passage goes beyond others in speaking of a "new covenant," but it can be paralleled by Psalms 37:31, 40:8, and Deuteronomy 30:14, 6:6. and 11:18 in its reference to the law contained in the heart—with none of these latter passages ruling out the presence of the external Law. Indeed, there are even expectations in the Old Testament that some type of external and divine teaching would continue to be valid in "the latter days." The parallel passages of Isaiah 2:1-5 and Micah 4:1-5 and the Servant passage of Isaiah 42:1-4, accepting the relation of the Servant to that of the Son of Man and the Messiah,[17] assert such an anticipation. Davies

---

sitional" principles, and condemns any reference to such as a return to "Pharisaic Judaism" (*ibid.*, p. 138) and a "sub-ethical position" (*ibid.*, p. 141).

[15] Cf. P. P. Bläser, *Gesetz bei Paulus,* pp. 234-43, and Sung Bum Yun, *Römer 7, 25 und der Pneumatikos* (Seoul, Korea: Tong, 1958), for extremely strong assertions of this position that Christian pneumatic guidance and any type of external principles stand as diametrically opposed.

[16] W. D. Davies, *Torah in the Messianic Age,* p. 85. J. Klausner's argument that all such evidence for the Jewish expectation of a new Torah is of late date and influenced by Christian thought, and therefore not of importance for the understanding of first-century Jewish thought, is found in *Messianic Idea in Israel,* pp. 446-49. Cf. S. Zeitlin's similar argument in his note to N. Wieder's article, "The Idea of a Second Coming of Moses," *J. Q. R.,* Vol. XLVI, No. 4 (Apr., 1956), p. 365.

[17] Cf. W. Manson, *Jesus the Messiah,* pp. 171 ff.

further quotes from the Targums on Isaiah 12:3 and Song of Songs 5:10, Song of Songs Rabbah 2.13, Midrash Qoheleth 2.1 and 12.1, and Yalqut on Isaiah 26 showing that there was the expectation that, in the words of the Targum on Isaiah 12:3, "You shall receive a new teaching with joy from the chosen of Righteousness."[18] As to why the earlier Gemaras and Midrashim show no explicit trace of such an expectation, Davies concludes that this "may be due to deliberate surgery."[19] As he points out, we do know from Justin's Dialogue[20] and such Talmudic passages as Deut. R. 8.6 and b. Shab. 104a[21] that "the question of the New Torah agitated Judaism"[22] and that the rabbis answered Christian propaganda with obvious polemic intent. And thus the possibility of deliberate surgery is very real.

In the discoveries at Qumran there is further evidence that the expectation of a new lawgiver and Torah was a part of the common Messianic thought of Judaism. We have long known that this group was awaiting "him who will teach righteousness."[23] But now, with the discovery of the one page of biblical "Testimonia" beginning with Deuteronomy 18:18 ff. and the knowledge that the sect anticipated at least some prophetical element in the realization of the Messianic hope,[24] we must more readily agree with Davies' temperate conclusion

[18] Davies, *Torah in the Messianic Age,* pp. 70-74.

[19] *Ibid.,* p. 86. Cf. N. Wieder: "The Rabbis suppressed it for polemical reasons" ("The 'Law-Interpreter' of the Sect of the Dead Sea Scrolls: The Second Moses," *J. J. S.,* Vol. IV, No. 4 [1953], p. 175).

[20] Justin, Dialogue with Trypho, XI (Ante-Nicene Fathers, ed. A. Roberts and J. Donaldson [Buffalo: Christian Literature Pub. Co., 1886], Vol. I, pp. 199-200). Justin insists that in Christ has come "an eternal and final law" which "has abrogated that which is before it" (*ibid.*).

[21] Deut. R. 8.6, which appears to be a direct rebuttal to Paul's interpretation of Deut. 30:11-14 in Rom. 10:6 ff.: " 'For this commandment . . . it is not in heaven (XXX, 11 f.)'. Moses said to Israel: 'Do not say: Another Moses will arise and bring us another Torah from heaven'; I therefore warn you, 'It is not in heaven,' that is to say, no part of it has remained in heaven."

b. Shab. 104a: "These are the commandments, that a prophet may henceforth [i.e., after Moses] make no innovations."

[22] Davies, *Torah in the Messianic Age,* p. 87.

[23] CDC 6.11 (8.10); trans. M. Burrows, *The Dead Sea Scrolls.*

[24] Four views as to the relation of "a prophet" and "the annointed ones of Aaron and Israel" in 1QS 9.11 have been advanced:

1. The prophet is the Messiah, while the annointed ones are his followers. See W. H. Brownlee, "The Dead Sea Manual of Discipline," *B.A.S.O.R.—S.S.,* Nos. 10-12, pp. 35-36, 50.

2. The prophet is the forerunner, while the Messiah to follow would combine

that "we can at least affirm that there were elements inchoate in the Messianic hope of Judaism, which could make it possible for some to regard the Messianic Age as marked by a New Torah."[25]

But while Judaism seems to have contained this thought in at least its embryonic form, the records we have from the hands of the early Church bring it out more strongly. And the background of the early Church was probably more influential on Paul's thought at this point than that of Judaism. In both Peter's sermon on Solomon's porch and Stephen's defense before the elders it is emphasized that there is some sort of providential continuity between Moses and Christ, by the quotation of Deuteronomy 18:15: "A prophet shall (the Lord) God raise up unto you from among your brethren, like unto me."[26] Similarly, as C. H. Dodd points out, "it is not the least remarkable feature of the Gospels as historical documents that although they all—even Mark—are written under the influence of a 'high' Christology, yet they all—even John—represent Jesus as a teacher with His school of disciples."[27] This is seen most dramatically in Matthew's presentation of the Sermon on the Mount, but it is also evident in the titles *Rabbi,*[28] *Rabbouni,*[29] *Didaskale,*[30] and *Epistata*[31] applied to Jesus throughout the Gospels. Many passages indicate that Jesus was regarded by the populace as a prophet with a teaching

---

in his person both priestly and kingly functions. See T. Gaster, *Scriptures of the Dead Sea Sect,* pp. 15 and 108, n. 71.

3. The prophet is the forerunner, while both a priestly Messiah and a kingly Messiah were expected to follow. See K. G. Kuhn, "The Two Messiahs of Aaron and Israel," *Scrolls and the N. T.,* ed. K. Stendahl, pp. 54-64; Burrows, *Dead Sea Scrolls,* pp. 264-65.

4. The prophet and the annointed ones of Aaron and Israel are three aspects of the one Messiah. See A. Dupont-Sommer, *Jewish Sect of Qumran and the Essenes,* p. 55.

[25] Davies, *Torah in the Messianic Age,* p. 85. Cf. Wieder's articles advocating that Judaism expected a second Moses: "The 'Law-Interpreter,'" *op. cit.,* pp. 158-75, and "The Idea of a Second Coming of Moses," *J. Q. R.,* Vol. XLVI, No. 4 (Apr., 1956), pp. 356-66.

[26] Acts 3:22, 7:37.

[27] C. H. Dodd, "Jesus as Teacher and Prophet," *Mysterium Christi,* ed. G. K. A. Bell and A. Deissmann (New York: Longmans, Green, 1930), p. 53.

[28] John 1:38, 49, 3:2, 26, 6:25.

[29] John 20:16.

[30] John 3:2, 11:28, 13:13-14; Matt. 8:19; Mark 4:38.

[31] Luke 5:5, 8:24, 45, 9:33, 49, 17:13.

ministry[32]—by some even as "*the* prophet"[33]—and that Jesus encouraged this conception.[34] And the Fourth Gospel, which can least be accused of Judaistic tendencies, presents Christ as at least thrice exhorting His disciples to keep His commandments[35] and as setting forth His person as in some sense a new Torah.[36] Further, there seems to be indirect evidence in at least two passages that the Gospel writers and Jesus' critics understood His claim to Messiahship to include that of being "a prophet like unto Moses." The first passage is the account of the mocking of Jesus in Mark 14:65, where He is veiled and called upon to prophecy—possibly taunting Him with the accusation that in His silence He is not like the veiled Moses but like the veiled Balaam.[37] The second is the objection of the Pharisee in Luke 7:39 that Jesus was not "the prophet"[38] because He allowed a woman of the street to touch Him.

The significance of "the Law of Christ" for Paul. In two passages Paul presents the idea of a "law of Christ": (1) in Galatians 6:2 he says that in bearing one another's burdens the Christian is fulfilling "the law of Christ" (*ton nomon tou Christou*), and (2) in I Corinthians 9:21 he speaks of himself as not being without law before God but as being "under the law of Christ" or "in-lawed to Christ" (*ennomos Christou*). Admittedly, both passages are exceedingly difficult to interpret. But the question must be asked: Is there in Paul's use of the phrase any thought of a standard in the Christian life which possesses an external significance and validity?

Modern interpretations of these expressions take one or the other of the following forms, both of which I believe to be erroneous:

1. That in his reference to "law" there appears the old pre-Christian mode of thought which Paul used almost subconsciously and without intending the term to be taken literally.[39]

2. That this "law" referred to is the law of the Spirit and must be

[32] Mark 6:15, 8:28; Luke 7:16, 13:33, 24:19.

[33] Matt. 21:11; John 6:14.

[34] Mark 6:4; Luke 4:24, 13:33; John 13:13.

[35] John 14:15, 21, 15:10. The use of *entolē* in the "new commandment" of love in 13:34 and 15:12 is possibly a figurative one.

[36] John 14:6.

[37] Note Num. 24:3. Cf. Dodd, "Jesus as Teacher and Prophet," *op. cit.*, p. 57.

[38] Accepting the reading of B.

[39] Cf. J. Weiss, *Primitive Christianity*, Vol. II, p. 554.

understood to refer to inward and nonpropositional guidance.[40] But there are factors which stand as weighty evidence for the position that Paul viewed "the law of Christ" to be more than simply acting in a Christian spirit and to be different in some respects from what is spoken of as "the law of the Spirit."[41]

Oscar Cullmann has pointed out that Paul was not opposed to using the word "tradition" (*paradosis*) for the instruction and teaching of Christ and the Church,[42] even though (1) that term carried the idea of external authority within Judaism, (2) Jesus had strongly denounced "the tradition of the elders" as being "the tradition of men,"[43] and (3) Paul himself had abandoned "the traditions of my fathers."[44] Thus, though the slogan of the pious Jew was "hold fast the traditions,"[45] the Apostle likewise exhorted his converts to "hold fast the traditions which you were taught"[46] and praised them when they did "hold fast the traditions."[47] Though he opposed what he called "the tradition of men,"[48] it does not follow that he also opposed the external validity of all traditions and principles.

In fact, as C. H. Dodd says, "maxims which formed part of the tradition of the sayings of Jesus are treated as if they were in some sort elements of a new Torah."[49] While in discussing the problems of marriage in I Corinthians 7, Paul may claim for his own view the direction of the Spirit and contrast it favorably with what Christ has said on the subject; yet it appears that what Christ has said "remains

[40] Cf. Bläser, *Gesetz bei Paulus,* pp. 234-43; R. Bultmann, *Theology of the N. T., Vol.* I, pp. 328 ff.

[41] Rom. 8:2; though actually there is never a reference to "the law of the Spirit" as such, it is "the law of the Spirit of life in Christ Jesus."

[42] O. Cullmann, " 'KYRIOS' as Designation for the Oral Tradition Concerning Jesus," *S. J. T.,* Vol. III (1950), pp. 180-86.

[43] Matt. 15:1-9; Mark 7:1-13.

[44] Gal. 1:14.

[45] Mark 7:8-9.

[46] II Thess. 2:15. Cf. II Thess. 3:6; I Cor. 15:2; Col. 2:6; I Tim. 6:20; II Tim. 1:14.

[47] I Cor. 11.2. Cf. I Thess. 2:13.

[48] Col. 2:8.

[49] C. H. Dodd, "ΕΝΝΟΜΟΣ ΧΡΙΣΤΟΥ," *Studia Paulina,* ed. W. C. van Unnik and G. Sevenster (Haarlem: Bohn, 1953), p. 107. Cf. H. Riesenfeld, *The Gospel Tradition and Its Beginnings* (London: Mowbray, 1957), pp. 19 ff.

uniquely authoritative."[50] Similarly, he explicitly quotes his Lord in such matters as the maintenance of the Christian preacher,[51] the institution of the Lord's Supper,[52] and the blessedness of giving[53] as though such words of Jesus carried a decisive validity. Also, there are at least eight passages in the hortatory section of Romans where, though Christ is not explicitly credited, "Paul is clearly dependent upon the words of Jesus" and uses them as valid external guidance for the Christian life:[54]

1. Romans 12:14. "Bless them which persecute you: bless, and curse not." (Cf. Matt. 5:44.)

2. Romans 12:17. "Recompense to no man evil for evil." (Cf. Matt. 5:39 ff.)

3. Romans 12:21. "Be not overcome of evil, but overcome evil with good." (Cf. Jesus' teaching on nonresistance.)

4. Romans 13:7. "Render therefore to all their dues: tribute to whom tribute is due; custom to whom custom; fear to whom fear; honor to whom honor." (Cf. Mark 12:13-17; Matt. 22:15-22; Luke 20:20-26.)

5. Romans 13:8-10. "Owe no man anything, but to love one another: for he that loveth another hath fulfilled the law. For this, Thou shalt not commit adultery, Thou shalt not kill, Thou shalt not steal, Thou shalt not bear false witness, Thou shalt not covet; and if there be any other commandment, it is briefly comprehended in this saying, namely, Thou shalt love thy neighbor as thyself. Love worketh no ill to his neighbor: therefore love is the fulfilling of the law." (Cf. Mark 12:28-34; Matt. 22:34-40; Luke 10:25-28.)

6. Romans 14:10. "But why dost thou judge thy brother?" (Cf. Matt. 7:1; Luke 6:37.)

7. Romans 14:13. "Let us not therefore judge one another any more; but judge this rather, that no man put a stumblingblock or an occasion to fall in his brother's way." (Cf. Matt. 18:7; Mark 9:42; Luke 17:1-2.)

[50] Dodd, "ΕΝΝΟΜΟΣ ΧΡΙΣΤΟΥ," *op cit.*, p. 105 Cf. I Cor. 7:10 with Matt. 19:4-9; Mark 10:3-9; Luke 16:18.

[51] Cf. I Cor. 9:14 with Matt. 10:10, Luke 10:7.

[52] Cf. I Cor. 11:23-25 with Matt. 26:26-29; Mark 14:22-25; Luke 22:19 f.

[53] Cf. Acts 20:35 with the substance of Luke 14:12-14.

[54] W. D. Davies, *Paul and Rabbinic Judaism*, p. 138.

8. Romans 14:14. "I know, and am persuaded by the Lord Jesus, that there is nothing unclean of itself." (Cf. Matt. 15:11; Mark 7:15.)

One must therefore agree with C. H. Dodd that "it is not, then, so clear, after all, that Paul intended to repudiate the understanding of Christianity as a new law."[55]

Luther indeed insisted that Christ "is no Moses, no exactor, no giver of laws, but a giver of grace, a saviour, and one that is full of mercy,"[56] but that statement must be viewed in its context of justification by faith alone and as a reaction to the schoolmen and "merit-mongers" who commercialized righteousness. Similarly, the Pauline proclamation that "Christ is the end of the law in its connection with righteousness for all who believe" and that the Christian is "not under law but under grace" must not be pushed to what seems a logically consistent interpretation of the Apostle; i.e., that thus the Christian is to receive guidance in his life only from the inward direction of the Holy Spirit. While the Apostle's use of the word "law" is not identical with Judaic usage, it is not accidental. He possessed and proclaimed a tradition of Christ's person and teaching which he regarded as an external and authoritative norm and pattern for the outworking of Christian liberty. It is certainly a mistake to consider "the law of Christ" as the equivalent of the rabbinic Halakah or to confine its designation only to the teaching of Jesus. Yet it remains that "even for Paul, with his strong sense of the immediate governance of Christ through His Spirit in the Church, that which the Lord 'commanded' and 'ordained' remains the solid, historical and creative nucleus of the whole."[57]

THE CORRELATION OF THE TWO FACTORS

Recognizing, therefore, that guidance in the Christian life has both an external and an internal aspect in Paul's thought, the question

[55] C. H. Dodd, *Gospel and Law* (Cambridge, Eng.: The University Press, 1951), p. 66.

[56] M. Luther, *Galatians,* p. 178 on Gal. 2:20.

[57] Dodd, "ΕΝΝΟΜΟΣ ΧΡΙΣΤΟΥ," *op cit.,* p. 110. Note the decided change in Dodd's position at this point from that in his earliest writing, *Meaning of Paul,* where he asserted that in the Pauline literature Jesus is "not . . . referred to as an outside standard" (p. 146) for Paul's message is "autonomy for the Christ-inspired conscience" (p. 148), to that contained in such later works as the above article and as in chapter four of *Gospel and Law.*

arises as to the correlation of these two elements in the working out of the believer's liberty. If there be in reality two normative factors in the direction of liberty, how does Paul view their interrelationship and function?

The directing principles of the Law of Christ. The law of Christ stands as the standard of God for Paul. He views the teaching of Christ as the embodiment and one true interpretation of the Old Testament, as is indicated by his use of *kata tas graphas* in I Corinthians 15:3, where the Christian interpretation of the Old Testament prophecies came about in the first instance through the instruction of Jesus.[58] And also he considers the person of the historical Christ to be the tangible portrayal and example of the divine standard, as is evident in his significant phrase *kata Christon*[59] and his frequent appeals to the example and character of Christ Himself.[60] Thus the Law of Christ must be understood in the thought of Paul as not only the teaching of Christ but also the example of the person of Christ; both comprising the new Torah.[61]

But it is significant that wherever the Apostle brings to bear on a particular ethical situation the authoritative teaching or example of Christ, he never represents that new Torah as being a detailed code which has a ready-made answer for every circumstance. Any interpretation of Paul which views him as merely exchanging the Halakah of the rabbis for the Halakah of Jesus fails to appreciate his thought regarding the Law of Christ. Even the definite command of the Lord regarding marriage is not considered by Paul to be "law" in the Jewish sense of a detailed code covering every exigency. Instead, it partakes of the nature of a principle; a principle which points the way to the solution in the particular circumstance but which must be applied anew

[58] Cf. G. W. H. Lampe's argument that the hermeneutical principles of the New Testament writers stem from the earthly instruction of Jesus Christ Himself, "The Reasonableness of Typology," *Essays on Typology* (London: S. C. M. Press, 1957), p. 25. See also Riesenfeld, *Gospel Tradition and Its Beginnings*, esp. pp. 28-30.

[59] Rom. 15:5; II Cor. 11:17 (*kata kurion*); cf. Col. 2:8.

[60] Rom. 15:3, 7, 8; I Cor. 11:1; II Cor. 8:9; Eph. 5:2, 25, 29; Phil. 2:5-11; Col. 3:13; I Thess. 1:6.

[61] Note the insistence of Justin Martyr that in the New Covenant "an eternal and final law—namely, Christ—has been given to us, . . . He is the new law, and the new covenant, ..." (Dialogue with Trypho, 11; trans. M. Dods *et al.*, Ante-Nicene Christian Library, Vol. II, p. 100).

to differing situations. Thus, though Christ taught that the non-separation of husband and wife is the principle which God has established from the beginning,[62] He said nothing specific about ascetic separation within the married state[63] or how this principle works out when the relationship between husband and wife has been altered through the conversion of one party.[64] These are matters which Paul places under the controlling principle explicit in the Law of Christ, but for which he also recognizes that specific direction must be sought from another source.

The Law of Christ is thus viewed as a standard which in its negative aspect objectively passes judgment on the self-assertion and waywardness of the Christian and in its positive purpose gives direction through authoritative principles. Paul would have agreed with E. F. Scott's understanding of the ethical teaching of Jesus at this point:

> Instead of framing laws he stated principles, and made them so few and broad and simple that no one could overlook them. . . . It is true that he enounced a large number of precepts which appear to bear directly on given questions of conduct. . . . But when we look more closely into the precepts we find that they are not so much rules as illustrations. In every instance they involve a principle on which all the stress is laid; but it is applied to a concrete example, so that we may not only grasp it as a principle but judge for ourselves how it works.[65]

Similarly, C. H. Dodd has remarked:

> I suggest that we may regard each of these precepts as indicating, in a dramatic picture of some actual situation, the *quality* and *direction* of action, which shall conform to the standard set by the divine *agapē*.[66]

Assuming that Paul knew of the words and actions of his Lord, it is significant that he never fell into the fallacy of a false precision in urging his converts to forgive exactly "seventy times seven,"[67] and no more, or in advocating that the example of prayer which Jesus gave

[62] I Cor. 7:10, 11b.
[63] I Cor. 7:3-6.
[64] I Cor. 7:12-16.
[65] E. F. Scott, *Ethical Teaching of Jesus,* p. 27. Cf. *Man and Society in the New Testament* (New York: Scribner, 1947), pp. 52, 62.
[66] Dodd, *Gospel and Law,* p. 73.
[67] Matt. 18:22; cf. Luke 17:4.

to His disciples was to be binding in its order and phraseology for a truly proper intercession.[68] And there is evidence that even his Lord considered the concrete situations contained in His teaching as dramatic illustrations of the principle involved rather than binding requirements, for in the records of the trial there is no indication that he literally offered the other cheek—though He certainly was true to the principle contained in Matthew 5:39. Indeed, that Jesus taught so much in parables—so much so that of His public ministry it could be said that "he spoke nothing to them without a parable"[69]—evidences the fact that the principles were the vital elements while the concrete situations in which those principles were encased were meant to be only illustrative. Nor is there in Paul's appeal to his converts to "walk in love, even as Christ loved us and gave himself for us"[70] or in his praise of the Thessalonians that they "became imitators . . . of the Lord"[71] any thought other than that of following the principles of Christ's example. Certainly he is not exhorting them to repeat the sacrifice of Christ or praising them for their punctilious conformity to the external activity of the Lord's ministry. Paul, who insisted that "the written code killeth,"[72] was not prepared to view the Law of Christ as more than authoritative principles set in concrete illustrations.

While on the one hand we must argue that the Law of Christ was for Paul no legalistic code of ethics,[73] on the other we must also insist that he understood its purpose to be more than merely to convey an impression of the atmosphere of the new life.[74] C. H. Dodd is true to the Apostle's thought when he says that

> the ethical precepts of the gospels serve two purposes. On the one hand, they help towards an intelligent and realistic act of "repentance," because they offer an objective standard of judgment upon our conduct, so that we know precisely where we stand in the sight of God, and are in a position to accept His judgment upon us and thereby to partake of His forgiveness. On the other hand, they are intended to offer positive moral

[68] Matt. 6:9-13; Luke 11:2-4.
[69] Matt. 13:34.
[70] Eph. 5:2, 25.
[71] I Thess. 1:6.
[72] II Cor. 3:6.
[73] As H. Windisch asserts, *Meaning of the Sermon on the Mount, passim.*
[74] As R. Bultmann insists, *Jesus and the Word,* pp. 92-94.

guidance for action, to those who have, in the words of the gospels, received the Kingdom of God.[75]

Paul viewed the Law of Christ as both propositional principles and personal example, standing as valid external signposts and bounds for the operation of liberty and concerned with the quality and direction of Christian liberty.

The pneumatic guidance of the Mind of Christ. And yet, Luther has rightly insisted that "it is not enough nor is it Christian, to preach the works, life and words of Christ as historical facts, as if the knowledge of these would suffice for the conduct of life."[76] In spite of the importance of the Law of Christ in the Apostle's thought, if we view this as the sole source for the direction and guidance of liberty we cannot claim to have truly interpreted Paul's message. In fact, to go only this far would be to agree more with Stoicism than with distinctive Christianity. For while the Law of Christ is a definite factor in the direction of Christian liberty, it is not the most distinctive factor nor that which actually produces the Christian ethic. Without the Mind of Christ through the activity of the Spirit at work in the believer, the principles of the Law of Christ remain remote and unattainable. In a slightly different context, James S. Stewart has pertinently remarked regarding "that type of modern religion which is content to regard Jesus merely as example":

Were there no more than this, the contemplation of the perfect holiness of Jesus could only breed despair. No shining example, cold and remote as the stars, can cleanse the conscience that has been defiled, or break the

[75] Dodd, *Gospel and Law,* p. 64. Cf. O. Cullmann, *Christ and Time,* p. 229, and K. Lake, *Paul: His Heritage and Legacy,* p. 48 for similar expressions.

[76] M. Luther, "A Treatise on Christian Liberty," *Works of Martin Luther,* Vol. II, trans. W. A. Lambert, p. 326. Many have viewed Luther in this statement, and in such expressions as "I have need of nothing, except that faith exercise the power and dominion of its own liberty" (*ibid.,* p. 324), as renouncing all validity to the external Word in the direction of Christian liberty. But, as R. H. Bainton points out: "Here is the question of religious authority. The mystic finds it in inward experience, not in a book or creed. So Luther sometimes talked as if God or the Spirit operated directly. But more commonly, even in the beginning, he was unwilling to divorce the Spirit from the outward Word; and so increasingly after the conflict with the radicals, Luther even went so far as to attribute to the Word an effectiveness practically *ex opere operato*" ("The Development and Consistency of Luther's Attitude to Religious Liberty," *H. T. R.,* Vol. XXII, No. 2 [Apr., 1929], pp. 126-27).

octopus grip which sin gets upon the soul. The evangel of an ethical example is a devastating thing. It makes religion the most grievous of burdens.[77]

And it is true as well in the matter of Christian guidance. For Paul, the believer's life must ultimately be guided and empowered by the Spirit if it is to be truly Christian. The words of Jesus concerning the Spirit well represent Paul's thought as well at this point: "He will guide you into all truth; . . . for he will take what is mine and declare it unto you."[78]

The precise function of the Spirit in this matter of the exercise of Christian liberty is probably best summed up in the Apostle's use of the word *dokimazō*—i.e. testing, determining, proving. Cullmann has pointed this out in saying,

> The working of the Holy Spirit shows itself chiefly in the "testing" (*dokimazein*), that is, in the *capacity of forming the correct Christian ethical judgment at each given moment,* and specifically of forming it in connection with the knowledge of the redemptive process, in which, indeed, the Holy Spirit is a decisive figure.
>
> This "testing" is the key to all New Testament ethics. . . . Certainty of moral judgment in the concrete sense is in the last analysis the one great fruit that the Holy Spirit, this factor in redemptive history, produces in the individual man.[79]

Hence, whereas in the Old Covenant the individual was to *"determine* the things which are best being instructed out of the law,"[80] in the New Covenant the Christian is to *"test* all things"[81] and *"determine* the things which are best"[82] by reference to the working of the Holy Spirit in his life.[83] Thus Paul exhorts: "Be transformed by the renewal of your mind, that you may *determine* what is the good and acceptable and perfect will of God."[84]

The guidance of the Christian in his liberty is thus in Paul's mind a

[77] J. S. Stewart, *Man in Christ,* p. 168.
[78] John 16:12-15.
[79] Cullmann, *Christ and Time,* p. 228.
[80] Rom. 2:18.
[81] I Thess. 5:21.
[82] Phil. 1:10.
[83] Note the close proximity of the exhortations "test all things" of I Thess. 5:21 and "quench not the Spirit" of I Thess. 5:19.
[84] Rom. 12:2.

matter involving both the Law of Christ (*nomos Christou*) and the Mind of Christ (*nous Christou*). Neither the objective nor the subjective element of this relationship is productive of the Christian life if that one element is really considered to stand alone. It is not without significance that the two elements of the Law of Christ and Spirit-directed testing are joined so closely together in the opening verses of Galatians 6, and that they are both subsumed under the broader heading of "walking by the Spirit." Nor should we fail to notice that the same epistle of I Corinthians which so stresses the Mind of Christ also contains the reference to being "in-lawed to Christ." Thus the "spiritual man," i.e., the man who not only notes the principles and example of the Law of Christ but who also allows the Mind of Christ to make application to his ethical judgment at each given moment, "judges all things."[85] Such a man recognizes that as he is true to the general direction given in the Law of Christ and obedient to the Mind of Christ, he need not be too concerned regarding the adverse opinion of men; for, as Paul insisted in his own case, "it is a very small thing that I should be judged by you or by any human court. . . . It is the Lord who judges me."[86] Likewise he realizes that the same freedom of ethical decision which is his under the Law of Christ and the Mind of Christ must be allowed to his fellow Christian. He may see his brother taking a different course of action. But as his brother is desirous of acting within the bounds of the Law of Christ and of being guided by the Mind of Christ, he recognizes in Christian love —even though he might be "persuaded in the Lord Jesus"[87] of the correctness of his own convictions—that "it is before his own Lord that he [i.e., the Christian brother] stands or falls."[88] Liberty is not only based in Christ, it is also directed and judged by Christ.

APOSTOLIC AND ECCLESIASTICAL AUTHORITY

But in stating that liberty receives its guidance only from Christ, the question immediately arises regarding the validity of apostolic and ecclesiastical instruction and ethical pronouncements. Emil

[85] I Cor. 2:15a.
[86] I Cor. 4:3-4; cf. I Cor. 2:15b; II Cor. 10:7; Col. 2:16.
[87] Rom. 14:14.
[88] Rom. 14:4; cf. Rom. 14; I Cor. 2:15b; II Cor. 5:10.

Brunner, in apparent consistency with Paul's Christological emphasis, insists that thus "not even an Apostle can tell you what you ought to do."[89] And many have followed his lead to assert that "any reimposition of do's and don'ts—even though imposed in the name of Christ —is less than Christian, for Christ knows no taboo." Yet, while this emphasis has captured a vital element in Paul's teaching, it has not fully represented his thought; for the Apostle did consider it his and the Church's legitimate function to exhort and make ethical pronouncements. And he himself spoke authoritatively regarding even specific situations.[90] Many have considered this a great inconsistency,[91] but evidently Paul did not think it so. It is far beyond the scope of this work to enter into an extended discussion regarding Paul's consciousness of his own ministry and his thought regarding the nature and function of the Church. But his thought on this more limited matter of the place of an apostle and the Church in the guidance of the believer's liberty must be considered.

The responsibility of an apostle and the Church. Paul certainly considered himself possessed of an authority, which he said "the Lord gave for building you up and not for destroying you."[92] While he readily stated that his authority was not to enslave[93] or lord it over the faith of his converts,[94] he also insisted that he could legiti-

[89] Brunner, *Divine Imperative,* p. 118.

[90] Dodd speaks of "the downright peremptory tone which Paul adopts." He goes on to point out that the Apostle "neither argues nor offers tactful advice. He gives 'orders'; the term which he employs is the term used for army orders. This may come as something of a shock to those who have been accumstomed to think of Paul as the apostle of liberty, and even of what is nowadays called 'Christian anarchism' " (*Gospel and Law,* pp. 13-14).

[91] E.g., F. C. Burkitt, who, after treating "the high Paulinist doctrine" of liberty, goes on to say: "What, however, is also clear is that (like most theoretical anarchists) he did not always live up to it. In other moods Paul issues his own Decrees, and I do not find them always convincing" (*Christian Beginnings* [London: University of London, 1924], p. 122). W. L. Knox says that in I Cor. Paul "is forced to introduce an elementary form of a Christian moral code, but it is entirely inconsistent with his theology in Romans and Galatians" (*St. Paul and the Church of Jerusalem,* p. 318, n. 3; cf. *St. Paul,* pp. 94-95). Even Dodd, in his earliest work, declared that Paul's "occasional attempts at a dictation" were "really not consistent with his principles" (*Meaning of Paul,* p. 147).

[92] II Cor. 10:8. Cf. I Tim. 2:7.

[93] II Cor. 11:20-21.

[94] II Cor. 1:24.

mately reprove,[95] discipline,[96] instruct,[97] and even command.[98] And that which he claimed for himself in this matter of the exercise of liberty, he expected of the Church. Thus the Church also was to rebuke error,[99] discipline flagrant wantonness,[100] and decide in particular matters where the welfare of the community was at stake.[101] He even assures the church at Corinth that in such matters it assembles, and undoubtedly acts, "with the power of our Lord Jesus."[102] Therefore he exhorts his converts to be subject to their leaders,[103] for, in the words of Hebrews 13:17, "they are keeping watch over your souls as those who will have to give account." He considers that both he and the Church have a rightful authority in this matter of liberty's direction.

The key to the understanding of the problem of how Paul could proclaim that Christ was the only guide in the exercise of the believer's liberty and yet could believe himself and the Church to be responsible in some measure for that liberty seems to be found in the transition between chapters 2 and 3 of I Corinthians. In the closing verses of chapter 2, he speaks of the spiritual (*pneumatikos*) man who has no need of a religious authority to aid him in knowing the will of God; indeed, for him such an authority would simply be superfluous. In chapter 3, however, he opens by declaring that those he is addressing were not spiritual men (*pneumatikoi*) but rather were fleshly beings (*sarkikoi*); and thus he begins to instruct and command them in matters regarding their liberty. These were Christians (*adelphoi,* not those of the *psuchikoi*[104]) who had left the principles and example of the Law of Christ, and who evidently were not obedient to the Mind of Christ. And as such, they needed to be called back from the following of their own fleshly desires to the lordship of Christ. Implicit throughout the Pauline teaching is this thought

[95] II Cor. 13:2.
[96] I Cor. 5:3-8; I Tim. 1:20.
[97] E.g., I Thess. 4:2 ff.
[98] Philemon 8.
[99] I Tim. 1:20; Titus 2:15.
[100] I Cor. 5:4-8; II Cor. 2:6; II Thess. 3:14-15.
[101] I Cor. 6:1-6.
[102] I Cor. 5:4.
[103] I Cor. 16:16.
[104] I Cor. 2:14.

that the apostolic and ecclesiastical rebukes, instructions, and commands are only necessary because of spiritual immaturity. True, because of the temporal tension in the present outworking of redemptive history, full maturity is still a goal with all; and thus the need for a constant awareness of the Law of Christ as well as an experiencing of the Mind of Christ. But spiritual men need not be rebuked or commanded, nor need the Apostle dwell upon the Law of Christ in addressing them. Thus, to those churches and individuals he considers well within the framework of the Law of Christ and desirous of being guided by the Mind of Christ, e.g., the churches of Thessalonica and Philippi and his "beloved fellow worker" Philemon, he primarily appeals (*parakaleō*), encourages (*paramutheomai*), and beseeches (*marturomai*) to "lead a life worthy of God" and of "the gospel of Christ."[105] But to those churches which he feels are not spiritual, e.g., the church at Corinth, and to those of which he has no certain knowledge because of lack of personal acquaintance, e.g., the church at Rome and those addressed in the so-called Ephesian letter, he gives commands in the first case and instructions in the principles of Christ in the second—as well as his usual exhortations to be directed by Christ and follow the guidance of the Spirit. Paul seems to have made a similar distinction as is contained in the ancient Jewish fable, the Story of Ahikar: "My son, send a wise man and give him no orders; but if thou wilt send a fool, go rather thyself and send him not."[106]

Now certainly the conception of a two-stratum religious society wherein the more spiritually mature are authorized to instruct and even command the less mature can be criticized on the grounds that not only is it undemocratic, but too often it leads to blind obedience and tyranny. Such criticism is often voiced, even though such stratification finds many accepted parallels in normal family and societal life. And the fact that the officers and members of the "visible" Church are still human makes the point of this criticism a real possibility. Whether it be bishop, presbyter, or the will of the congregation—a matured individual, matured individuals, or the matured opinion of the whole—there is always the twofold danger that in the process of ecclesiastical guidance the less mature will only blindly conform to

[105] I Thess. 2:11-12; Phil. 1:27; Philemon 9-10.
[106] The Story of Ahikar, 2.41.

the dictates of that religious authority and the authority itself will take on the character of a tyrant. While this danger may be lessened in the more democratic types of religious structure, it is not nullified. Despite Rousseau's maxim that "by giving myself to all I give myself to none," the authority of the sovereign group can be just as tyrannical as that of a sovereign. Paul recognized these dangers, and thus insisted that the *normal* Christian life was lived "by the Spirit"[107] and that those who restored the wayward and less mature were to do it in gentleness, humility, and love.[108] But he still taught that *hoi pneumatikoi* were in some manner to aid in the outworking of their less mature brothers' liberty: "You who are spiritual restore such a one."[109]

The manner in which this responsibility is to be carried out. We cannot leave this question without attempting some answer to the further problem of just how Paul conceived that this responsibility of an apostle and the Church should be carried out. Of course there are no explicit procedures which Paul lays out in this regard. It would have been entirely non-Pauline for him to give a set of rules for the restoration of saints. Yet we can gather certain suggestions from his letters as to how an apostle and the Church should function in this matter of the exercise of liberty.

Four legitimate functions in the execution of this responsibility seem to be recognized:

1. The censuring of action which is beyond the general direction of the Law of Christ. Paul's own rebuke of the ethical excesses at Corinth[110] and his exhortations to the churches likewise to discipline and rebuke[111] reveal his thought at this point.

2. The reiteration of the principles and example of the Law of Christ to those who are new in the faith or who tend to be wayward. Thus Paul gave ethical instruction to his new converts[112] and filled the exhortations of Romans 12-14 with reminiscences of the teaching of Jesus.

[107] E.g., Gal. 5:16-25.
[108] E.g., Gal. 6:1-5; II Cor. 2:1-11; II Tim. 2:25.
[109] Gal. 6:1.
[110] I Cor. 5:3-5; II Cor. 13:1 ff.; I Tim. 1:20.
[111] I Cor. 5:4-8; II Cor. 2:6; II Thess. 3:14-15; I Tim. 5:20.
[112] I Thess. 4:2.

3. The urging of obedience to the Mind of Christ. This appeal to "put on the Lord Jesus Christ," "have this mind in you which is also in Christ Jesus," and "walk by the Spirit" he evidently considered the highest ethical appeal possible.

4. The interpretation of the will of Christ for specific problems affecting the corporate life of the community in a particular area and at a particular time. This Paul did in those matters of lawsuits, marriage, meats offered to idols, the veiling of women in church, and the collection for the saints, which were disrupting questions and of great concern to the whole church at Corinth.

It is this fourth point which seems most problematic, for here he infringes upon that area which he proclaims is the exclusive domain of the Spirit. He seems to feel, however, that since that church has shown itself to possess an element of carnality by the very fact of its divisions and strifes, it is incumbent upon him as an apostle entrusted with the care of the churches to speak with the authority given him of God for the sake of the corporate life of the community. Thus he gives instructions and even commands for the particular situation to those whom he feels are in their present state not responsive to the Mind of Christ. And this he does for the sake of the corporate life of the Church.

But in all of this it must be noticed that he does not consider this really normal. It is abnormal because of his converts' abnormal spiritual condition. Similarly, he seems to recognize that in every pronouncement of this kind his words must be considered an interpretation. While they are given with apostolic authority, and thus must be heeded, they can never take the place of or be equal in rank with the express directives of the Lord nor the guidance of the Spirit. This distinction seems evident in his following statements:

I Corinthians 7:6. "But I say this by way of concession, not by way of command."

I Corinthians 7:25. "I have no command of the Lord, but I give an opinion as one mercifully commissioned by the Lord to be trustworthy."

I Corinthians 7:40. ". . . according to my opinion. And I think that I have the Spirit of God [on this matter]."

II Corinthians 8:8. "I say this not by way of command."

Further, these were apostolic interpretations for a specific time and a specific circumstance, not eternally valid principles. They were the Mind of Christ, he believed, for that circumstance. Paul would be the first to insist that they are true for later and other situations only in the sense that the principle which they apply remains constant, and only as the Spirit applies that principle anew to new situations in the same manner. He explicitly states that one of his opinions was conditioned by "the present distress,"[113] and it seems that he recognized the temporally and circumstantially bound nature of his other pronouncements as well. We need not suppose, for instance, that he would have continued to argue for the inconsequential character of eating meat offered to idols when at a later time such an act acquired the connotation of a renunciation of Christ.

Thus as a father in maturity and an apostle in rights he applies the Mind of Christ as he knows it to the specific situation of those who are less mature and for whom he is responsible, insisting all the while that such action on his part was only an interim measure until they came to maturity and taken for the sake of the corporate community.

THE CONDITIONING OF LIBERTY

But there is also another vitally important element present in the Pauline teaching regarding liberty, and that is the concept of love as the conditioning factor in the exercise of Christian liberty. Much has been written regarding the signficance of *agapē* and its distinction from the less meaningful *philia* and the nonbiblical *erōs,*[114] but it is impossible to overemphasize its importance in Paul's thought. With only a very slight extension of meaning to the words in his Song of Songs the Apostle could just as easily have said: Though I have all knowledge of the will of God and have not love, I am nothing. Paul's thought regarding the exercise of liberty contains both elements: (1) the knowledge of the will of God through the Law of Christ and the Mind of Christ, and (2) the conditioning of that knowledge as it is put into practice through love.

[113] I Cor. 7:26.

[114] E.g., A. Nygren, *Agape and Eros,* trans. P. S. Watson (London: S.P.C.K., 1953), pp. 30 ff.

As with many points in Paul's theology—and for that matter in the Christian life itself—these two concepts of the will of God and the love of God are so intimately joined that they can only be separated in practice at the cost of total destruction to the Christian ethic. Certainly to do the will of God truly is to act in love; while to act in a Spirit-inspired love is to fulfill the expressed Law of Christ and undoubtedly often to be in conformity to the Mind of Christ. Yet Paul does not simply equate the two conceptions, as is the manner of so much theological thought today. He does not speak of love so much as directing the Christian's liberty as of conditioning it. It is not that love is primary in giving guidance to the believer, for actions stemming from the best of motives and intentions can at times result in turmoil, harm, and anything but the will of God. Rather, love stands as the qualifying factor to that ethic which has received its guidance from Christ. The love which compelled and controlled God's action on behalf of man "has been poured into our hearts by the Holy Spirit,"[115] with the result that now love, in both its divine manifestations and its human responses, has become also the motivation for and the modifying element in the Christian ethic. As the will of God, expressed through the interaction of the Law of Christ and the Mind of Christ, is central in the guidance of liberty, so the love of God, both His love to us and our response, is central in its conditioning. It is this conditioning factor of love together with the pneumatic guidance of the Mind of Christ that makes operative in the particular situation the principles and example of the Law of Christ; and it is the union of these factors that results in the will of God being done in specific and differing situations.

Love to those within the community. The necessity of love within the Christian community is so basic to Paul's thought and teaching that he can say to the Thessalonians: "But concerning love of the brethren you have no need to have any one write to you, for you yourselves have been taught by God to love one another."[116] While the Pauline correspondence has less explicit reference to brotherly love than does the Johannine literature,[117] the conception of such love

[115] Rom. 5:5.

[116] I Thess. 4:9.

[117] Paul's explicit exhortations to brotherly love are found in Rom. 12:10, 13:8; Gal. 5:13; Eph. 5:2.

lies basic to Paul's ethical teaching and, as will be pointed out in the following chapters, finds its best illustration in the Apostle's practice.

The Johannine emphasis that love of God means also love of the brethren finds its counterpart in Paul's presentation of the unity that exists between Christ and the Church, and thus between Christians themselves. As many have pointed out,[118] it is probable that Paul first learned of the solidarity of Christ and Christians on the Damascus road in the words: "Saul, Saul, why persecutest thou me?" Henceforth there rang in his heart the gist of the reported saying of Jesus: "Inasmuch as you did it to one of the least of these my brethren, you did it to me."[119] Thus he used the strong metaphor "the body of Christ" in describing the corporate fellowship of Christians in Christ.[120] We need not insist that this expression is to be taken realistically or ontologically.[121] The close relation between symbol and reality which is a feature of Hebrew thought must be taken seriously as a warning against the too exact and exclusive identification of "the body of Christ" with the Church.[122] Yet we must not minimize the strength of this metaphor in signaling the intense unity of fellowship that exists between Christ and the members of His Church. Without asserting such an ontological union, it still remains true that the Apostle could not "look into the eyes of a Christian without meeting there the gaze of Christ."[123] Therefore he tells the

[118] E.g., J. A. T. Robinson, *The Body*, p. 58; E. Best, *One Body in Christ*, p. 184.

[119] Matt. 25:40.

[120] I Cor. 12:27; cf. I Cor. 10:17, 12:12-30; Eph. 1:23, 4:12; Col. 1:18.

[121] As J. A. T. Robinson, *The Body*, and Catholic interpreters.

[122] Best has cogently argued: "Jer. 50:17, 'Israel is a scattered sheep,' does not imply reality but metaphor; so likewise, Jer. 50:6, 'My people hath been lost sheep,' and Isa. 5:7, 'For the vineyard of the Lord of Hosts is the house of Israel, and the men of Judah his pleasant plant.' Cf. Ps. 80:8; Hos. 10:1; Isa. 52:2. Israel is 'this' or 'that'—and the references could be indefinitely extended—but no one seriously believes that in these references anything more than a metaphor is implied. The word denoting comparison is just customarily omitted. It is true of descriptions of Yahweh in the Old Testament: Ps. 91:2, 'I will say of the Lord, He is my refuge and my fortress'—which does not mean that the Lord is an inanimate castle but that in certain aspects of his being he behaves like such a castle. So it is in the case of the description of the Church as the Body of Christ" (*One Body in Christ*, p. 99).

[123] J. A. T. Robinson, *The Body*, p. 58, quoting E. Mersch, *The Whole Christ*, p. 104.

Corinthians that in "sinning against the brethren and wounding their weak conscience you are sinning against Christ,"[124] and in making the Lord's Supper a gluttonous feast and through it even shaming the Christian poor you are "not discerning the body."[125] In this case, the latter phrase probably refers both to not discerning in the supper the divine significance of the things partaken of, the Lord's broken body and shed blood, *and* to not discerning in the supper the divine fellowship that has been and is established in Christ and among the members of His Body, the Church.[126]

It is because of this corporate relationship of believers in Christ that Paul speaks of his fellow Christian as a brother, a term which testifies to the closeness of the believer to other believers and which is exceeded in the figure of the family only by the words describing marriage itself—which are normally reserved in biblical terminology for the relationship of the Lord and His people. Similarly, while Paul's use of the preposition *en* designates the believer's personal relation to his Lord, his use of the prefix *sun* illustrates his thought regarding his own unity with other Christians and the believer's corporate relation within the community of Christ; e.g., *sunergos* (fellow worker),[127] *sugkoinōnos* (partner),[128] *summimētēs* (fellow imitator),[129] *sundoulos* (fellow slave),[130] *sustratiōtēs* (fellow soldier),[131] and *sunaichmalōtos* (fellow-prisoner).[132]

Thus the Christian's liberty within the community of Christ is to be conditioned by the love of God; a love which manifests itself in concern for the welfare of the fellow believer,[133] and which motivates and controls every attempt in edification[134] and restoration.[135] If the

[124] I Cor. 8:12.
[125] I Cor. 11:29.
[126] Cf. J. Moffatt, "Discerning the Body," *E. T.*, Vol. XXX, No. 1 (Oct., 1918).
[127] Rom. 16:3, 9, 21; I Cor. 3:9, 16:16; II Cor. 8:23; Phil. 2:25, 4:3; Col. 4:11; Philemon 1, 24.
[128] Phil. 1:7.
[129] Phil. 3:17.
[130] Col. 1:7, 4:7.
[131] Phil. 2:25; Philemon 2.
[132] Rom. 16:7; Col. 4:10; Philemon 23.
[133] Gal. 6:2; Phil. 2:4.
[134] I Cor. 12-14, esp. 13.
[135] II Cor. 2:5-11; Gal. 6:1.

will of God is to be truly done and the Christian's liberty truly exercised, all that is done must be done in love.[136] That same love which motivated God to give the gift of freedom in Jesus Christ must likewise motivate the Christian to waive his given rights of liberty wherever necessary for the sake of the corporate ideal.

Love to those outside the community. History has witnessed many groups who emphasized the distinctive reality of the brotherhood of believers in Christ and the obligation of love within the brotherhood, but who arbitrarily limited the requirement of love for the Christian to those within the community. And this is a common human tendency. Thus there develops a double standard of love: one for the brethren and one for those outside the fold. But this one-sided emphasis finds no justification in Paul. Though he did say that the Christian's goodness is to be directed "especially to those who are of the household of faith," the Apostle prefaced that statement by saying: "Let us do good to all."[137] And this same balance of love to both Christian and non-Christian is presented in Romans 12, where verses 3-13 deal with action within the Christian fellowship and verses 14-21 with the believer's attitude toward those without. The same intensity of love is to condition the Christian's action in both spheres, for the believer is to be interested in the welfare of all, whatever their spiritual condition.

In spiritual matters, one way in which this love is manifested to the world is in a willingness to restrict one's personal liberty in matters which are of secondary importance for the sake of the Gospel. Paul explicitly states this principle in a series of balanced clauses in I Corinthians 9:19-23. There he says that to the Jew he voluntarily "became as one under the law," even though as a Christian he holds himself to be free from the Law, and to the Gentile he "became as one outside the law [i.e., the Law of Moses]," for in truth he was done with that law—though for different reasons than his Gentile audiences. Since for Paul the Law had lost its connection with righteousness in the coming of Christ and now only carried nationalistic significance, it had become less than secondary to the central issue

[136] I Cor. 16:14.
[137] Gal. 6:10.

of his message. This meant, on the one hand, that he was not going to alienate his Jewish hearers and thus frustrate his ministry and the essential point of his message by a rash disregard of the national traditions. And, on the other, that he was not going to cast a stumbling block before his Gentile audiences by lauding what to him and to them (but for different reasons) were only national traditions.

David Daube has pointed out that Paul's action of being "all things to all men" on secondary issues in order that he might stress the primary matter "had formed part of Jewish missionary practice long before Paul."[138] He cites the case of Hillel's acceptance of a proselyte who would accept only such written law as contained the most fundamental ethical principles, the great teacher feeling that in such an acceptance the main point was won and the rest would come in time.[139] Thus, "at the decisive moment of conversion, he [i.e., Hillel] fell in with the notions of the applicant" in order to gain his major objective.[140] Similarly Daube cites the Letter of Aristeas 257, where, when the king asks how he might meet with acceptance when traveling abroad, the answer is given: "By becoming equal to all." In its context, this is advice for the traveler and has a political sense; and yet "it may be assumed that, as early as the time the Letter was composed, this was also a slogan of proselyte-makers. The author of the Letter himself was a Jewish propagandist."[141] Thus Daube argues that "Paul, when he wrote the passage from I Corinthians . . . (i.e., I Cor. 9:20-23), was drawing on a living element in Jewish religion."[142] But while this background may be true, Paul's attitude in I Corinthians 9:19, "for though I am free from all I have made myself a servant to all, in order that I might win the more," seems to have more the reminiscence of the example of Jesus than that of Hillel. In Philippians 2:6-11 and Galatians 4:4-5 he presents Jesus as being truly free of all men and yet as having taken the form of a servant under the Law in order that He might redeem those who were under the Law. In other words, Christ subjected Himself to the very

[138] D. Daube, *N. T. and Rabbinic Judaism,* p. 336.
[139] b. Shab. 31a, Aboth de-R. Nathan 15.
[140] D. Daube, *N. T. and Rabbinic Judaism,* p. 336.
[141] *Ibid.,* p. 341.
[142] *Ibid.,* p. 341.

limitations which He came to break in order to lay the foundations of the Gospel. And the fact that in Romans 15:8 and Ephesians 5:2 Paul holds up this example of Christ in becoming "a servant to the circumcised" as worthy of emulation indicates that even Paul's methods were Christologically based. Luther seems to have best and most succinctly caught the Apostle's thought in saying, "I will therefore give myself as a Christ to my neighbor, just as Christ offered Himself to me."[143] For Paul, the truly liberated man is the one who, like Christ, is free from evil and the possessor of God-given rights; yet who, like Christ, willingly re-enters the arena of conflict and voluntarily relinquishes his rights in nonessential matters in order to aid his fellows in the discovery of true freedom.

Thus the Christian's liberty in the sphere outside the fellowship of Christ, as well as within the community, is to be conditioned by the love of God; a love manifesting itself in concern for the welfare and salvation of those outside Christ, and motivating and controlling every action in the realization of that purpose. That same love which motivated God to give and Christ to bring the gift of liberty must also motivate the Christian to control his liberty in matters of secondary importance for the sake of the central message of liberty in Christ. This conditioning factor of love in the exercise of the Christian's liberty is best exemplified in the Apostle's own practice. To that practice we must turn in the following chapters.

[143] Luther, "Treatise on Christian Liberty," *op. cit.*, p. 337.

Practice

IX

Paul and the Jerusalem Church

SINCE THE PUBLICATION of F. C. Baur's *Paulus* in 1845, the practice of Paul has been considered by many the chief enigma in the study of the Apostle. His relations with the Jerusalem Church and its leaders, his practice in the Gentile mission and pastoral ministry, and his personal acceptance of distinctly Jewish customs while confessedly the Apostle of Gentile liberty have been subjects of much dispute. The difficulties of understanding his practice as represented in Acts and as suggested in some of his own statements have brought about a serious re-evaluation of the reliability both of the Acts account and of the moral character of Paul himself. It is to these problems that we must now turn if we would view aright the historical profile of Paul.

The first question of importance here—regarding Paul's relations with Jerusalem Christianity—has stood for over a hundred years as one of the most prominent problems in New Testament studies. Probably more scholarly effort has been expended upon it than on any other. And while the Tübingen proposals held the ascendancy through the nineteenth and early twentieth centuries, the past few decades have witnessed a growing majority in opposition to Baur's solution.[1] Little that is new can be added to the discussion of many years' duration. But we must review the issues and try to discern the most reasonable conclusions, so as better to understand the Pauline practice.

[1] Though see H. J. Schoeps, *Paul,* pp. 126-67 and *passim,* for a revival of Tübingen's distinction between Jewish Christianity and Paul regarding Jesus Christ and a continuation of the *Religionsgeschichte* explanation of the Pauline message.

Methodologically, it will be wise to confine our evidence to the letters of Paul. I agree with Baur that "the two first chapters of the Epistle to the Galatians form a historical document of the greatest importance in our investigations into the true standpoint of the Apostle and his relations to the elder Apostles."[2] Certainly highest priority in any historical or biographical inquiry must be given to such personal reflections, even though we need not agree that these portions alone ought to be held as authentic. This chapter will therefore deal with the relations between the Apostle to the Gentiles and the church of Jerusalem as they are evidenced in the Pauline epistles, leaving further questions regarding his practice to the following chapters.

THE JUDAIZERS

Whether or not we view Paul's career as a lifelong conflict with Judaizing antagonists, it is at least certain that we would have very little information from Paul himself regarding his relation to the Jerusalem church and its leaders if he had not had to combat the Judaizers. The threat from these opponents to the Pauline mission—or at least his remembrance of that threat—is the occasion for most of the Apostle's references to Jerusalem Christianity. If we are to understand these references, we must first have some knowledge of the Judaizers: we must ask who they were, what backing they had from the leaders in Jerusalem, and what influence they exerted within their own community.

Identity of the Judaizers. In attempting to understand the Judaizers, we cannot begin by assuming a common identification between (1) the "false apostles" of Corinth, who claimed to be both "apostles of Christ" and "Hebrews,"[3] (2) those whom Paul had in mind as adversaries to the Gospel in Rome, who would "cause dissensions and difficulties" in that church,[4] and (3) the heretics of Galatia. Although it is probable that a basic similarity unites all these Pauline opponents in such scattered localities as Galatia, Corinth, and Rome, the identification of the Judaizers must depend primarily upon their description

[2] F. C. Baur, *Paul,* Vol. I, p. 105.
[3] II Cor. 11:13, 22.
[4] Rom. 16:17.

in the letter where their activity is most clearly evident; i.e., Galatians. Nor need we be detained in consideration of the merits or improbabilities of Lütgert's and Ropes' "two-front theory" in identification of the opponents in Galatia.[5] Whether there were legalists and libertarians in Galatia or only legalists, at least there were those who proclaimed a so-called Jewish-Christian legalism; and it is only with the legalists that we are here concerned. Nor does it seem at all possible that such legalistic influence as was exerted on Paul's converts came only from the local synagogue—i.e., that Paul's opponents were simply Jews advocating Judaism. The Christians of Galatia, who before their conversion had spurned the full ministry of the synagogue, were not now prepared to render greater due to the Jewish practices than their own Apostle taught them—unless they had been encouraged to do so by Christian preachers claiming a fuller Christian message. These Pauline opponents in Galatia cannot be viewed as any other than those claiming to be Christians.

In the early thirties, E. Hirsch and W. Michaelis proposed the view that these heretics were strictly Gentiles who had been converted in a pre-Pauline time, circumcised before their baptism, and now were actively advocating the necessity of the same to Paul's converts.[6] Using a quite different approach, J. Munck has also insisted upon the Gentile character of these legalists. He believes them to be Pauline converts who agreed with their spiritual father's central message but felt it "safer to take over everything from the Jerusalem section of the church, though the leaders in Jerusalem had given the Gentile Christians freedom to follow Paul's Gospel."[7] The purpose of this chapter does not allow a detailed confrontation of either of the above views. Suffice it here to say that from Paul's manner of speaking of the situation in Galatians 1-2, it is difficult to picture these Judaizers as anything but Jewish Christians—in fact, Jewish Christians claiming to represent the official position of the

[5] W. Lütgert, *Gesetz und Geist* (Gütersloh: Bertelsmann, 1919); J. H. Ropes, *The Singular Problem of the Epistle to the Galatians* (Cambridge, Mass.: Harvard University Press, 1929).

[6] E. G. Hirsch, "Zwei Fragen zu Galater 6," *Z. N. W.*, Vol. XXIX, Heft 3/4 (1930), pp. 192-97; W. Michaelis, "Judaistische Heidenchristen," *Z. N. W.*, Vol. XXX, Heft 1 (1931), pp. 83-89.

[7] J. Munck, "Israel and the Gentiles in the New Testament," *J. T. S.*, Vol. II, Pt. 1 (Apr., 1951), p. 10.

Jerusalem church. From Paul's anathema in 1:8-9 upon even an angelic messenger if the message of such a being should be different from that which he had proclaimed to them, we may infer that these trouble-makers came with high qualifications. From his strong denial in 1:11-24 that his gospel was dependent for its source upon the Jerusalem disciples, it appears that this was exactly what his opponents claimed. And from his own claim in 2:1-10 of an independent authority which the elder apostles also recognized, it can only be supposed that the heretics asserted the contrary. Here were opponents claiming high qualifications and insisting that the Jerusalem apostles were both the source of Paul's gospel and the final authority before whom he must bow. All these implications, together with the fact that in Paul's reference to the parallel incident of the Antioch episode in 2:11-21 he closely joins "the ones from James" with "those of the circumcision party" of whom Peter was afraid,[8] strongly suggest that the heretics of Galatia were none other than Jewish Christians claiming the authority of their home church in Jerusalem. In all probability they were members of the strict law-abiding group in the Jerusalem church, of which James was officially the leader.[9]

Relation of the Judaizers to the Jerusalem apostles. But in accepting the Judaizers to be members of the Jerusalem church, the old problem arises of their relation to the Jerusalem apostles. F. C. Baur and his followers, greatly dependent upon the Clementine literature and viewing Simon Magus as a veiled representation of Paul, made it their major theme that the leaders of the Jewish church were at one with Paul's opponents and often clashed with him themselves. They insisted that the whole church at Jerusalem was united in opposition to the Pauline message.[10] Others, though at many points removed from the Tübingen position, have likewise viewed the elder apostles as standing behind and with the Judaizers. Eduard Meyer did not accept the Clementine evidence, but strictly on the basis of Galatians 1-2 and the other Pauline letters insisted that Peter, and

[8] It seems evident that in Paul's mind, though the Galatian question and the Antioch episode had superficial differences, these two cases dealt with basically the same issue.

[9] See Appendix, pp. 272-73.

[10] Baur, *Paul*, Vol. I, pp. 113, 119-30.

no other, was the leader of the legalistic agitation and actively led the campaign against Paul in all the Gentile churches.[11] Hans Lietzmann believed that the Jerusalem apostles were not actively engaged in that opposition, but that they did stand in agreement with the Judaizers. And by so giving their support to Paul's adversaries they were "very dangerous opponents behind his back."[12] Lietzmann saw James as the one who was mainly responsible in encouraging the errorists in the Gentile churches (for he "belonged at bottom to those who were strangers to Jesus"[13]) and Barnabas as the one who actively opposed Paul in Galatia.[14] Of late the influence of this Tübingen dialectic has waned and there has been a growing feeling among scholars that the radical emphasis of Baur is a lost cause. Echoes of old Tübingen, however, have resounded in S. G. F. Brandon's assertions that "there can be no real doubt" and the evidence is "irresistible and the conclusion must accordingly be accepted that Paul's real opponents were the leaders of the Jerusalem Church."[15]

And yet, though the Judaizers possibly possessed "letters of commendation"[16] from the Jerusalem church and certainly highly extolled the merits and authority of the Jerusalem leaders, there is no real evidence against, and even some for, the view that these antagonists of the Pauline gospel were taking a line of their own. Such positive evidence as exists for the basic agreement between Paul and the earlier apostles will be better considered in the next section of this chapter. Negatively, however, it must be pointed out that while Paul has only the sharpest words of rebuke for the heretics, "he utters not a single word" about the Jerusalem leaders who have been thought to stand behind them.[17] In fact, as Lietzmann confesses, it is only as we "look more closely and are able to read be-

[11] E. Meyer, *Ursprung und Anfänge des Christentums* (Stuttgart: Cotta, 1925), Vol. III, esp. p. 434; cf. also pp. 424-26, 432-36, 441-42, 455-59, 464, 493-500.

[12] H. Lietzmann, *Beginnings of the Christian Church,* p. 143.

[13] *Ibid.,* p. 83.

[14] H. Lietzmann, *An die Galater,* H.N.T. (Tübingen: Mohr, 1923), p. 38.

[15] S. G. F. Brandon, "The Crisis of 70 A.D.," *H. J.,* Vol. XLVI (Oct., 1947—July, 1948), pp. 222-23.

[16] II Cor. 3:1.

[17] Lietzmann, *Beginnings of the Christian Church,* p. 143.

tween the lines of his letters, [that] we perceive behind the servants of Satan, the false apostles, and the spurious brethren, the shadows of the great figures in Jerusalem."[18] But such reading between the lines cannot be accepted on a par with positive evidence. If one were simply to try to imagine what went on, then Lightfoot's suggestion seems to carry greater likelihood:

In all revolutionary periods, whether of political or religious history, the leaders of the movement have found themselves unable to control the extravagances of their bigoted and short-sighted followers: and this great crisis of all was certainly not exempt from the common rule. St Paul is constantly checking and rebuking the excesses of those who professed to honour his name and to adopt his teaching: if we cannot state this of St James with equal confidence, it is because the sources of information are scantier.[19]

There does not seem to be any real evidence for the position that the Jerusalem apostles were in agreement with the work of the Judaizers; and thus we must agree with the insistence that "man die Fiktion gänzlich aufgeben muss, hinter der Häretikern in Galatien stehe die Autorität der Jerusalemer Führer."[20]

Both Baur's insistence that the Judaizers must be identified with the whole Jerusalem church and Munck's that there were no Judaizers in that church are extreme positions. Nor need we agree with the implication of Schmithals' thesis that these were Jewish-Christian Gnostics, who, because of their Gnosticism, would not be controlled by churchly authorities though they could at the same time highly extol the Jerusalem leaders in debate.[21] Though they may have possessed Gnostic tendencies, our knowledge of Jewish Gnosticism is too meager to make possible such a precise identification. All that really seems evident is that, while these were members of the Jerusalem church, they were too shortsighted to share in the vision of their leaders. They probably considered themselves as conscientious and acting from the best principles and motives, though Paul viewed them as motivated by fear of persecution and the desire for au-

[18] *Ibid.,* p. 143.
[19] J. B. Lightfoot, *Galatians,* p. 371.
[20] W. Schmithals, "Die Häretiker in Galatien," *Z. N. W.,* Vol. XLVII (1956), p. 36.
[21] *Ibid.,* p. 38.

thority.[22] As they remained within the confines of Palestinian Jewish Christianity, they were probably indistinguishable from the rest of the brethren. But when they traveled abroad, their true colors as "false apostles" and "spurious brethren" were manifest. On the basis of their evident Christian faith and godliness in Jerusalem, they had probably received general letters commending them to all Christians abroad. But it seems that they used these recommendations to their own purpose.[23] In their visit to Antioch they appear to have had a real mission from James. But we need not suppose more than that they took a line of their own in the episode Paul relates.

Influence of the Judaizers on the Church. In all probability, the Galatian Christians were won back to the Pauline gospel.[24] The very fact that the Apostle's letter to them was preserved favors this view, as does also Paul's reference at a later date to the churches of Galatia as joining in the collection for the poor Christians of Jerusalem.[25] Likewise, it seems that in the Galatian battle the main thrust of the Judaizers' attack in Pauline circles had been broken. While the legalists probably attempted to continue their policy of disruption among the Gentile Christians,[26] and Paul was constantly aware of the danger from this source,[27] it appears that in the latter part of the Pauline

[22] Gal. 6:12, 13.

[23] Cf. E. F. Scott: "It does not appear that the leading Apostles were in sympathy with their attitude, much less with their onslaught on Paul; yet those obviously earnest men could not be refused 'letters of commendation' (I Cor. iii. 1) which certified that they were highly esteemed in the Jerusalem church. This it was that made their propaganda so dangerous. Wherever they went they were able to represent themselves as spokesmen for the mother-church, duly accredited by the foremost Apostles" (*The First Age of Christianity* [London: Allen & Unwin, 1926], p. 140).

[24] Cf. A. S. Peake, *Paul and the Jewish Christians* (Manchester: Manchester University Press, 1929), pp. 28-29.

[25] I Cor. 16:1; cf. Acts 20:4.

[26] Whether or not Paul countered Judaizing influence in his Roman epistle, at least the Judaizers' presence in some of the other Gentile churches seems evident by statements in II Cor. 11, Phil. 3, and the Pastorals (cf. P. P. Bläser, *Gesetz bei Paulus,* pp. 81-88).

[27] Peake speaks of the outburst against the Judaizers in Phil. 3:2—4:1 as "one of the fiercest which has come to us from his pen" (*Paul and the Jewish Christians,* p. 32). This need not be an interpolation from an earlier time, since Eph. 2:11 ff. and Col. 2:11 ff. indicate that at least the remembrance of the Judaizing conflict was still in Paul's thoughts; cf. I Tim. 1:7; Titus 1:10-16, 3:9.

ministry their influence was held in check and their attack not made in quite the same manner as in Galatia. Whether this was the result of Paul's action, the decision of the Jerusalem Council, or both —or even of other factors—need not trouble us here. The interesting question arises, however, concerning the influence of the Judaizers within their own mother church.

One gains the impression in scrutinizing the church of Jerusalem that the rank and file within its membership became more zealous for the Law and more strict in its practice as time went on. It appears that the stricter type of Jewish Christianity gained more of an influence over the community than did that of *am haarez* Christianity.[28] In the earlier days, James seemed less fearful to speak out against Christians of the Pharisaic party who opposed Paul.[29] Paul argued as though his position was the characteristic view of the primitive church[30] and came to the Jerusalem Council as though confident of the outcome.[31] Later, however, James seemed to speak at the instigation of those zealous for the Law,[32] and Paul had fears that the Jerusalem church might not accept his labor for them in the collection he had made.[33] We can only guess the reasons why. But it does seem that the type of mentality from which the Judaizers originated had a greater influence upon the Jewish church itself than it did on the Gentile churches during the same period.

[28] Regarding "Scrupulous" and *am haarez* Jewish Christianity, see Appendix, pp. 271-73.

[29] Acts 15:13-21.

[30] E. F. Scott points out in regard to Paul's recital of Peter's position in Gal. 2 that, "It is commonly assumed that these sentiments of Peter—if Paul is correct in his judgment of them—were peculiar to Peter himself. . . . But we miss the significance of the whole incident when we read in it nothing more than the individual attitude of Peter. Paul, it is evident, means us to think of Peter as representing the view which was characteristic of the primitive church, although it had been perverted by the influence of the 'false brethren.' It is this that gives point to Paul's rebuke of the older Apostle. He appeals not so much to his private conscience as to his knowledge of the true position of the church. Peter, it is suggested, must know in his heart that this practice which he is countenancing is the later innovation, while Paul has taken his stand on the genuine primitive tradition" (*Beginnings of the Church* [New York: Scribner's Sons, 1914], p. 121).

[31] There is a seeming note of eagerness in Paul's decision to go to Jerusalem, as recorded in Acts 15:2.

[32] Acts 21:20-25.

[33] Rom. 15:31.

PAUL AND THE "PILLAR" APOSTLES

We must now bring together the various scattered hints and references so as to deal more formally and completely with the question of the relations between Paul and the Jerusalem apostles.

Basic differences between them. It cannot be assumed that, because the elder disciples in Jeruslem were not in agreement with the Judaizers, they were completely at one with Paul. The fact that "the disciples were first called Christians in Antioch"[34] indicates that even the pagan world could recognize some difference between the Christianity proclaimed by Paul and the Jewish Christianity of the early apostles, and thus between the apostles themselves.

We must, however, insist that those differences were not over such questions as: (1) the circumcision of Gentile Christians, or (2) communion between Jewish and Gentile Christians within the Church. While many have argued that Paul did have Titus circumcised in deference to the wishes of the Jerusalem leaders,[35] the same advocates of this view have quite honestly admitted that from an exegetical standpoint they must return "a verdict of 'not proven' " for their position—and that the opposite view is not impossible.[36] To argue from the omission of *hois oude* in Galatians 2:5 of Codex Bezae, thus getting the sense of "we yielded," is to argue from the least attested text.[37] Nor can it be said that the circumcision of Timothy and that of Titus are truly analogous situations.[38] Undoubtedly there was a real distinction in the minds of most Jews, including the Jewish Christians of Jerusalem and the Apostle Paul, between one who was a half-Jew and one who was purely a Gentile. Paul nowhere disputed the right—or even the necessity, because of the circumstances and views of the Jerusalem church—of Jewish Christians to continue the

[34] Acts 11:26.

[35] Esp. K. Lake, *Beginnings,* Vol. V, pp. 196-98; F. C. Burkitt, *Christian Beginnings,* p. 118; W. L. Knox, *St. Paul and the Church of Jerusalem,* pp. 182-83.

[36] Cf. Lake, *Beginnings,* Vol. V, p. 198; Knox, *St. Paul and the Church of Jerusalem,* p. 190, n. 19.

[37] All the manuscripts stand in opposition to D at this point, though Irenaeus, Victorinus, Tertullian, Ambrosiaster, Primasius, and the Old Latin agree.

[38] As Lake makes them, *Beginnings,* Vol. V, pp. 197-98.

practice of circumcision. But he strongly opposed it as a religious practice for Gentile converts. Timothy probably came under the classification of a Jewish Christian in the eyes of many. But Titus was definitely a Gentile believer. Nor is the statement of Galatians 2:3 —"But not even Titus, who was with me, was compelled to be circumcised, though he was a Greek"—most naturally read: Titus was circumcised, but not by any compulsion.[39] While it might be suitable in regard to Timothy who possessed Jewish blood, such a concession in the case of the Gentile Titus, even if made under no compulsion, would undermine Paul's whole polemic and make Galatians 2 more bluster than argument. As many have insisted, "we must give proper weight to Paul's actual statements, which cannot without violence be accommodated to the view that Titus was circumcised."[40]

There is no real evidence that on the question of the circumcision of Gentile Christians there was any difference between Paul and the elder apostles. Paul's refusal to mention these leaders as his opponents is significant. And the fact that he brought at least one uncircumcised Gentile believer with him on his last visit to Jerusalem[41] indicates that he had no fear that the leaders of the Jerusalem church could be pressured into asking for the circumcision of his Gentile converts and Christian companions—even though there was a rising element of legalism within Jewish Christianity. Similarly, Paul believed that the Jerusalem apostles stood at one with him on the question of communion between Jew and Gentile within the Church. It is significant that he does not rebuke Peter for acting from wrong principles, but for being untrue to his own principles.[42] As Paul saw it, Peter's action in breaking fellowship between Jewish and Gentile Christians at Antioch was an act of hypocrisy and a failure to apply accepted doctrines consistently. Although those who precipitated the disturbance at Antioch were "from James," and Peter acted more out of regard for the welfare of his Jewish brethren than for the larger good of

[39] Knox admits that the greatest argument against his position is that the opposite view "gives a more natural interpretation of the Greek of vv. 3-5" (*St. Paul and the Church of Jerusalem,* p. 190, n. 19).

[40] Peake, *Paul and the Jewish Christians,* p. 13, n.

[41] I.e., Trophimus, Acts 21:29. Possibly also those of Acts 20:4.

[42] C.f., e.g., Lightfoot, *Galatians,* pp. 354-55; F. J. A. Hort, *Judaistic Christianity* (London: Macmillan, 1894), pp. 77-78.

the Gospel,[43] Paul did not consider the Antioch episode as manifesting any basic difference of doctrine or principle between himself and the Jerusalem leaders.

What differences there were between Paul and the elder apostles seem to stem, in the first place, from their different conceptions of their own missions. We need not agree with J. Munck that the apostles differed in their view of the pattern of redemptive history; i.e., that Paul viewed God's program as being the conversion of a representative number of Gentiles first, then the conversion of Israel, and then the *parousia,* as opposed to the Jerusalem church's conviction of Israel first, then the *parousia,* and only then the conversion of the Gentiles.[44] Certainly Munck has done a service in pointing out Paul's thought of his mission as an indirect ministry to Israel[45] and in emphasizing anew his abiding concern for his own nation. But in his main thesis, Munck has gone to the same length as F. C. Baur in allowing his presuppositions to control his sources. Any presentation that discredits certain portions of the evidence—even the account of Acts—simply because they do not fit into the thesis of the historian, must be looked upon with a bit of suspicion. Rather than there being a difference between the apostles regarding the pattern of redemptive history, it seems all we need insist upon is that there was a difference between them regarding each one's own special mission within the over-all redemptive program. There does not seem

[43] Many have understood Peter's action at Antioch to be an endeavor to protect the Jewish Christians of Jerusalem, probably those back home who would be subjected to antagonism by the Jews when the Judaizers' report of conditions in Antioch reached Jerusalem (cf. *ibid.,* p. 78), or less likely the emissaries from James themselves who would be subjected to persecution by the Jews in Jerusalem if it had been known that they ate with Gentiles (cf. B. Reicke, "Der geschichtliche Hintergrund des Apostelkonzils und der Antiochia-Episode," *Studia Paulina,* p. 177).

[44] J. Munck, *Paulus und die Heilsgeschichte.*

[45] Though E. Stauffer has better characterized Paul's thought as to how God would use his ministry for the benefit of Israel: "God accepts the Gentiles into the people of Christ in order to make the people of God under the old convenant jealous. . . . Indeed, the apostle's mission to the Gentiles itself appears in this light as the only possible, if indirect service he can render to the future of his people. In divine emulation the apostle brings the Gentiles into the Church so as to make the people of the old covenant 'jealous' on their part, and so to prepare the way for their salvation and return" (*N. T. Theology,* p. 191).

to be any real reason to reject the witness of the Gospels and the Acts regarding the Jewish church's consciousness of the universal import of the Gospel even while it continued to insist that its special mission was solely to Israel, or Paul's approach to his own nation in each city even when he proclaimed himself an apostle to the Gentiles.[46] All that seems evident is that while the apostles recognized the validity of each other's orders, they also insisted that each had been assigned a special responsibility. This is all that need be implied in Paul's recital of the events that led to and included "the right hand of fellowship" given by James, Cephas, and John to Paul and Barnabas.[47] They bound themselves to partnership in the general redemptive program of God and to mutual recognition of one another's labors. Not that they parceled out the area of the Empire geographically between them because they could only agree to disagree and desired to stay out of each other's hair, but they pledged themselves to respect each other's commission and methods.[48]

But while this difference seems to have been amicably resolved, both parties recognizing their particular mission to be only one part of the over-all redemptive plan of God and not the whole of that program, it appears that their difference regarding the nature of the Church was more tolerated than settled. For both the Jerusalem apostles and Paul, the Church was at least in some sense the new and true Israel. But the consequences of this view took opposite directions for them.[49] To distinctively Jewish Christianity, the Church as the new Israel implied that the new community was bound to retain its ties with the nation at almost any cost; and in practice this meant that Jewish Christians, wherever situated, should retain their basic allegiance to national customs. As the later Tanaanitic rabbis of Judaism attempted to separate the religious from the national communities of Israel, preserving the religious while the national fell to ruin, so the Jerusalem Christians seem to have attempted a like separation. Only in this case the Jerusalem leaders attempted to preserve

[46] *Infra,* pp. 252-53, 283-84.
[47] Gal. 2:6-10.
[48] Cf. J. Weiss, *Primitive Christianity,* Vol. I, p. 268.
[49] Cf. E. F. Scott, *Beginnings of the Church,* pp. 35-42.

the national customs while allowing the religious connotations of old Judaism to fall, in that they were superseded by or incorporated into Christianity. To Paul, the Church as the new Israel meant that while the Church must always be conscious of its historical roots, it had no necessary commitment to continue putting forth its foliage in the same manner as old Israel. When used in a religious context, the name "Israel" for Paul was emptied of all necessary reference to a nation and retained only a spiritual content.[50]

This difference between the apostles had no practical effect when it came to relations within a purely Jewish or a purely Gentile church. But the clash of ideologies became apparent in the case of Jewish Christians within a Gentile fellowship. While the Jerusalem leaders were quite willing to permit communion between circumcised Jews and uncircumcised Gentiles within the Church, they were unwilling to see the Diaspora Jewish Christians forget their distinctive sign of Jewish nationality or relinquish the basic customs of the nation. This is forcefully illustrated in James' statement to Paul that there was a fear within the Jerusalem church that Paul had really been doing what his antagonists said he had, i.e., "teaching all the Jews who are among the Gentiles to forsake Moses, telling them not to circumcise their children or observe the customs."[51] The very accusation implies that his opponents had caught his emphasis upon the nonessential significance of external matters. They had seen that the logical implication of such teaching as "neither circumcision counts for anything nor uncircumcision"[52] was the relegation of Jewish practices to the category of purely optional matters devoid of all religious significance. Probably Paul let his hearers draw their own conclusions as to what he really thought of Jewish Christians continuing to circumcise their children and practicing the basic customs of the Jewish nation. But it appears that had it not been for the Jerusalem church's mission to the nation and its strong feeling that as the new Israel it must continue tied to the national customs, he would have carried out his message to its logical conclusion and let the old practices of Judaism

[50] Cf. the Hagar-Sarah allegory of Gal. 4:21-31.
[51] Acts 21:21.
[52] I Cor. 7:19.

drop in his own life and in those of his Jewish converts. But here was a case like that of meat offered to idols, as recorded in I Corinthians 8-10. Thus, for the sake of those who are overly scrupulous, he continues to be scrupulous himself and to teach the Jewish Christian of the Diaspora to "remain in the state in which he was called."[53] And in this case Paul's action was taken both for the sake of the Jerusalem church's mission and for the sake of not causing the "weak" and superscrupulous Christians of Jerusalem to stumble.[54]

Their Christological agreement as the basis for unity. But while the apostles conscientiously, and no doubt from premises which each considered unassailable, differed in their ecclesiology, it must be remembered that they were at one in their Christology. Paul's rebuke of Peter at Antioch was certainly recorded to reveal Peter's inconsistency of action. Yet we lose at least half the point to the Galatians if we do not see that in the narration of that episode Paul also insisted upon the basic bond of unity between Peter and himself in the matter of doctrine. Similarly, Paul's incorporation into his letters of early Church Christology in at least I Corinthians 15:3-4 and Philippians 2:6-11, and the sermons recorded of the early Church in Acts, reveal that there was a basic Christological agreement between him and the Jerusalem apostles. Some have disparagingly insisted that "the agreement between Paul and the Eleven was really confined to the place which Jesus holds in the world of history and in the life of his people."[55] But such an agreement is by no means incidental.

[53] I Cor. 7:20. Similarly in the question of slavery. The Gospel certainly is implicitly opposed to it. But it seems that if Paul saw this implication, he was willing to ignore it for the time being, so that the primary element in the Gospel message of reconciliation with God should not be obscured. Whether consciously or unconsciously, Paul took the course of emphasizing the theological aspect of the Gospel message while allowing many of the social implications to work themselves out at a later time from a basic Christian consciousness.

[54] This seems to be the answer to the great difficulty many have regarding Paul's presentation of the Law, as best expressed by Albert Schweitzer: "Some passages take for granted its observance by the Jews as unquestionably right and proper, and only seek to maintain the freedom of the Gentiles in regard to it, whereas others reject it in principle, in such a way that Paul would be obliged to maintain also the emancipation of the Jews . . . if the rules of logical inference are to be applied. As it is, however, there is a want of congruence between the negative theory and the limitation of the practical demand" (*Paul and His Interpreters*, p. 146).

[55] W. M. MacGregor, *Christian Freedom*, p. 180.

To agree regarding Christ and to center one's life in Him is to carry the distinctive stamp of Christian which unites in spite of all differences.

It is entirely false to continue the Tübingen fiction that Paul and the Jerusalem apostles could never agree on basic principles. While he was never one to seek agreement by a thinning out of convictions and was quite prepared to stand staunchly for what he considered to be the essence of the Gospel proclamation, Paul also realized the basic oneness that exists between believers in Christ and the need to preserve and strengthen that fellowship which has been established through Him. To view the actions of James and Peter as a continual campaign to bring about Paul's "complete overthrow"[56] and Paul's whole missionary activity as an attempt to silence the voice of Jewish Christianity by the majority voice of Gentile Christendom[57] is to ignore this basic and controlling Christological agreement. Paul shows no evidence of such a tension in his relations with the elder apostles. In his report of the agreement with the Jerusalem leaders, it seems that "Paul is convinced that their intentions were honorable: the expression 'right hand of fellowship' is cordial and affectionate."[58] We may see sinister motives in the apostles' words and actions if we so desire. But it is important to note that while Paul differed at times with his fellow apostles in Jerusalem, he wrote of them with an attitude of respect. Even when dealing with the divisions in Corinth, a matter in which Peter was probably not personally involved though his name was being used, "he treats the name of Cephas with a delicate courtesy and respect which has almost escaped notice."[59] As J. B. Lightfoot further pointed out, "when he comes to argue the question, he at once drops the name of St. Peter: 'While one saith, I am of Paul, and another, I am of Apollos, are ye not carnal? What then is Apollos, and what is Paul?' "[60] And it seems that he thought enough of Peter as a Christian, a fellow apostle, and a witness of

[56] As Brandon, "Crisis of 70 A.D.," *op. cit.*, p. 226.

[57] As Knox, *St. Paul and the Church of Jerusalem*, pp. 194-96. Knox observes that while his view is based on what appears to be the most probable interpretation of the available evidence, . . . [it] has no direct authority from the original narrative of the Acts."

[58] Weiss, *Primitive Christianity*, Vol. I, p. 268.

[59] Lightfoot, *Galatians*, p. 351.

[60] *Ibid.*

the life, death, and resurrection of the Lord to go up to Jerusalem to see him—probably both to establish fellowship with him and to hear from his own lips about the historical Jesus.[61]

Perhaps Silas stands as the best symbol for the basic unity and fellowship that existed between the Apostle to the Gentiles and the apostles of the Jerusalem church. Here was a Jerusalemite prophet who was in good standing in his own church, who joined Paul when the issues of his Gentile mission were certainly clear, who shared with Paul the work of founding the churches in Macedonia and Achaia, and who later appears in close connection with Peter.[62] Just why Paul originally took him and why Silas disappears entirely in the Acts account after the missionary journeys are not known. But it is significant that, so far as can be seen in the records, no discord arose between the two.[63] Some have considered it "remarkable that Paul took with him a native of Jerusalem, because Silas was probably accustomed to treat the tradition of the life of Jesus in a manner quite different from his own."[64] It seems better, however, to interpret this easy association of Silas with both the Jerusalem apostles and Paul as just another evidence of the basic unity that existed between the two sections of early Christianity and their respective leaders.

We must conclude, therefore, that though he disclaimed any dependence upon the Jerusalem apostles for his essential message, and

[61] Gal. 1:18 is a much debated verse. Paul's insistence is that he did not go to Jerusalem *didachthēnai* by Peter, but *historēsai Kēphan.* But that does not necessarily mean, as Hort suggested, that he only went up "to 'explore' St. Peter, to find out how he would be disposed to treat the persecutor now become a champion" (*Judaistic Christianity,* p. 56). With Paul's strong emphasis upon the unity of believers in Christ, he would quite naturally desire to establish fellowship with Peter; and while being with the foremost of Jesus' earthly companions, he could not have failed to be interested in a first-hand portrayal of the earthly life of Jesus (cf. G. D. Kilpatrick, "Galatians 1:18 ΙΣΤΟΡΗΣΑΙ ΚΗΦΑΝ," *New Testament Essays,* ed. A. J. B. Higgins, pp. 144-49). The fact that Paul waited three years before making an attempt to visit Peter need not indicate an aloofness from or disagreement with this disciple even in the earliest days. Peake's suggestion at this point is as good as any: "Jerusalem would not be the safest place for Paul to visit after he had not merely failed to fulfill his commisison from the High Priest but had gone over to the Christians" (*Paul and the Jewish Christians,* p. 8, n. 1).

[62] Cf. I Pet. 5:12.

[63] Cf. A. Harnack's treatment of Paul and Silas, *The Mission and Expansion of Christianity,* Vol. I, pp. 78-79.

[64] Weiss, *Primitive Christianity,* Vol. I, pp. 277-78.

though he appears a bit irritated to have to agree with the Judaizers that the elder apostles were "pillars" (*stuloi*) when in some ways he considered them most weak,[65] Paul was entirely prepared to accept the apostles of Jerusalem both as fellow apostles in the work of Christ and as those who had been entrusted with the primary responsibility of witnessing concerning the resurrection.[66] As both fellow workers and indispensable connecting links between the historical Jesus and the community of the New Age, Paul saw it to be his duty and privilege to maintain fellowship with them at almost any cost to himself personally.

AN EXPRESSION OF UNITY

Before closing this chapter regarding the relations between Paul and the Jerusalem church, it is well to note one point wherein the Apostle shows himself willing to expend himself for the sake of Jewish as well as Gentile Christianity; i.e., in the collection for the saints of Jerusalem.

Though Acts has a great deal of detailed information regarding this collection and Paul's determination to present it personally, the Apostle's own thoughts concerning it are better seen in his letters. In Romans 15 he declares that he has earnestly desired for a long time to go to Rome, and from there to Spain. Yet, even though he is relatively near, he feels it his bounden duty to retrace his steps and return to Jerusalem in order to deliver the contribution of the Gentile Christians to the poor of the Jerusalem church. And this in spite of the fact that he fully realizes that such a project is fraught with great personal danger. Even if we could not trust the long section of Acts where Paul is represented as fully realizing that "imprisonment and afflictions" await him at Jerusalem,[67] the touching request of Romans 15:30-32—"I appeal to you, brethren, . . . to strive together with me in prayers to God on my behalf, that I may be de-

[65] For the view that there is a relative, not absolute, disparagement in Paul's voice in his reference to *hoi dokountes stuloi einai* in Gal. 2:9, see J. G. Machen, *The Origin of Paul's Religion*, pp. 120-21; C. K. Barrett, "Paul and the 'Pillar' Apostles," *Studia Paulina*, pp. 1-2.

[66] "Paul also could reckon himself a witness of the resurrection, but only as an exception—an *ektrōma* (I Cor. 15:8)" (Barrett, *ibid.*, p. 18, n. 1).

[67] Acts 20:17-21:14.

livered from the disobedient in Judea and that my service for Jerusalem may be acceptable to the saints"—indicates that he was willing to go "even to the length of martyrdom" in the fulfillment of this mission.[68]

But the question arises: Why did Paul feel himself duty-bound to present such a collection, and at such great personal risk? Some have viewed him as under a binding commitment to the Jerusalem leaders, and here only fulfilling it; i.e., this contribution to their church was the price he had to pay for their recognition of his ministry and of the validity of Gentile Christendom.[69] Others insist that he viewed the Jerusalem church as the successor to the Temple, and that thus it was necessary for all Christians to support it in much the same manner as Judaism supported its central sanctuary with the annual temple tax.[70] J. Munck argues that Paul's great concern to take the collection to Jerusalem stems from his view of the pattern of redemptive history; i.e., since "Jerusalem and Israel are the central part of the history of salvation," he must bend every effort in his Gentile mission for the welfare of Jerusalem Christianity.[71] And yet, as A. S. Peake has said, all these interpretations seem to make

> far too much of what was essentially a spontaneous expression of Christian philanthropy and brotherly love. The initiative in this had originally been taken by the Church of Antioch. It does not seem to have been a response to a claim that assistance to the mother Church might be rightfully demanded. The Apostles know from experience the sympathetic interest of Paul and Barnabas and the Church at Antioch, and they appeal that their help may be continued.[72]

As with the earlier famine relief to Judea in which Paul took a leading part, so it seems this larger collection was originally meant as an expression of Christian love to brethren in more difficult straits

[68] A. Harnack, *The Date of the Acts*, p. 64.

[69] E.g., H. Achelis: "Das war der Preis, mit dem Paulus bezahlt hat: er gab die äussere Abhängigkeit für die innere Freiheit" (*Das Christentum in den ersten drei Jahrhunderten* [Leipzig: Quelle & Meyer, 1912], Vol. I, p. 48).

[70] E.g., W. L. Knox, *St. Paul and the Church of Jerusalem*, p. 298.

[71] Munck, "Israel and the Gentiles," p. 7.

[72] Peake, *Paul and the Jewish Christians*, p. 15, n. 1. Lightfoot has put it concisely: "His past care for their poor prompted this request of the elder Apostles. His subsequent zeal in the same cause was the answer to their appeal" (*Galatians*, p. 111).

financially. Paul's desire to aid his Jewish Christian brethren springs most naturally from his teaching regarding a love-conditioned liberty and the Church as the Body of Christ in which all members "have the same care for one another."[73] And it is on this basis of mutual concern and responsibility within the Body of Christ that he represents the collection to his Romans readers, in the words: "For if the Gentiles have shared in their spiritual blessings, they ought also to minister to them in material blessings."[74]

But such a gift would not necessitate his personal appearance in Jerusalem, and thus the placing himself in great danger of Jewish reprisals. His words in I Corinthians 16:3-4 indicate that he had contemplated only sending the gift on by representatives from the various churches. For some reason, however, he felt more and more strongly as the time approached that he must accompany the delegates and present the gift personally. It seems that that reason lay in the increasing estrangement of the rank and file within the Jerusalem church from Gentile Christianity, an estrangement which appears to have been brought about by the increasing influence in the church at Jerusalem of the more scrupulous-minded Christians.[75] He is not trying to buy favor from the mother church for his mission or his converts, but he does desire that the collection which was gathered in love should be viewed by its recipients as a real token of love and a definite symbol of unity between Gentile and Jewish Christianity. And this seemed to him to require his presence as well as the money. Thus, in one sense, it can truly be said that the collection for the Palestinian Christians was an endeavor to preserve the unity of the Church.[76] And in his determination to present the contribution personally, we see his willingness to sacrifice himself, if need be, for the unity and welfare of the Church.

[73] I Cor. 12:25; cf. 12:12-30.
[74] Rom. 15:27.
[75] See Appendix, p. 276.
[76] Cf. P. I. Bratsiotis: "Es ist sogar nicht übertrieben zu sagen, dass das gesamte Wirken dieses Apostels als ein Kampf für die Einheit der Kirche verstanden werden könnte" ("Paulus und die Einheit der Kirche," *Studia Paulina,* ed. W. C. van Unnik and G. Sevenster, p. 29.

X

All Things to All Men

IN THE EFFORT TO understand Paul's practice, it is to the Apostle's activity within the Gentile church that we must first turn. As F. C. Baur said, "He can only have been a Jew unto the Jews in the same manner in which he was a Gentile to the Gentiles."[1] At this point Baur is certainly right; though his understanding of what Paul taught and was like in a Gentile situation led to the distortion of the Pauline profile. We must therefore view anew the Apostle's methods and actions within his own sphere of labor. And since a proper historical method must always begin with a consideration of the documents closest to the object of study, and in view of the criticisms against Acts, it is best at this point to center our attention exclusively upon the Apostle's practice in the Gentile world as revealed in his own letters. Of necessity, the principle enunciated in I Corinthians 9:22 will be the dominant theme of this chapter; for in Paul's declaration of being "all things to all men" for the sake of the Gospel and the salvation of men, we have, as Lightfoot long ago insisted, "the key to all seeming inconsistencies in different representations of his conduct."[2]

IN THE GENTILE MISSION

From the days of the Fathers, Paul's Athenian experience as recorded in Acts 17 has been cited as the illustration of the "all things to all men" principle as it worked out in the Gentile situation. But there are also other evidences in the Pauline correspondence—par-

[1] F. C. Baur, *Paul*, Vol. I, p. 131.
[2] J. B. Lightfoot, *Galatians*, p. 348.

ticularly in I Corinthians—of his practice within the Gentile church which are not usually considered in dealing with this subject. And one factor in his approach and method in the Gentile mission which stands out clearly and is pertinent here is his personal frugality.

In I Corinthians 9:1-18, the passage just preceding the "all things to all men" exclamation, Paul insists that as an apostle—and especially so to the Corinthians themselves—he has the right to support at the cost of the Church, and that, if he were married, his wife would rightfully share in this privilege. He justifies this right to maintenance by reference to the analogy of wages paid those who serve in worldly affairs; to the Old Testament statement and practice; and to the command of Christ. And yet, while he insists that this right of maintenance is the privilege of every apostle, he declares that he has not made use of it. And the fact that in II Corinthians 11:7-15 he must defend himself against those who would discredit his apostleship by implying that he was ashamed to accept an apostle's due indicates that at least at Corinth he did indeed deny himself this right. Precisely why he took this action is a little difficult to ascertain. He speaks of it as a practice that was needful for the sake of the Gospel[3] and his service to the Corinthians,[4] motivated by love for those to whom he ministered,[5] and meant to benefit the Corinthian church[6] and to undermine the claims of false apostles.[7] He even speaks of this refusal of his full right in the Gospel, and thus his offering of the Gospel *gratis,* as his boasting and his reward.[8] It is possible that the willingness so to deny himself was early learned in the school of Gamaliel I, for Hillel and his immediate descendants were known for going beyond the call of duty in applying the more stringent rulings to themselves and the more lenient to the people.[9] Probably the need for such action arose from the Greek suspicion of the sophists among the traveling philosophers of the day who ex-

[3] I Cor. 9:12.
[4] II Cor. 11:8.
[5] II Cor. 11:11.
[6] II Cor. 11:7-9.
[7] II Cor. 11:12-15.
[8] I Cor. 9:15-18; II Cor. 11:10.
[9] Cf. Mish. Yom Tob (Betzah) 2.6, Mish. Eduy. 3.10: "What shall we infer from thy father's household [i.e. Gamaliel I's], which applied the stringent ruling to themselves but the lenient ruling to Israel?" Cf. also Mish. Ber. 2.5-7, Mish. Yom Tob (Betzah) 3.2, Mish Bab. Mez. 5.8.

tracted payment in advance for their services and were not willing to live on voluntary contributions.[10] But the significant factor here is that in so refusing his full rights, Paul was but manifesting in action a real element of his doctirne of Christian liberty; i.e., that the indicative of our liberty in Christ must always be conditioned by a love that is willing to sacrifice for the sake of the Christian's central message and purpose. Thus he declares in I Corinthians 9:24-27 that for the sake of his message and purpose he exercises self-control in all things, and in II Corinthians 6:3 ff. that he seeks in the exercise of his liberty to "give no occasion of offense in anything, in order that the ministry be not blamed."

TO THE LIBERTINES

It is also instructive to note how the Apostle deals with the problems within the Corinthian church, for here too his famous confession explains his approach to many situations.[11] In chapters 5 and 6 of I Corinthians, Paul strongly censures the immorality present in the church and the readiness of some of its members to go before pagan courts with a brother rather than be deprived of their rights. It will probably continue to remain uncertain whether he was speaking to one "party" in the Paul-Apollos-Cephas-Christ division, or dealing with a situation and mentality that cut through two or more of these groups. In any case it is clear that he is here concerned with Gentile Christian libertines whose watchwords seem to have been "All things are lawful for me!" and "Food for the stomach and the stomach for food!"[12] And while he censures their excesses in 5:1—6:11, he deals with their underlying thought in 6:12-20.

The interesting factor to note here is that in dealing with their thought, he begins by unhesitatingly accepting their fundamental position that the Christian is free from all earthly restraint. Whether "All things are lawful for me!" are Paul's own words, misused by his converts, or the natural inference of his Corinthian converts from what he has proclaimed to them, the point is that the Apostle begins

[10] Cf. R. H. Strachan, *II Corinthians,* M.N.T.C. (London: Hodder & Stoughton, 1935), p. 23.

[11] Cf. H. Chadwick, "All Things to All Men," *N. T. S.,* Vol. I (1954-55), pp. 261-75.

[12] I Cor. 6:12-13.

by agreeing with them in what had probably become current among the Corinthian libertines as a trite maxim. Similarly with the expresion "Food for the stomach and the stomach for food!" As the pagan world could speak of "the sword to the scabbard, and the scabbard to the sword,"[13] and mean by that "the male and the female, and the passion of each for intercourse with the other, and the faculty which makes use of the organs which have been constructed for this purpose,"[14] so, it seems, the libertine Christians in Corinth joined the popular expressions of their pagan culture to their perverted idea of Christian liberty and made "food for the stomach and the stomach for food" a specious plea for sexual laxity.[15] But even here Paul begins by agreeing with their basic tenet.

The Apostle could easily be charged with being unscrupulous at this point. And if his agreement with his erring pupils' basic claim was really not sincere, then he certainly cannot be relieved of such a charge. But in actuality, Paul did agree with them—though only up to a point. In effect he says to these libertine Christians that, if one considered only the indicative of Christian liberty, then indeed "all things are lawful"; if the Gospel proclamation was only that Christ has freed us for our full expression, then even immorality would be proper. But, like Epictetus' argument on this same question that "use is one thing, and understanding another,"[16] Paul went on to insist that the question of Christian liberty is not ended in simply a consideration of what is lawful. Rather, the fact that "all things are lawful for me" must be constantly tempered by (1) the realization that "not all things are profitable," and (2) the determination that "I will not be enslaved by anything."[17] In the first qualification the Apostle seems to have in mind the Christian community, declaring that liberty is limited "by reference to the moral or religious life of all those who are concerned, viz. the agent and those whom his conduct may influence."[18] In the second he views the individual, urging

[13] Epictetus, Dissertations, I. 6. 6.

[14] *Ibid.*, I. 6. 9.

[15] Cf. J. Moffatt, *I Corinthians,* M.N.T.C. (London: Hodder & Stoughton, 1938), pp. 68-69.

[16] Dissertations, I. 6. 13.

[17] I Cor. 6:12.

[18] A. Robertson and A. Plummer, *I Corinthians,* I.C.C. (Edinburgh: T. & T. Clark, 1911), p. 122.

that "we must beware of using liberty in such a way as to lose it."[19] Or, in terms of the presentation of Paul's teaching in chapters VII and VIII of this work, he begins by agreeing that the Gospel indicative is indeed a declaration that all things are lawful to the Christian. But he goes on to insist that:

1. The imperative of the Gospel to "stand fast, therefore, and do not submit to a yoke of slavery" must be heeded, a factor the libertines had ignored—and thus were perverting Christian liberty—in their slavery to their own sinful passions.
2. The direction of liberty must be from Christ, whose direction the libertines had abandoned in their giving over to a harlot what rightfully belongs to Christ and in their following of their own fleshly desires.
3. The exercise of liberty must be conditioned by love, which is not manifested—and true liberty thus not exercised—in flagrant moral promiscuity.

Paul's earlier words in Galatians 5:13 are apt for this situation as well: "For you were called unto liberty, brethren; only use not your liberty as an opportunity for the flesh, but through love be servants of one another."

Thus the Apostle truly agrees with his erring converts when they stress the indicative of the Gospel message, but he insists that the doctrine of liberty in Christ is more than just the acceptance of the indicative of that liberty if it is to be truly Christian liberty. He begins on their own ground, at the point where he finds agreement with them, and leads them on from there.

The question is often raised as to why Paul did not merely quote the last clause of the Jerusalem Decree regarding "unchastity" (*porneia*) in settling the issue; for whether the Decree be considered a three-clause ethical pronouncement or a four-clause enactment covering both food and ethical questions, the final clause regarding immorality remains and would bear directly on this situation at Corinth. We must deal at length with the Jerusalem Decree in the next chapter; suffice it to say here that omission of the final item of the Decree in Paul's letter to Corinth is no evidence either against the existence of the decree or of Paul's refusal to accept it whole-

[19] *Ibid.*, p. 122.

heartedly. The Apostle is here dealing with the libertine mentality. It is probable that those to whom he is writing are the same Christians as those reflected in II Corinthians as criticizing him for being too bound by earthly considerations and not taking a really spiritual view. Whether or not the Decree existed or was accepted by Paul, to quote any ecclesiastical pronouncement to those ultraspiritualists who considered all such statements as sub-Christian would have immediately labeled him as beneath them in spirituality and would have closed the door to his endeavor to lead them on in true Christian liberty. It could just as well be argued that part of the criticism against Paul in the Corinthian church arose within the libertine group because he had originally delivered the Decree to them as that because he did not quote its last section in I Corinthians 6 the Decree is spurious, known to Paul only after his third journey or unacceptable to him. Whether or not the Decree existed and was delivered and/or accepted, Paul thought too much of these libertine Christians to revolt them and thus cause them to stumble by bringing in what they believed to be a sign of immaturity when it was not absolutely necessary to do so. He is dealing with Christians whose outlook is so warped that they can call moral laxity an exercise in spiritual liberty and ecclesiastical guidance a fleshly function; but even here he is "all things to all men" in order to lead them on to a true understanding and expression of the liberty that is in Christ Jesus.

TO THE ASCETICS

In I Corinthians 7, the Apostle turns to the first of those matters which had been asked him in the letter from Corinth: the question regarding marriage. It is not necessary for our purpose here to consider the whole question of Paul and marriage,[20] nor even to attempt

[20] The majority opinion seems to be that Paul "shows a surprising lack of appreciation of the spiritual possibilities in the marriage relation, in fact, a rather abysmal and embarrassing ignorance of the total meaning of marriage" (J. Knox, *Chapters in a Life of Paul* [New York: Abingdon-Cokesbury, 1956], p. 105). But note also O. Michel, "Wie spricht Paulus über Frau und Ehe?" *Theologische Studien und Kritiken,* Vol. CV, Heft 2 (1933), pp. 215-28, and Chadwick, "All Things to All Men," *op. cit.,* pp. 263-70, for an emphasis upon the external situation at Corinth as affecting the manner in which the apostle casts his words.

an identification of those within the Corinthian church who had sent him this question and/or for whom it was a real problem. It will be sufficient at this point to note the mentality to which he addresses himself and the approach he takes.

Whereas in I Corinthians 5 and 6 Paul dealt with libertine thought, he now turns to the Christian ascetic.[21] And here he confronts a more difficult situation in many ways; for while the libertine movement would appear to many outside its ranks as merely licentiousness clothed in piety, rigid asceticism usually gains the reputation of being eminently religious. Thus the Apostle, if he is to gain those who stand outside the ascetic group—but view it with respect—as well as earnest ascetics themselves, must use the utmost Christian tact in the matter. This must be recognized, for it probably explains the care and some of the intricacies involved in the Pauline argumentation of this chapter.

Again, the interesting factor to note in Paul's approach to the question is that he begins in agreement with those he seeks to correct. Nowhere in the chapter does he bring in the Hebraic argument of Creation for the order and function of the sexes, for he evidently realizes that such an argument would carry no weight with the dualistically tainted ascetic mentality. Rather, he begins his discussion with those points on which they can both agree: "It is well for a man not to touch a woman," as in verse 1; and "It is well for them [i.e., the unmarried and widows] to remain [single] even as I," as in verse 8. In these two expressions Paul, as in the case of the libertines, again seems to be quoting back to a group of Corinthian converts their own declarations. The first appears to be their motto, while the second is evidently their attempt to give a Christian justification to their thought through the example of Paul himself.

Now Paul truly did agree with the ascetics—at least up to a point. He could never have thought of them as "these blind buzzards [who] cannot discern things which are the good creatures of God from vices,"[22] for Christian liberty also includes the right to abstain from

[21] Note Robertson and Plummer, *I Corinthians,* p. 132 on I Cor. 7:1, and J. Weiss, *Der erste Korintherbrief* (Göttingen: Vandenhoeck & Ruprecht, 1910), p. 169 on I Cor. 7:1.

[22] As Luther said regarding the ascetics of his day (*Galatians,* p. 213 on Gal. 3:3); though Luther's invective was against those who based their right-

legitimate pursuits if one be convinced in his own mind that this is the will of Christ for him personally. And in Paul's own case, it seems that he believed himself divinely directed along lines similar to those of his ascetic addressees. It will probably never be conclusively settled whether or not Paul was ever married, but it seems most probable that he was not.[23] The argument that as a member of the Sanhedrin he must have been a married man, and a father as well, is not strong; for this rule,[24] made in the interests of clemency within the council, is from a later period. Similarly, Clement's theory that he was married, but left his wife at Philippi so as not to interfere with his travels, and that he addresses her in the words "true yoke-fellow" of Philippians 4:3,[25] may be safely set aside. How could he agree with the ascetics that the unmarried and widows should "remain even as I" if he had all the while been married? That the ascetics could point to the example of Paul as substantiation for their views on continence indicates that he was unmarried rather than a widower. Similarly, his statement expressing the wish "that all were as I am myself" is more understandable as a desire that all possessed the gift of continence than that all should be widows and widowers or should simply remain unmarried whatever the situation. In this, as indicated by his own personal practice, the Apostle did agree with the ascetics; i.e., he agreed that the best procedure, *if* one possessed the gift of continence, was to remain single. The gift of continence was probably especially valuable for the Christian amid the moral excesses in the pagan world of that day, and celibacy "for the sake of the kingdom of heaven" had been praised by Christ Himself.[26] But Paul entirely disagreed with the ascetics in their reason for sexual abstinence and in their insistence that this should be the normal experience of every truly spiritual Christian.

For Paul, abstinence from sexual expression within marriage could only be enjoined, and the gift of continence was only given,

---

eousness upon their works of abstinence, and thus the asceticism of Luther's attack and that of Corinth are not truly parallel.

[23] Cf. Robertson and Plummer, *I Corinthians,* pp. 138-39 on I Cor. 7:8.

[24] B. Sanh. 36b.

[25] Cf. Robertson and Plummer, *I Corinthians,* pp. 138-39 on I Cor. 7:8.

[26] Matt. 19:11-12.

(1) in the case of a desire to fulfill a specific purpose for the glory of God,[27] (2) in view of "the present distress,"[28] and/or (3) in anticipation of the imminent coming of Christ.[29] He agrees with the ascetics that difficulties and troubles accompany marriage, and he would spare his converts that.[30] But he insists that no sin is involved in marrying.[31] Nowhere does he speak of marriage as subspiritual because of the material aspect in it causing defilement. Nor could Paul agree that celibacy was to be the normal or even the best procedure for every Christian. If the Corinthians were to accept such a tenet, they would become "slaves of men" rather than freemen in Christ.[32] Both celibacy and marriage are callings of God.[33] And while Paul believed that the gift of continency which he and some of the Corinthians possessed was the best gift for the furtherance of the Christian mission in that particular period in God's redemptive history,[34] he did not account marriage as essentially sinful or as less than a calling of God.

We see, therefore, in Paul's approach to the Christian ascetics of Corinth that same application of the principle "all things to all men" as we saw in his dealings with the libertines. He begins at the point where he finds agreement with them, acknowledging that the indicative of the Gospel allows them to manifest their liberty in Christ in a rigid asceticism if they so choose. And he agrees with them that he personally has found the single state—with its necessary accompanying gift of continence—to be the best. But he goes on to undermine their dualistic justification for abstinence from sexual relations by offering what he believes to be true Christian reasons, and he renounces the view that such abstinence is alone truly Christian. Thus he agrees with them that liberty in Christ allows for a Christian asceticism. But he goes on to argue that:

[27] E.g., giving oneself to prayer (I Cor. 7:5) and devoting oneself to difficult missionary endeavor involving physical risk (as seems true in Paul's case). But within the married state, such sexual abstinence was only to be temporary and to be agreed upon by both partners.

[28] I Cor. 7:26, so translating *tēn enestōsan anagkēn.*

[29] I Cor. 7:29, 31.

[30] I Cor. 7:28b, 32.

[31] I Cor. 7:28a, 36b, 38a.

[32] I Cor. 7:23.

[33] I Cor. 7:12-24.

[34] I Cor. 7:6, 38.

1. Continence must be considered a gift, not an obligation; else we enslave men to our ideal and do not allow them to stand in the liberty to which Christ has set them free.

2. Abstinence from sexual expression in marriage can be justified only in light of our Christian purpose, the present circumstances, and/or our expectation of Christ's imminent return, but never on the ground that sexual relations within marirage are evil *per se*.

3. The obligation of permanent abstinence, without the gift of continence, can set one "aflame with passion" and be a "temptation to immorality"; thus causing havoc within the Christian community and displaying, by the ascetics' insistence upon it as an obligation for all, a failure on their part to condition their own Christian liberty by love.

TO THE "STRONG"

In I Corinthians 8:1—11:1, Paul takes up another point of real tension in the Corinthian church: the matter of eating meat which has been previously consecrated to an idol. Two factions had formed within the church on this issue. The one group insisted that liberty in Christ meant freedom from the old Jewish prejudice against eating meat which had been previously offered to idols, and evidently taunted the other group with the nickname "the Weak."[35] The other group felt that to eat such meat was to participate at least to some extent in idolatry, and thus to deny their exclusive oneness with Christ. Just who these eaters and noneaters were is not our problem here. In all likelihood, however, the noneaters had been influenced by Jewish thought, if not actually former Jews or Jewish proselytes,[36] while the eaters seem to be purely Gentile Christians closely approx-

[35] A. S. Geyser has suggested that while the eaters looked down upon the noneaters and called them *hoi asthenountes,* the noneaters' nickname for the eaters was, with a play on words, *hoi esthiontes*—which the eaters changed to *hoi ischuroi* ("Paul, the Apostolic Decree and the Liberals in Corinth," *Studia Paulina,* p. 124).

[36] What is meant for a Jew to eat meat offered to an idol is indicated by R. Simeon b. Gamaliel, the son of Paul's teacher, in his discussion of "the sacrifices of the dead" (Ps. 106:28) in Mish. Ab. Zar. 2.3: "Flesh that is entering in unto an idol is permitted, but what comes forth is forbidden, for it is as 'the sacrifices of the dead.' " Cf. Mish. Aboth 3.3 for another early indication of the Jewish horror of such meat.

imating, if not actually identical with, the libertines discussed previously. Nor need we attempt to define the relationship between the strong and the weak of I Corinthians 8—10 and the strong and the weak of Romans 14.[37] While the passage in Romans does speak of disputations over foods, and while the same types of thought and similar issues may lie behind those conflicts as at Corinth, the problems as stated in the two accounts are sufficiently varied—meats that have been offered to idols in I Corinthians and vegetarianism in Romans[38]—to prohibit an absolute identification of the groups at Corinth with their counterparts in the Roman epistle. Our task at this point is not to determine precisely who Paul's addressees were at Corinth, but how he deals with them.

Judging from the brief and general treatment given to the matters dividing the strong and the weak at Rome, such questions, though probably constantly arising, were not burning and disruptive issues in that church.[39] But at Corinth this division regarding meats offered to idols seems to have threatened the very fabric of the Christian community. And to Paul the issue was grave not so much because of the immature view of "the weak" but because of the spirit of those he rather ironically refers to as "the Strong"[40] in condemning their less knowledgeable brethren. Thus Paul deals not so much with the problem of the rightness or wrongness of eating such meat, or with those he believes have failed to see the full implications of their liberty. Rather, he seeks to correct those who agree with him in their view of idolatry and meats but would use their knowledge in a manner damaging to the welfare of their brethren. He is troubled not so much over immaturity and the failure to be theologically consistent as over the spirit that would condemn these shortcomings in spiritual pride.

[37] For representative discussions, see J. H. Ropes, "The Epistle to the Romans and Early Christianity," *Studies in Early Christianity,* ed. S. J. Case, who opposes the equation of the two sets in each city, and P. P. Bläser, *Gesetz bei Paulus,* p. 86, who advocates their great similarity if not actual identity.

[38] Though the problem of demon-contaminated meat may lie in the background of the question in Rom. 14, it is not so stated and must be read into that passage in order to make the problems identical.

[39] Assuming that Rom. 14 was meant for the Christians at Rome and not, as Renan suggested, that it was a part of a letter meant for members of the Ephesian, Thessalonian, and other unknown churches.

[40] I Cor. 10:22.

But again, it is instructive to note how he approaches these supposedly knowledgeable Christians. Indeed, there is no quotation of an ecclesiastical edict. Many have seen in this fact conclusive proof that the Jerusalem Decree, which dealt with this very question of "things sacrified to idols" (*eidōlothuta*), was either unknown to Paul at this time or unacceptable to him, or must be considered simply fictional.[41] Others argue that since the Decree was addressed only to "the brethren who are of the Gentiles in Antioch and Syria and Cilicia," it could not legitimately be applied to this similar case in Europe.[42] Some, believing it to be "a rather drastic expedient" to argue either that the Decree was spurious or that it was unknown to the Apostle, and unconvinced by the proposal that the Decree was meant only for a limited area, have left the question unsettled, simply stating that "it is perhaps better to recognize that no quite satisfactory solution of the problem has yet been discovered."[43] But, though this again anticipates a later discussion of Paul's acceptance of the Jerusalem Decree, it will perhaps be helpful to note the character of the Apostle's addressees in Corinth, for at least a partial and possible solution to the dilemma. Here are those who pride themselves in being strong and possessing knowledge. Here are those who believe they stand as equals with any—so much less are they ready to submit to a Jewish-Christian desire when they see that the Judaistically influenced Christians of their own city lack in maturity and knowledge. It may be, as W. L. Knox has suggested, that Paul was also thinking of "the Weak" and thus could not mention the Jerusalem Decree lest such a reference be "interpreted as an admission of the superiority of the Christians of Palestine and therefore of their leader, Peter, to Paul himself."[44] But it is also just as possible that the Apostle had "the Strong" primarily in mind, and that he would not raise—assuming for the moment that the Decree existed and was known to the Apostle—

[41] E.g., J. Weiss: "The discussions in I Corinthians about eating meat offered to idols are unintelligible if Paul had been in the position of being able simply to appeal to the decree" (*Primitive Christianity,* Vol. I, p. 260). Cf. also H. Lietzmann, *Beginnings of the Christian Church,* p. 143.

[42] E.g., Lightfoot, *Galatians,* p. 308; F. J. A. Hort, *Judaistic Christianity,* pp. 74-76; J. G. Machen, *Origin of Paul's Religion,* pp. 94-95; Geyser, "Paul, the Apostolic Decree and the Liberals in Corinth," *op. cit.,* pp. 136-37.

[43] A. S. Peake, *Paul and the Jewish Christians,* p. 22.

[44] W. L. Knox, *St. Paul and the Church of Jerusalem,* p. 316.

an argument that savored to them of legalism and would close the door to his further endeavors on their behalf. The fact of Paul's silence regarding such a churchly pronouncement on this question is no evidence that he was ignorant of or refused to accept it. It could just as well be argued that the Corinthian assertion that "all of us possess knowledge" was a reaction to an original deliverance by the Apostle of the Decree.[45] Paul is "all things to all men" here as well, starting at the point where he can find agreement with his converts in order to lead them on to a fuller understanding and expression of their Christian liberty.

Thus the Apostle begins by agreeing with "the Strong" in their inferences from the indicative of the Gospel that "all of us possess knowledge" and that "an idol has no real existence" since "there is no God but one."[46] But he goes on to insist that in their refusal to condition their liberty by love for the sake of their weaker brethren,

[45] Cf. Moffatt: "If at Corinth they were told of the Jerusalem decree against eating *eidolothuta,* they probably resented or scorned the idea that they should be hampered by any local edict of the Palestinian churches which enforced such irrelevant scruples. 'We Christians know better; an idol is nothing to us' " (*I Corinthians,* p. 102).

[46] Weiss (*Primitive Christianity,* Vol. I, p. 326) and W. L. Knox (*St. Paul and the Church of Jerusalem,* p. 113, n. 13) assert that Paul's view of idolatry in I Cor. 8 is fundamentally different and opposed to his position on the same matter in I Cor. 10. Weiss views this as evidence that these two chapters were written at different times with different purposes in mind, while Knox argues rather that the apostle was just unsuccessful in attempting to unite two incompatible theories regarding idolatry.

But Paul's presentation is paralleled, illuminated, and explained by the teaching of Gamaliel II in Mish. Ab. Zar. 3.4: "Proklos the son of Philosophos asked Rabban Gamaliel in Acre while he was bathing in the Bath of Aphrodite, and said to him, 'It is written in your law, "And there shall cleave nought of the devoted thing to thine hand." Why (then) dost thou bathe in the Bath of Aphrodite?' He answered, 'One may not make answer in the bath' [because it is forbidden to speak words of the Law while naked]. And when he came out he said, 'I came not within her limits: she came within mine! They do not say, "Let us make a bath for Aphrodite," but "Let us make an Aphrodite as an adornment for the bath." Moreover if they would give thee much money thou wouldest not enter in before thy goddess naked or after suffering pollution, nor wouldest thou make water before her! Yet this goddess stands at the mouth of the gutter and all the people make water before her. It is written, "Their gods," only; thus what is treated as a god is forbidden, but what is not treated as a god is permitted.' "

The significance of this parallel is heightened when we realize that "tradition probably contains many sayings of Gamaliel I which are erroneously ascribed to his grandson of the same name" (W. Bacher, "Gamaliel I," *J. E.,* Vol. V, p. 559).

they are giving offense to those they are endeavoring to win outside the Church, working havoc within the Church, and not glorifying God in the exercise of their so-called Christian freedom.[47] And, as with the libertines, he argues that while "all things are lawful," "not all things are helpful," and "not all things build up."[48]

TO THE ECSTATICS

"The typically Pauline method of outclassing his opponents on their own ground"[49] is seen also in the Apostle's treatment of the ecstatics in the church at Corinth. We would probably never have known the nature and variety of Paul's ecstatic experiences had the Apostle not had to deal with the Corinthian spiritualists; for though he highly valued visions and revelations as a dynamic factor and sign of his apostleship, he hesitated to speak of them in any detail. He himself says that the Church could gain nothing by his repetition of such strictly personal ecstatic occurrences.[50] But in dealing with those who were overemphasizing and misusing the pneumatic element in Christianity, Paul meets them on their own ground. Thus he agrees that the gift of tongues is a genuine supernatural "charisma"[51] and that revelatory visions possess real validity.[52] In fact, he counters his addressees' claims by declaring: "I thank God that I speak in tongues more than you all";[53] and he tells of a time "fourteen years ago" when he was "caught up into Paradise" (*heōs tritou ouranou*) and given an "abundance of revelations."[54] These assertions were not manufactured. Evidently Paul was a true ecstatic. But the fact that he mentions these experiences nowhere so fully as he does in the Corinthian letters indicates that in that correspondence he has a definite purpose in referring to his own prophetic ecstasies. From the tone of I Corinthians 12—14 and II Corinthians 12, that purpose can hardly be other than to confront his misguided converts on their own ground.

[47] I Cor. 8:7-13, 10:24-32.
[48] I Cor. 10:23.
[49] Chadwick, "All Things to All Men," *op. cit.*, p. 272.
[50] II Cor. 12:1, 6.
[51] I Cor. 12:10, 28.
[52] II Cor. 12:1-4.
[53] I Cor. 14:18.
[54] II Cor. 12:2 ff.

This he does in order to gain a hearing for his main thesis that spiritual gifts are given by the Spirit, "who apportions to each one individually as he wills," and "for the common good."[55] Hence his plea is for the Corinthian Christians not to exalt the gift of tongues out of all proper perspective, but (1) to make love their aim, (2) to seek the spiritual gifts as the Spirit gives them, and (3) to use such gifts as are given for the upbuilding and edification of the Church. But the point here is: in order to win his ecstatically minded addressees, his approach is that of an ecstatic to ecstatics.

In all these instances in Paul's pastoral ministry to the Corinthian church, it cannot be said that the Apostle is acting merely opportunistically—if we mean by that taking advantage of a situation without regard for principle or ultimate consequences.[56] He is attempting no deception in his approach to his converts. In every case he recognizes them to be real Christians, but Christians who in grasping an aspect of the Gospel proclamation have perverted the truth they possess into an error through an exclusive emphasis upon that element and/or through an attitude of spiritual pride. In every case he seeks to work from the one element of truth which they have grasped to a fuller understanding and expression of their liberty in Christ. Far from disregarding ultimate consequences, his whole purpose is to strengthen his converts and the Church as a whole. And by beginning with them at the point where there is common agreement and omitting such matters and arguments as will cause unnecessary offense, he is but manifesting his missionary and pastoral principle of being "all things to all men." Here is a legitimate flexibility of approach and elasticity of attitude which needs to be more characteristic of every Christian pastor, missionary, scholar, and statesman. Here is a man ready to forego some personal privileges, desirous not to offend needlessly, and willing to approach those with whom he differed on a point of common agreement; all for the sake of the Gospel and the Body of Christ. With this insight into the character of Paul, we are better able to tackle some of the very knotty problems regarding his practice as represented in the Book of Acts.

[55] I Cor. 12:4-11.

[56] Chadwick speaks of Paul's "apostolic opportunism," though he seeks to disinfect the expression of all evil connotations ("All Things to All Men," *op. cit.*, p. 264).

XI

The Problem Practices of Acts

IT IS TO THE PROBLEM practices of Paul as represented in the Book of Acts that we must now turn, for these actions have been variously interpreted. Continental theologians early viewed the seeming discrepancy between Paul's teaching in his letters and his practice in Acts as the weightiest argument against the veracity of the Acts account. Their insistence was that it is "unjust that the picture of the Apostle's character which we gain from his Epistles should be distorted by the misrepresentations of an author who lived long after the Apostolic period, and wrote in the interests of a party."[1] Of those who accept the Acts portrayal of Paul's activity, many—primarily British scholars—have tended to view his actions as evidence that the Apostle was just too ingenious to be hampered by logic; while some have argued that only Acts should be trusted as truly representing the Apostle's thought, and that from these practices we see that he "in no way quitted the faith of his fathers."[2] And between these positions there is no want of diversified interpretation.

My argument here is not meant to be primarily a defense of the authenticity of the Book of Acts. Certainly other factors must also be considered in a truly critical study of that work; though, of course, the conclusions arrived at in this chapter will have a direct bearing on many of the introductory problems associated with the Acts. Nor is it my desire to smooth out possibly inherent rough places in the Pauline profile or gloss over real inconsistencies. But it is my conviction that much of the criticism against the represented practices and stated methods of the Apostle is in reality only the debris remaining

[1] F. C. Baur, *Paul,* Vol. I, p. 210.
[2] J. Parkes, *Judaism and Christianity,* p. 84.

long after the main structure of the Tübingen theory has fallen. Such criticism, I believe, stems from a failure to understand aright the Apostle's teaching regarding Christian liberty.

JEWISH VOWS AND CUSTOMS

It is in its narration of the Apostle's continued practice of Jewish vows and customs that the Acts presentation seems to run most contrary to the principles of its central character. The circumcision of Timothy,[3] the cutting of his hair at Cenchrea in token of a vow,[4] and the joining of four Jewish Christians in a week-long temple ritual of purification, meditation, and offering in fulfillment of a vow[5] are the most prominent of these disputed actions. And here we must begin our discussion of the problem practices of Acts.

The credibility of these practices. Baur's argument was based upon the logical premise that since the Apostle could not consistently have performed these acts, he therefore could not have done them. But since Harnack's work on the problem, scholars have increasingly viewed his actions less suspiciously. Those who have defended the credibility of Paul's performance, notably A. Harnack and J. B. Lightfoot, have argued:

1. Since Paul had to defend himself in Galatians 5:11 against the charge of preaching circumcision, there must have been something in either his preaching or his practice, or in both, which when misunderstood could give rise to such an accusation.

2. For an apostle who declared that his missionary practice was to be "all things to all men," such action was certainly possible.

3. In a theology which lays great stress upon the essential oneness of believers and the need for Christians to restrict their liberty for

[3] Acts 16:3.

[4] Acts 18:18.

[5] Acts 21:23 ff. W. M. MacGregor quotes Hausrath, *Der Apostel Paulus,* p. 453, as saying: "One could as well believe that Luther, in his old age, made a pilgrimage to Einsiedeln, walking on peas, or that Calvin on his deathbed vowed a golden robe to the Holy Mother of God, as that the author of Romans and Galatians stood for seven days in the outer court of the Temple, and subjected himself to all the manipulations with which rabbinic ingenuity had surrounded the vow, and allowed all the liturgical nonsense of that age to be transacted for him by unbelieving priests and Levites" (*Christian Freedom,* p. 71).

the sake of their brethren, such action could be expected.

4. From the fact that Acts states that the Jerusalem vow failed in its effort to pacify the Jews, and implies from its silence that it also failed in the reconciliation of the stricter Jewish Christians to Paul, the recital of such actions—and in such detail as in the case of the Jerusalem vow—is absolutely wanton in character if those actions were merely invented by a later author to show that harmony existed between Paul and Jerusalem.[6]

All these arguments have validity in countering the old Tübingen position. But there still remains one significant point which has been consistently overlooked. Harnack bemoans the fact that while Paul's letters show him willing to omit the Mosaic Law in his work with Gentiles, we do not have any instance reflected in his own correspondence where he came under that Law for the sake of his Christian mission, his nation, or his Jewish Christian brethren. As Harnack says:

> Unfortunately, we are unable to produce any instance from his epistles to illustrate the latter situation, and we do not know either how far he went in his observance of Jewish laws or how often he found himself so placed. There is thus a serious gap in our first-hand knowledge of this side of St Paul's conduct; but that this side existed there can be no doubt.[7]

But there is one statement in his letters in which he explicitly says that in a certain matter he submitted to the old Jewish Law in his Christian ministry, and submitted for the sake of the Gospel. And in this action it appears that he submitted in a far greater measure than he ever did in the taking of vows, the continuance of any customs, or the circumcising of any of his companions.

In II Corinthians 11:24 we find the statement: "From the Jews five times I received forty [lashes] less one." There is no doubt but that these lashes were received in the synagogue and administered at the hands of the officials of Judaism.[8] Now as a Roman citizen, a Jew could escape the synagogue whippings for heresy or misconduct by an appeal to the imperial authorities—though to do so would be not only to gain immunity from Judaism's jurisdiction but also to

[6] A. Harnack, *Date of the Acts*, pp. 67-89; J. B. Lightfoot, *Galatians*, pp. 347-48.

[7] *Date of the Acts*, p. 55.

[8] Cf. L. N. Dembitz, "Stripes," *J. E.*, Vol. XI, pp. 569-70.

sever oneself from the ministry and fellowship of the synagogue.[9] Undoubtedly Rabbi Saul, even though he possessed Roman citizenship, would never have thought of such an appeal had there ever come a time when he was to be judged for a breach of the Law. But what was it that kept the Christian Paul so tied to the synagogue as to endure lashing, when theologically he was separate from Judaism and politically he could escape the ordeal? Evidently it was not an absolute tie; for when it became evident that to submit to Jewish legislation toward the close of his ministry meant death and the cessation of that ministry, he did appeal to imperial protection and judgment. Whether most of these synagogue whippings occurred in the early fourteen years of his Christian life or during his ministry as recorded in Acts in circumstances of which we have no account cannot be determined from either his letters or the record in Acts.[10] Nor is such a determination necessary to the present argument. The point here is that this is one of the afflictions which in II Corinthians 11:23 Paul subsumes under the heading of things he suffered as a servant of Christ. In the case of these five whippings we have explicit evidence from the Apostle's own letters that at least at this point he did submit to Judaism's legislation even though he could theologically justify his escape from such punishment and could politically effect his release. And when we realize that the Apostle was willing to go to this length in being "to those under the law . . . as one under the law," the seeming strangeness of any further Jewish practice which Acts might record of him fades into insignificance. One must insist, therefore, that the Acts representation of the Apostle's practice is entirely credible.

The rationale behind these practices. How then can such practices be explained? Many have viewed Paul as only acting according to expediency; i.e., in not allowing consistency to come between himself and action.[11] On this interpretation, he was willing to be inconsistent

[9] Cf. W. L. Knox, *St. Paul and the Church of Jerusalem,* p. 322, n. 12.

[10] "Some of these incidents may be connected with the fourteen years of which we know nothing. In other cases, where Luke merely reports that the opposition secured his expulsion, there may have been an actual trial before the synagogal authorities, and a formal condemnation of his teaching by them" (J. Parkes, *Jesus, Paul and the Jews,* p. 113). M. Dibelius argues for a pre-Acts ministry in Tarsus, during which time these whippings took place (*Paul,* p. 70).

[11] E.g., C. G. Montefiore, *Judaism and St. Paul,* pp. 182-83; W. D. Stacey, *Pauline View of Man,* p. 16.

if such action could further his mission, smooth over tensions, and/or relieve antagonisms. A. Schweitzer saw the Apostle's practice as the practical result of his eschatological theology; i.e., since his Lord would shortly return, he believed it to be his mission only to proclaim preparedness for that coming and not to attempt any change in the *status quo*.[12] A minority believe that Paul could have easily performed these acts because in reality he never departed from Judaism. According to this latter view, the Apostle has been misinterpreted by most of Christendom; and to an extent Paul himself is responsible for this confusion, since his words regarding the Law have more bluster and passion in them than real truth. Thus his actions reveal that the strong denunciations of the Law in his letters were not an essential or permanent part of his message.[13] Some have even interpreted these practices as a sentimental return to the old days, which, though contradictory to his teaching, must be excused on the basis of emotional ties.[14]

Behind these practices, however, lies an explanation more basic than any of the above. If the charge of inconsistency were removed from the interpretations of expediency and eschatology, we could justly say that those positions are grasping onto truth. But expediency and eschatology were only elements of a broader ethical basis in the life of the Apostle. His doctrine of Christian liberty included both elements, and upon it his practice was firmly grounded.

Undoubtedly the Apostle was convinced that his message, by comparison with that proclaimed by the Jerusalem apostles, better presented the work and teaching of Jesus Christ. He had not only caught the dominant themes of the Christian message, i.e., that in the work of Christ righteousness has now become a matter dependent only upon Christ, entirely apart from the Law, and that in the Body of Christ there can be no distinction of fellowship between Jew and

[12] A. Schweitzer, *Mysticism of Paul,* pp. 193-94.

[13] E.g., Parkes, *Judaism and Christianity* and *Jesus, Paul and the Jews, passim.*

[14] E.g., MacGregor says: "The historian should take his hero as he finds him, with all his inconsistency and his weakness; for the very fact that a great man cultivates somewhere a secluded garden of sentiment and old prejudice, may count for something in the impact of his character when at work" (*Christian Freedom,* p. 71). And again: "Logically he was done with vows and all their associated formalities, but emotionally he clung to them; and where the interests of his work were not involved, he found pleasure and even, perhaps, a certain advantage in the old observances" (*ibid.,* p. 72).

Gentile; but he had also seen the implication that thus the Jewish law has no necessary claim upon the Christian as a form of religious expression or a manner of life. But his sweeping insistence that "neither circumcision counts for anything nor uncircumcision" could only be partially assented to by the Jerusalem church. While the "pillars" agreed with him that circumcision was neither a necessity for salvation nor a basis for fellowship, they could not agree with the implication of his statement that the Jewish Law was not a necessary *Lebensform* for those who were still Jews.[15] As a member of the true remnant of Israel whose primary responsibility it was to witness to the nation, the Jewish Christian was expected to retain the national practices.[16] It seems that Paul could applaud the desire of the Jerusalem Christians to witness to their own nation, but he could never accept the ecclesiological thought that stood behind the desire and thus made Jewish legality a necessary manner of life for every Jewish Christian. And yet, though "such scruples might be a mark of weakness, . . . they were none the less to be respected; in any case they were less reprehensible than the spirit which condemned them."[17]

Here we find the working out of Paul's teaching that the believer's liberty must be conditioned by love if it is to be truly an exercise of Christian liberty; and that this love manifests itself within the Christian community in a willingness to restrict one's own liberty for the sake of a weaker brother. The same principles found explicitly stated in I Corinthians 8—10 seem also to be the basis for Paul's action when in contact with the Jerusalem church. In the one case, his personal conviction was that "an idol is nothing" and "meats are nothing." In the other, it was that "circumcision is nothing" and the Temple has lost its significance in view of the person and work of Jesus Christ. But in both cases he seems to have realized that "there is not in every man that knowledge."[18] Thus in both cases he restricted his personal liberty for the sake of the weaker brother. At Corinth he abstained from certain practices for the sake of certain local Christians, while for the sake of the Jerusalem Christians he

[15] For this distinction of the Law as necessary for righteousness and the Law as a *Lebensform* or *Lebensnorm,* cf. P. P. Bläser, *Gesetz bei Paulus,* pp. 74 ff.

[16] See Appendix, pp. 280-81.

[17] W. L. Knox, *St. Paul and the Church of Jerusalem,* p. 349.

[18] I Cor. 8:7.

performed certain actions. In both situations he viewed the matters in question as entirely neutral in themselves to the man set free by Christ. But in both cases he refused to allow these neutral and purely secondary matters to cause a brother to stumble, and work havoc in the Church. He had no doubts but that at least the majority of the members of the Jerusalem church were earnest Christians desiring to do their Lord's will. Similarly, he fully realized the external pressures upon these believers, for he had personally both persecuted and been persecuted in Jerusalem.[19] Thus, while he strongly denounced those who asserted that the Law was necessary for righteousness and/or for fellowship within the Church, he also tolerated in Christian love those who were true believers and yet who viewed the Law as a necessary form of religious expression and manner of life for all with a Jewish background.[20] Indeed, as Luther said, "he chose a middle way, sparing the weak for a time, but always withstanding the stubborn, that he might convert all to the liberty of faith."[21]

Paul would have agreed that "the truly emancipated man is not in bondage to his liberty."[22] Thus, though it seems that his desire was not merely "to keep the gentiles free from the law . . . but also to win the Jews over to the new freedom of the children of God,"[23] he limited the very liberty he proclaimed for the sake of those both within and outside the Church. In Corinth he abstained from meat in deference to the overscrupulous believers whom he might otherwise cause to stumble. For the sake of similarly overscrupulous Christians at Jerusalem and for the sake of the Jewish mission he allowed him-

[19] I Thess. 2:14-16: "The Jews . . . who killed the Lord Jesus and the prophets, and drove us out."

[20] Luther's distinction between the fundamentals and the adiaphora in the dispute regarding the date of Easter is entirely Pauline; for while he argued strongly for the position of the Eastern Church as against his own Church, he also insisted: "Therefore my advice is to let it alone and let it be kept as it now is, and patch and tear the old coat, and let Easter see-saw back and forth until the Last Day, or until the monarchs agree to change it together, in view of these facts. It breaks no one's legs and St. Peter's boat will not be hurt by it, since it is neither heresy nor sin, but only a solecism, or error, in astronomy" ("On the Councils and the Churches," *Works of Martin Luther,* Vol. V, trans. C. M. Jacobs, p. 186).

[21] M. Luther, "A Treatise on Christian Liberty," *Works of Martin Luther, op. cit.,* Vol. II, pp. 339-40.

[22] F. F. Bruce, *The Acts of the Apostles* (London: Tyndale Press, 1951), p. 35.

[23] H. Lietzmann, *Beginnings of the Christian Church,* p. 200.

self to be severely lashed five times by the synagogue authorities, circumcised one of his companions who was half-Jewish, took upon himself Jewish rites and vows when circumstances demanded, and generally continued his personal practice of the national customs.[24] "Naturally, his fellow-countrymen did not understand, indeed could not understand, such freedom! But the Apostle was not therefore a hypocrite."[25] He could only be charged with hypocrisy and inconsistency if he had acted in opposition to his own principles or had professed to believe these practices essential when he really thought otherwise. But in actuality, "no one held to great principles more consistently."[26] His wide diversity of practice springs most naturally from his doctrine of Christian liberty.

CONTINUED PREACHING TO THE JEW

A survey of Paul's missionary procedures reveals the fact that Acts portrays the Apostle as usually beginning his ministry in a city by preaching in the local synagogue;[27] and this despite the repeated declarations in his letters that he is an apostle to the Gentiles.[28] As if this were not enough, the Acts account represents him as telling the Jews of Iconium that "it was necessary that the word of God should be first spoken to you"[29] and as taking the initiative in calling together the Jewish leaders in Rome to present the Gospel to them.[30] It is this great interest in Jews on the part of one who declared plainly that he had been "entrusted with the gospel to the uncircumcised even as Peter [had been commissioned] to the circumcised"[31] which has caused many to doubt the historicity of the Acts account,[32] a few to view Paul as still within the framework of Judaism,[33] and some to argue that in each city he really only turned to the Gentiles because

[24] Note Acts 22:17-21.

[25] Harnack, *Date of the Acts,* p. 81.

[26] F. J. Foakes-Jackson, *Life of St. Paul* (London: Cape, undated), p. 15.

[27] Acts 13:5 (Salamis); 13:14 (Antioch in Pisidia); 14:1 (Iconium); 17:1 (Thessalonica); 17:17 (Athens); 18:4 (Corinth); 19:8 (Ephesus).

[28] E.g., Gal. 1:16, 2:7-9; Rom. 11:13, 15:16, 18. His mission to the Gentiles is also referred to in Acts 9:15, 13:47, 26:17-18.

[29] Acts 13:46.

[30] Acts 28:17 ff.

[31] Gal. 2:7; cf. 2:9.

[32] See J. Weiss, *Primitive Christianity,* Vol. I, p. 210.

[33] E.g., Parkes, *Judaism and Christianity,* p. 79.

he found that his Jewish mission had failed.[34] And indeed, the question is pertinent: Could the Apostle who declared so definitely that his ministry was to the Gentiles have been so careful to begin his labors in each city with the Jews?

Many have argued that to view this as a contradiction between the Epistles and the Acts "is to overlook the fact that the likeliest audience, even for the missionary to the Gentiles, was to be found at the divine service in the synagogue, where he would meet former pagans who had been converted to Judaism, i.e., proselytes, and, above all, the non-Jewish attenders, the so-called 'God-fearing Gentiles.' "[35] This is certainly true. Yet this explanation does not entirely cover Paul's practice of first approaching the synagogue and his evident interest in the conversion of Jews living in the Diaspora. In addition to this factor, we must recognize that the concordat of Galatians 2:7-10 was neither a strictly geographical division of area nor a strictly ethnic division of responsibility. The Apostle who yearned over his own nation as in Romans 9—11,[36] saw his Gentile mission as an indirect ministry to Israel in causing his own people to become jealous for the blessings of God,[37] declared the Gospel to be "to the Jew first and also to the Greek,"[38] and believed that there is no distinction before God between Jew and Gentile,[39] cannot be blamed if he interpreted the agreement recorded in Galatians 2 as designating only primary responsibility and not exclusive concern. This is what is indicated in Acts' representation of the Lord's words to Ananias: "Go, for he is a chosen instrument of mine to carry my name before the Gentiles and kings and the sons of Israel."[40] Paul had no doubt that he was commissioned to be an apostle to the Gentiles, but he never interpreted this call as meaning a total disregard for the Jew. Rather, he was attempting to follow his Lord's practice and command of putting the Jew first[41]—but never allowing that order to stand in his way or detain him from *his* primary responsibility to the Gentile.

[34] E.g., Schweitzer, *Mysticism of Paul,* p. 181.
[35] Dibelius, *Paul,* p. 85.
[36] Esp. Rom. 9:1-3 and 10:1.
[37] Rom. 11:11, 14.
[38] Rom. 1:16.
[39] E.g., Rom. 2:11, 3:9, 3:22.
[40] Acts 9:15.
[41] E.g., Acts 1:8.

ACCEPTANCE OF THE JERUSALEM DECREE

The account of the Jerusalem Council in Acts 15 stands as the watershed in the design and construction of the narrative in Acts. And in that account, "the most serious difficulty is to fit an acceptance of the Decree with the ethical system championed by S. Paul, for whereas most of the other difficulties come from our comparative ignorance, this comes from the express statements of the Apostle himself."[42] The problem is twofold: (1) Did Paul actually accept the Jerusalem Decree? And (2), if we believe he did, was he compromising his own teaching of liberty in Christ in so doing?

The text of the Decree. Before going further, it is necessary to raise the question regarding the nature of the Decree. As is well known, there is an important textual variation between the Neutral Text and the Western Text at this point. The received text lists four prohibitions: abstinence "from things sacrificed to idols and from blood and from things strangled and from unchastity" (*apechesthai eidōlothutōn kai haimatos kai pniktōn kai porneias*).[43] The text of D and its Latin associates omit "and from things strangled" (*kai pniktōn*), giving the other three and also including the Golden Rule in negative form. If the four-clause text is accepted, we have a mixture of ceremonial, dietary, and ethical injunctions. If the three-clause version be viewed as original, then it might possibly be said that the Decree is an ethical pronouncement. I need not repeat all the arguments both pro and con on this question, which has rightly been called "one of the most tangled problems in the history of the early Church."[44] But some summary and indication of the conclusions accepted here must be presented if we are to proceed further.

It was not until 1905 that the text of Codex Bezae for the Decree began to be looked upon by scholarship as offering a real alternative to the received text. In that year Gotthold Resch, continuing the work of Hilgenfeld, published *Das Aposteldekret nach seinen ausserkanonischen Textgestalt,* in which he argued that the Western Text, with both its omission of "things strangled" and its inclusion of the negative

[42] F. C. Burkitt, *Christian Beginnings,* p. 112.
[43] Acts 15:20, 29, 21:25.
[44] A. S. Peake, *Paul and the Jewish Christians,* p. 17.

Golden Rule, was original. This work so influenced Harnack that he changed his previously published opinion and strongly supported the three-clause text—except that he took the negative Golden Rule to be a later insertion.[45] In close succession, Kirsopp Lake joined Harnack and advocated that the Neutral "things strangled" and the Western Golden Rule were both additions attempting to clarify the shorter but ambiguous original version.[46] And since 1911 there have been others who have agreed with Harnack and Lake in accepting the three-clause text of D while deleting its addition of the Golden Rule.[47] Most agree because they feel that the three clauses of the Western Text, interpreted as prohibitions against idolatry, murder, and impurity, better fit into a Pauline acceptance than the four ceremonial, dietary, and ethical injunctions of the Neutral Text. But the acceptance of the Western reading cannot in any sense be called the "generally accepted view."[48]

To view the Jerusalem Decree as a bit of basic moral legislation, so elemental in its ethical propositions that Paul could easily have expressed his approval, is indeed tempting. The sins of idolatry, murder, and moral impurity were often grouped together by Judaism and the early Church as the three basic heinous sins of the world,[49] and it would not be too hard to project this thought into the considerations of the Jerusalem Council. But on a textual basis, it is very difficult to justify the abandoment of the received version. We have no real evidence that there ever existed a short form of the text without both "things strangled" and the Golden Rule;[50] and if the Western

[45] A. Harnack, *Acts of the Apostles,* pp. 248-63.

[46] K. Lake, *Earlier Epistles,* pp. 48-60.

[47] E.g., J. Jocz, *Jewish People and Jesus Christ,* p. 68; P. Carrington, *The Early Christian Church* (Cambridge, Eng.: The University Press, 1957), Vol. I, p. 104.

[48] As Jocz speaks of it, *Jewish People and Jesus Christ,* p. 68.

[49] E.g., b. Yoma 9b: "Why was the first Sanctuary destroyed? Because of three (evil) things which prevailed there: idolatry, immorality, bloodshed." Mish. Aboth 5:11: "Captivity enters the world on account of idol-worship, fornication and bloodshed." B. Sanh. 74a: "Any sin denounced by the Law may be committed by a man if his life is threatened, except the sins of idolatry, fornication and murder." B. Erech. 15b: "Whoso slandereth his neighbour committeth sins as great as idolatry, fornication and murder." Rev. 22:15: "Without are the fornicators, and the murderers, and the idolaters."

[50] K. Lake insists that Tertullian's exclusion of both "things strangled" and the Golden Rule "is the extremely important exception" (*Earlier Epistles,* p. 49, n. 1).

Text "is wrong in its addition, it lies under the suspicion of being wrong in its omission."[51] Similarly, while it is usually best to prefer the shorter reading, in this case the shorter reading appears in a text which, since the radical rejection of the Western Text by Wescott and Hort, generally does not highly commend itself to all. Nor can it be said that the Western Text really gets around the ceremonial and dietary nature of the Neutral version, for to interpret *haima* as murder is to avoid the more natural sense of "the eating of blood" for the term. Since, therefore, the arguments for the three-clause text are rather inconclusive and can establish no more than a mere possibility for the genuineness of that text, since the four-clause text appears in the generally more acceptable Neutral group of texts, and since the problem of ceremonial and dietary injunctions is really not set aside by an acceptance of the Western Text, it seems best to read the Jerusalem Decree as prohibiting: "things offered unto idols" (*eidōlothuta*), "[the eating of] blood" (*haima*), "[the eating of] things strangled" (*pnikta*), and "unchastity" (*porneia*).[52] The fact that the Western texts present it as an ethical pronouncement coupled with the Golden Rule is probably due to a remodeling of the Decree to make it a rule for the whole Church at a later time when the prohibitions of "blood" and "things strangled" had lost their meaning.

Arguments against Paul's acceptance of the Decree. The major argument against Paul's acceptance of the Jerusalem Decree is that it "was by no means an insignificant legal requirement" and cannot be reconciled with the Apostle who "undisturbedly . . . pushed along the straight road of freedom from the law."[53] And evidence in support of this view that he refused to accept the Decree, or at best gave only a careless and passive consent to it in the interests of peace,[54] has been seen in both what is said and what is omitted in the Pauline literature. The incident of Peter's vacillation at Antioch and the statement of James in Acts 21:25 have convinced many that the Decree was sent out without consulting Paul, some time after the conference

[51] Peake, *Paul and the Jewish Christians,* pp. 18-19.

[52] For excellent discussions of this question, note J. G. Machen, *Origin of Paul's Religion,* pp. 87-91, and Peake, *Paul and the Jewish Christians,* pp. 17-20.

[53] Lietzmann, *Beginnings of the Christian Church,* p. 142.

[54] As W. Sanday's position, "The Apostolic Decree," *Theologische Studien Theodor Zahn dargebracht* (Leipzig: Deichert, 1908), p. 332.

at Jerusalem and without Paul knowing of its existence until much later.[55] Similarly, the fact that "he writes not a single syllable about the Apostolic Decree"[56] in either his Corinthian correspondence or his Galatian letter has been seen as proof that either he knew nothing of it or—assuming that he agreed to it at the Jerusalem conference or heard about it shortly afterward—could not wholeheartedly accept it.[57] One is not so interested here in the date of the Decree, though that question is inseparably bound up with the other. Our concern at present is whether the above-mentioned "evidence" can really be considered as proof of Paul's disparagement of the Decree. The following section will consider the main problem regarding the relation of the Decree to the Apostle's doctrine of liberty.

It has already been noted that there was a real reason for the omission of the Decree from the Corinthian correspondence.[58] Paul could not quote any type of ecclesiastical statement to those supraspiritualists of Corinth if he desired to win them over to a truer understanding and expression of their Christian liberty. His method even in his churches was that of being "all things to all men," and it seems that he would not have used a churchly pronouncement in such a case—even if he had written it himself.

But his failure to mention the Decree in his Galatian letter cannot be explained along similar lines; despite the theory of Lütgert and Ropes regarding the errorists in Galatia, and Schmithal's synthesis of that view.[59] The solution to the problem of the omission in Galatians seems to be that the Apostle wrote this epistle *before* attending the conference at Jerusalem. I agree with Wm. Ramsay, F. C. Burkitt, J. G. Machen, G. S. Duncan, W. L. Knox and others that "the most natural interpretation of the biographical statements in Galatians

[55] E.g., Weiss, *Primitive Christianity,* Vol. I, pp. 260-61, 274-75.

[56] Lietzmann, *Beginnings of the Christian Church,* p. 143.

[57] E.g., *ibid.,* p. 143; Weiss, *Primitive Christianity,* Vol. I, pp. 5, 260; MacGregor, *Christian Freedom,* pp. 31, 142.

[58] *Supra,* pp. 234-35, 241-42.

[59] W. Lütgert (*Gesetz und Geist*) and J. H. Ropes (*Singular Problem of the Epistle to the Galatians*) saw a similar group of pneumatic converts in the Galatian churches as at Corinth, while W. Schmithals ("Die Häretiker in Galatien," *Z. N. W.,* Vol. XLVII [1956], pp. 25-67) views the heretics of Galatia and Corinth as Jewish-Christian Gnostics possessing both the pneumatic and supraspiritual traits which come out so strongly in the Corinthian letters.

i and ii is that they were written before the 'Council' at Jerusalem."[60] This implies acceptance of the South Galatian theory and the correlation of Galatians 2:1-10 with Acts 11:30, subjects which cannot be treated extensively here. But while there are problems in dating Galatians before the Council, there seem to be greater historical difficulties in dating it later. The most evident difficulty in the early date concerns the relation of Galatians to Romans. But, as J. Weiss has said, the latter writing of the Apostle "is in some degree rather a great monologue that a letter, . . . a cross-section of his mental life which could have come equally well from almost any period of his life."[61] To insist, however, that Galatians was written after the conference is to introduce confusion and difficulty at many points in the relation of Galatians to Acts. I agree with P. Carrington that "the arguments which perplexed the older theologians and still go on in the schools were due in no small degree to the fact that they accepted the later date of Galatians, which was traditional in their time."[62] When the events and statements of Acts cannot be correlated with those of Galatians, there is another solution besides a scepticism of the veracity of Acts. The early dating of Galatians is not so lacking in support that it can be easily set aside. And it produces a workable union between Galatians and Acts.

We may therefore conclude that Paul's lack of reference to the Jerusalem Decree is no real evidence that he was unaware of it or refused to accept it. Nor is there any conclusive evidence that the Decree was not formulated at the Jerusalem Council, as represented in Acts 15. Accepting the early date for Galatians, Peter's vacillation was also earlier that the Council and does not therefore have a bearing on the question at hand. And James' statement to Paul in Acts 21:25 may be viewed just as easily as a reassurance of the elder apostles' recognition of Gentile independence within a context of brotherly forbearance as that James was telling Paul something he did not know, which was really done behind his back.

[60] Burkitt, *Christian Beginnings,* p. 116. Cf. Wm. Ramsay, *St. Paul the Traveller and the Roman Citizen,* p. xxxi, and *The Teaching of Paul in Terms of the Present Day* (London: Hodder & Stoughton, 1914), pp. 372 ff.; Machen, *Origin of Paul's Religion,* pp. 78-87; G. S. Duncan, *Galatians,* M. N. T. C. (London: Hodder & Stoughton, 1934), pp. xviii-xxxii; W. L. Knox, *St. Paul and the Church of Jerusalem,* pp. 220-27.

[61] Weiss, *Primitive Christianity,* Vol. I, p. 363.

[62] Carrington, *Early Christian Church,* Vol. I, p. 91.

Christian liberty and the Decree. But if it be insisted that there is no reason to believe that Paul refused to accept the Decree, is there any reason to believe that he could have approved it without compromising his own teaching regarding Christian liberty? In discussing this question, two factors must be recognized:

1. That in the Council of Jerusalem two different types of "necessary things" were considered. First, the theological necessity of circumcision for righteousness was discussed, and rejected. Second, the practical necessity of Gentile abstinence from certain practices for the sake of Jewish-Gentile fellowship within the Church and for the sake of the Jewish mission was considered, and approved. The major work of the conference had to do with the vindication of Gentile freedom, while the secondary matter was concerned with an expression of that freedom in regard to the scruples of others.[63]

2. That in the teaching of Paul a definite place was given to apostolic and ecclesiastical authority in the guidance of Christian liberty. As noted in chapter VIII, Paul believed that when there is a division of the Church regarding the will of God for a particular situation, and when that division threatens the welfare of the Christian community, then it is the responsibility of the apostles and the Church to attempt to interpret the Mind of Christ for that specific condition in the interests of the life of the Church and the preservation of liberty.

Taking these two factors into consideration, I can see no reason why the Apostle would not have willingly accepted the Jerusalem Decree. On the primary question of the fact and recognition of Gentile liberty, his point was won. But on the problem of how this Gentile liberty was to be expressed in view of the scruples of both the Jewish Christians and the unconverted Jews, there seems to have been real confusion within the churches. One cannot believe that this problem only arose later among the Gentile Christians at Corinth, or that the fears of the Christian Pharisees in the Jerusalem conference were entirely unfounded.[64] Here was a condition which, in view of

[63] Cf. Luther's excellent treatment of the Jerusalem Council, "On the Councils and the Churches," *op. cit.*, esp. pp. 150-54, 188, 193-95.

[64] Note Lightfoot's suggestion: "It is strange indeed that offences so heterogeneous should be thrown together and brought under one prohibition; but this is perhaps sufficiently explained by supposing the decree was framed to meet some definite complaint of the Jewish brethren. If, in the course of the hot

the uncertainty within the churches regarding it and the vital necessity to preserve a fellowship among believers and a contact with the Jewish people,[65] made it necessary for the apostles to give what they believed to be a correct interpretation of the Mind of Christ for the specific situation. This seems entirely within the range of Paul's thought as previously outlined.[66] Thus I agree with F. C. Burkitt's conclusion that "as a rule of life it was such as St. Paul would approve, or at least be quite ready to comply with, so long as it was understood by intelligent Christians to be a concession to the scruples of others, not a positive Divine ordinance."[67]

CLAIMS IN DEFENSE

I have argued that in his missionary activity, his pastoral ministry, and his interchurch relations, as presented in both his letters and the Acts account, the Apostle Paul was but consistently working out his own teaching of Christian liberty. But one further point is pertinent in discussing the relation of his practice to his teaching, and that has to do with the claims which Acts represents Paul as making in his speeches of defense. Could the Apostle of liberty have said:

1. "I am a Pharisee, a son of Pharisees,"[68] when he certainly did not practice a policy of exclusivism in his Gentile mission?
2. "With respect to the hope of the resurrection of the dead am I being judged,"[69] when he was really being questioned for his preaching regarding the resurrection and person of Jesus Christ?
3. "I went up to worship at Jerusalem,"[70] whereas he hardly came for the primary purpose of worshiping in the Temple?
4. "I came to bring alms and offerings for my nation,"[71] when he

---

dispute which preceded the speeches of the leading Apostles, attention had been specially called by the pharisaic party to these detested practices, St. James would not unnaturally take up the subject and propose to satisfy them by a direct condemnation of the offences in question" *Galatians,* p. 306.

[65] Acts 15:21 states that the Decree was needful in view of Jewish scruples. See Gen. 9:4 regarding the prohibition; also Jubilees 6:7, 10, 7:28, 21:5-6.

[66] *Supra,* pp. 197-202.

[67] Burkitt, *Christian Beginnings,* p. 134. Cf. Machen, *Origin of Paul's Religion,* p. 93.

[68] Acts 23:6; cf. 26:5.

[69] Acts 23:6, 24:21, 26:6-8.

[70] Acts 24:11.

[71] Acts 24:17.

really was bringing a collection for the poor Christians of the Jerusalem church?

Can we believe that Paul's Christian liberty and his missionary tactic of being "all things to all men" allowed him to go to the length of what appears to be outright dishonesty? Is liberty in Christ entirely without principle, so that it matters not how we accomplish our purpose so long as the end is achieved?

Many have agreed with J. Weiss that "we must be on our guard against spoiling the portrait of Paul by the impressions we receive from the speeches of the Apostle which have been interpolated, especially the speeches in the defence during his trial."[72] J. Parkes, on the other hand, fully accepts these statements as evidence that the Apostle never really broke with Judaism.[73] Of those who accept Paul as a genuine Christian and these claims as Pauline, most interpret him as playing the *enfant terrible* before rather unworthy opponents. But even if we attribute the most evil intentions to his accusers, there still appears to be something not quite straightforward in Paul's replies. It still appears that the Apostle used his liberty as an occasion for an adroit maneuver which was not really sincere.

But much of our suspicion regarding these claims must be credited to our own ignorance of (1) the Judaism of Paul's day, (2) the manner in which the author of Acts condensed the speeches he included, and (3) the thought of Paul regarding his nation. Although the Talmudic literature represents the Pharisees as practicing a strict exclusivism, it is quite possible that this was not so strictly carried out in earlier times.[74] In the Gospels, while the Pharisees looked askance at Jesus for eating with publicans and sinners[75] and for allowing His disciples to eat with unwashed hands,[76] they are also presented as inviting Him to dinner[77] and arranging a temporary alliance with the Herodians.[78] In all likelihood, Pharisaism in this earlier day was not so stereotyped as it later became under rabbinic

[72] Weiss, *Primitive Christianity,* Vol. I, p. 148.

[73] *Judaism and Christianity,* pp. 79 ff.

[74] Cf. W. L. Knox, *St. Paul and the Church of Jerusalem,* p. 21, n. 41 and p. 22, n. 47.

[75] Matt. 9:10-13; Mark 2:15-17; Luke 5:29-32.

[76] Matt. 15:1 ff., Mark 7:1 ff.

[77] Luke 14:1 ff.

[78] Mark 3:6.

development. Probably Paul could still have been considered a Pharisee because of his belief in the resurrection and his personally scrupulous observance of the Law, even though he did not separate himself from Gentiles and the *am haarez*.

The claim that "with respect to the hope of the resurrection of the dead am I being judged" has been especially criticized. But here we must realize that probably "whenever the Resurrection was spoken of, our Lord, as a matter of course, formed for St Paul, for St Luke, and for the listeners the efficient cause."[79] This is demonsrated in the reporting of Paul's Athens address, for there, after speaking in 17:31 of God's "raising him [i.e., Jesus] from the dead," the Acts account continues in 17:32 with the words: "But when they heard of the resurrection of the dead, some mocked; . . ." Here, at least, the phrase "the resurrection of the dead" carries the connotation of the resurrection of Jesus Christ from the dead as well as the more general doctrine of a resurrection. Acts presents Paul throughout his defenses before the imperial authorities as making clear that it was the resurrection of Jesus Christ he meant,[80] and that his Roman judges clearly understood this.[81] And thus when the single phrase "the resurrection of the dead" is used by Paul and/or Luke, even before Jewish judges, it seems to refer to the whole doctrine of the resurrection—especially as it has been validated and illustrated by the resurrection of Jesus Christ. There does not seem to be any deceit here on Paul's part. Luke may have been condensing the Apostle's speech to the extent of leaving out the obvious, as it seems was done in Acts 17:32. But as Harnack argued, "We may even believe that St Paul, at the beginning of his discourse, said roundly, 'Touching the Resurrection of the dead I stand here called in question'; for Luther also declared a hundred times that he was called in question touching the merits and the honour of Jesus Christ, while his opponents asserted that these things did not come at all into the question."[82]

Nor need we see a touch of insincerity in the declarations "I went up to worship at Jerusalem" and "I came to bring alms and offerings for my nation." Though Acts 24:11 records Paul as saying that he

[79] Harnack, *Date of the Acts,* p. 87.
[80] Acts 24:14, 24:24, 26:23.
[81] Acts 25:19.
[82] Harnack, *Date of the Acts,* p. 87.

"went up to worship at Jerusalem," only three verses later, in 24:14, the account represents him as continuing: "But this I admit to you, that according to the Way which they call a sect, I serve the God of our fathers." No deceit was intended, as the clarification shows. Similarly, the same Paul who said in Rom. 15:31 that the collection he was making for the Jewish Christians was "my service which is *for Jerusalem*" (*eis Ierousalēm*) could also say that "I came to bring alms and offerings *for my nation*" (*eis to ethnos mou*). What he did, he did not only for the relief of the Christian poor in the Jerusalem church and not only for the unity of the Church universal, but also "for *all* Israel; he had ever before his eyes the nation *in its entirety*.... The conversion of the whole nation was the ultimate aim of all his exertions."[83] And by aiding that branch of the Church whose mission it was to call the nation to its Messiah, he was indirectly engaged in a mission to his own nation.

Of all the practices of Paul in the Book of Acts, the claims made in defense are probably the most susceptible of being interpreted as a false representation by a later author or a compromise by the Apostle himself of his own high ethical teaching. But even here, we need not posit any real contradiction between the teaching and the practice of the Apostle Paul.

[83] *Ibid.*, p. 74 (italics his).

Conclusion

LIFE, RELIGION, AND HOPE for Paul were centered in Jesus Chirst, as the Apostle declares in Philippians 1:21: "For me to live is Christ." It was the Damascus road identification of the crucified Jesus with the Messiah of Israel's hopes that altered his whole course of life. It was his realization of the person and work of Christ that brought him to view Jewish nomism, as well as all forms of legalism, as invalid before God. It was in the work and fellowship of Christ that he found the basis for true liberty. It was through the interaction of the Law of Christ and the Mind of Christ that he came to know the will of God in his life. It was in the divine love manifested in and through Christ, and thus also in and through those who are "in Christ," that he found the conditioning factor for all life. And it was his realization of the central importance of Jesus Christ in the history of redemption and the life of every believer that influenced his actions, both in staunchly withstanding those who in their doctrine or action would minimize the significance of Christ's person and work and in willingly tolerating those who knew the centrality of Christ in their own lives but who were weak and immature in other matters. Paul's faith was Christologically orientated. And in his Christian teaching and practice he allowed nothing to obscure the centrality of Jesus Christ—whether a form of legalism or the exercise of Christian liberty.

But what can be said regarding the relevance of Paul's message to our day? Is his teaching merely of historical and antiquarian interest? Not at all! As one called to the office of an apostle[1] and "commissioned by the Lord to be trustworthy,"[2] his words are authorita-

[1] E.g., Rom. 1:1.
[2] I Cor. 7:25.

tive for the Christian Church. And in his message there is a real corrective to constantly arising legalism. In a day when the "Christian graces" are stressed without any thought of the centrality of Christ, and men seek divine favor through human effort and take comfort in self-justification, Paul's proclamation that salvation is of the Lord is pertinent.[3] Likewise wherever ethical instruction or ecclesiastical pronouncement usurp the Gospel of Christ—even though the Church must instruct and guide because of carnality and immaturity—the Apostle's doctrine is relevant. Similarly so in the often confused relationship between Stoic inwardness, which is really a form of humanism, and Christ-centered inwardness. The Gospel is not Stoic teaching in a religious guise, as it is too often presented in our churches. The Gospel breaks even the inner legalism of Stoicism. W. R. Inge has well said: "Christianity cannot live on moral aphorism, or on a 'galvanisation' of Platonism or Stoicism in Christian dress, but only on the 'Christus-mystik' which was the heart of St. Paul's religion, and which led him to lay increasing emphasis on the brotherhood of believers in 'the body of Christ.' "[4] Personal knowledge of and fellowship with Christ is at the heart of the Gospel proclamation. And wherever formal theological knowledge, mental assent to a creed, ascetic practices, the performance of ecclesiastical rites, ethical behavior, or love to one's neighbor are viewed as man's action in the attainment of salvation and sanctification—good as many of these are in their proper place—we have brought the Gospel within the orbit of what Paul meant by "works." "We must not," as James Denney aptly said, "eke out faith by works or love, any more than we must make good the deficiencies of the objective Christ by stray thoughts on the Spirit or the sacraments. Faith is the appropriation

[3] "He must be blind indeed who denies the relevance of this to an age like our own, in which so many modern substitutes for the Gospel—secularism and humanitarianism and moralism and legalism—have appeared on the field, and so many voices are declaring that Abana and Pharpar are better than all the waters of Israel. Even among Christians the attempt to develop Christian graces (which are the circumference of religion) without having first faced up to the question of self-surrender and rightness with God (which is religion's centre) is not unknown; and as long as this is so, Paul's doctrine of justification, so far from being an obsolete survival of merely historical and antiquarian interest, will remain a living word of God, challenging and convincing and convicting, and mighty to save" (James S. Stewart, *Man in Christ*, p. 245).

[4] W. R. Inge, *Christian Ethics and Modern Problems*, p. 385.

of Christ, and apart from Christ and faith, not only works and love, but sacraments and Spirit, are words without meaning."[5]

Paul's doctrine has pertinence also for that thought which stands at the other extreme in its reaction to legalism: the kind of thought termed by Luther *Schwärmerei* and *Enthusiasmus.* Christian liberty is not to be defined as "self-mastery," "obedience to a law which we prescribe to ourselves," "the understanding of what is necessary and what is contingent," "rational self-direction,"[6] or "the discriminating response of an educated affection."[7] It is Christ-mastery, not self-mastery. Nor is it to be viewed as devoid of external principles and guidance. Though based in and directed by Christ, it is not therefore separated from the Scriptures or the Church. C. H. Dodd has insisted that "Christianity recognizes no spiritual revelation which is not directly related to the historical reality of Jesus";[8] and has correctly pointed out that

> it would thus be a mistake to regard primitive Christianity as a "religion of the Spirit" *sans phrase,* over against religions of authority or of tradition. The early Church was no society of the "inner light," dependent for its doctrine and its ethical standards upon mystical promptings. Spiritual experience may interpret, supplement and enlarge the original content of faith, but it is not an independent source of truth. It is all controlled by the central and common tradition of the Gospel of Christ and the Law of Christ.[9]

Thus Paul would teach us that (1) freedom from the letter (*gramma*) is not also freedom from the Scriptures (*graphai*);[10] (2) liberty in Christ is not only personal but also carries corporate implications, in that the believer is part of the Body of Christ; and (3) Christian liberty is not devoid of propositional truths and ecclesiastical guidance, though its vital nature is not grasped if only these are accepted.

And in the Apostle's practice we have an example worthy of emulation. While he certainly did not anticipate many of the modern problems connected with interchurch relations and the personal exercise of liberty, Paul did demonstrate forcibly in his own life at least

[5] J. Denney, *Christian Doctrine of Reconciliation,* p. 166.
[6] I. Berlin, *Two Concepts of Liberty,* pp. 19-29.
[7] T. E. Jessop, *Law and Love* (London: S.C.M. Press, 1940), p. 155.
[8] C. H. Dodd, *History and the Gospel,* p. 58.
[9] *Ibid.,* pp. 58-59.
[10] Cf. O. Michel, *Paulus und seine Bibel,* pp. 174 ff.

two principles: (1) the need to stand firmly for the central significance of Jesus Christ in the redemptive program of God and in the reconciliation of men to the Father; and (2) the need to manifest true Christian love and brotherly tolerance to those who know personally the person of the Gospel proclamation but with whom we cannot fully agree regarding matters of lesser importance. Of course, the cases are legion wherein we need to apply these principles in our own daily lives. We would not, and could not, attempt to formulate rules as to how these principles should be applied in every exigency. We can only pray that in each personal decision we may be in conformity to the Law of Christ and have the Mind of Christ, and that in every church deliberation the Spirit may control.

Appendix

Christianity in Jerusalem

AT MANY POINTS in the body of this study the tangent subject of Jerusalem Christianity has arisen. Aspects of the branch of early Christendom that carried the distinctively Jewish stamp have been treated in passing, but it will be profitable to outline here the circumstances and thought of Christians in the Holy City. Such a summary sketch of Jewish Christianity will enable us better to understand Paul in his relation to his brethren and his nation.

CONSTITUENCY

In the early days of its existence, Jerusalem Christianity encompassed three types of Jews. These can conveniently be designated by the names of their best-known representatives: Peter, James, and Stephen. As time went on the three were narrowed to two, and later still it appears that of the remaining two, one became dominant.

The am haarez. The first followers of the Lord were those classified by the Jews as the *am haarez,* i.e., "the people of the land" who practiced the minimum standards of the Law but made no real attempt to be Pharisaically scrupulous. It was this class, "the common people" (*ho polus ochlos*) of Mark 12:37, who heard Jesus gladly. And certainly the original twelve, drawn as they were from such occupations as fishing and tax-gathering in which a Pharisaical keeping of the Law can hardly be expected, were of this type.

In the early gatherings of Christians in Jerusalem, this group undoubtedly predominated numerically. To whatever extent we view the Galilean disciples of the Lord as returning to their homes after the events of Passion week, at least a nucleus remained at Jerusalem and there joined the Judean followers in forming the first Christian community in that city. Though these early believers had never devoted themselves to a detailed legal observance in their pre-Christian days, either because of the demands of earning a living or for lack of inclination, they were nonetheless loyal Jews both nationally and religiously. And now as Christ's followers, while their observance of the Law had not increased through their new allegiance, at least it was not diminished. Peter, for instance, still ignored the principles of separation established in the rabbinical schools in his missionary activity when left to himself,[1] yet he never renounced the basic national customs and practices. He frequented the Temple as before;[2] and while there is no mention in Acts of any but those who were "zealous for the law"[3] making vows and sacrificing, in all likelihood his type of Jewish Christianity at least joined in the basic offerings of the Temple. *Am haarez* Christianity in Jerusalem gave no appearance of change in its relation to the Law. While its central doctrine of the Messiahship of Christ did not increase its law-abiding qualities, neither did that belief make its practice any less Jewish than it had been. Thus the populace seems to have looked upon this group with favor, while the Pharisees seem to have tolerated the Christians because of their unchanged practice of the basic national laws. But the Sadducees, despite the *am haarez* Christians' continuance in the national customs, must have always viewed with grave suspicion their teaching concerning Jesus as an authority greater than that of the Temple authority.

The scrupulous. As "the number of the disciples multiplied greatly in Jerusalem, . . . a great many of the priests"[4] and "those of the party of the Pharisees"[5] came into the Jerusalem church. Also we read of the legally scrupulous James becoming one of the "pillars" in the church and later apparently taking charge of affairs. We need

[1] E.g., in his residence with one whose business was tanning hides (Acts 9:43), his ministry to the Samaritans (Acts 8:14-25), and his eating with Gentile Christians at Antioch previous to the arrival of those from James (Gal. 2:12). Paul implies, in Gal. 2:14, that this was Peter's regular custom when left to himself.

[2] Acts 2:46, 3:1—4:4, 5:20-26, 5:42.

[3] Acts 21:20.

[4] Acts 6:7.

[5] Acts 15:5.

not assert that James was an ascetic[6] or a legalist in the sense in which that term has been used in this study,[7] nor that his rise in the church was the occasion of a return to legalism within the Jewish Christian community. It would be unfair to simply credit his position in the church to a Jewish materialistic and legalistic veneration of one who was related to the Lord. Probably it is more accurate to say that his rise came as the result of the need for one to lead this growing section of scrupulous-minded Christian priests and Pharisees in the church, and that his relation to Jesus, his Davidic descent, his strict observance of the Law and his personal qualities eminently fitted him to this task of interesting, holding, and governing those who would undoubtedly have looked down upon *am haarez* leadership.[8] It seems that even the Jerusalem church, to a limited extent, was endeavoring to be "all things to all men" in its mission to the Jewish populace. The character and thought of this group must be more exactly designated in the following pages. Suffice it now to note that here were Christians who, like the *am haarez* type, continued their Jewish practices in much the same manner and to much the same extent as they had done before their conversion.

The Hellenists. From the beginning of the Christian community in Jerusalem, those designated the "Hellenists" (*Hellēnistai*) in Acts were present in the church. Discussion has long continued as to just who is signified by this term. Most have accepted it as referring to Greek-speaking Jews from the Diaspora who settled in Jerusalem.[9] Others interpret it to mean simply Gentiles of the Greek-cultured

[6] The tradition quoted from Hegesippus (Eusebius, Ecclesiastical History, II. 23. 4-7) probably is no more than a guess and an attempt to magnify James, though it is often accepted; e.g., F. C. Burkitt, *Christian Beginnings,* pp. 57-65, P. Carrington, *Early Christian Church,* Vol. I, pp. 104-105.

[7] As, e.g., H. Lietzmann, *Beginnings of the Christian Church,* p. 83.

[8] A. Schlatter has pertinently commented: "The fact that, prior to the Crucifixion, James had not been able to throw in his lot with Jesus did not weaken his position in the Church. James' experience was the same as everyone else's. For all alike the Resurrection constituted the turning point and transformation in their relationship to Jesus. There was no one in the Church who did not recall with penitence his former conduct; they all knew that they had found occasion of stumbling" (*The Church in the New Testament Period,* trans. P. P. Levertoff [London: S.P.C.K., 1955], p. 12).

[9] E.g., F. J. A. Hort, *Judaistic Christianity,* p. 48; Lietzmann, *Beginnings of the Christian Church,* p. 88. The major problem with this interpretation is why, then, Paul called himself a Hebraicist when he was also from the Diaspora.

world,[10] some Jewish proselytes,[11] and a few a radical reforming "gentilistic" party within Judaism which accepted the moral precepts of the Law but was set against sacrificial worship.[12] Lately, C. F. D. Moule has suggested that these were "simply Jews (whether by birth or as proselytes) who spoke only Greek and no Semitic language, in contrast to *Hebraioi,* which would then mean the Jews who spoke a Semitic language in addition, of course to Greek."[13] Such a definition seems an advance in the explicit meaning of the term. Certainly it hurdles the difficulty in the traditional interpretation of why Paul called himself a Hebraicist when he was also from the Diaspora, explains why Hellenistic synagogues were needed in Jerusalem, and offers an insight into the problem of why the seven deacons of the early Church appear as evangelists within their own Hellenistic circles when they were appointed for the supervision of material matters. But, judging from Paul's Corinthian opponents' assertion that they were "Hebraicists" and not "Hellenists"—and the Apostle's emphatic rejoiner "So am I!"[14]—the terms *Hebraios* and *Hellēnistēs* denote more than mere language differences. They seem also to connote the ideas of a Jew trained in the best traditions of his fathers as opposed to a Jew whose basic mentality is that of Hellenism.

[10] E.g., J. H. Ropes, *Beginnings,* Vol. III, p. 106. It is difficult, however, to visualize purely Gentile Christians in the Jerusalem church at such an early date—if, indeed, at any time during the first century. The case of Cornelius is related as being quite exceptional. Probably, being a Roman soldier, he did not long remain in Palestine to cause embarrassment to the native Christians.

[11] E.g., E. C. Blackman, "The Hellenists of Acts vi. 1," *E. T.,* Vol. XLVIII, No. 11 (Aug., 1937), pp. 524-25. But the fact that in Acts 6:5 special attention is drawn to only one of the seven as a proselyte seems fatal to this view that all seven were proselytes.

[12] E.g., M. Simon, *St. Stephen and the Hellenists,* and O. Cullmann, "The Significance of the Qumran Texts for Research into the Beginnings of Christianity." *Scrolls and the N. T.,* ed. K. Stendahl, pp. 18-32. But evidence for such a party is lacking. Nor is such evidence forthcoming in the Dead Sea finds. The only possible suggestion of a Gentile interest in the Qumran texts is the mention of proselytes as one of the four ranks within the community in CDC 14.3-6 (17.1-4), and this probably only refers to Jewish candidates for membership who were undergoing probation (cf. M. Burrows, *Dead Sea Scrolls,* p. 263). Further, it cannot be said that the Qumran community was set against sacrificial worship *per se* (*supra,* pp. 80-81, 135). These religious separatists still hoped to "succeed in reoccupying their native soil" CDC 13.20-21 (16. 10-11), and to share in a purified temple worship.

[13] C. F. D. Moule, "Once More, Who Were the Hellenists?" *E. T.,* Vol. LXX, No. 4 (Jan., 1959), p. 100.

[14] II Cor. 11:22.

Most of the Hellenists probably returned to the homeland out of religious ardor. Some probably found the religion of the homeland to be entirely satisfying; others possibly reverted to the fundamentalism of the rabbis and priests in a blind reaction to the liberalism they had witnessed in the Diaspora; while undoubtedly there were those who in returning had their idealistic dreams broken by the casuistry and hair-splitting they witnessed in many quarters. Those who blindly held to their new-found legal scrupulousness as the only safeguard to a more liberal spirit possibly appear in the Acts as those who disputed with Stephen and stirred up the opposition against him. Those who had become disillusioned with the legalism of Jerusalem were probably those who, if they became Christians, were most vociferous in speaking out against that legalism. We need not speak of the Christian Hellenists as approximating the Pauline preaching. In the speech attributed to Stephen, there is no indication of a mission to the Gentiles or an offer of an absolutely law-free gospel—though there is a strong rebuke of Israel's constant missing the significance of the working of God because of its emphasis upon externals. But the significant point for our consideration here is that in this group we find Jews within the Jerusalem church who differed from the others in that church in two ways: (1) linguistically, and (2) in their relation to the Law. Their linguistic differences probably resulted in separate meetings being held for Aramaic- and Greek-speaking Christians.[15] This in itself could have branded them as inferiors in the Jerusalem church, both to those outside the church and to some of those within. But their changed relation to the Law resulted in their expulsion from the city itself. Here were those who were naturally under suspicion by their Hebraic Jewish brethren as being contaminated with a liberal spirit; and here were those who had come to Palestine with the declared purpose of practicing the faith of their fathers in the strictest possible manner, but who now as Christians desired only to live as the *am haarez*. And not only so, but they were

[15] A. S. Peake attributed this need for such a division primarily to conservative versus liberal differences (*Paul and the Jewish Christians,* p. 4), but such a separation could have taken place merely on a linguistic basis. While undoubtedly some of both sides were equally conversant in either Aramaic or Greek, and certainly all the Hellenists knew a minimum of Aramaic, probably the native Christians felt most at home under instruction given in Aramaic while most of the Hellenists would prefer their worship and teaching in Greek.

vociferous in their opposition to Pharisaic principles. The Pharisees could tolerate the *am haarez* Christians, for they had always been *am haarez* and even as Christians did not speak against a rigid observance of the Law. But these Hellenists, who had entered the land under the guise of returning pilgrims, were not only ceasing their strict devotion but also spreading about in the Holy City itself that religious liberalism which the Hebraicists detested in the Diaspora. The religious leaders could do little to stamp out that dangerous spirit where it already existed in the Diaspora and in Palestine itself, but they could preserve the Holy City from contamination and thus, they believed, best prepare the way for the Messiah.

It seems best, therefore, to interpret the persecution recorded in Acts 8 as directed primarily against the Hellenists,[16] though undoubtedly the Hebraic Christians also took this as an occasion to become as inconspicuous as possible in the countryside about Jerusalem. We are told that the whole Church was scattered throughout Judea and Samaria, "except the apostles." But evidently only the Hellenistic Christians felt it inadvisable to return to Jerusalem at some later time. Thus the Jerusalem Church was narrowed to two Aramaic-speaking groups, both of which were quite willing to retain that relation to the Law which they had practiced before their conversion. Exactly how these two groups interacted with one another we are not told. Yet it does seem that Acts represents the stricter as increasing in strength and influence from the time of their defeat in Acts 15 to their pressure in Acts 21 for some sign from Paul himself that he still observed the Law. Indeed, as J. T. Milik suggests, it may be possible that this increasing influence of the stricter party within the Jerusalem church was in part the result of "a perpetual increase in Essene influence on the early Church."[17]

ESSENTIAL THEOLOGY

In realizing that at Jerusalem there existed a type of Christianity which claimed to be distinctively Christian and yet continued those

[16] As, e.g., Lietzmann, *Beginnings of the Christian Church,* p. 90.

[17] J. T. Milik, *Ten Years of Discovery,* p. 142. Milik believes that we can see this Essene influence "almost taking over and submerging the authentically Christian doctrinal element; indeed, it may be considered responsible for the break between the Judeao-Christians and the Great Church" (*ibid.,* pp. 142-43).

practices which were distinctively Jewish, and evidently without feeling that there was any inconsistency in such a dual loyalty, the question arises regarding the theology of this community. We need not investigate every point of their thought, but at least the following four doctrines must be considered if we are to form a faithful outline of their essential theology: Christ, the Church, the Law, and eschatology.

Christology. Many Jewish and some Christian scholars, noting that the Jerusalem church continued to observe the Jewish rites and customs, have asserted that Jewish Christianity intended to be no more than a conventicle within the synagogue, i.e., a sect of Judaism, and that had it not been for the Pauline antinomianism Christianity could have continued to the present day under the wing of its parent religion.[18] But to look upon Christianity in Jerusalem as only a sect of Judaism is to fail in appreciation of that radically new factor which had drawn these Jews together: the person of Jesus Christ. James Parkes and R. Travers Herford have viewed the difference between the Church and the synagogue as primarily that of the respective attitudes toward the Torah, rather than that of their views of Christ.[19] George F. Moore has minimized the significance of their Christological beliefs in insisting that the Jerusalem church "was not a schismatic body; its leaders and the mass of their followers were, aside from their peculiar messianic and eschatological beliefs, observant Jews, as their teacher had been."[20] But, though they observed the Jewish law, this does not mean that they intended to be no more than observant Jews.[21] For them, the central significance of history was not still to be anticipated in the coming of a future Messiah, but to be seen in the Messiah who had come in the person of Jesus

[18] J. Parkes even insists that it was Paul's intention as well for the Church as a whole to remain within the fold of Judaism—or at least for Jewish Christendom so to remain (*Judaism and Christianity*).

[19] *Ibid.*, p. 78; R. T. Herford, *Pharisaism,* p. 146.

[20] G. F. Moore, *Judaism,* Vol. I, p. 187.

[21] E. F. Scott has remarked that while it seems that they had no intention of breaking with the nation, "it does not follow, however, that the disciples aimed at nothing more than to constitute a sect within the parent religion. With the fullest consciousness that they had come into possession of somehing new, they may yet have sought to retain their hold on the system they had inherited and to construe their new faith by the categories which it supplied" (*Beginnings of the Church,* p. 111).

Christ.[22] The primary function of true religion was not now the keeping of the Law in anticipation of the coming Messiah, but the knowledge of and fellowship with the Christ who has come unto His own. These were not observant Jews who also possessed "peculiar messianic and eschatological beliefs"; these were those who were primarily Christ's, but also Jews. The Church's difference with the synagogue "was not about secondary matters such as the Golden Rule or the relation of intention and deed or even the nature of Messianic activity, but about the affirmation by the Church and denial by the Synagogue of Jesus' Messiahship and divinity."[23] The person of Christ was "the one great special point" [24] that distinguished the Jewish Christians from Judaism even while they continued the Jewish practices.

S. G. F. Brandon has recently insisted that the basic distinction between Gentile and Jewish Christianity was also Christological, in that the Jerusalem Church accepted only "the Jesus of History," "the Jewish Messiah," whereas Paul proclaimed "the Christ of Faith," "a universal Saviour-god."[25] But, as James S. Stewart says, "it is a point of first-class importance" that the records do not present "any disagreement between the primitive Christian community and Paul on the ground of Christology."[26]

> The circumstance that his Christology stood unchallenged means that nothing in it was felt to be alien to the fundamental tenets of the Church. He was simply making explicit what had been present in germ in the Christian attitude to Jesus from the first. Even pre-existence was less an arbitrary importation than an inference from acknowledged fact.[27]

[22] O. Cullmann has pertinently stated: "He who does not see that the radically new thing in the New Testament is the Primitive Christian shifting of the center of time can understand Christianity only as a Jewish sect" (*Christ and Time*, p. 86).

[23] D. Daube, *N. T. and Rabbinic Judaism,* p. viii. For a similar emphasis, see J. Jocz, *Jewish People and Jesus Christ, passim;* W. D. Davies, *Paul and Rabbinic Judaism,* pp. 323-24; H. Danby, *The Jew and Christianity* (London: Sheldon Press, 1927), *passim.*

[24] C. G. Montefiore, *Judaism and St. Paul,* p. 135.

[25] S. G. F. Brandon, "The Crisis of 70 A.D.," *H. J.*, Vol. XLVI (Oct. 1947—July 1948), p. 225, and *The Fall of Jerusalem and the Christian Church* (London: S.P.C.K., 1951), pp. 4, 54-87.

[26] J. S. Stewart, *Man in Christ,* p. 294. Cf. J. G. Machen, *Origin of Paul's Religion,* pp. 129-36.

[27] J. S. Stewart, *ibid.,* p. 296.

And not only is there no evidence that the Jewish church opposed Paul's Christology, but there are indications that Paul really believed that both Gentile and Jewish Christianity stood together at this point. The incorporation into his teaching of some Christological confessions of the early Church[28] and his representation of Peter as agreeing with him that "a man is not justified by the works of the law but through the faithfulness of Christ Jesus,"[29] are significant items in the Apostle's testimonial to the basic orthodoxy of Jewish Christendom's Christology.

Ecclesiology. In addition to the consciousness that their distinctiveness lay in their acknowledgment of and relationship to Christ, the Jerusalem Christians were aware of their own special existence as the *ekklēsia* of God. It is important to recognize that whereas the majority of Jews in those early years probably regarded Jewish Christianity as only a sect of Judaism, the church at Jerusalem considered itself the true Israel. These Christians were not a party or school of thought within Israel; they were Israel. Or, in words probably truer to their thought, they were the faithful remnant within the nation who alone could truly be called the *ekklēsia* of God.[30] They were a minority, it is true. But they could look back on every vital movement of God within the nation—the prophetic revivals, the pneumatic psalmody, the Hasidic resistance—and note that at the heart of matters stood a small minority which was well aware of its own numerical insignificance. "Just as Israel had always been a small band living among the great peoples of the earth, but not ashamed of its smallness, so within the small band there was at many times a smaller band."[31] But, "on each occasion the minority in question held itself to be the true representative of Israel's heritage and mission, and sought to appeal to the conscience of other Jews, to awaken them, and to bring them into line."[32]

The consciousness of their own nature as the true Israel, the faith-

[28] Cf. C. H. Dodd, *Apostolic Preaching and Its Developments,* pp. 19-29, and O. Cullmann, *Earliest Christian Confessions.*

[29] Gal. 2:16. Cf. *supra,* pp. 149-52, regarding *pistis* when applied to Christ.

[30] Cf. E. F. Scott, *Beginnings of the Church,* pp. 35-42. J. Jeremias points out that "the idea of the Remnant is of central significance for late Judaism. Here beats the heart of piety at the time of Jesus" ("The Qumran Texts and the New Testament," *E. T.,* Vol. LXX, No. 3 [Dec., 1958], p. 69).

[31] A. D. Nock, *St. Paul,* p. 52.

[32] *Ibid.*

ful remnant within the nation, lies as the implicit presupposition behind the actions of the Jerusalem Christians. Hence, at least partially, must be understood (1) the urgent need to replenish the number of apostles to the number corresponding to the tribes of Israel,[33] (2) the importance of making Jerusalem their headquarters, and (3) the need to obey God rather than men in standing as the prophetic remnant in calling back rebellious Israel. Here, though without the separatist and ascetic bent of mind that drove the covenantors of Qumran away from what they highly esteemed, is a parallel between the Jerusalem church and the Essenes. The Jerusalem Christians and the Essenes both claimed, as R. H. Charles said of those in CDC, "to be the true Israel: hence the Temple was their Sanctuary, Jerusalem their holy city, and the cities of Israel the sphere of their missionary effort."[34]

The Law. In considering the thought of the Jewish church regarding the Law, we find our records strangely silent. Even in Acts 15, where there is the record of a council which met regarding the question of Gentile Christianity and the Law, there is no suggestion that the correlary subject of Jewish Christianity and the Law was ever raised—it being of course assumed that the latter would go on keeping it. But nowhere is there an attempt to express the rationale behind such observance. Perhaps this very omission is an indication that the Jerusalem Christians, knowing the temperament of their brethren and remembering the persecution of the Hellenistic Christians, were hesitant to consider the subject. But it would be unfair to assert from the silence that the Jewish Christians never atttempted to correlate their Christian theology with their Jewish practice. Probably the more enlightened members of the mother church, believing the Law to be a yoke which the Jews had never borne successfully and salvation for the Jew as well as the Gentile to be found only in Christ,[35] justified their continued adherence to the Law in one or more of the following ways:

[33] Acts 1:15-26.

[34] R. H. Charles, *Ap. and Ps.*, Vol. II, p. 793.

[35] See Acts 15:10-11; Gal. 2:15-16. Cf. B. H. Branscomb, *Jesus and the Law of Moses,* pp. 104-106, regarding the nonobligatory character of the Law for righteousness for even Jewish Christians, and E. F. Scott, *Beginnings of the Church,* pp. 120-21, regarding Paul's belief that the catholic spirit was the spirit of the whole Jerusalem church.

1. On a religious basis. As members of the new and true Israel, which is to pre-Christian Judaism as the flower to the stalk, they were duty bound to keep their ties with old Israel. They could also argue that since "Israel," "religion," and "life" possessed new significance to the believer in Christ, so the practices of Judaism could be viewed in a new light and used as expressions of devotion to Christ. While relation with God is not to be gained by such observance, certainly the liberty which is in Christ allows the Christian to express that relation through old forms which have been given a new significance. At least it is evident that, from a religious perspective, the Jerusalem Christians still regarded the Law as "an appropriate vessel into which their own devotion could be poured."[36]

2. On a nationalistic basis. As members of the nation they felt duty-bound to render allegiance to those unifying practices of national Israel. As J. B. Lightfoot argued, to the Jewish Christian the Law "was a national institution, as well as a divine covenant. Under the Gospel he might consider his relations to it in this latter character altered, but as embodying the decrees and usages of his country it still demanded his allegiance. To be a good Christian he was not required to be a bad citizen."[37]

3. On a practical basis. As members of the remnant of Israel commissioned to call the rebellious sons of Israel to repentance, they were duty-bound to continue their practice of the Law if they were to remain in a position to gain a hearing for their central message. If they really believed that in view of the person and work of Christ the Law had taken its place as a purely secondary matter religiously, then they could reasonably insist that the performance or nonperformance of that matter should not be made to interfere with the vital element of the Christian Gospel.

I am not attempting to manufacture reasons to justify them. The above proposals are only attempts to penetrate the silence and understand the action and thought of the Jewish Christians from their perspective. Undoubtedly other reasons were brought forward. But, judging from what we know of Jewish Christianity from the New Testament, these at least seem to have been advanced.

Eschatology. We have noted that the central significance of history

[36] J. Weiss, *Primitive Christianity,* Vol. I, p. 54.

[37] J. B. Lightfoot, *Galatians,* p. 312.

for Jewish Christianity was no longer the anticipated Messiah, but the revealed Messiah. But while their spiritual focus had shifted in their conversion, their hopes for the kingly coming of Christ were in no way lessened. While they based their faith on the past work and present fellowship of Jesus Christ, they still looked to the future for the second coming of their Lord.

This expectation also stands behind many of their actions. Their continuance in the Temple, for instance, was not at first the result of a dominant legalism within the church. Nor did it stem only from their ecclesiology, their mission, or the example of their Lord in His earthly ministry. These are all factors, but in themselves not fully explanatory. Their great hopes of an early return of their Lord, who "shall come suddenly to his temple,"[38] must also be considered in explanation of why they "continued steadfast with one accord in the temple."[39] Probably, "like Simeon in the Gospel story, they resorted every day to the temple, believing, like him, that they would there witness the coming of the Lord's Christ."[40] Similarly, their willingness to have "all things in common"[41] was probably motivated in part by their expectation of the coming *parousia*. And this hope of and early consummation of history in the coming of the Christ in power and majesty was probably one reason why the Jewish Christians felt no great compulsion to define their relation to the Mosaic Law. When their Lord came, He would settle this difficult question. Until then they would continue to emphasize matters of prime importance while using the forms at hand for the expression of their faith.

MISSION

It is almost self-evident that the Jerusalem church considered its mission to be to the house of Israel. The promise to the disciples that they would "sit upon twelve thrones judging the twelve tribes of Israel"[42] is somewhat enigmatic, for it leaves unresolved questions

[38] Mal. 3:1.
[39] Acts 2:46.
[40] E. F. Scott, *Beginnings of the Church,* p. 22. Cf. also Branscomb, *Jesus and the Law of Moses,* p. 271; Lietzmann, *Beginnings of the Christian Church,* p. 77.
[41] Acts 4:32.
[42] Matt. 19:28; Luke 22:30.

concerning what is meant by "judging" and how the judgment of the disciples "in the new social order" (*en tē paliggenesia*) relates to the judgment of Christ. But at least it indicates a special and indissoluable association of the disciples with Israel as a nation. Jewish Christendom knew that its Lord had confined His earthly ministry to the nation,[43] as He declared in the words "I am not sent but unto the lost sheep of the house of Israel"[44]—and as even the Apostle to the Gentiles confessed in calling Jesus "a minister of the circumcision."[45] And the disciples had previously been explicitly directed to confine their ministry to "the lost sheep of the house of Israel,"[46] while the last words of Christ before his ascension also put the premium on the Church's witnessing first "in Jerusalem and in all Judea."[47] Thus theologically as well as nationally, their interests were directed almost exclusively to their own people.

This is not to deny their recognition of the appropriateness of a Gentile mission, nor even of the existence of a non-Mosaic, Gentile church.[48] If the record of Acts can be trusted at all, and I believe it can, the preaching of the Jerusalem church in the early years contained the universal note struck by Peter: "The promise is to you and your children and to all that are afar off, even as many as the Lord our God shall call unto Him."[49] Likewise, the Jerusalem church appears to have given its official approval to the conversion of Cornelius,[50] the proclamation of the Gospel in Samaria,[51] the exist-

[43] Only three cases of extra-Jewish relations are recorded of Jesus in the Synoptics: the Centurion, the Syro-Phoenician woman, and probably the Gadarene demoniac. The Fourth Gospel adds only the incident of the Greeks (proselytes?) who sought Jesus and the friendly contact with the Samaritans. While His teaching (e.g. Matt. 8:11-12; Luke 13:28-29; Matt. 25:31-46; John 10:16; John 12:32) and certainly His work foreshadowed a universal extension of the Gospel, His actual extra-Jewish contacts appear sporadic and almost accidental. C. H. Dodd has interestingly remarked: "His concentration upon Israel is the more marked because, according to a well-attested saying, He divined that He would have found a more ready response in Tyre and Sidon" (*History and the Gospel,* p. 131).

[44] Matt. 15:24.

[45] Rom. 15:8.

[46] Matt. 10:6.

[47] Acts 1:8.

[48] Cf. Hort, *Judaistic Christianity,* pp. 41-42; Schlatter, *Church in the N. T. Period,* p. 20.

[49] Acts 2:39.

[50] Acts 11:18.

[51] Acts 8:14 ff.

ence of the church at Antioch,[52] and the message of Paul.[53] But though this is true, the Jerusalem Christians felt it to be their special commission to bring the message of the grace of God in Christ Jesus to men and women of their own nation and thus lead Israel back to God by gathering her around her Messiah. The fact that they were the true Israel, the faithful remnant, meant that they possessed a primary responsibility for their brethren "according to the flesh." "Come out from among them and be separate"[54] was not a maxim of the Christian mission in Jerusalem. Even Peter's "save yourselves from this perverse generation"[55] was not meant in the sense of withdrawal, but of repentance. While the Jerusalem church realized its distinctness from Judaism and recognized that the Gospel was meant to have a broad application, it also felt its responsibility to its own nation.

RELATIONS WITH THE NATION

But how did Jewish Christianity fare within the nation? To what extent was it accepted, and what impact did it have? While many details of its history are uncertain, yet the broad outline seems fairly clear.

In its earliest days. As has been noted, both *am haarez* and strict Jewish Christianity continued in the national rites and customs in much the same manner as they had done before their conversion, while the Hellenists allowed their new faith to change their practice in relation to the Law. It was this fidelity to the Law on the part of the native Palestinian Christians that kept Christianity from being "strangled in the cradle."[56] That same tolerance of thought which allowed Jesus to teach in the open air, in the synagogues,[57] and in the courts of the Temple[58] was also directed towards His followers in those early days of the Church's existence. Judaism's adherents were

[52] Acts 11:22 ff.
[53] Gal. 2:9.
[54] II Cor. 6:17.
[55] Acts 2:40.
[56] E. F. Scott, *First Age of Christianity,* p. 118.
[57] Cf. I. Abrahams, *Studies in Pharisaism and the Gospels,* pp. 12-13.
[58] The Synoptics are agreed that He taught "daily" in the Temple when He was in Jerusalem (Matt. 26:55; Mark 14:49; Luke 22:53 and 19:47), and there are frequent references to His teaching as given there (e.g., Mark 12:35; Luke 20:1, 21:37; John 7:14, 7:28, 8:20).

trained to demand orthodoxy of practice, but not necessarily orthodoxy of theology.[59] Thus, as long as Jesus' followers continued in the national practices, it seems that the populace was willing to tolerate—and even listen to—this new teaching. Official Judaism was certainly not as willing to condone the views of the Christians as were the people. But the officialdom of the nation was unable to present a strong opposition to this new theology, being torn within by party strife, subject to the rule of Rome, and restrained by the voice of the people. The Pharisees were undoubtedly opposed to the Messianic claims of the Church, and must have been at least a bit suspicious of the new movement's keeping of the Law. But they were steeped in a tradition of moderation[60] and unwilling to join their hated Sadducean rivals in a suppression of "misguided" but law-abiding people who were in many ways closer to Pharisaism than were the Sadducees. The latter probably would have welcomed the opportunity to persecute the followers of Christ. But though they had within their ranks the titulary rulers of the nation, they could not fully express their desires because of the tolerance of the people, the moderation of the Pharisees, and the desire for peace in the land on the part of the Roman government. Thus the early believers in Jerusalem seem to have been left relatively free to pursue their own course.[61] Undoubtedly economic and social pressures were constantly brought to bear upon them from various sources, but official and national enmity seem to have broken out in these earliest days only sporadically and under certain conditions.

The rising persecution. It was the attack of the Hellenistic Christians upon externalism and scrupulous Law-observance that publicized Christianity's separateness from Judaism and brought about the first persecution of the infant Church. In this, the Pharisees came to realize that the worst of their fears were well founded; and the Pharisees and Sadducees were brought together in a common effort to stamp out this Diaspora-like liberalism and punish offenders who attempted to pollute

[59] "Judaism was more of a life, and less of a creed, than Christianity has ever been. Provided a Jew worshipped the true God and lived according to the Law, he could believe or teach any nonsense he liked. Sensible men might exclude him from their society, but he was not outside the Synagogue of Israel" (K. Lake, *Paul: His Heritage and Legacy*, pp. 35-36).

[60] See *supra*, p. 33 *n*.

[61] Cf. W. L. Knox, *St. Paul and the Church of Jerusalem*, pp. 1-3.

the Holy City under the guise of religion. Thus the death of Stephen and the inquisition that followed. This persecution seems to have been directed primarily against the Hellenists themselves, though the native Christians felt its effect as well because of their countenancing of the Hellenistic heresy. The Jewish leaders evidently took advantage of a momentary abatement of imperial authority in Jerusalem, and possibly in Judea as well, to carry out their plans.[62] But with the returning control of Rome, the continuing Law-observance of the native Christians, and the loss of the leader of the Sanhedrin's forces to the very cause he was persecuting,[63] official Jewish antagonism to the Jerusalem church was held in check. On the wave of this anti-Christian feeling, Herod sought to gain favor with Jewish officialdom by instigating his own persecution of the Christians.[64] And he did succeed in killing James, the brother of John. But the Roman desire for peace prevailed. The Jewish church had learned a bitter lesson concerning how it must conduct itself if it were to continue in its appointed mission. And from this time, through a combination of its own caution and the imperial desire for peace and order, it managed to avert an open break with the nation for almost a quarter-century.

But in the rising tide of Jewish nationalism the moderation of the Pharisees held less sway and the tolerance of the people was growing thin. Sadducees and Zealots spoke more and more for the people, while the church at Jerusalem came more and more into disfavor for its countenancing of the Law-free gospel of Paul. In the year A.D. 62, in the interim between one Roman governor and the arrival of his successor, the High Priest Annas took the opportunity to rid himself of the leader of the Christian community, James.[65] It is significant that the Pharisees so objected to this act as to cause Annas to be deposed by the Roman government. But the tide of nationalism was moving decidedly against the Jewish Christians. Whether they left Jerusalem to take up residence in Transjordanian Pella primarily because of the death of James, the rising tide of antagonism against them, or the approach of the Roman armies—or because of

[62] See Eusebius, Ecclesiastical History, II. 23.2.

[63] Since Paul figured so prominently in this persecution, "it may be conjectured that his withdrawal would in any case have led to its abandonment" (W. L. Knox, *St. Paul and the Church of Jerusalem*, p. 60, n. 50).

[64] Acts 12:1 ff.

[65] Cf. Danby, *Jew and Christianity*, p. 15.

all these factors—and exactly when they left, are questions which cannot be answered with any degree of certainty. They would surely not have left Jerusalem until they felt it absolutely necessary. But just when that point was reached is not clear.[66] By A.D. 68, at any rate, they found this dual loyalty to both Jesus and nation brought to the point of an either/or decision by the national leaders and the populace, and they were forced to leave their nation and stand aside in its conflict with Rome. This was the decisive step which ended their endeavor to be both earnest Christians and practicing Jews. And in the fall of the city and its sanctuary, the decision to stand apart from the nation was decisively sealed. As Harnack said:

> No Christian, even supposing he were a simple Jewish Christian, could view the catastrophe which befell the Jewish state, with its capital and sanctuary, as anything else than the just punishment of the nation for having crucified the Messiah. Strictly speaking, he ceased from that moment to be a Jew; for a Jew who accepted the downfall of his state and temple as a *divine* dispensation, thereby committed national suicide.[67]

The fall of Jerusalem broke the last link for most Jewish Christians with their nation and shoved them into the stream of catholic Christianity. Yet, almost illogically it seems, human feelings linked to a powerful tradition still caused some to attempt a reconciliation. This was not an easy task. After the revival of Judaism at Jamnia, Christians were denounced as *minim*—i.e., heretics.[68] And now they were hated not only for their theological heresies, but also for their disloyalty to the nation. In a desire for religious unity amidst national chaos, Gamaliel II, about A.D. 80, revised the 18 Benedictions so that the *minim* would automatically exclude themselves from the worship of the synagogues rather than be forced to confess what would mean a denunciation of Christ.[69] And in the Jewish revolt of A.D. 132-35 the remnant of Jewish Christianity was again confronted with an acid

[66] Cf. Jocz, *Jewish People and Jesus Christ,* pp. 165-66, for a review of opinions ranging from immediately after the death of James in A.D. 62 (Jocz's) to A.D. 68 (Harnack's).

[67] A. Harnack, *Mission and Expansion of Christianity,* Vol. I, p. 63.

[68] For treatments of the "minim" in Talmudic literature advocating that they were primarily Jewish Christians, see: R. T. Herford, *Christianity in Talmud and Midrash,* pp. 155-56, 365-81; Jocz, *Jewish People and Christ,* pp. 45-57, 174-90; Daube, *N. T. and Rabbinic Judaism,* pp. 142, 444.

[69] B. Ber. 28b; b. Meg. 17b. See Herford, *Christianity in Talmud and Midrash,* pp. 127-35, for a discussion regarding the date of the Benedictions.

test of their loyalty: either the nation, which at this time included the Messianic claims of Simon ben Kosebah,[70] or Christ. For those who chose Christ there was no possibility of a return to the nation. Jewish Christianity, except as continued in the Nazarene sect and as some of its tenets found expression in the Ebionites and later in Islam, received its deathblow in the first destruction of Jerusalem, and its burial in the Messianic claims of Simon ben Kosebah. Thereafter a Gentile bishop presided in Jerusalem.[71]

[70] In the Wadi Murabbaat texts, this appears as the Hebrew form of the name which his Aramaic-speaking followers evidently changed to Bar Kokhbah, "Son of the Star," and his enemies to Bar Kozebah, "Son of the Lie"; see Burrows, *Dead Sea Scrolls,* p. 58, and A. Dupont-Sommer, *Jewish Sect of Qumran and the Essenes,* p. 10. According to Justin Martyr, ben Kosebah took vengeance on the Christians when they refused to deny Jesus as the Messiah: "For in the Jewish war which lately raged, Barchochebas, the leader of the revolt of the Jews, gave orders that Christians alone should be led to cruel punishments, unless they would deny Jesus Christ and utter blasphemy" First Apology, XXXI (Ante-Nicene Fathers, ed. A. Roberts and J. Donaldson [Buffalo: Christian Literature Pub. Co., 1886], Vol. I, p. 173).

[71] Eusebius, Ecclesiastical History, IV. 6. 4.

General Index

This index gives principal references to topics and names discussed at length; complete references to passages and names will be found in the Index of Names and the Index of Scripture and Ancient Writings.

Index of Names

Numbers in boldface type designate pages on which complete bibliographical data for an author's works are given. The works of many ancient authors will be found in the Index of Scripture and Ancient Writings.

Index of Scripture and Ancient Writings

I. OLD TESTAMENT

II. NEW TESTAMENT

III. APOCRYPHA

IV. PSEUDEPIGRAPHA

V. PHILO

VI. JOSEPHUS

VII. CHURCH FATHERS

VIII. RABBINICAL WRITINGS

IX. DEAD SEA SCROLLS

X. OTHER ANCIENT WRITERS